T0375404

THE VALUE OF
UNCERTAINTY

Dealing with Risk in the Equity Derivatives Market

THE VALUE OF UNCERTAINTY

Dealing with Risk in the Equity Derivatives Market

George Kaye

CEO, Derivitec Ltd

Imperial College Press

Published by

Imperial College Press
57 Shelton Street
Covent Garden
London WC2H 9HE

Distributed by

World Scientific Publishing Co. Pte. Ltd.
5 Toh Tuck Link, Singapore 596224
USA office: 27 Warren Street, Suite 401-402, Hackensack, NJ 07601
UK office: 57 Shelton Street, Covent Garden, London WC2H 9HE

British Library Cataloguing-in-Publication Data
A catalogue record for this book is available from the British Library.

THE VALUE OF UNCERTAINTY
Dealing with Risk in the Equity Derivaties Market

Copyright © 2013 by Imperial College Press

All rights reserved. This book, or parts thereof, may not be reproduced in any form or by any means, electronic or mechanical, including photocopying, recording or any information storage and retrieval system now known or to be invented, without written permission from the Publisher.

For photocopying of material in this volume, please pay a copying fee through the Copyright Clearance Center, Inc., 222 Rosewood Drive, Danvers, MA 01923, USA. In this case permission to photocopy is not required from the publisher.

ISBN 978-1-84816-772-8

Printed in Singapore.

To Rika and Archie

Preface

When I began writing this book, in the spring of 2010, the world was starting to pull out of one of the greatest financial disasters it had ever experienced. Unlike previous crashes, however, this one appeared to have been driven, at least in large part, by exotic derivatives, an area in which I myself had spent a decade as a quantitative analyst. Suddenly 'models' had become the villain, with 'over-reliance on the Gaussian copula' being touted in the media as the cause of all our woes. As someone who had built trading models for banks, and analysed the significance of the basic assumptions going into them, this compelled me to write something from the point of view of the practitioner. For a start, what do we actually *mean* by a model? What sorts of assumptions are we actually making when we construct them? What does the market actually tell us, both historically and from traded prices? Perhaps most interestingly, where and why should we care? Before we rush off and blame our assumptions, it seems reasonable at least to address these sorts of questions in a structured manner. That is what I have attempted to do in this book, albeit confined to my own area of knowledge, equity derivatives.

This book can be read either from start to finish, as a 'deep dive' into equity derivatives modelling, or can be dipped into depending on the branch of modelling that happens to be of interest. Likewise, those more interested in the overall regulatory and risk management aspects underlying model risk might be content to read the first and last chapters only, where I hope to have explained why model risk is important, and what, if anything, we can do about it. At the risk of re-iterating, however, this is a quant's take on the problem. I have attempted to address questions on equity derivative model risk in terms of the parts of the stock evolution process a quant would naturally consider. The book is structured as follows.

Chapter 1 is an introduction to the field of derivative pricing, no arbitrage theory, and exactly why no arbitrage pricing is so difficult. I have presented a derivation of the classical Black–Scholes pricing equation, underlined the assumptions inherent to it, and shown why the market indicates that the theory is insufficient for consistent derivative pricing. Through this discussion, I have presented my own take on what a model actually is, and what we mean by model risk. I have then provided an outline of how regulation entered into this problem, and how model risk itself thereby became a vital question in the management and control of exotic derivative portfolios.

Chapter 2 presents the Dupire model of local volatility, one of the first consistent models for pricing exotics in line with the so-called 'vanilla' market. Whilst the weaknesses of the model are presented, the importance of the model as a basis for more realistic approaches is also illustrated.

Chapter 3 starts to drill down into the first assumption underlying the Dupire model, namely the stock growth. More precisely, we look at the importance of our assumption of dividend payments being proportional to stock price, and discuss various approaches for incorporating the more natural view that short-term dividends tend to be stock price independent. Having derived an extension to the Dupire model which allows for such a view, we demonstrate the impact of dividends on barrier and lookback options, and highlight the central importance that vanilla option price calibration has to play in the analysis of model risk.

Chapter 4 moves onto the second moment of the stock price diffusion, and looks at our assumption of state dependent local volatility. Allowing for one source of idiosyncracy to the volatility itself, we derive another extension to the Dupire model to incorporate *stochastic* local volatility consistently. We then apply this to some 'prime suspects', namely options on realised variance, cliquets and barrier options, and contrast our findings on the latter with those of Chapter 3.

Chapter 5 explores departure from diffusion and considers the impact of jumps, through company default and jump to zero. As this falls very much into the field of equity-credit hybrid derivatives, we illustrate the importance of a calibrated model of default to equity default swaps and convertible bonds.

Chapter 6 relaxes the catastrophic assumptions of Chapter 5, and considers jumps to an indeterminate level, over and above a Dupire style diffusion. Having re-derived the Dupire formalism to incorporate this so-called 'jump diffusion', we apply the model to variance swaps, constant proportion portfolio insurance (CPPI) strategies, cliquets and the investigation of implied volatility surface dynamics.

Chapter 7 dives into the one remaining term in the Black–Scholes formulation, namely the risk-free rate itself, and presents a brief discussion on interest rate derivative modelling, and how it can be applied consistently to equity processes. Again, we re-derive the Dupire formalism, this time in the context of stochastic interest rates, and demonstrate the importance of rate stochasticity on variance swaps, callable and auto-callable options, and equity-rate hybrid products.

Chapter 8 moves away from the single asset products examined in the preceding chapters and looks at the importance of *correlation* between those assets. For simplicity, we return to the Dupire model for the underlying process, but allow correlation itself to become stochastic, and correlated with the returns on the assets. This drew particular attention in the crash of 2008, when the tendency of stocks to fall together was shown to be manifestly correlated with the fall in the market itself. A simplistic model is derived, and applied to a simple set of 'multi-asset' exotics, namely rainbow style options, covariance swaps and correlation swaps.

In the final, ninth chapter, we try to address the question about what, if anything, can be done about model risk. The various existing approaches of limits and reserves are discussed, but we also present attempts at 'model independent' pricing, which attempt to derive consistent prices for exotics based only on direct market observables, such as the dynamics of *implied* rather than local volatility.

This book is, then, a step-by-step guide into the various parts of the equity process which matter to a practitioner. No single book, or indeed compendium of books, could ever cover this subject fully, but we hope that the questions and examples raised are at least interesting, and form the basis of profitable discussion for the future.

George Kaye

Disclaimer

The opinions and statements expressed in this book are those of the author and are not necessarily the opinions of any other person, including UBS AG. UBS AG and its affiliates accept no liability whatsoever for any statements or opinions contained in this book, or for the consequences which may result from any person relying on any such opinions or statements.

Acknowledgments

First and foremost, my deepest thanks to my former colleague, Nuno Antunes, for his invaluable review, suggestions and comments on this work. If this book turns out to be useful to those with an interest in equity derivatives, it will be in no small way due to him. Many thanks Nuno, it was a privilege and pleasure discussing this subject with you in such great detail.

I would also like to thank Jacqueline Downs and Lance Sucharov, of Imperial College Press, for their seemingly inexhaustible supplies of editorial patience throughout the long period of writing and discussion. Their understanding of the tortuous process of technical composition made the process of producing this book that much easier. I also gratefully acknowledge the support of Riccardo Rebonato, Alex Lipton, Edward Lockhart, Parameswaran Gopikrishnan, Olivier Garcia and Ibrahim Lemniei Khouli, for kindly reading and commenting on the intermediate drafts, and to my friend and former colleague, David Pottinton, for suggesting the title.

Contents

    3.1   History of dividend modelling   52
           3.1.1   Discrete proportional dividends   54
           3.1.2   Discrete cash dividends   56
           3.1.3   Mixed dividend modelling   61
    3.2   How do dividends actually evolve? Historical analysis . .   63
    3.3   The mixed dividend model   68
    3.4   Barrier options and lookbacks   74
           3.4.1   Basic barrier and lookback valuation   75
           3.4.2   Barrier   options   priced   with   different
                    dividend models   79
           3.4.3   What have we learned?   85
    3.5   Conclusions   86
    3.6   Exercises   87

4. Volatility   89

    4.1   Historical analysis of realised volatility   90
    4.2   Historical analysis of implied volatility   94
           4.2.1   Vega hedging in a volatile environment   97
    4.3   Stochastic volatility modelling   104
    4.4   Stochastic Local Volatility   111
           4.4.1   Initial observations   115
    4.5   Trading realised volatility: Variance swaps   120
           4.5.1   Definition and trading rationale   120
           4.5.2   Pricing   122
    4.6   Trading implied volatility: Cliquets   130
    4.7   Barriers revisited   143
    4.8   But does it make sense?   149
    4.9   Conclusions   150
    4.10   Exercises   151

5. Default   153

    5.1   How to model default   155
           5.1.1   Structural models of default   156
           5.1.2   Reduced form models of default   159
    5.2   The Andersen–Buffum model   164
           5.2.1   Calibration   170
    5.3   Equity Default Swaps   174

Chapter 1

Introduction

This is a book about model risk in the equity derivatives market. From the crash of 1987, until the crash of 2008, the outstanding notional in interest rate, credit and equity derivatives grew from just under USD 1 trillion to USD 451 trillion [ISDA (2009)], equivalent to over seven times global GDP [IMF (2009)]. So-called 'exotic' derivatives made a significant contribution to this growth, so much so that the 'vanilla' market failed to keep step and provide a sufficient basis for hedging and price discovery. This resulted in model *choice*, based on one view of unobservable dynamics or another, becoming a major source of uncertainty. This book focuses on the significance of such model choices to valuation. Of the many lessons we may learn from this analysis, principal among them is how much there is still to learn. Instruments we might expect to be exquisitely sensitive to certain model choices in fact turn out not to be, whilst conversely, instruments deemed to be essentially vanilla, and thereby insensitive to model choice, turn out to be even more sensitive than their more exotic looking counterparts. In the field of derivatives, possibly the most untrustworthy of all our faculties is our intuition. It is hoped, nonetheless, that this book may go some way to improving that faculty, and at least provide some tools for testing it.

1.1 Equity, fairness and arbitrage

Equity, by definition, is supposed to be fair. It entitles the holder to a percentage of the income distributed by the associated company equal to the percentage of stock held. Shareholders do not have *equal* voting rights in the decisions of the company; that would clearly be unfair. Why would someone who'd invested twice as much as someone else only have an equal say? On the contrary, shareholders have *equitable* rights in the company,

1

their vote carries proportionally to the amount invested. Such a scheme is clearly fair from a democratic point of view, but is this the same as *financially* fair? Let us define the latter as follows:

Definition 1.1. In the context of a financial transaction, a *fair* transaction is one in which neither the buyer nor seller is able to make a riskless profit.

Such a definition is equivalent to the statement that the transaction is free from *arbitrage*. Note that the transaction must yield a profit greater than or equal to zero with *certainty* to be classified as an arbitrage. A simple example would be a coin tossing game between two people, call them A and B, where A receives two dollars if the coin falls heads, and B receives 1 dollar if the coin falls tails. As the game is obviously more attractive to A than B, B should clearly demand payment to enter into it. Suppose that the coin is fair, and that interest rates are zero, then the transaction would be fair provided neither A nor B would be guaranteed a profit. Clearly, if A pays B 2 dollars or more, the game is an arbitrage for B. Conversely, if B somehow ends up paying A 1 dollar or more, the game is an arbitrage for A. Defining the amount paid by A to B as P, the game would be fair provided $-1 < P < 2$. Note the distinction with expectation. We might think that the fair price for this game should simply be $1/2$, as for this price $E[P] = 0$. If we played this game a large number of times, and paid the *average* profit to the profit taker, then as the number of games tended to infinity, this would indeed be the fair price, as the variance of the profit would tend to zero, making the game riskless. For a finite number of games, however, the fair price must necessarily exist over a range. Whilst the example is obviously somewhat contrived, it does serve to illustrate an important aspect of valuation theory, namely that the fair price for a transaction is, in general, *unique* only under idealised circumstances, such as infinite portfolio diversification, or infinitesimal transaction time. We will examine this in more detail in the rest of this chapter.

For a stable financial system to exist, parties within it must be able to transact freely and agree on a price. The more they transact, the faster any opportunities for immediate wealth creation will be eroded, so that indeed, in a fully transparent, liquid, continuously traded system, the market should always be fair. Such a theory is an example of an efficient market hypothesis, of which there are three forms. The *strong efficient market hypothesis* [Fama (1965)], maintains that the prices of traded assets reflect all possible information, including 'insider' information (such as how much dividend a stock is going to pay in a year's time). The *semi-strong efficient market hypothesis*, maintains that the prices of traded assets reflect all *publicly* available information (such as the next announced dividend on a stock) is more reasonable. The *weak efficient market hypothesis* maintains that the prices of traded assets reflect only all *past* available information (for example, the financial health of a company and how its performance has compared to its peers). Until Black and Scholes published their seminal paper [Black and Scholes (1973)], one of the most popular methods for determining the fair price of a security was based on the *Capital Asset Pricing Model* (CAPM) introduced originally by Jack Treynor in 1961 [Treynor (1961)], and later developed independently by William Sharpe [Sharpe (1964)], John Lintner [Lintner (1965)] and Jan Mossin [Mossin (1966)]. CAPM itself, however, can be seen as a special case of the more general *Arbitrage Pricing Theory* (APT), introduced by Stephen Ross in 1976 [Ross (1976)], which we will now describe.

1.2 Arbitrage Pricing Theory

Fundamental to APT is the idea that the rate of return on any security is a linear function of k factors:

$$r_i = E_{\mathbb{P}}[r_i] + \sum_k b_{ik} F_k + \varepsilon_i \tag{1.1}$$

with $E_{\mathbb{P}}[F_k] = E_{\mathbb{P}}[\varepsilon_i] = 0 \ \forall \ i, k$, and ε_i uncorrelated with F_k. Note that the expectation is considered under $\mathbb{P}$, the *physical* measure denoting the actual probability distribution of asset returns. We will use the notation $E[x] = E_{\mathbb{P}}[x]$ for the remainder of the section. We assume furthermore that markets are perfectly competitive and frictionless (such that any arbitrage opportunity will be immediately eliminated), that investors have homogeneous beliefs that the returns on the set of assets under consideration are governed by (1.1), and that the number of assets n under consideration is $\gg k$. We now construct an *arbitrage portfolio*, which (a) uses no wealth, and (b) is riskless. From our definition of arbitrage in the previous section, these conditions imply that the portfolio must earn no return on average. Denoting w_i the change in the dollar amount in the i-th asset as a percentage of the individual's total invested wealth, the condition (a) gives:

$$\sum_{i=1}^{n} w_i = 0 \tag{1.2}$$

Using (1.1) we can write for the additional portfolio return:

$$r_P = \sum_{i=1}^{n} w_i \left[E[r_i] + \sum_k b_{ik} F_k + \varepsilon_i \right] \tag{1.3}$$

Now we use the fact that the number of assets in the portfolio is *large*. This gives $w_i \simeq 1/n$ and $Var[\sum_i w_i \varepsilon_i] \to 0$ as $n \to \infty$. We are also free to choose the weights w_i such that all systematic risk is eliminated, i.e.

$$\sum_i w_i b_{ik} = 0 \tag{1.4}$$

making the return on our portfolio riskless as $n \to \infty$. The no arbitrage condition then states that r_P itself must be zero, i.e.

$$\sum_i w_i E[r_i] = 0 \tag{1.5}$$

Combined with (1.4), (1.5) implies a solution:

$$E[r_i] = \lambda_0 + \sum_{j=1,k} \lambda_j b_{ij} \tag{1.6}$$

If we now incorporate a riskless asset $i = 0$ with a riskless rate of return r_f, then from (1.1) $b_{0j} = 0 \; \forall \; j$ and

$$E[r_0] = r_f = \lambda_0 \tag{1.7}$$

with the last equality following from (1.6). If we now define $\bar{\delta}_j$ as the expected return on a portfolio with unit sensitivity to the j-th factor, and zero sensitivity to the other factors, we can combine (1.7) and (1.6), and rewrite the latter to give:

$$E[r_i] = r_f + \sum_{j=1,k} [\bar{\delta}_j - r_f] b_{ij} \tag{1.8}$$

Interpreting (1.8) as a linear regression equation, we end up with the estimate of b_{ij} given by:

$$b_{ij} = \frac{Cov(r_i, \delta_j)}{Var(\delta_j)} \tag{1.9}$$

i.e. the correlation between r_i and δ_j. Now, in the simplest model, where there is only one systematic factor M, with rate of return r_M we end up with the Capital Asset Pricing Model:

$$E_{\mathbb{P}}[r_i] = r_f + [E_{\mathbb{P}}[r_M] - r_f]\beta_i \qquad (1.10)$$

where β_i is the correlation between r_i the *market return* r_M.

If we now consider a single period payoff, paying $S_i(T)$ at time T then using $r_i = S_i(T)/S_i(0) - 1$, we can solve (1.10) to give:

$$S_i(0) = \frac{E_{\mathbb{P}}[S_i(T)]}{1 + r_f + [E_{\mathbb{P}}[r_M] - r_f]\beta_i} \qquad (1.11)$$

So, if we have a measure of β_i, r_f and $E_{\mathbb{P}}[r_M]$, and some estimate for $E_{\mathbb{P}}[S_i(T)]$, then the price of our asset, for this simplified single period case, is determined. In practice β_i and r_f are found by regression of r_i vs r_M over a long time period of non-overlapping return windows (e.g. monthly over a 25-year period [Modigliani and Pogue (1974a,b)], with $E_{\mathbb{P}}[r_M]$ calculated off the same data set.

We could view (1.11) as a statement about the pricing of an instrument which pays the stock price at some time in the future T. Of course, as such a contract would just deliver the stock, this must be valued at the stock price today. Let us now consider a *forward* contract, which pays $S_T - F$ for a unit of stock at time T. As this contract is equivalent to a long position in a risky asset paying S_T and a short position in a riskless one paying F then, assuming that the stock pays no dividends, the CAPM price for this contract V_0 would simply be:

$$
\begin{aligned}
V(0) &= \frac{E_{\mathbb{P}}[S_T]}{1 + r_f + [E_{\mathbb{P}}[r_M] - r_f]\beta} - \frac{F}{1 + r_f} \\
&= S_0 - \frac{F}{1 + r_f}
\end{aligned}
$$

where β is the correlation between the return on the contract and the market. In practice, these contracts trade at zero value, giving $F = S_0(1 + r_f)$.

We could have come to the same answer via a different argument. Assume that we short the stock, and use the proceeds to buy the forward contract, at V_0 and F units of a risk-free zero coupon bond, paying unity at time T, priced at $P(0, T)$. At T the forward contract will simply pay the difference between $S_T - F$, the value of buying the stock at the agreed forward price. At expiration we exercise the forward contract, buy back the stock we've shorted, and receive F from the bond. Our final position is thus net zero stock, zero cash, with *certainty*. For this to be a fair transaction, the value of the portfolio today must be zero, giving a *unique* price for the forward contract $V_0 = S_0 - FP(0, T)$. In other words, we have *replicated* the forward contract through a long position in stock and a short position in bonds. For this to trade at zero value, we must have $F = S_0/P(0, T) = S_0(1 + r_f)$ as before.

1.3   The Black–Scholes model

In 1973, Fischer Black and Myron Scholes provided a radically new method for providing a unique fair price for options and corporate liabilities based on the replication arguments used in the previous section [Black and Scholes (1973)]. Driving this theory is one central idea:

- In the limit of continuous trading, and assuming no market frictions, the net change of a costless portfolio consisting of an option and a replicating position in stocks and bonds is identically zero, for *any* realised path of the underlying assets.

In their original paper, the only source of randomness was considered to be the stock price underlying the option. Moreover, the stock itself was considered to be a geometric Brownian motion with constant drift and volatility, with the risk-free rate also constant. The argument then worked like this:

(1) Construct a replicating portfolio of α_0 stocks and β_0 zero coupon, riskless bonds, such that the option price at time T_0 is equal to $-\alpha_0 S_0 - \beta_0 B(0)$. The net portfolio Π is manifestly costless.

(2) At every single subsequent time t, between T_0 and expiry T, compute the amount of stock α_t we need to hold such that the *variance* of the change in portfolio value over the interval $[t, t + dt]$ is zero in the limit of continuous sampling $(dt \to 0)$.

(3) Use the proceeds from stock trading to adjust our net cash position such that the portfolio remains costless.

Let's see how this works, step-by-step. At time t_0 we have $\Pi_0 = 0$, with a holding of α_0 of stock and $\beta_0 B_0 = -(V_0 + \alpha_0 S_0)$ of zero coupon bonds, where α_0 is chosen to ensure that the variance of the portfolio is zero over the time-step $[t_0, t_1]$. The stock is assumed to obey the geometric Brownian motion:

$$\frac{dS_t}{S_t} = \mu dt + \sigma dW_t$$

where dW_t is a normally distributed increment $\sim \mathcal{N}(0, dt)$. At the next time-step, our bond has accrued to $\beta_0 B_0 \exp(r(t_1 - t_0))$ and our option value and stock value changed to V_1 and S_1 respectively. At this point, we then buy a further $(\alpha_1 - \alpha_0)S_1$ of bonds to change our stock position to $\alpha_1 S_1$ of stock ensuring that the variance in our portfolio over the next time-step $[t_1, t_2]$ continues to be zero. We also want to ensure that our portfolio remains at zero value, requiring us to change our bond position to $\beta_1 B_1 = -(V_1 + \alpha_1 S_1)$. The net Profit and Loss (P&L) from this rebalancing is:

$$d\Pi_1 = -(\alpha_1 - \alpha_0)S_1 - [\beta_1 B_1 - \beta_0 B_0 \exp(r(t_1 - t_0))]$$

Using the fact that the new portfolio is perfectly balanced, we can rewrite this as:

$$d\Pi_1 = V_1 + \alpha_0 S_1 - (V_0 + \alpha_0 S_0) \exp(r(t_1 - t_0))$$

In general, the P&L at the n-th rebalance date will be:

$$d\Pi_n = V_n + \alpha_{n-1} S_n - (V_{n-1} + \alpha_{n-1} S_{n-1}) \exp(r(t_n - t_{n-1}))$$

so that, in the limit of small $dt = t_n - t_{n-1}$, denoting $t_{n-1} = t$, $t_n = t + dt$, we can write this as:

$$d\Pi(t) = V(t + dt) + \alpha(t)S(t + dt) - (V(t) + \alpha(t)S(t))(1 + rdt)$$

Taylor expanding to second order:

$$V(t + dt) - V(t) = \frac{\partial V}{\partial t} dt + \frac{\partial V}{\partial S} dS_t + \frac{1}{2} \frac{\partial^2 V}{\partial S^2} dS_t^2$$

We thus have:

$$d\Pi(t) = \frac{\partial V}{\partial t} dt + \left[\frac{\partial V}{\partial S} + \alpha(t) \right] dS_t + \frac{1}{2} \frac{\partial^2 V}{\partial S^2} dS_t^2 - (V(t) + \alpha(t)S(t))rdt$$

Now, in the continuous trading limit $dt \rightarrow 0$, $Var[dS_t^2] \rightarrow 0$ for a geometric Brownian motion, leaving only the linear term in dS_t contributing to the variance of $d\Pi(t)$. To ensure zero variance in the continuous trading limit (a.k.a *risk-neutrality*) we require:

$$\alpha(t) = -\frac{\partial V}{\partial S}$$

Secondly, we want the option price to be *fair*, i.e. there can be *no* profit or loss from this trading strategy. This determines the *self-financing* condition $d\Pi_t = 0$, giving:

$$\frac{\partial V}{\partial t}dt + \frac{1}{2}\frac{\partial^2 V}{\partial S^2}dS_t^2 - \left(V(t) - \frac{\partial V}{\partial S}S(t)\right)rdt = 0$$

In the limit $dt \rightarrow 0$, $(S(t+dt) - S(t))^2 \rightarrow \sigma^2 S(t)^2 dt$. We thus recover the classic Black–Scholes equation:

$$\frac{\partial V}{\partial t} + rS\frac{\partial V}{\partial S} + \frac{1}{2}\sigma^2 S^2 \frac{\partial^2 V}{\partial S^2} - rV = 0$$

for $t_0 \leq t < T$. The implications of this result were staggering.

(1) With a little bit of algebra (see exercise), this equation can be reduced to the diffusion equation:

$$\frac{\partial u}{\partial \tau} = \frac{\partial^2 u}{\partial x^2}$$

for $u = u(x, \tau)$. For a given set of boundary conditions (or in the terminology of derivatives: 'payoffs') the solution to this equation is *unique*. This trading strategy guarantees a *single* option price on which all parties can transact fairly and risklessly. The solution to this equation, for a call option, is given by:

$$C(T_0, K) = e^{-r(T-T_0)} \int_0^\infty \phi(S_T)(S_T - K, 0)^+ dS_T \tag{1.12}$$

where

$$\phi(S_T) = \frac{1}{S_T\sqrt{2\pi\sigma^2(T-T_0)}} \exp\left[\frac{-\left[\log\left(\frac{S_T}{S_0}\right) - (r - \sigma^2/2)(T-T_0)\right]^2}{2\sigma^2(T-T_0)}\right]$$

corresponding to a stock distributed *log-normally* with mean $\log(S_0) + (r - \sigma^2/2)(T - T_0)$ and variance $\sigma^2(T - T_0)$. We refer to the probability measure[1] corresponding to this distribution as the *risk-neutral measure*, in contrast to the *physical measure* (a.k.a *real-world measure* or *objective measure*) corresponding to the distribution $\log(S_T/S_0) \sim \mathcal{N}((\mu - \sigma^2/2)(T - T_0), \sigma^2(T - T_0))$. Note that only the effective drift is different between the two measures, and indeed the *Cameron–Martin–Girsanov theorem* expresses this exactly [Baxter and Rennie (1997)]:

Theorem 1.1. *If W_t is a $\mathbb{P}$ Brownian motion, and γ_t an $\mathcal{F}$-previsible process[2] satisfying the boundedness condition $E_{\mathbb{P}} \left[\frac{1}{2} \int_0^T \gamma_t^2 dt \right] < \infty$, then there exists a measure $\mathbb{Q}$ such that:*

(a) $\mathbb{Q}$ is equivalent to $\mathbb{P}$
(b)

$$\frac{d\mathbb{Q}}{d\mathbb{P}} = \exp\left(-\int_0^T \gamma_t dW_t - \frac{1}{2} \int_0^T \gamma_t^2 dt \right)$$

(c) $\widetilde{W}_t = W_t + \int_0^t \gamma_s ds$ is a $\mathbb{Q}$-Brownian motion

The quantity $d\mathbb{Q}/d\mathbb{P}$ is termed the *Radon–Nikodym* derivative, characterising the change of measure from $\mathbb{P}$ to $\mathbb{Q}$. In other words, for a diffusive process which is driftless in one measure, we can transform the probability space of the process in such a way that only its drift is altered. Equation (1.12) is in fact a special case of a general property of the risk-neutral measure, namely, for any *tradable* instrument V_t, i.e. one that can be replicated with instruments for which there exists a market price, we have:

$$\frac{V_t}{B_t} = E_{\mathbb{Q}} \left[\frac{V_T}{B_T} \bigg| \mathcal{F}_t \right]$$

where

$$B_t = \exp\left[\int_0^t r_s ds \right]$$

---

[1] Formally, a real-valued function μ defined on a set of events I in a probability space which (a) satisfies countable additivity, $\mu\left(\bigcup_{i \in I} E_i \right) = \sum_{i \in I} \mu(E_i)$ for disjoint sets E_i and (b) returns results in the unit interval $[0, 1]$, returning 0 for the empty set and 1 for the entire set of possible outcomes.

[2] A process dependent only on its history up to one time tick earlier.

is sometimes referred to as the *money-market account* and defines the *numeraire* characterising the risk-neutral measure $\mathbb{Q}$. We use the notation $E_{\mathbb{Q}}[X_T|\mathcal{F}_t]$ as a shorthand denoting the expectation of X_T in the measure $\mathbb{Q}$ conditional on the *filtration* $\mathcal{F}_t$ (the history of X_t up to time t) at time t. We will show in Chapter 7 that a simple, and powerful, relationship exists between the Radon–Nikodym derivative and the *numeraires* of the respective measures, which will prove essential in pricing derivatives in a stochastic rate environment.

(2) The actual growth of the stock μ has absolutely no bearing on the price – it gets cancelled via the trading strategy itself. At a stroke, forecasts of future stock performance were rendered irrelevant to the pricing of options. This of course is a natural corollary of the result that the price of the option is unique.

In a sense then, the Black–Scholes delta hedging strategy can be regarded as the embodiment of financial fairness defined at the beginning of the chapter. No one wins, no one loses, and this happens with *certainty*. So did finance suddenly die in 1973? Happily for the author (who coincidentally was born in the previous year), the answer was no. The Black–Scholes model is an exceptionally elegant and beautiful model. It just happens to be insufficient for the world we live in.

1.4   The problems of the real world

1.4.1   *Discrete hedging*

The first, obvious problem, with the Black–Scholes formalism is the assumption that we can hedge continuously. In the over-the-counter (OTC) market at least, most delta hedging is performed at market close. One could, in principle, hedge more often than that, but the transaction costs would necessitate option pricing at uncompetitive levels. In his 2010 paper [Sepp (2010)], Sepp derives approximate forms for jump-diffusion models with discrete hedging times, and non-zero transaction costs, some of the results of which we will outline in this section. Suppose we continue with the Black–Scholes assumption that the diffusion parameters of the stock process are constant over time, but that the stock diffuses with volatility σ, whilst the option is *marked* with volatility $\hat{\sigma}$. For the buyer of the option, it is straightforward to show (see exercise), that the change in the portfolio value over a finite time interval $\delta t_n = t_n - t_{n-1}$ is given, to second order in spot, by the 'gamma leakage':

$$\delta\Pi(t_n) \simeq \frac{1}{2}\left(\sigma^2 - \hat{\sigma}^2\right)\delta t_n S^2(t_{n-1})\frac{\partial^2 V(t_{n-1}, S(t_{n-1}))}{\partial S^2}$$

The total accrued P&L is given by accruing these portfolio losses and gains at the risk-free rate, i.e.

$$P(T) = \sum_{n=1}^{N} e^{r(T-t_n)}\delta\Pi(t_n) = \sum_{n=1}^{N}(\sigma^2 - \hat{\sigma}^2)\delta t_n \Gamma(t_{n-1}, S)$$

where we define the *cash-gamma* as:

$$\Gamma(t, S) \equiv \frac{1}{2}e^{r(T-t)}S^2(t)\frac{\partial^2 V(t, S(t))}{\partial S^2}$$

and $t_N = T$. This allows us to see immediately that, under the real-world measure $\mathbb{P}$, the expected P&L is given by:

$$E_\mathbb{P}[P(T)] = \sum_{n=1}^{N}(\sigma^2 - \hat{\sigma}^2)\delta t_n E_\mathbb{P}[\Gamma(t_{n-1}, S)]$$

Sepp goes on to show that, in the case where the diffusion of the stock under the real-world measure $\mathbb{P}$ and risk-neutral measure $\mathbb{Q}$ are the same, that $E_\mathbb{P}[\Gamma(t_{n-1}, S)] = \Gamma(t_0, S)$. Like this, we can approximate the expected P&L by:

$$E_\mathbb{P}[P(T)] \simeq (\sigma^2 - \hat{\sigma}^2)T\Gamma(t_0, S)$$

Interestingly, this does *not* depend on the number of hedging fixings N between t_0 and the expiry of the option T. The result also seems intuitive: if we price an option at an implied volatility above the *actual* stock volatility, we should expect to end up with a negative P&L, i.e. we've paid too much for the option. We will look at this problem in more detail in the next section.

Assuming we've actually priced the option with the implied vol equal to the realised vol, we would still expect the transaction to be profitless, *on average*. But Black–Scholes states that the transaction should be profitless *with certainty*. In the absence of transaction costs, assuming for the moment that realised volatility equals implied volatility, it can be shown [Derman (1999b); Sepp (2010)] that $Var[P(T)] \propto 1/N$. So, even in the case where our implied volatility guarantees zero expectation for P&L, we are not in fact risk neutral. This behaviour is shown in Figures 1.1 and 1.2 for the P&L distribution of a *daily* hedged at the money (strike = spot) call with 2-year expiry, vs that for the same call but hedged *monthly*. The implied volatility is set equal to realised volatility (20%) with the risk-free rate and real-world stock drift set to zero. One thousand simulations were used.

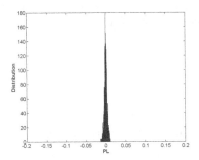

Fig. 1.1   Distribution of realised P&L, 2Y ATM call, daily hedging, 20% implied vol.

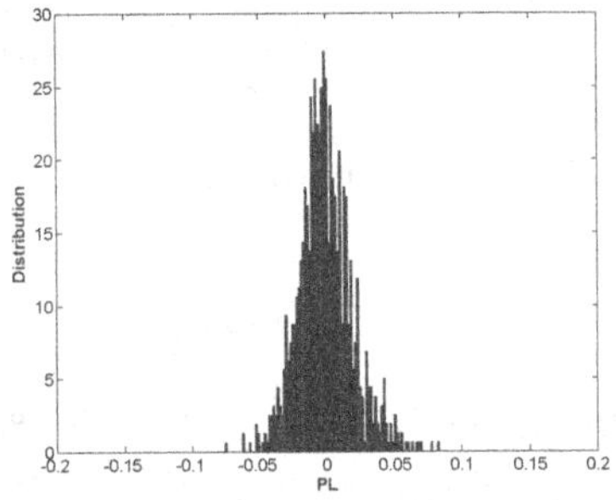

Fig. 1.2   Distribution of realised P&L, 2Y ATM call, monthly hedging, 20% implied vol.

In both cases, the mean of the realised P&L is close to zero, as expected, but the risk-neutrality of the scheme deteriorates with decreasing hedging frequency, as predicted. It is unlikely, however, that our implied volatility will be exactly in line with realised volatility. Figures 1.3 and 1.4 show the P&L distributions for options priced with 15% implied vol and 10% implied vol respectively.

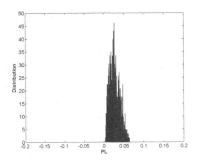
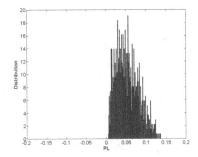

Fig. 1.3   Distribution of realised P&L, 2Y ATM call, daily hedging, 15% implied vol.

Fig. 1.4   Distribution of realised P&L, 2Y ATM call, daily hedging, 10% implied vol.

Two things appear to happen. As expected, the mean of the P&L distribution manifestly becomes positive to the option holder, as the price paid lies below the fair value. The standard deviation of the distribution also increases with decreasing implied volatility.

1.4.2 *Transaction costs*

A related problem to the impact of hedging in discrete time is the problem of transaction costs. This is also covered in Sepp's framework, where he introduces both fixed transaction costs (as a percentage of the trade value) and costs proportional to the total value of shares traded. The latter was considered as far back as 1985 by Leland [Leland (1985)], where he introduced a drag on the rebalancing P&L:

$$\Theta_n = \frac{\kappa}{2}S(t_n)|\Delta(t_n, S) - \Delta(t_{n-1}, S)|$$

(where, as per Γ, we employ the shorthand $\Delta(t_n, S) = \Delta(t_n, S(t_n))$). Unsurprisingly, this reduces the expected P&L. Sepp estimates that the effect goes as $-\Gamma(t_0, S)\kappa\sqrt{2\sigma^2 TN/\pi}$, i.e. the more frequently we hedge, the more volatile the stock, and the longer dated the option, the worse our transaction losses become. The frequency effect is illustrated in Figures 1.5 and 1.6 for the same option as above, for daily vs monthly hedging, at a transaction cost κ of 2%. The implied volatility is taken equal to realised at 20%.

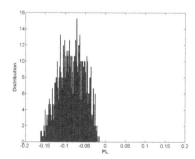

Fig. 1.5 Distribution of realised P&L, 2Y ATM call, daily hedging, 2% transaction cost.

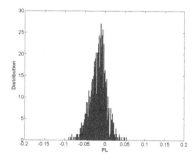

Fig. 1.6 Distribution of realised P&L, 2Y ATM call, monthly hedging, 2% transaction cost.

The example is somewhat extreme. A transaction cost of around 20bps would be more realistic, but it illustrates the point. Where the investor is long-the-call, a reduction in the implied volatility is required to break even (i.e. bring the expected P&L back to zero), and vice versa if short-the-call. In the latter case Leland [Leland (1985)] calculated an adjustment $\delta\hat{\sigma}$ given by:

$$(\hat{\sigma} + \delta\hat{\sigma})^2 = \sigma^2 + \kappa\sigma\sqrt{\frac{2N}{\pi T}}$$

1.4.3   *The breakdown of log-normality*

In all of the above discussion of how the Black–Scholes model deviates from absolute fairness, we made the simplifying assumption that the underlying stock propagates with constant diffusion volatility and drift, and that rates also are constant. The extension to a term structure of all of these parameters is not in itself hugely problematic for the model, it simply results in the *implied* market parameters being different from the model parameters. For the more general model [Merton (1973)], we have for the stock process in the real-world measure:

$$\frac{dS_t}{S_t} = \mu(t)dt + \sigma(t)dW_t^{\mathbb{P}}$$

and in the risk-neutral measure:

$$\frac{dS_t}{S_t} = r(t)dt + \sigma(t)dW_t^{\mathbb{Q}}$$

where $E_{\mathbb{P}}[dW_t^{\mathbb{P}}] := 0$ and $E_{\mathbb{Q}}[dW_t^{\mathbb{Q}}] := 0$. Indeed, if we want to factor in a continuous dividend yield $q(t)$ this expression is modified to:

$$\frac{dS_t}{S_t} = [r(t) - q(t)]dt + \sigma(t)dW_t \qquad (1.13)$$

(see Chapter 2). The corresponding partial differential equation for the option price $V(t)$ can be written:

$$\frac{\partial V}{\partial t} + [r(t) - q(t)]S_t\frac{\partial V}{\partial S} + \frac{1}{2}\sigma^2(t)S_t^2\frac{\partial^2 V}{\partial S^2} - r(t)V(t) = 0 \qquad (1.14)$$

For which the solution for a call, $V(T) = \max(S_T - K, 0)$ is given (see exercise) by the Black–Scholes formula:

$$C(K,0) = e^{-\bar{r}(T)T} \left[F(T)N(d_1) - KN(d_2) \right] \tag{1.15}$$
$$F(T) = S_0 e^{(\bar{r}(T) - \bar{q}(T))T}$$

$$d_1 = \frac{\log(F(T)/K)}{\widehat{\sigma}(T)\sqrt{T}} + \frac{\widehat{\sigma}(T)\sqrt{T}}{2}; \; d_2 = d_1 - \widehat{\sigma}(T)\sqrt{T}$$

$$\bar{r}(T) = \frac{1}{T} \int_0^T r(t)dt$$

$$\bar{q}(T) = \frac{1}{T} \int_0^T q(t)dt$$

$$\widehat{\sigma}^2(T) = \frac{1}{T} \int_0^T \sigma^2(t)dt$$

Note that $F(T)$ is the fair strike of the *forward* contract introduced earlier, though now generalised to continuous dividend yield. The result can likewise be derived from a simple hedging argument (see exercise). In the original Black–Scholes model, where all model parameters are constant, we trivially have that the implied rate, dividend yield and volatility $\bar{r}(T)$, $\bar{q}(T)$ and $\widehat{\sigma}(T)$ are equal to their associated model parameters r, q and σ. The associated risk-neutral stock price distribution $\varphi(S_T, T)$ at maturity T can be derived simply by considering the integral form of the undiscounted call value $\widetilde{C}(K, T) = e^{\bar{r}(T)T}C(K,T)$[3]:

$$\widetilde{C}(K,0) = \int_0^T \max(S_T - K, 0)\varphi(S_T, T)dS_T$$

Differentiating twice by K we arrive at (see exercise):

$$\frac{\partial^2 \widetilde{C}}{\partial K^2} = \varphi(K, T)$$

If we apply this to (1.15) we obtain:

$$\varphi(K, T) = \frac{n(d_2)}{K\sqrt{\widehat{\sigma}^2(T)T}}$$

where $n(x) = \sqrt{1/2\pi}e^{-x^2/2}$. This is simply the probability density of a variable whose logarithm is distributed normally $\sim \mathcal{N}(\log(F) - \widehat{\sigma}^2T/2, \widehat{\sigma}^2T)$, a.k.a the *log-normal distribution*. Note that the implied volatility derived

---

[3]Strictly speaking, this is the distribution in the so-called T-forward measure, equivalent to the risk-neutral measure when rates are deterministic. This will be presented in detail in Chapter 7.

from this time varying but *deterministic* process has no dependence on the strike level. As we shall explore in Chapter 2, this is almost never the case. A typical equity implied volatility surface (in this case 1Y-5Y options on the S&P500) is shown in Figure 1.7.

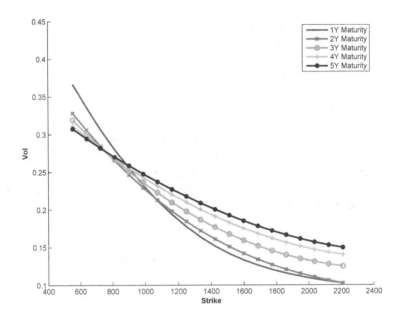

Fig. 1.7   1Y-5Y volatility surface slices for the S&P500, as of 1/3/2010.

Since the crash of 1987, equity options have tended to show a so-called 'negative volatility skew', i.e. the market tends to pay more for puts than calls, of the same *moneyness* $\log(K/F)$. This has led some commentators to refer to equity options as 'options on fear', highlighting the fact that trading in equity derivatives is strongly driven by the fear of downside stock moves. We will return to this subject repeatedly throughout this book, but for the moment, what does this imply about the equity process in general? Applying the chain rule to the undiscounted call option price $\widetilde{C}(K,T) = \widetilde{C}(K, \widehat{\sigma}(K,T), T)$, we have:

$$\varphi(K,T) = \left.\frac{\partial^2 \widetilde{C}}{\partial K^2}\right|_{\widehat{\sigma}} + 2 \left.\frac{\partial^2 \widetilde{C}}{\partial K \partial \widehat{\sigma}}\right|_{\widehat{\sigma},K} \frac{\partial \widehat{\sigma}}{\partial K} + \left.\frac{\partial \widetilde{C}}{\partial \widehat{\sigma}}\right|_K \left.\frac{\partial^2 \widehat{\sigma}}{\partial K^2} + \frac{\partial^2 \widetilde{C}}{\partial \widehat{\sigma}^2}\right|_K \left(\frac{\partial \widehat{\sigma}}{\partial K}\right)^2$$

(1.16)

The implications of this expression are profound. For *any* implied volatility slice $\hat{\sigma}(K, T)$ with strike dependence, the implied risk-neutral probability distribution cannot be log-normal. The latter is given by the first term in (1.16) only. But we know that a deterministic geometric Brownian motion of the type (1.13) must necessarily result in a log-normal distribution. The inescapable conclusion then is that the stock process *cannot* follow a deterministic geometric Brownian motion. The problem for practitioners in the market, and all interested parties then is simple to pose, but impossible to answer fully: if the stock does not follow a deterministic geometric Brownian motion, what process *does* it follow? The reason why the question is impossible to answer fully is that there are, as we shall see, an infinite number of possible processes which do indeed match vanilla option prices perfectly, a handful of which we will explore in detail in this book. You might think that this is all a bit academic. If we match the market, who cares what model we use? Again, the answer is simple: the market cares which model we use to match the market.

1.5 The importance of model choice

1.5.1 *Wrong hedge, wrong price*

In derivatives, it is not sufficient merely to match market prices. As we move from day to day, the model parameters underlying those prices will be recalibrated, so that they themselves become volatile. As we shall explore in Chapter 2, the Dupire local volatility model is a case in point. In essence, the model essentially says that, as of today, for a given realised spot price at some point in the future, we know *exactly* what the instantaneous volatility (a.k.a the *local volatility*) will be, conditional on that spot price. The model can be written as follows:

$$\frac{dS_t}{S_t} = \mu(t)dt + \sigma(S_t, t)dW_t$$

At first glance such a model appears to be quite unrealistic. In finance (almost) nothing is certain. Why should we magically know everything there is to know about stock dynamics merely by looking at the market today? Of course we don't, but such an approach turns out to have the enormous advantage that the dynamics can be derived directly from market implied volatilities, without recourse to expensive integration and calibration routines. Indeed, as we shall derive, the local volatility at spot $S_T = K$ at time T is given by:

$$\sigma^2(K,T) = \frac{\frac{\partial \widetilde{C}}{\partial T} - \mu(T)\left[\widetilde{C} - K\frac{\partial \widetilde{C}}{\partial K}\right]}{\frac{K^2}{2}\frac{\partial^2 \widetilde{C}}{\partial K^2}}$$

where $\widetilde{C}(K,T)$ corresponds to the undiscounted call price at strike K and maturity T. After some algebra, this equates to:

$$\sigma^2(z,T) = \frac{\frac{\partial}{\partial T}\big|_z \left(\hat{\sigma}^2 T\right)}{1 + \hat{\sigma}T\frac{\partial^2 \hat{\sigma}}{\partial z^2} + Td_1 d_2 \left(\frac{\partial \hat{\sigma}}{\partial z}\right)^2 - \frac{2z}{\hat{\sigma}}\frac{\partial \hat{\sigma}}{\partial z}}$$

where $z = \log[K/F(T)]$ with $F(T)$ the forward at maturity T and $\hat{\sigma}$ corresponds to the *implied* volatility at strike K and maturity T. We will discuss the significance of this expression in terms of arbitrage later, but for the moment, notice what it says. Conditional on knowing the implied volatility for all possible strikes and all possible maturities, we can exactly state how the stock evolves at all points in the future. Logically then, we should be able to compute the local volatility surface $\sigma(S,t)$ *once*, and hedge all derivatives on the associated stock through simple delta hedging (as the only source of randomness is the stock price) perfectly for all time. The reality of course is that this is far from the truth. For a start, the change in the implied volatility surface with spot that this model implies is unrealistic compared to actual market moves, so the model needs to be *re-calibrated* every day. In effect, the change in option value predicted by this model with spot is just incorrect, so our delta hedge is wrong. Even though we will indeed match to market prices every day, the hedging P&L on our overall portfolio will not be zero, even in the continuous limit. We also indeed will not be risk-neutral, i.e. the P&L of our portfolio will clearly not have zero variance. Let's illustrate this with another example.

Suppose that we have an option with flat implied volatility, and we simply delta hedge the option as per Black–Scholes. But now, let's make the more realistic assumption that local volatility is in fact volatile (we will demonstrate this in Chapter 4). We have for the evolution of the option:

$$dV_t = \frac{\partial V}{\partial t}dt + \frac{\partial V}{\partial S}dS_t + \frac{\partial V}{\partial \sigma}d\sigma_t + \frac{1}{2}\left[\frac{\partial^2 V}{\partial S^2}dS_t^2 + 2\frac{\partial^2 V}{\partial S\partial\sigma}dS_t d\sigma_t + \frac{\partial^2 V}{\partial \sigma^2}d\sigma_t^2\right]$$

Thus, for the evolution of our full, delta hedged portfolio $\Pi = V - \Delta S + B$, we have, assuming zero dividend yield:

$$d\Pi_t = dV_t - \frac{\partial V}{\partial S}dS_t + dB_t$$

So that, again, taking the portfolio to be perfectly rebalanced at every time-step, such that $B_t = \Delta(t)S_t - V_t$, using $dB_t = B_t r_t dt$, we have for the re-balancing P&L:

$$d\Pi_t = \frac{\partial V}{\partial t}dt + \frac{\partial V}{\partial \sigma}d\sigma_t + \frac{1}{2}\left[\frac{\partial^2 V}{\partial S^2}dS_t^2 + 2\frac{\partial^2 V}{\partial S \partial \sigma}dS_t d\sigma_t + \frac{\partial^2 V}{\partial \sigma^2}d\sigma_t^2\right]$$
$$+ r_t\left(\frac{\partial V}{\partial S}S_t - V_t\right)dt$$

Now, as we are pricing and hedging the option according to a Black–Scholes volatility $\widehat{\sigma}$, we have:

$$\frac{\partial V}{\partial t} + r_t\frac{\partial V}{\partial S}S_t + \frac{1}{2}\frac{\partial^2 V}{\partial S^2}S^2\widehat{\sigma}^2 = r_t V_t$$

If, for the sake of argument, we assume that our local volatility process also follows a geometric Brownian motion $d\sigma_t/\sigma_t = \kappa dt + \xi dW_t^\sigma$, where $E[dW_t^\sigma dW_t^S] = \rho dt$ our expression for the rebalancing P&L simplifies to:

$$d\Pi_t = \left[\frac{\partial V}{\partial \sigma}\sigma_t \kappa dt + \frac{1}{2}\left(\frac{\partial^2 V}{\partial S^2}(\sigma_t^2 - \widehat{\sigma}^2) + 2\frac{\partial^2 V}{\partial S \partial \sigma}\rho\xi S_t\sigma_t + \frac{\partial^2 V}{\partial \sigma^2}\xi^2\right)\right]dt$$
$$+ \xi\sigma_t dW_t^\sigma$$

Our strategy is thus clearly no longer self-financing, has non-zero expected P&L, and non-zero variance, even in the continuous limit. Whilst, based on our observation of vanilla option prices, we might have hoped a flat local volatility model to be appropriate, the realities from *stochastic* volatility could be quite costly to us. Indeed, if our position had a strong negative sensitivity of *vega* ($\partial V/\partial \sigma$) to volatility itself (*vol gamma*), or indeed if vega has a strong positive sensitivity to spot (*vanna*), and spot were negatively correlated with volatility, our *mis-hedge* could result in a significant negative realised P&L[4]. Supposing now that we were a little more sophisticated and had actively hedged away the volatility risk of the portfolio, would all be fair again?

---

[4]We will show in Chapter 4 that, for European options, this leakage can be absorbed in a volatility smile. Options priced on flat implied volatility under a stochastic volatility regime, as in this example, would necessarily be mis-priced.

1.5.2   *Right hedge, wrong price*

As we shall see in Chapter 4, stochastic volatility is not in itself a problem to hedge, at least theoretically. If we assume that the volatility is driven by only one source of randomness, as per the above example, we can actually hedge away the stochasticity with another instrument. This is derived in detail later, but it suffices for now to quote the result. The partial differential equation for the option price, where we *are* risk-neutral and self-financing, is given by:

$$\frac{\partial V}{\partial t} + r_t S_t \frac{\partial V}{\partial S} + g_t \sigma_t \frac{\partial V}{\partial \sigma} + \frac{1}{2} \left[\frac{\partial^2 V}{\partial S^2} \sigma_t^2 S_t^2 + 2 \frac{\partial^2 V}{\partial S \partial \sigma} S_t \sigma_t^2 \rho \xi + \frac{\partial^2 V}{\partial \sigma^2} \xi_t^2 \sigma_t^2 \right] = r_t V_t$$

As per delta hedging, the real-world drift of the volatility process has disappeared. *Unlike* delta hedging, however, the resultant risk-neutral expression does *not* uniquely identify a risk-neutral drift for the volatility. We could choose anything we like for g_t in the above expression and still be perfectly hedged. The reason for this, in essence, is that we can't buy the local volatility directly. We can see this by considering a world in which the stock could not in fact be hedged directly. As before, we'd construct a costless portfolio but now with another derivative, rather than the stock itself, i.e. $\Pi_t = V_t + \alpha(t) V_t' + \beta(t) B_t = 0$. The change in this portfolio would then be:

$$dI\!I_t = \frac{\partial V}{\partial t} dt + \frac{\partial V}{\partial S} dS_t + \frac{1}{2} \frac{\partial^2 V}{\partial S^2} dS_t^2 +$$
$$\alpha(t) \left[\frac{\partial V'}{\partial t} dt + \frac{\partial V'}{\partial S} dS_t + \frac{1}{2} \frac{\partial^2 V'}{\partial S^2} dS_t^2 \right] - r_t dt (V_t + \alpha(t) V_t')$$

To make this delta-neutral, we have:

$$\alpha(t) = -\frac{\partial V / \partial S}{\partial V' / \partial S}$$

giving us for $dI\!I_t = 0$:

$$\frac{\frac{\partial V}{\partial t} + \frac{1}{2} \frac{\partial^2 V}{\partial S^2} \sigma_t^2 S_t^2 - r_t V_t}{\partial V / \partial S} = \frac{\frac{\partial V'}{\partial t} + \frac{1}{2} \frac{\partial^2 V'}{\partial S^2} \sigma_t^2 S_t^2 - r_t V_t'}{\partial V' / \partial S} \qquad (1.17)$$

This expression could then be satisfied, in general, if both sides are simply set to some general $-g_t$, giving:

$$\frac{\partial V}{\partial t} + g_t \frac{\partial V}{\partial S} + \frac{\partial^2 V}{\partial S^2}\sigma_t^2 S_t^2 - r_t V_t$$

The stock 'growth' in this market is completely unspecified, though the hedging strategy is perfect. On the other hand, where we *can* trade the stock, we can have $V' = S$, taking the right side of (1.17) to $-r_t S_t$, *uniquely* specifying $g_t = r_t S_t$ and re-establishing Black–Scholes. Regrettably, though products such as volatility swaps, short-term forward rate agreements, or correlation swaps do exist, and are actively marketed, they do not *exactly* allow us to trade in local volatility, the short rate, or local correlation, respectively. For most of the model parameters which concern us then, a perfect hedge does not guarantee a unique price. And therein lies the essence of model risk, which we will now define as follows:

Definition 1.2. The model risk of a financial instrument is the uncertainty of the price of that instrument given the uncertainty in its model parameters.[5]

We will also define a *model* as:

Definition 1.3. A model is a set of stochastic processes applied to the underlying assets of a trade.

We note that this definition is considerably more restrictive than that recently proposed by the Federal Reserve [OCC (2011)], which defines a model as:

...a quantitative method, system, or approach that applies statistical, economic, financial, or mathematical theories, techniques, and assumptions to process input data into quantitative estimates.

Such a definition would effectively incorporate all of the following into the definition of model risk:

---

[5]Note that this definition incorporates the uncertainty in the sensitivity of price to market parameter shock. A strong area of interest, within the field of model risk, is the extent to which a portfolio might be better hedged through the greeks being better reflective of 'true' market dynamics by virtue of a model which more accurately captures those dynamics. This area, however, namely the relative *merits* of one model over another from a risk management perspective, would form another book in its own right, and will not be covered in this volume.

- **Market risk**. The sensitivity of an instrument to implied volatility, or interest rate shocks, or implied correlation moves, is the risk to market *observables*, a.k.a 'greeks'. By contrast, model risk, by our definition, is the sensitivity of an instrument to model *unobservables*. The fact that an instrument may have high implied volatility sensitivity (for example, a near expiry at the money digital), tells you little about its sensitivity to volatility of local volatility.

- **Calculator risk**. Trades can be priced more or less accurately depending on the adequacy of the numerical scheme employed. A continuous barrier option, for example, will on the whole have a more accurate price (and certainly more accurate greeks) if computed through finite difference techniques rather than Monte Carlo ones. Any trading entity will inevitably have some uncertainty in the price and greeks of its instruments coming from the noise in the numerical simulation, but this is quite distinct from the risk to the model parameters (though more complicated models may exacerbate the problem).

- **Scenario risk**. The exposure of a portfolio to a market crash scenario, for example, where spots decline by 30%, vols spike by 30% and correlations approach 100%, is an essential metric for any effectively risk-managed business, but again, falls outside the definition of model risk used here.

- **Operational risk**. Earlier papers on model risk [Kato and Yoshiba (2000)] frequently defined model risk as the risk of model *error*, e.g. from errors in market data, or discretisation errors in the calculator. This sort of risk, whilst important, is really the joint responsibility of model validation and product control. The former would check, for example, that the analytic limits of an exotic model are correct, that the model converges properly and is stable under perturbation, whilst the latter would check that the market data inputs line up with consensus estimates and/or traded prices. The error in the behaviour and inputs to the model is essentially an operational risk, with little or nothing to do with the *uncertainty* in the price of a product deriving from lack of model parameter transparency.

Whilst, subject to the wider definition of model used by regulators, these may all be seen as valid aspects of model risk, they will not be the subject of this book. Again though, does price uncertainty due to model really matter? After all, if we agree on the price of an instrument at the start of the trade, and hedge it perfectly until expiration, who cares if different banks might value it differently through the life of the trade? Well for a start, the regulators. In the early part of the last decade, the Financial Accounting Standards Board (FASB) and the International Accounting Standards Board (IASB) released their respective statements, FAS 133 and IAS 39, which largely involved disclosure of derivative positions on public financial statements, in contrast to the prior regime where derivatives were an 'off balance sheet' item in the footnotes of the accounts. The instruments were, moreover, required to be booked at 'fair value', namely the price at which the instrument could be sold, a.k.a the 'exit price', rather than 'book value', a.k.a. the 'entry price'. For exchange traded investments, such as stocks and government bonds, such a requirement presents no particular problems. The market price can simply be taken from the exchange. For derivatives however, notably exotics, the market for the instrument is not active. To clarify fair value treatment in these cases, the FASB issued statement FAS 157 [FASB (2008)] in September 2006, effective for financial assets and liabilities on statements issued for fiscal years beginning after 15th November 2007. The fair value was again defined as *the price that would be received by the holder of the financial asset in an orderly transaction (an exit price notion) that is not a forced liquidation or distressed sale at the measurement date*, but prioritises the inputs used to measure fair value into three levels:

- **Level 1**: unadjusted, quoted prices for identical assets or liabilities in active markets (e.g. exchange traded investments, futures and actively traded debt).
- **Level 2**: inputs, other than quoted prices within level 1, that are observable for the asset or liability, either directly or indirectly through corroboration with observable market data (e.g. vanilla interest rate swaps and credit default swaps, whose values are derived on yield curves or credit spreads, respectively).
- **Level 3**: unobservable inputs for the asset or liability, that is, inputs that reflect the reporting entity's own assumptions about the assumptions market participants would use in pricing the asset or liability (including assumptions about risk), developed on the best information available in the circumstances (e.g. any exotic derivative).

Level 1 pricing, where the direct market quote for the instrument is used, is referred to as *mark-to-market* pricing. For level 2 inputs, the common approach to valuation is to employ so-called *mark-to-matrix* pricing where similar, benchmark securities are used to interpolate fair value. For example, a vanilla interest rate swap of a less liquid tenor and maturity might be computed from a yield curve built from more liquidly traded swaps. Both mark-to-market and mark-to-matrix approaches are referred to in FAS 157 as *market approaches* to valuation, where one uses prices and other relevant information generated by market transactions involving identical (for mark-to-market) or comparable (for mark-to-matrix) assets or liabilities. Clearly, for bespoke exotic derivatives, such approaches are inapplicable. The valuation method, where one discounts future expected cashflows, with the latter based on a model, is referred to in FAS 157 as the *income approach*, and is essentially a *mark-to-model* price. Note, however, that the directive suggests that the model price is based on the *best* information available in the circumstances. This little clause is actually fundamental to the material impact of model risk. As an example, consider the pricing of a Napoleon cliquet, a highly exotic structure popular around the first half of the last decade where the holder receives a fixed coupon plus the *worst* return on a stock, floored at some level (commonly zero). The returns are calculated on a regular schedule (e.g. every month). We will look at this structure in detail in Chapter 4, but suffice to say for the moment that the product is highly sensitive to our assumptions on volatility of volatility by virtue of the strong sensitivity of its vega risk to volatility itself. A model which uses the best information available will, at the very least, calibrate to European option prices. It turns out that we can specify what we like for volatility of volatility, so that in the absence of a transparent market for the latter, the uncertainty in the price of this instrument due to the uncertainty in volatility of volatility could be large. Suppose then we had, based on historical analysis of realised volatility time series, for example, estimated a vol of vol of 100%. Now move to a world where options on the realised variance of the same stock, covering the maturity of the Napoleon cliquet, become actively traded. Suddenly the market would price at a revised vol of vol level, revising the 'fair value' of the instrument. But as we're required to report the instrument *at* fair value, we could suddenly be exposed to a balance sheet write down. Another scenario, which in fact occurred on these structures in 2003, is that the instrument itself becomes traded by a large enough number of banks to suggest a new consensus price. This phenomenon in fact forms the basis of Rebonato's definition of model risk [Rebonato (2002b)]: *Model risk is the risk of occurrence of a significant difference between the mark-to-model value of a complex and/or illiquid instrument, and the price at which the same instrument is revealed to have traded in the market.* Firms whose models consistently priced away from that consensus were forced to revise their models and write the asset down [Jeffery (2004)]. Note, moreover, that firms tend to take a one-sided position on exotics. In the case of exotic cliquets, for example, most investment banks were short the product. For one particular firm, short around EUR 200 million of reverse cliquets (see later) and Napoleons losses from 'mis-pricing' of equity exotics were so severe that the firm itself was wound down [Lyon (2005)]. In other words, the best guess of the value of an equity exotic is more than just an academic exercise. The effects of not accounting for model risk can be fatal.

1.6 The approach of this book

To make a statement about the magnitude of model risk in a firm, or even a single trading book, is a highly complex task. It requires an integrated pricing system where whole portfolios can be moved from one model to another, and the impact of stressing of new model parameters on valuation broken down and analysed. A large number of different trade types, with a plethora of different characteristics, need to be sifted out and their reaction to the model explained, with the largest contributors to the valuation impact dealt with in detail. Even if we had access to a real trading portfolio, a model risk analysis of this nature would clearly breach the confidentiality of the related institution, and would in fact not be that educational. The approach we will be adopting to model risk in this book then is *illustrative*. We will take a small set of models, calibrated to European options as far as possible, and compare the impact of their model parameters on the value of a small set of commonly traded equity exotics. The latter will, as far as possible, be chosen for their relevance to the model risk under investigation. For example, in our analysis of the valuation effects of dividend modelling, we will investigate lookback and barrier options. In our analysis of stochastic volatility we will look at realised volatility products like variance options, and implied volatility products like cliquets. In our analysis of correlation modelling we will look at realised correlation products and structured baskets such as worst-ofs. The aims of this approach are four-fold:

(1) To illustrate why enhanced models are required, by reference to historical and market data.

(2) To demonstrate how a model incorporating an enhanced set of dynamics can be created such that calibration to European option values is straightforward and precise.

(3) To demonstrate how certain well-known exotics react to the enhanced model, both before calibration to European option data, and afterwards.

(4) To build up a step-by-step understanding of why the exotics chosen for analysis react to the new model as they do, with the aim of developing a methodology for model risk analysis on real portfolios.

Note that the models chosen are a long way from being exhaustive. They form, rather, a small set of possible extensions to the Black–Scholes model. For example, our analysis of stochastic volatility considers only the multiplication of the local volatility by an exponential stochastic variable, with only one stochastic driver. The process will remain diffusive. By contrast, our analysis of jump processes will assume that the diffusive component adopts a deterministic local volatility process. We will not attempt to combine the two approaches into a stochastic volatility with jumps process. Likewise, our stochastic rate model will assume a simple short rate process, though a fully fledged market model for the rate evolution could equally well be considered. Like this, the book can be considered an illustration and discussion of *first-order model risk*, which we will distinguish from *second-order model risk* as follows:

- **First-order model risk**: the uncertainty in valuation given the uncertainty in model parameters addressing a *new* model aspect (e.g. deterministic state dependent correlation vs static correlation).
- **Second-order model risk**: the uncertainty in valuation given the choice of model addressing the *same* model aspect (e.g. state correlated stochastic correlation vs deterministic state dependent correlation).

Second-order model risk is rather more subtle than first-order model risk, and will not be addressed in this book. Merely explaining the first-order effects of an enhanced model on valuation, once the effects of calibration have been factored in, is complicated enough, even for apparently simple payoffs. Likewise, as the title of this book suggests, we address the question of the impact of enhanced modelling on *value*. The impact on greeks is no less important, but tends to be much more complex. One is essentially attempting to address the question of how the new value of an instrument, under a new model, reacts to a shock in the value of calibration instruments. Such an analysis is of course fundamental to the change in risk management of an exotic under a new model, but again, will not be addressed in this book.

So, having laid the groundwork for some model risk analysis, let us proceed, starting with the simplest of all models to match to vanilla instruments[6].

1.7   Exercises

(1) Consider a forward contract, where the buyer is under the *obligation* to purchase one unit of stock at some future time T, for an agreed price K. Consider first the case of no dividends or borrow costs. Show, that by shorting one unit of stock at a price S_0 today, and investing the proceeds in zero coupon bonds paying unity at T, the fair strike for the contract is given by:

$$K = \frac{S_0}{P(T_0, T)}$$

where $P(T_0, T)$ is the value of the zero coupon bond paying unity at expiry. In the case where rates r_t are deterministic, show that the bond price is given by:

$$P(T_0, T) = \exp\left[-\int_{T_0}^{T} r(t)dt\right]$$

(Hint: consider shorting the bond and investing the proceeds in a cash account accruing interest at rate $r(t)$.)

Now consider the case where the stock pays a *continuous* dividend yield, such that the dividend paid out to a stock holder over the interval $[t, t+dt]$ is given by $S_t q(t)dt$. By considering a *total return* strategy, where the dividend is continuously reinvested into stock, show that the starting short position in stock consists of $n(0) = \exp\left[-\int_0^T q(t)dt\right]$ shares. Use this result to show, in the case where both the dividend yield and rates are deterministic, that the fair strike of the forward contract is given by:

---

[6]Note: Unless otherwise stated, all instrument prices calculated in this book will be quoted on unit notional.

$$K = S_0 \exp \left[\int_{T_0}^{T} (r(t) - q(t))dt \right]$$

(2) Starting from the Black–Scholes equation:

$$\frac{\partial V}{\partial t} + rS\frac{\partial V}{\partial S} + \frac{1}{2}\sigma^2 S^2 \frac{\partial^2 V}{\partial S^2} - rV = 0$$

Show that the transformations $\tau = \frac{1}{2}\sigma^2(T - t)$, $x = \log S$ and $V = ue^{-\alpha x - \beta \tau}$ yield the diffusion equation:

$$\frac{\partial u}{\partial \tau} = \frac{\partial^2 u}{\partial x^2}$$

where:

$$\alpha = \frac{a}{2}$$

$$\beta = 1 + a + \frac{a^2}{4}$$

$$a = \frac{2r}{\sigma^2} - 1$$

(3) Consider a call option priced with implied volatility $\hat{\sigma}$ where the actual stock volatility is given by σ. By considering the evolution of the portfolio $\Pi_t = C_t - \Delta_t S_t + B_t$ together with the Black–Scholes equation applied to the option's price, show that the expected change in the portfolio value is given by:

$$E_{\mathbb{P}}[d\Pi_t] = \frac{1}{2}\Gamma_t S_t^2(\sigma^2 - \hat{\sigma}^2)dt$$

(4) Transform the time dependent version of the Black–Scholes equation (a.k.a the Black–Scholes–Merton equation):

$$\frac{\partial V}{\partial t} + [r(t) - q(t)]S_t\frac{\partial V}{\partial S} + \frac{1}{2}\sigma^2(t)S_t^2\frac{\partial^2 V}{\partial S^2} - r(t)V(t) = 0$$

to log space $x_t = \log S_t$, and $\tau = T - t$. Consider now the Fourier transform of the option price:

$$\widetilde{V}(\xi, \tau) = \int_{-\infty}^{\infty} V(x, \tau)e^{i\xi x}\,dx \qquad (1.18)$$

and the inverse transform:

$$V(x,\tau) = \frac{1}{2\pi} \int_{-\infty}^{\infty} \tilde{V}(\xi,\tau)e^{-i\xi x}d\xi \tag{1.19}$$

where $V(x,0)$ is the payoff of the option at expiry in x. Apply (1.19) to the transformed equation derived above to show that:

$$\tilde{V}(\xi,\tau) = \tilde{V}(\xi,0)\exp\left[-\int_0^\tau \left(r(s) + i\mu(s)\xi + \frac{\sigma^2(s)}{2}\xi^2\right)ds\right]$$

where $\mu(t) = r(t) - q(t) - \sigma^2(t)/2$. By considering the solution for flat rates, dividend yield and volatility, show that the solution to the call payoff is given by the Black–Scholes formula with *implied* rate, dividend yield and volatility given by:

$$\bar{r}(T) = \frac{1}{T}\int_0^T r(t)dt$$

$$\bar{q}(T) = \frac{1}{T}\int_0^T q(t)dt$$

$$\hat{\sigma}^2(T) = \frac{1}{T}\int_0^T \sigma^2(t)dt$$

(5) Show that the second derivative with respect to strike of the call payoff $f(S_T, K) = (S_T - K, 0)^+$, at expiry T is given by:

$$\frac{\partial^2 f}{\partial K^2} = \delta(S_T - K)$$

where $\delta(S_T - K)$ denotes the Dirac delta function, satisfying the property;

$$\int_{\mathbb{R}} f(x')\delta(x - x')dx' = f(x)$$

for a function f of a real variable x. Use this property to show that, for the undiscounted call price $\tilde{C}(K,T) = \int_0^\infty f(S_T, K)\varphi(S_T, T)dS_T$:

$$\frac{\partial^2 \tilde{C}}{\partial K^2} = \varphi(K,T)$$

Chapter 2

Preliminaries

As discussed in the previous chapter, the art of model risk analysis lies in stressing assumptions on the underlying processes driving valuation, whilst at the same time preserving close agreement with market observables. To this end, the world of financial modelling roughly falls into two camps: that which seeks to make the underlying processes as 'clean' as possible, whilst allowing for a degree of disagreement on the less liquidly traded areas of market data; and that which demands full calibration at the expense of the purity of the underlying processes. The argument in favour of the first approach is that it has greater 'explanatory power', and may even point to 'better' marks for more illiquid data, whilst the argument in favour of the second is essentially that the market is always right. In this book we propose a somewhat modified thesis in favour of the second approach, namely that, when it comes to model risk analysis, it is helpful to have a common starting point around which model assumptions can be stressed flexibly and meaningfully. Models which sacrifice calibration accuracy in favour of purity, whilst they are indeed useful in terms of calculation speed, suffer from the major drawback that the model parameters tend to be fixed in one go at the calibration stage. Moreover, if a new model assumption is to be applied on top of the old, it tends to be very difficult to recover a new consistent set of *implied* market data. Like this, a clear like-for-like comparison between different model variants is made that much harder. As it happens, the Dupire model of local volatility [Dupire (1994)] (also known as the Derman–Kani model [Derman and Kani (1994)] due to the discovery of essentially the same model in the same year by Bruno Dupire at Paribas Capital Markets, and Emanuel Derman and Iraj Kani at Goldman Sachs) not only calibrates to observable market data *automatically*, but it also, as pointed out later by Emanuel Derman [Derman and Kani (1998)], serves as an *effective* model on which extensions can be consistently built. This second point, which we will discuss in some detail later in this chapter, is crucial to a model risk framework. Though, as we will demonstrate, the Dupire model is somewhat contrived and implies unrealistic market dynamics, it serves as an invaluable backbone on which basic model assumptions can be stressed, whilst at the same time preserving a close fit to market observables.

2.1   Mathematical formulation

Central to the Dupire model is the idea of a *deterministic* relationship between spot and volatility. Put simply, if I know the spot price at some point in the future, I know exactly what the corresponding volatility will be. This is a powerful assumption. It implies that if I simply take a snap shot of the market today, then, somehow, the dynamics on that market are frozen for all eternity (or at least until the market ceases to be...) Mathematically, this reduces to the following:

$$\frac{dS_t}{S_t} = \mu(t)dt + \sigma(S,t)dW_t$$

where W_t describes a Wiener process $\sim \mathcal{N}(0, dt)$. Note also the 'fx-style' description of growth here. The stock is assumed to describe a continuous process. We can pay dividends, but they're assumed to be continuously compounding, i.e. distributed continuously in time with the law $q(t)S(t)dt$. The Dupire model can also be made to work in the more realistic discrete dividend world, but this will be investigated further in Chapter 3.

There are numerous ways of deriving the Dupire result for the local volatility $\sigma(S,T)$, which we will distinguish carefully from the implied Black–Scholes volatility for an option of strike K and maturity T, $\hat{\sigma}(K,T)$, one of which is left as an exercise at the end of this chapter. The one we will favour here is rather more involved than it strictly needs to be, but serves as a more powerful machinery for model extensions used in the remainder of this book. To begin, let's construct the Black–Scholes hedging argument.

As the only source of uncertainty is the stock price diffusion dW_t, we only need to construct a simple delta hedged portfolio of an option $V(S,t)$, $\alpha(t)$ units of stock S_t and $\beta(t)$ units of bond $B(t)$:

$$\Pi(t) = V(S,t) + \alpha(t)S_t + \beta(t)B(t) \tag{2.1}$$

where the bond is assumed to grow at the risk-neutral rate $dB(t) = r(t)B(t)dt$. The portfolio is self-financing and entered into at zero cost, giving us:

$$d\Pi(t) = 0 \qquad (2.2)$$

for the first statement, and by implication

$$\beta(t)B(t) = -V(S,t) - \alpha(t)S_t$$

for the second. Following the arguments of Chapter 1, we can derive the hedge rebalancing P&L as before, but now have an additional term due to the dividend paid out on the stock position:

$$d\Pi_n = V_n + \alpha_{n-1}S_n - (V_{n-1} + \alpha_{n-1}S_{n-1})\exp(r(t_n - t_{n-1}))$$
$$+ \alpha_{n-1}S_{n-1}q_{n-1}(t_n - t_{n-1})$$

In the limit of small $dt = t_n - t_{n-1}$, denoting $t_{n-1} = t$, $t_n = t + dt$, we can write this as:

$$d\Pi(t) = V(t + dt) + \alpha(t)S(t + dt)$$
$$- (V(t) + \alpha(t)S(t))(1 + rdt) + \alpha(t)S(t)q(t)dt$$
$$= dV(t) + \alpha(t)dS_t + \alpha(t)S(t)(q(t) - r(t))dt - V(t)rdt$$

Taylor expanding, eliminating the term in dS_t and employing the self-financing condition (2.2) as before, we arrive at the modified Black–Scholes equation for an option on a stock with continuously compounded dividend yield:

$$\frac{\partial V}{\partial t} + [r(t) - q(t)]S\frac{\partial V}{\partial S} + \frac{1}{2}\sigma^2(S,t)S^2\frac{\partial^2 V}{\partial S^2} - r(t)V(S,t) = 0 \qquad (2.3)$$

We will refer to (2.3) as the *backward Kolmogorov equation* for $V(S,t)$. In general, we know the payoff of the option at expiry T for some stock level S_T. We could refer to this payoff as $V(S_T, T; S_T, T)$. This equation is essentially allowing us to project the value at expiry back to some earlier time $V(S_t, t; S_T, T)$. Supposing that we had an option which paid $\delta(S_T - e^z)$ at expiry, i.e. paid only if we hit some predefined stock level (this is referred to as an *Arrow–Debreu price*). As rates are assumed to be deterministic, let us also consider the undiscounted value of this option (we will revise this in the chapter on stochastic rates). We will also find it more straightforward to transform (2.3) to log spot space $x = \log(S_t)$:

$$\frac{\partial \widetilde{V}}{\partial t} + \left[\mu(t) - \frac{1}{2}\sigma^2(x,t)\right]\frac{\partial \widetilde{V}}{\partial x} + \frac{1}{2}\sigma^2(x,t)\frac{\partial^2 \widetilde{V}}{\partial x^2} = 0 \qquad (2.4)$$

denoting $\widetilde{V}$ as the undiscounted option value and $\mu(t) = r(t) - q(t)$ as the risk-neutral stock growth. We have simply for the Arrow–Debreu option:

$$\widetilde{V}(x,t) = G(x,t;z,T)$$

where $G(x,t;z,T)$ is the Green's function encapsulating the probability of evolving from state (x,t) to state (z,T). To derive the Dupire formula for local volatility we would actually like to know the differential equation for G in terms of z and T rather than x and t. This will allow us to compute the stock price distribution at a later time given its value at an earlier time, and analogously is referred to as the *forward* Kolmogorov equation. We proceed as follows. In general the solution to (2.4) is given by:

$$\widetilde{V}(x,t) = \int G(x,t;x',t')\widetilde{V}(x',t')dx' \qquad (2.5)$$

for *any* time $t' \geq t$. This is a statement of the martingale property of undiscounted option prices evolving in the risk-neutral measure $\mathbb{Q}$: $\widetilde{V}(x,t) = E_{\mathbb{Q}}[\widetilde{V}(x',t')]$ the proof of which we leave as an exercise at the end of this chapter. Let us write (2.4) as:

$$\frac{\partial \widetilde{V}}{\partial t} + \mathfrak{L}_{x,t}\widetilde{V} = 0 \qquad (2.6)$$

where $\mathfrak{L}$ denotes the backward equation operator $\mathfrak{L}_{x,t} = \left[\mu(t) - \frac{1}{2}\sigma^2(x,t)\right]\frac{\partial}{\partial x} + \frac{1}{2}\sigma^2(x,t)\frac{\partial^2}{\partial x^2}$. Applying this operator with respect to x' and t' to (2.5) gives:

$$\frac{\partial \widetilde{V}(x',t')}{\partial t'} + \mathfrak{L}_{x',t'}\widetilde{V}(x',t') = 0$$

allowing us to write:

$$\int G(x,t;x',t')\left[\frac{\partial \widetilde{V}(x',t')}{\partial t'} + \mathfrak{L}_{x',t'}\widetilde{V}(x',t')\right] = 0 \qquad (2.7)$$

We know from (2.5), however, that:

$$0 = \int \left[\tilde{V}(x',t') \frac{\partial}{\partial t'} G(x,t;x',t') + G(x,t;x',t') \frac{\partial}{\partial t'} \tilde{V}(x',t') \right] dx'$$

We also have the definition of the adjoint operator A^*, $\langle Ax, y \rangle = \langle x, A^*y \rangle$, with $\langle \ldots \rangle$ denoting the inner product. Together, this allows us to write (2.7) as:

$$\int \tilde{V}(x't') \left[-\frac{\partial}{\partial t'} G(x,t;x',t') + \mathcal{L}^*_{x',t'} G(x,t;x',t') \right] dx' = 0$$

giving us the relationship that, for the backward equation on the Green's function $G(x,t;x',t')$ given by:

$$\frac{\partial G(x,t;x',t')}{\partial t} + \mathcal{L}_{x,t} G(x,t;x',t') = 0$$

the corresponding forward equation is given by:

$$-\frac{\partial G(x,t;x',t')}{\partial t'} + \mathcal{L}^*_{x',t'} G(x,t;x',t') = 0$$

To figure out what the adjoint operator actually is, we integrate by parts:

$$\int dx' G(x,t;x',t') \mathcal{L}_{x',t'} \tilde{V}(x',t') =$$

$$\int dx' G(x,t;x',t') \left[\tilde{\mu}(x',t') \frac{\partial \tilde{V}}{\partial x'} + \frac{1}{2}\sigma^2(x',t') \frac{\partial^2 \tilde{V}}{\partial x'^2} \right] =$$

$$\int dx' \tilde{V}(x',t') \left[-\frac{\partial}{\partial x'} [\tilde{\mu}(x',t') G(x,t;x',t')] \right]$$

$$+ \frac{1}{2} \int dx' \tilde{V}(x',t') \left[\frac{\partial^2}{\partial x'^2} [\sigma^2(x',t') G(x,t;x',t')] \right]$$

using $\tilde{\mu}(x',t') = \mu(t) - \frac{1}{2}\sigma^2(x',t')$ and the assumption that both the value of G and the x' derivatives of G vanish as $x' \to \pm\infty$. So we have finally:

$$\frac{\partial G(x,t;x',t')}{\partial t'} + \frac{\partial}{\partial x'} [\tilde{\mu}(x',t') G(x,t;x',t')] = \frac{1}{2} \frac{\partial^2}{\partial x'^2} [\sigma^2(x',t') G(x,t;x',t')]$$

Transforming back to spot space gives us the somewhat better known Fokker–Planck equation:

$$\frac{\partial G(S_t, t; S_T, T)}{\partial T} =$$

$$-\frac{\partial}{\partial S_T}[\mu(T)S_T G(S_t, t; S_T, T)] + \frac{1}{2}\frac{\partial^2}{\partial S_T^2}[\sigma^2(S_T, T)S_T^2 G(S_t, t; S_T, T)]$$

(2.8)

Now we can complete the Dupire formulation. Writing for the undiscounted call price:

$$\widetilde{C}(S_t, t; K, T) = \int_0^\infty [S_T - K, 0]^+ G(S_t, t; S_T, T) dS_T \qquad (2.9)$$

and applying (2.8) gives:

$$\frac{\partial \widetilde{C}}{\partial T} = \int_0^\infty dS_T [S_T - K, 0]^+$$

$$\times \left[-\frac{\partial}{\partial S_T}[\mu(T)S_T G(S_t, t; S_T, T)] + \frac{1}{2}\frac{\partial^2}{\partial S_T^2}[\sigma^2(S_T, T)S_T^2 G(S_t, t; S_T, T)] \right]$$

Again, integrating by parts and noting $\frac{\partial}{\partial S_T}[S_T - K, 0]^+ = \mathbf{1}(S_T - K)$ and $\frac{\partial^2}{\partial S_T^2}[S_T - K, 0]^+ = \delta(S_T - K)$, we get:

$$\frac{\partial \widetilde{C}}{\partial T} = I_1 + I_2$$

where:

$$I_1 = \mu(T) \int_0^\infty S_T G(S_t, t; S_T, T)\mathbf{1}(S_T - K)dS_T$$

$$= \mu(T) \int_0^\infty (S_T - K + K)G(S_t, t; S_T, T)\mathbf{1}(S_T - K)dS_T$$

$$= \mu(T) \left[\widetilde{C}(K, T) + K \int_K^\infty G(S_t, t; S_T, T)dS_T \right]$$

and

$$I_2 = \frac{1}{2} \int_0^\infty \sigma^2(S_T, T) S_T^2 G(S_t, t; S_T, T) \delta(S_T - K) dS_T$$

$$= \frac{1}{2} K^2 \sigma^2(K, T) G(S_t, t; K, T)$$

Finally, differentiating (2.9) with respect to K we have the identities:

$$\frac{\partial \widetilde{C}}{\partial K} = -\int_K^\infty G(S_t, t; S_T, T) dS_T$$

$$\frac{\partial^2 \widetilde{C}}{\partial K^2} = G(S_t, t; K, T)$$

We thus obtain a forward equation (referred to hence as the *Dupire equation*) for the call price in terms of K and T:

$$\frac{\partial \widetilde{C}}{\partial T} = \mu(T) \left[\widetilde{C} - K \frac{\partial \widetilde{C}}{\partial K} \right] + \frac{1}{2} K^2 \sigma^2(K, T) \frac{\partial^2 \widetilde{C}}{\partial K^2}$$

whence we arrive at the expression for the local volatility

$$\sigma(K, T) = \sigma(S = K, t = T)$$

with:

$$\sigma^2(K, T) = \frac{\frac{\partial \widetilde{C}}{\partial T} - \mu(T) \left[\widetilde{C} - K \frac{\partial \widetilde{C}}{\partial K} \right]}{\frac{K^2}{2} \frac{\partial^2 \widetilde{C}}{\partial K^2}} \tag{2.10}$$

Let's pause for a moment to consider the impact of this expression. In a nutshell, given a continuum of European option prices $C(K, T)$, for all strikes and maturities, we have a *complete* definition of the stock price process, without any need for iterative calibration. The impact on the financial industry was revolutionary. Suddenly, we had an easily computable method for pricing *any* instrument, using a methodology which, provided we used the same forward curves and volatility surfaces, would yield the same price. We will see in the next section, however, that there is a considerable price to be paid for such simplicity. Nonetheless, the importance of this work cannot be understated. *All* models have drawbacks, but a model which is simple, robust and easily extendible, which all practitioners can comfortably use, is a model worth supporting.

2.2   Volatility surface arbitrage

To begin, let's take a closer look at the form of the expression in (2.10). For our process to be well-defined, the local variance must be greater than or equal to zero. A negative local variance would yield an imaginary volatility term causing any numerical solution to become unstable. We thus require that either the numerator and denominator of the fraction be both positive, or both negative. The latter is in fact unacceptable in that, whilst the process will be well-defined, its integration will not recover input option prices. A well-defined process must necessarily result in a well-defined probability distribution. Integration of such a system would then result in a set of option prices convex in strike, contrary to the option price inputs. We thus require both the numerator and denominator to be positive for a well-defined process which integrates back to the option price inputs. As stated, the positivity of the denominator is equivalent to the implied probability distribution $G(S_t, t; S_T, T)$ being positive everywhere at T. Were this not to be the case, it would imply that simply by trading a butterfly spread with strikes spanning the region of negative probability would necessarily make money for the seller. This is referred to by the picturesque name *butterfly spread arbitrage*. The proof is left as an exercise at the end of this chapter. What about the numerator? At this point it's helpful to rewrite (2.10) in terms of implied volatility.

First, let's transform to $z(T) = \log[K/F(T)]$ where the forward at time T is given by $F(T) = S_t \exp\left[\int_t^T \mu(t)dt\right]$. We have:

$$K\frac{\partial C}{\partial K} = \frac{\partial C}{\partial z}$$

$$\frac{\partial C}{\partial T} = \left.\frac{\partial C}{\partial T}\right|_z - \mu(T)\left.\frac{\partial C}{\partial z}\right|_T$$

Putting these into the numerator of (2.10) gives for the numerator:

$$num = \frac{\partial C}{\partial T} + K\mu(T)\frac{\partial C}{\partial K} - \mu(T)C = \left.\frac{\partial C}{\partial T}\right|_z - \mu(T)C$$

We can then also write $C(z, T) = F(T)\tilde{c}(z, T)$ where:

$$\tilde{c}(z,T) = N(d_1) - e^z N(d_2)$$
$$d_1 = -z/s(z,T) + s(z,T)/2$$
$$d_2 = -z/s(z,T) - s(z,T)/2$$
$$s(z,T) = \hat{\sigma}(z,T)\sqrt{T}$$

and $\hat{\sigma}(z,T)$ is the implied volatility for an option of maturity T and strike $F(T)e^z$. This gives:

$$\left.\frac{\partial C}{\partial T}\right|_z = \mu(T)C + F(T)\left.\frac{\partial \tilde{c}}{\partial T}\right|_z$$

reducing the local variance numerator to:

$$num = F(T)\left.\frac{\partial \tilde{c}}{\partial T}\right|_z$$

This can be solved to give:

$$num = \frac{n(d_1)}{2s(z,T)}\left.\frac{\partial s^2(z,T)}{\partial T}\right|_z$$

So now we have an interpretation for the numerator of the Dupire local variance. In order for our process to be well-defined, the implied variance $s^2(z,T)$ at constant *moneyness* z must be monotonically increasing. This is in fact a statement that *calendar arbitrage*, where one nets cash by selling early maturity options and buying longer maturity options of the same moneyness, should be impossible for a well-defined process (see exercise). Not only then is the Dupire model simple to construct, it has a clear financial interpretation in terms of arbitrage opportunities in time and space (strike). For completeness, we give the full expression in terms of implied volatility:

$$\sigma^2(z,T) = \frac{\left.\frac{\partial}{\partial T}\right|_z (\hat{\sigma}^2 T)}{1 + \hat{\sigma}T\frac{\partial^2 \hat{\sigma}}{\partial z^2} + Td_1d_2\left(\frac{\partial \hat{\sigma}}{\partial z}\right)^2 - \frac{2z}{\hat{\sigma}}\frac{\partial \hat{\sigma}}{\partial z}}$$

One point to note in passing, which we will dwell on more in the chapter on dividends: for the local variance to be finite, the implied variance must be continuous in time for a given level of moneyness z. In practice, we have neither a continuum of option prices against strike nor against maturity, and have to construct a so-called *volatility surface* from a discrete set of points in both directions. This equation tells us that, for this scheme to be stable, any time interpolation we come up with should be continuous in variance against moneyness. It also tells us that implied volatility must be finite to second order of differentiation. Any splining we perform to imply the unobservable 'wing' data (deeply out-of-the-money (OTM) puts and calls) from the observable range of strikes must therefore be continuous to second order. And herein lies one of the costs of the Dupire formalism. Whilst indeed it is autocalibrating, *any* volatility surface can be fed in to calculate the local variance. For local variance to be well-defined at all, however, the fitted surface must be continuous to second order in strike and first order in variance against moneyness in time. To be positive and integrate back to the input surface, however, both the numerator and denominator of the local variance fraction need to be positive *everywhere*. If you now couple in the requirements that the fit be stable from one day to the next, transform benignly under vol surface perturbation (e.g. slope steepening, curvature increase), and be based on a surface with a minimal set of marking parameters, e.g. to allow extrapolation to long-dated maturities not traded over-the-counter (OTC) or on the exchange, you quickly see that getting the Dupire model to work practically in a financial institution, typically trading order of 100–500 stocks on anything from vanilla options to highly customised structured products, is a huge challenge, and one which keeps practitioners busy on a daily basis.

2.3   Implied volatility surface dynamics

At the beginning of this chapter, we pointed out that the Dupire model of local volatility assumed a deterministic relationship between spot and volatility known for all time given a snapshot of the market today. This is obviously unrealistic, but taken at face value, what does it imply? Let us illustrate by means of a somewhat contrived example on some stock with a vol surface marked out to one year only, as shown in Figure 2.1 (strike K, maturity T in days). The resultant local volatility surface is shown in Figure 2.2.

Now, supposing we take the Dupire model as read. If we perturb the spot, we should be able to derive a new volatility surface purely based on integrating up the given local vol surface. This regime is sometimes referred to as 'sticky local volatility'. The result for the 1Y slice is shown in Figure 2.3.

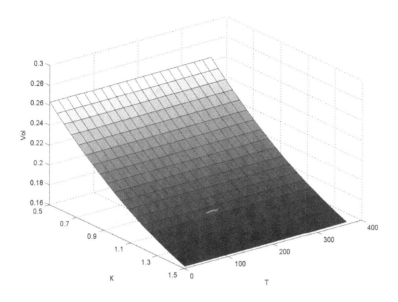

Fig. 2.1 Simple volatility surface.

This is a well-known move, commented on significantly in the literature in the context of delta hedging within a local vol environment. Pat Hagan *et al.* demonstrated [Hagan *et al.* (1999, 2002)] that if the local volatility model is of the form:

$$\sigma(S_t, t) = \sigma(S_t)$$
$$dS_t = S_t \sigma(S_t) dW_t$$

then the implied volatility at spot price S_0 and strike K is linked to the local volatility by the singular perturbative expansion:

$$\hat{\sigma}(S_0, K) = \sigma(\overline{S}) \left\{ 1 + \frac{\sigma''(\overline{S})}{24\sigma(\overline{S})} (S - K)^2 \right\}$$

where $\overline{S} = \frac{1}{2}[S_0 + K]$ and $\sigma''(x) = d^2\sigma/dx^2$. The authors point out that the first term accounts for approximately 99% of the actual implied volatility, giving us the simple approximation:

$$\hat{\sigma}(S_0, K) \simeq \sigma\left(\frac{1}{2}[S_0 + K]\right) \tag{2.11}$$

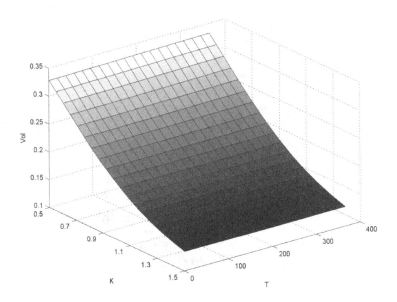

Fig. 2.2   Corresponding local volatility surface.

If then we freeze the local volatility surface we must have for the implied vol surface at the new spot height $S_0 + \delta S$

$$\hat{\sigma}(S_0 + \delta S, K) = \hat{\sigma}(S_0, K + \delta S) \qquad (2.12)$$

In other words, the smile should move to the left as spot moves to the right, as seen in Figure 2.3. Indeed, defining the at-the-money (ATM) vol to be $\hat{\sigma}_0(S) = \hat{\sigma}(S, S)$, (2.12) implies:

$$\hat{\sigma}_0(S_0 + \delta S) = \hat{\sigma}(S_0, S_0 + 2\delta S) \simeq \hat{\sigma}_0(S) + 2 \left. \frac{\partial \hat{\sigma}}{\partial K} \right|_{K=S_0} \delta S$$

This is a well-known result. In a sticky local volatility model, the ATM vol moves by 'twice the skew' on spot bumping. Sadly, this is not borne out by reality, and indeed, Hagan *et al.* conclude [Hagan *et al.* (2002)]:

> ...*This is opposite to typical market behaviour, in which smile and skew move in the same direction as the underlying...*

A typical move is shown in Figure 2.4. What does this mean in practice? Essentially it means that every day you come into the office, you have to recompute the local vol surface to match to observed option prices. It

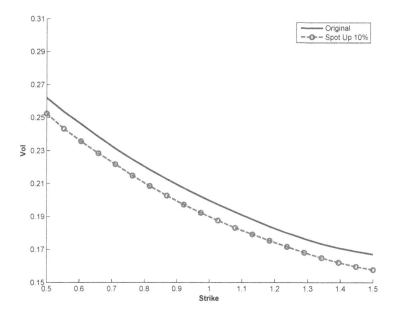

Fig. 2.3 1Y implied volatility slices, original and spot bumped assuming sticky local vol.

would in fact be rather remarkable were this not to be the case, but at a more fundamental level, it implies that the price derived from a pure local volatility model is not consistent with our hedge. If it were, we could simply delta hedge as demonstrated, leaving the implied volatility surface to move according to the static local vol surface. In practice traders tend to account for the 'skew delta' by incorporating a volatility scenario such as the one shown in Figure 2.4 into their delta calculation. Whilst the price will not indeed be consistent, the hedge will be a more accurate representation of observed market dynamics. This point, however, should be noted. When we start to look at extensions to the local volatility model, such as stochastic local volatility, or local volatility with stock price jumps, in addition to evaluating the impact on instrument price, we will also look at the impact on hedging. In some cases, calibrating to market data *dynamics* as well as market data itself is not only a powerful mechanism both for implying untransparent model inputs (e.g. jump-diffusion parameters), but also results in a model where pricing and hedging are better aligned. In the final chapter we will also mention some of the work done on taking this idea to its logical extreme, namely attempting to define a process *entirely* in terms

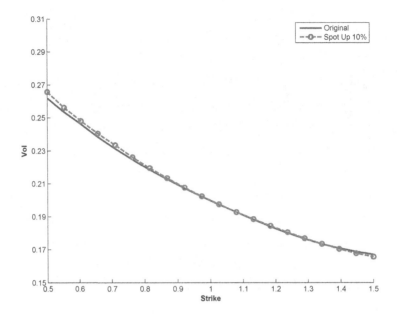

Fig. 2.4   Typical vol surface move for an upward spot bump.

of the observed dynamics of market observables [Schönbucher (1998)].

2.4   Implied forward volatility

In this section we make our analysis somewhat more realistic and look at the S&P500 vol surface introduced in Chapter 1, where the ATM slope now falls off with increasing maturity. Let us now price the following option $(S(T_2)/S(T_1)-\kappa,0)^+$, where $T_2 > T_1$, the option paying at T_2. We will refer to today as T_0 and assume a zero lag between fixing and payment. Such an option is referred to as a forward start option or 'clicklet' and forms the basis of a whole family of options on *returns* called 'cliquets'. The options were first marketed on the Chicago Board of Options Exchange in 1996 [Shparber and Resheff (2004)], and will form a substantial piece of our analysis of stochastic volatility and jumps later in this book. For the moment though, how would we price this? If we knew the implied volatility $\hat{\sigma}(\kappa, T_1, T_2)$, then assuming a model of proportional dividends, we could just write down the solution:

$$V = Df(T_0, T_2)[F(T_1, T_2)N(d_1) - \kappa N(d_2)]$$

$$d_1 = \frac{\log(F(T_1, T_2)/\kappa)}{\hat{\sigma}(\kappa, T_1, T_2)\sqrt{T_2 - T_1}} + \frac{\hat{\sigma}(\kappa, T_1, T_2)\sqrt{T_2 - T_1}}{2}$$

$$d_1 = \frac{\log(F(T_1, T_2)/\kappa)}{\hat{\sigma}(\kappa, T_1, T_2)\sqrt{T_2 - T_1}} - \frac{\hat{\sigma}(\kappa, T_1, T_2)\sqrt{T_2 - T_1}}{2}$$

$$F(T_1, T_2) = F(T_0, T_2)/F(T_0, T_1)$$

where Df denotes the discount factor in the currency of the underlyer. If $T_0 = T_1$, then we just have a regular European option with notional $1/S_0$ and strike $S_0\kappa$. Suppose we take T_2 as ΔT ahead of T_1: would we expect the forward implied vol surface $\hat{\sigma}(\kappa, T_1, T_1 + \Delta T)$ to look significantly different to today's implied vol surface $\hat{\sigma}(\kappa S_0, \Delta T)$? The common answer to this question is 'basically no'. Why should the future premium for OTM options of a given maturity and moneyness be significantly different from today? The local vol model, however, tells us that the further the start date of such an option, the cheaper that premium becomes. The effect is shown in Figure 2.5 for 1Y tenor forward starting options.

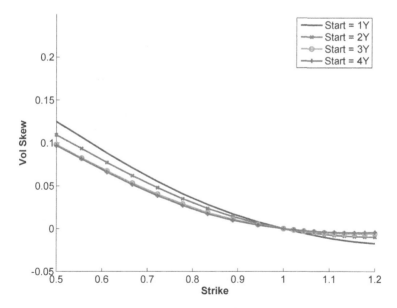

Fig. 2.5 Forward skew flattening in the local volatility model, as a function of strike κ.

The reason for this is straightforward. Inspection of (2.10) shows that the local vol surface and implied vol surface tend to look similar to each other close to the ATM point (in fact local vol tends to be roughly twice as steep, as implied by (2.11)). As the implied vol surface naturally flattens over increasing maturity, so does the local vol surface. As we go further into the future, precisely because the local vol surface is assumed static as a function of spot and maturity, the local vol surface remaining to us flattens, and the implied vol surface correspondingly. In fact, the flattening of today's implied vol surface as a function of maturity is a necessary no arbitrage condition. Roger Lee [Lee (2004)] demonstrates, on the basis of the work of Jim Gatheral [Gatheral (1999)] and Carr and Wu [Carr and Wu (2003)] that from no arbitrage constraints, for $K_1 < K_2$:

$$C(K_1) \geq C(K_2)$$
$$\frac{P(K_1)}{K_1} \leq \frac{P(K_2)}{K_2}$$

the ATM vol skew should decay as $O\left(\frac{1}{\sqrt{T}}\right)$ in the short-dated limit and as $O\left(\frac{1}{T}\right)$ in the long-dated limit. If then we have a well-defined local volatility process, the ATM volatility skew of forward starting options of a given maturity *must* get flatter the further out the start date. Essentially, we have been tripped up by our basic assumptions of determinism of the process driving implied volatility skew. Models where the local volatility is allowed to take on a degree of indeterminism, or where another process, such as a Poisson jump process, is added to the mix, reduce the dependency of forward skew on the local volatility itself, and allow a more realistic set of forward starting vol surfaces to be derived. This will be demonstrated in detail later in this book.

2.5   Local volatility as an effective model

In spite of our adulation of this model at the start of the chapter, we seem to have demonstrated that it's (a) difficult to implement practically, (b) gives the wrong implied volatility dynamics, (c) results in prices inconsistent with required hedging and (d) provides an unrealistic model for forward starting options, which, incidentally, form the basis of a large bulk of exotic equity products. Recall though what we said at the start of the chapter: the Dupire model of local volatility is an *effective* model allowing for exact calibration to observable market data. The model is no more realistic than the original Black–Scholes model. No one believes that vol is purely deterministic, and indeed the presence of volatility skew indicates that it can't be. However, this doesn't stop it being an excellent *mapping* from price space to currency independent space, on which all options can be compared. Similarly, as we will now show, the local vol model simply provides an invaluable *basis* on which more realistic models can be constructed. The fact that this basis derives from exact calibration to market data implies that any model built on top of it will calibrate similarly, provided the extra model inputs introduced don't themselves imply a new sort of arbitrage (see Chapter 5 on default modelling). Like this, we can compare the price impact of different models in a like-for-like manner. The central idea behind this concept is due to Gyöngy [Gyöngy (1986)], whose theorem can be exactly stated as follows:

Theorem 2.1 (Gyöngy, 1986). *Let W be an r-dimensional Wiener process, and*

$$dX_t = \mu_t dt + \sigma_t dW_t$$

be a d-dimensional Itō process where μ is a bounded d-dimensional adapted process[1], and σ is a bounded $d \times r$ adapted process such that $\sigma\sigma^T$ is uniformly positive definite[2]. Then there exist measurable deterministic function $\hat{\mu}$ and $\hat{\sigma}$ such that

$$\hat{\mu}(t, X_t) = \mathbb{E}[\mu_t | X_t] \ a.s. \ for \ each \ t \ and,$$
$$\hat{\sigma}\hat{\sigma}^T(t, X_t) = \mathbb{E}[\sigma_t \sigma_t^T | X_t] \ a.s. \ for \ each \ t$$

and there exists a weak solution[3] to the SDE:

$$d\hat{X}_t = \hat{\mu}(t, \hat{X}_t)dt + \hat{\sigma}(t, \hat{X}_t)d\widehat{W}_t$$

with $\mathfrak{L}(\hat{X}_t) = \mathfrak{L}(X_t)$ for all t, where $\mathfrak{L}$ denotes the law of a random variable and $\widehat{W}_t$ denotes another Brownian motion, possibly on another space.

The theorem effectively says that, if we have a process which depends on more than one variable, and for every realisation of the first variable we define a new drift and covariance given by the expectation of the drift

---

[1] An adapted process is one that cannot 'see into the future'. An informal interpretation is that X is adapted if and only if, for every realisation and every n, X_n is known at time n.

[2] Every eigenvalue is positive.

[3] A function for which the derivatives appearing in the equation may not all exist but which is nonetheless deemed to satisfy the equation in some precisely defined sense.

and covariance *conditioned* on the first variable, then we end up with a stochastic differential equation in terms of the first variable (and time) *only*, which *correctly reproduces the distribution from the original process*. The classic example is stochastic volatility. Supposing that the stock process evolved according to a one-dimensional Wiener process, as before, but the local volatility σ_t were not in fact deterministically related to spot, having rather some distribution for any given spot realisation. Gyöngy would then say that, if we project onto a process on S_t alone such that:

$$E[\sigma_t^2|S_t] = \hat{\sigma}^2(t, S_t)$$

the distribution of S_t from the projected process will match that from the original process. If, however, this projected process were the Dupire local volatility model, the *original* process would *de facto* calibrate to European options, provided of course that the resulting distribution of σ_t^2 were positive everywhere. This technique goes under the general title of 'Markovian projection', and is seeing increasing popularity across many areas of finance [Piterbarg (2007); Henry-Labordere (2009)]. The fact that there exists a simple projection for a wide range of complex processes which is accurate and simple to calculate makes the mechanics of equity model risk analysis tractable. The only question we now have to deal with is, what sorts of processes are 'meaningful'? We will operate under the following guidelines:

- **The process must be related to observed dynamics**. We know, for example, that volatility is stochastic, and to a certain extent we can measure how stochastic it actually is. We know, likewise, that indices do indeed jump, and can separate out the jump component from the diffusive. We know that dividend yield is stochastic but strongly anti-correlated with spot returns, and again, we can measure this. Models which relate to a measurable quantity both address hedging concerns and allow us to suggest plausible input levels.
- **The process must be related to actual instruments**. Models should be chosen in the light of what's actually trading. We have options on variance, we have ranked performance baskets, we have crash products. Each of these products will be strongly affected by one or another assumption in this book. We do not have variance swaps on dividends, however, so concerning ourself with the skew of dividend vol, whilst perhaps of intellectual interest, has little or no market data to which we can usefully calibrate.

- **The process should be widely applicable.** In this book we will necessarily confine our attention to a small number of underlyers and a small number of instrument types. However, a firm will need to run large-scale analysis across a wide set of different positions and underlyers. A model which takes an evening to calibrate a single underlyer, or result in wildly changing calibrated parameters, should be rejected up front.

These seem obvious, but in fact restrict the field of possible candidates quite powerfully. It is our hope that the models and examples chosen in the rest of this book address all of these guidelines, and allow some useful insights into the impact of model choice on instruments trading today.

2.6 Exercises

(1) Demonstrate that the solution to the backward equation (2.4) is given by (2.5). (Hint: apply Itō's lemma to the expectation of the option price.)

(2) Demonstrate that if a call at a lower strike of K_1 is less expensive than a call at a higher strike of K_2, a call spread where one shorts the higher strike call and goes long the lower strike call will always make money for the seller. (This is referred to as *call spread arbitrage.*) Derive the equivalent result for puts using put-call parity and discuss the meaning of the arbitrage in terms of the implied cumulative distribution of the stock at the relevant maturity.

(3) Demonstrate that for a continuum of call prices concave in strike over the region $[K_1, K_2]$, a butterfly spread consisting of a long call struck at K_1, a long call struck at K_2 and two short calls struck at $(K_1 + K_2)/2$ will always make money for the seller. Discuss the meaning of the arbitrage in terms of the implied probability distribution of the stock at the relevant maturity. (This is referred to as *butterfly spread arbitrage.*)

(4) Consider a deterministic interest rate model on a proportional dividend paying stock. Demonstrate that, if *per unit strike*, an undiscounted call of moneyness z and maturity T_1 is more expensive than an undiscounted call of the same moneyness and later maturity T_2, that shorting $1/K_1 P(0, T_1)$ of the earlier call and going long $1/K_2 P(0, T_2)$ of the later call will always make money for the seller, where $P(T_0, T_1)$ and $P(T_0, T_2)$ are the prices of the corresponding zero coupon bonds at time

T_0. Demonstrate that this implies that implied variance for constant moneyness must be monotonically increasing for all maturities. (This is referred to as *calendar spread arbitrage.*)

(5) The derivation of the Dupire local variance formula in this chapter was rather more involved than it needs to be (though the reasons for going down this route will become clear in Chapter 4). The faster method involves applying Itō's lemma to the payoff function $(S-K,0)^+$. Apply this method to come up with the same result.

(6) Extend the previous derivation to the case where local volatility is allowed to take on a degree of independence from the stock price, and demonstrate that $E[\sigma^2(S_T,T)|S_T = K] = \sigma^2_{Dupire}(K,T)$ for option calibration to hold.

Chapter 3

Dividends

In the previous chapter, we derived and discussed a simple model for a *continuous* stock price evolution whereby the volatility was deterministically related to the spot level. In practice, however, such an assumption of continuity tends to be at odds with reality. Stocks commonly pay out a share of the company's earnings in the form of a *dividend*. For the payment to be arbitrage free to the shareholder it should be accompanied by an exactly offsetting move in the share price itself. If not, either the shareholder would make a risk-free instantaneous profit, or someone shorting the shares would. So here is the first problem we need to deal with: stock price evolution is generally *not* continuous. The problem then is, in what way? Does the share price fall by a fixed amount unrelated to its current level, does it somehow scale, or is it some combination of the two? Is the movement in fact known with any degree of certainty at all, and if so, to what degree? In this chapter we will develop a simple model of dividends in the presence of a stock whose volatility continues to be a deterministic function of the stock price. We will show how such a model is a natural reflection of historical analysis, but will also demonstrate how different assumptions on the dividend process impact on the price of a subset of relatively simple exotics. The model will be simpler than those currently used in the industry, but will be designed to identify the dominant pricing considerations behind dividend assumptions as clearly as possible.

3.1   History of dividend modelling

The initial approach to dividends was in fact derived from another area, namely foreign exchange. In the latter, we have a simple relationship between the forward on an fx cross (say USD/JPY) and the spot fx, the risk-free rate on the payment currency (JPY) and the risk-free rate on the underlying. It works like this: say I enter into a contract to exchange USD 1 into JPY in a year's time (T). Rational investors would take a loan for USD 1 today (T_0), exchange it into JPY at the prevailing (spot) rate $f_{USD/JPY}$, then deposit the JPY amount in a Japanese account for one year. At the end of the year they'd then convert back into USD at the *agreed* forward rate specified in the contract, and pay back the US bank for the original loan. Mathematically this gives for the forward rate $F_{USD/JPY}$:

$$f_{USD/JPY}\, e^{\bar{r}_{JPY}(T-T_0)} / F_{USD/JPY} = e^{\bar{r}_{USD}(T-T_0)}$$

giving:

$$F_{USD/JPY} = f_{USD/JPY}\, e^{(\bar{r}_{JPY}-\bar{r}_{USD})(T-T_0)}$$

where

$$\bar{r} = \frac{1}{T-T_0}\int_{T_0}^{T} r(t)dt$$

Accordingly, we have for the risk-neutral process on the spot fx $f_{USD/JPY}(t)$:

$$\frac{df_{USD/JPY}(t)}{f_{USD/JPY}(t)} = [r_{JPY}(t) - r_{USD}(t)]\, dt + \sigma_t dW_t$$

giving $E_{\mathbb{Q}}[f(T)|T_0] = F(T_0, T)$ in the USD risk-neutral measure.

The nice thing of course is that, whilst we now have to consider two risk-free rates, the process on the fx is still continuous. Recalling from Chapter 2 that, as Dupire held for any risk-neutral drift $\mu(t)$, we can immediately deduce the local volatility from the implied volatility surface. Now let's consider the case of a dividend paying stock. A simple (but quite unrealistic) model for dividends is that they pay out *continuously* and *proportionally* to the stock price. Mathematically, over the interval $[t, t+dt]$:

$$div(t) = q(t)S_t dt$$

Now consider the forward contract on stock. A rational investor would want to eliminate exposure to stochastic dividends. The simple way to do this is to increase the short holding of stock against the forward continuously through time. Calling this amount $n(t)$, we must have:

$$dn(t) = n(t)q(t)dt$$

giving:

$$n(T) = n(T_0)\exp\left[\int_{T_0}^{T} q(t)dt\right] = n(T_0)\exp\left[\bar{q}(T_0,T)(T - T_0)\right]$$

The contract is to buy one share at forward price F though, giving $n(T) = 1$. We thus have for the static replication:

$$n(T_0)S_0\exp\left[\bar{r}(T_0,T)(T - T_0)\right] = F(T_0,T)$$

allowing us to buy one share with the cash accrued on account, and cancel the short position at zero cost. So using $n(T) = 1$ we now have:

$$F(T_0,T) = S_0\exp\left[(\bar{r}(T_0,T) - \bar{q}(T_0,T))(T - T_0)\right]$$

This looks exactly like the fx forward, replacing the underlying rate with the average continuously compounded dividend yield $\bar{q}(T_0,T)$. Likewise, we have for the risk-neutral stock diffusion:

$$\frac{dS_t}{S_t} = [r(t) - q(t)]\,dt + \sigma_t dW_t$$

allowing us to carry over all the machinery for dealing with fx skew straight into equity. Excellent, apart from two small problems:

- There's no such thing as a continuously compounded dividend yield, in reality at least.
- Dividends tend to be insensitive to stock price movement, unless the company runs into such difficulty that it has to cut dividends, or is doing so well that shareholders force a dividend hike.

Happily, neither drawback is unsolvable. Let's look at each in turn.

3.1.1   *Discrete proportional dividends*

For a start, as mentioned at the beginning of this chapter, dividend payment is a discrete event. To be more precise, on the date that someone
buying stock is no longer *entitled* to the dividend, referred to as the ex-
date, the stock price should fall by that amount. Were this not to be true,
an existing shareholder selling the stock to a new shareholder would record
an instantaneous profit or loss against the guaranteed dividend payment
occurring shortly afterwards. Notice that we immediately have a potential
problem: what if the stock price were *below* the dividend on the ex-date?
By the no arbitrage argument the stock would actually have to go *negative*
ex-dividend. This is obviously impossible. Apart from the fact that a negative stock price would imply shareholders pay back future dividend streams
to the company, it would also imply that the company would be allowed to
continue with its liabilities out-stripping its assets. Neither is economically
feasible. Worse still, negative stock price would break any model assuming
locally log-normal diffusion (which is obviously much worse...). One way
to deal with this problem is to assume that, whilst dividends are indeed
discrete, they vary in proportion to the stock price immediately *before* the
dividend ex-date (also referred to as the 'cum-dividend' price). We will use
the notation T_i^- to denote the ith cum-dividend time, and T_i^+ the corresponding ex-dividend time. So how would the forward replication work
now? Actually, in much the same way as with continuously compounded
dividends. Consider the number of shares held after reinvesting the dividend $div_i = q_i S(T_i^-)$. Reinvestment must necessarily occur just after the
stock price drops, so the number of shares on this date will change discon-
tinuously as:

$$n(T_i^+) = n(T_i^-)\left[1 + \frac{div_i}{S(T_i^+)}\right] = n(T_i^-)\left[1 + \frac{q_i S(T_i^-)}{S(T_i^-)(1 - q_i)}\right]$$
$$= n(T_i^-)/(1 - q_i)$$

So, we have in general that the number of shares shorted against our forward
position at time T is just:

$$n(T) = \frac{n(T_0)}{\prod_{T_0 < T_i \leq T}(1 - q_i)}$$

Again, setting this to unity and applying the forward static replication
argument gives:

$$F(T_0, T) = S_0 e^{\bar{r}(T_0,T)(T-T_0)} \prod_{T_0 < T_i \leq T} (1 - q_i) \qquad (3.1)$$

A typical forward profile is shown in Figure 3.1.

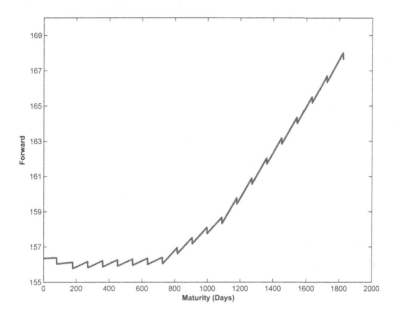

Fig. 3.1   Typical forward curve with discrete dividends.

How would the process for this work? As it happens, we can construct a continuous process around this, but obviously not on the stock. Denoting $Q(T) = \prod_{T_0 < T_i \leq T} (1 - q_i)$, we can write:

$$S_t = X_t Q(t)$$

where

$$\frac{dX_t}{X_t} = r(t)dt + \sigma_t dW_t$$

Integrating up this process, and taking expectation over S_T will trivially give the forward obtained in (3.1). We will see what this implies for the time interpolation of the implied vol surface on stock in the next section on local volatility re-derivation.

3.1.2   *Discrete cash dividends*

Now let's move onto the yet more realistic problem of dividends whose value is insensitive to stock price movements. To begin, why is this more realistic? On the whole, a company tends to pay out much the same dividend year after year. In times of crisis the dividend may be withdrawn, but if this goes on for too long the share price will eventually just tank and the company cease to exist. Equally, whilst equity holders need to be satisfied on an ongoing basis, all things being equal (i.e. excluding events which change the number of shares outstanding), a board of directors tends to keep dividends fixed in real economic terms. In general then, changes to dividends tend to be exceptional. The market view tends to be that, over a longer time scale, dividends are likely, *ultimately*, to follow share price movements, so that a share which has declined considerably over a number of years would be expected to pay a lower dividend, and vice versa, but in the immediate (generally < 2-year horizon), dividends can be considered fixed. This is commonly referred to as the cash dividend model. How would the forward look now? In this case, the strategy is rather different. As the dividend is simply a cash payment, it's simply paid to the shareholder from whom we've borrowed shares to build up a cash position, from that cash position. At time T the amount of cash we hold on account is given by:

$$S_0 \exp[\bar{r}(T_0, T)(T - T_0)] - \sum_{T_0 < T_i \leq T} div_i \exp[\bar{r}(T_i, T)(T - T_i)] \qquad (3.2)$$

Equation (3.2) assumes that the deal dates and payment dates of the problem are co-incident. A more complete expression would read:

$$\frac{S_0}{Df(\widetilde{T}_0, \widetilde{T})} - \sum_{T_0 < T_i \leq T} \frac{div_i}{Df(\widehat{T}_i, \widetilde{T})} \qquad (3.3)$$

where $\widetilde{T}$ corresponds to the date on which we actually exchange cash for the forward expiration, $\widetilde{T}_0$ the date on which we receive cash for shorting the stock, and $\widehat{T}_i$ the payment date of the ith dividend. For simplicity, we will take payment lags as zero. The above also assumes no charge for borrowing the stock (variously called *funding spread*, *borrow cost* or *product rate*). This has the effect of changing the effective cost of carry from r to $r - r_b$ for a borrow cost r_b, and again will be ignored for simplicity.

Definition of a process to match this forward is not unique. Broadly speaking, popular approaches to date have split into two camps: terminal spot models, where some accumulated dividend amount is added or subtracted to a dividend-*free* variable; and current spot models, where a single dividend is subtracted from the current spot level, leaving the volatility of the process unchanged. Let's look at each approach in turn.

3.1.2.1 *The spot model of cash dividends*

(For references see Wilmott [Wilmott (1998)] and Vandermark [Bos and Vandermark (2002)].)

The process can be written as follows:

$$dS_t = \left(r(t)S_t - \sum_i div_i \delta(t - T_i) \right) dt + \sigma_t S_t dW_t \qquad (3.4)$$

This can be thought of as a 'natural' approach to cash dividend modelling, in that the only effect of a dividend is to shift the terminal distribution of the spot process down by the ex-dividend amount. This gives two natural no arbitrage conditions:

- A call option with expiry just after the ex-dividend date should be worth the same as one just before, but with a strike shifted by the ex-dividend amount. This follows simply from (3.4):

$$E_\mathbb{Q}[(S(T_i{}^+) - (K - div_i), 0)^+] = E_\mathbb{Q}[((S(T_i{}^-) - div_i) - (K - div_i), 0)^+]$$
$$= E_\mathbb{Q}[(S(T_i{}^-) - K, 0)^+]$$

(The same is true for puts via put-call parity).
- A call option whose start date lies just before an ex-dividend date is worth the same as a call option, with the same expiry, whose start date lies just after the ex-div date, with the same strike. This of course must be the case from a simple trading argument: if the price of the option jumped down over a deal date, say, then one could instantly lock in a risk-free profit by selling just before and buying back the same option just afterwards. Consider the case of a single dividend D between now and expiry, with flat vol and rates for simplicity. Integrating (3.4), we have for the undiscounted value of a call, strike K and maturity T valued at $T_0{}^-$, just before the ex-date:

$$C(T_0^-, T, K) = \int \left[\left(S(T_0^-) - D \right) e^{\sigma W_{T-T_0} - \sigma^2 (T-T_0)/2} - K, 0 \right]^+$$
$$\phi(W)dW$$

where we have integrated over the Gaussian:

$$\phi(W) = \frac{1}{\sqrt{2\pi\sigma^2(T-T_0)}} e^{-W^2/2\sigma^2(T-T_0)}$$

Just after the dividend, at T_0^+ we have for the undiscounted value of the same option:

$$C(T_0^+, T, K) = \int \left[S(T_0^+) e^{\sigma W_{T-T_0} - \sigma^2 (T-T_0)/2} - K, 0 \right]^+ \phi(W)dW$$

But from no arbitrage conditions, $S(T_0^+) = S(T_0^-) - D$, so that $C(T_0^-, T, K) = C(T_0^+, T, K)$, as required. This is rather obvious, but not always obeyed by terminal spot models, as we shall see.

There are, however, two problems with this model. Whilst conceptually appealing (and indeed in line with observations of spot price dynamics), there is no closed-form solution for European options. Consider the case where today lies before a single dividend payment, at ex-date τ:

$$C(T_0, T, K) = \int \left[\left(S(\tau^-) - D \right) e^{\sigma W_{T-\tau} - \sigma^2 (T-\tau)/2} - K, 0 \right]^+ \phi(W_{T-\tau})dW_{T-\tau}$$
$$= \int \left[\left(S(T_0) e^{\sigma W_{\tau-T_0} - \sigma^2 (\tau-T_0)/2} - D \right) e^{\sigma W_{T-\tau} - \sigma^2 (T-\tau)/2} - K, 0 \right]^+$$
$$\times \phi(W_{T-\tau})\phi(W_{\tau-T_0})dW_{T-\tau}dW_{\tau-T_0}$$

This has the same sort of problem as an arithmetic Asian option, for example, where we pay out on the arithmetic average of stock observations against some strike. For log-normal processes, the arithmetic average is not log-normal. We can approximate the distribution of the average by, say, adding together two log-normals and matching the first four moments to the first four moments of the average [Krekel (2003)]. Another approach is to adopt a first-order perturbation approach to the terminal stock price [Bos and Vandermark (2002)]. For flat interest rates r and vol σ, it can be shown (and is left as an exercise at the end of this chapter), that we can approximate the stock at time t by:

$$S_t = (S_0 - D_n(T_0, T)) \exp\left[\left(r - \frac{\sigma^2}{2}\right)(t - T_0) + \sigma W_{t-T_0}\right] \quad (3.5)$$
$$- D_f(T_0, T) \exp(r(t - T_0))$$

where the present value of future dividends between t and expiry T is divided between a 'near' part $D_n(t, T)$:

$$D_n(T_0, T) = \sum_{T_0 < T_i \leq T} \frac{T - T_i}{T - T_0} div_i \exp(-r(T_i - T_0))$$

and a 'far' part: $D_f(t, T)$:

$$D_f(T_0, T) = \sum_{T_0 < T_i \leq T} \frac{T_i - T_0}{T - T_0} div_i \exp(-r(T_i - T_0))$$

This has the great advantage that the value of a call option expiring at time T can now be written as:

$$C(K, T) = C_0(S_0 - D_n(T_0, T), K + D_f(T_0, T)e^{r(T-T_0)}, \sigma, T)$$

where $C_0(S^*, K)$ is the Black–Scholes price of a dividend-free process S^*. It turns out [Bos and Vandermark (2002)] that this price is close, in practice, to the same price derived from the spot model through finite difference integration, allowing this to be used as a basis for deriving local volatilities given sets of option prices. Such an approach is, however, at best an approximation. Likewise, calibration of local vol on the spot model to option prices via numerical integration of the process will also suffer from the simplified form of the chosen local vol function, again preventing like-for-like comparison of proportional vs cash dividend models. The spot model will not therefore be used as the model of choice in this chapter.

3.1.2.2 *Terminal (forward) models of cash dividends*

The essential idea here has already been introduced in the previous section, where we approximated a model whose European prices were not closed-form, by one that was. The split far-near dividend model of Vandermark and Bos is one such approach. Simpler approaches can be split between the dividend subtraction method [Musiela and Rutkowski (1997)], and the dividend addition method [Buehler (2007); Frishling (2002); Hull (2008); Bos *et al.* (2003)]. In practice, the latter tends to be more popular. To allow closed-form European prices, we take some dividend-free process $X(T)$ and add or subtract some dividend amount to get a stock price whose expectation matches the forward. So, for dividend subtraction, we have:

$$S_T = X_T - D(T)$$
$$D(T) = \sum_{T_0 < T_i \leq T} div_i \exp[\bar{r}(T_i, T)(T - T_i)] \qquad (3.6)$$

whilst for dividend addition we have:

$$S_T = X_T + \widetilde{D}(T, T_H)$$
$$\widetilde{D}(T, T_H) = \sum_{T < T_i \leq T_H} div_i \exp[-\bar{r}(T, T_i)(T_i - T)] \qquad (3.7)$$

There are two problems with the subtraction method:

- For $X_T < D(T)$, $S_T < 0$.
- As our start date rolls over a dividend payment d we have just prior that the value of X_τ just after τ is given by $X_{\tau+} = S_{\tau+} + d = X_{\tau-}$, whereas just after $X_{\tau+} = S_{\tau+}$. In other words, whilst on any *given* start date, our process on $X(T)$ is continuous, that process itself changes as our start date rolls over a dividend. This will cause a pricing discontinuity and presents an arbitrage opportunity.

Conversely, the dividend addition method demands that we set some arbitrary horizon date T_H up to which the stock price is necessarily positive. Suppose we were just to take this date as an option expiry. This would present the same sort of problems as the start date roll in the subtraction method, namely that the spot of our dividend-free process would jump down as the maturity went over a dividend date (as $X_0 = S_0 - \widetilde{D}(T_0, T)$ in this case). So, for the same driving vol, we would expect the value of an American option, say, to jump downwards. This is exactly what we do see [Bos *et al.* (2003)], and presents another arbitrage opportunity. The solution to this problem is to fix the horizon date. At least in this case we have a *unique* process for valuing all our products. Note also that our process is unchanged as the start date of an option rolls through an ex-date, in contrast with the subtraction method. We still, however, have another problem. The longest dated expiry we might have could be such that the required spot for our dividend-free process is actually negative. The way to get round this is to mix proportional and cash dividend behaviour, described in the next section.

3.1.3 *Mixed dividend modelling*

In general, there is nothing to stop us assuming that dividend payment is somewhere between cash and proportional. A popular way of thinking about this is to assume that the dividend can be written as:

$$div_i = q_i S(T_i^-) + \widehat{div}_i$$

where we assume that the cash dividend component $\widehat{div}_i$ is paid immediately *after* the proportional dividend one. This gives for the forward:

$$F(T_0, T) = \widehat{F}(T_0, T)Q(T)$$
$$\widehat{F}(T_0, T) = S_0 \exp[\bar{r}(T_0, T)(T - T_0)]$$
$$- \sum_{T_0 < T_i \leq T} \frac{\widehat{div}_i}{Q(T_i)} \exp[\bar{r}(T_i, T)(T - T_i)]$$
$$Q(T) = \prod_{T_0 < T_j \leq T} (1 - q_j)$$

Mapping this expression to a regular cash dividend forward (3.2) with cash dividend $\widetilde{div}_i = E_\mathbb{Q}[div_i]$, and defining $\alpha(T_i) = \widehat{div}_i/\widetilde{div}_i$ gives $q_i = (1 - \alpha(T_i))\widetilde{div}_i/\left[F(T_i) + \widetilde{div}_i\right]$. We can thus consistently construct a mixed dividend model using only the market forward curve and some mixing parameter $\alpha(t)$. The new version of (3.6) reads as:

$$S_T = [X_T - D(T)]Q(T) \qquad (3.8)$$

where

$$D(T) = \sum_{T_0 < T_i \leq T} \frac{\widehat{div}_i}{Q(T_i)} \exp[\bar{r}(T_i, T)(T - T_i)]$$

The new version of (3.7) reads as:

$$S_T = [X_T + \widetilde{D}(T)]Q(T) \qquad (3.9)$$

where

$$\widetilde{D}(T) = \sum_{T < T_i \leq T_H} \frac{\widehat{div}_i}{Q(T_i)} \exp[-\bar{r}(T, T_i)(T_i - T)]$$

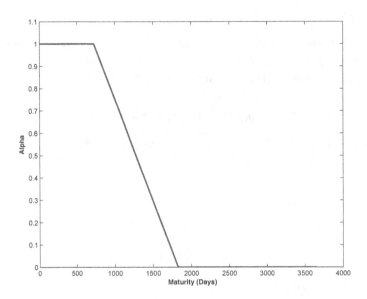

Fig. 3.2 Typical dividend mixing curve for a joint cash-proportional dividend model.

Commonly, the mixing curve $\alpha(T)$ has the form shown in Figure 3.2, pure cash out to 2Y, linearly mixed up to 5Y, then pure proportional thereafter.

This approach does at least ensure that the price change due to the changing character of the forecast dividend in (3.9) will be continuous. Unfortunately, there's still one remaining problem with (3.9): for the horizon date beyond the maturity of an option, dividends falling after the maturity will impact on the option's price, through calibration. We thus end up with dividend risk from payment which can have no possible impact. Such a problem clearly does not exist in (3.6), where no horizon date is required. Ultimately then, in spite of the apparent simplicity of the problem, cash dividend modelling throws up some fairly unpleasant choices:

- Should we adopt a spot model of dividends where the spot can fall below zero, and implied vol surface calibration is imprecise, but at least we have no problems with dividends after option expiry affecting option price, or option behaviour both for maturity and start date rolling over an ex-date?
- Should we opt for a model where vol surface calibration is precise, dividends after expiry have no effect on price, but the spot process

capable of falling below zero, and pricing arbitrageable every time our start date moves over a dividend date?

- Should we opt for model where vol surface calibration is precise, start date and maturity date behaviour non-arbitrageable, the spot process guaranteed positive, but where dividends falling after expiry impact option price?

For the purposes of model risk, rather than market risk discussion, lack of arbitrage, precise calibration and process positivity are, in the opinion of the author, non-negotiable. Nonetheless, for the sake of completeness, we will include both the additive and subtractive dividend models in the discussion of model risk for the remainder of this chapter. Though both models have their flaws, they do at least provide a reasonable framework for investigating the effect of switching from proportional to cash dividends.

3.2 How do dividends actually evolve? Historical analysis

Before we start to address the problems of re-calibrating a local volatility model under mixed dividend assumptions, it's useful to take a step back for a moment and see how dividends *actually* behave in relation to spot. Figure 3.3 shows how the actual dividend of a real US stock has changed in relation to spot level over the last ten years.

Two effects are immediately noticeable in this data:

- Dividends are reset intermittently, remaining constant for a considerable length of time, regardless of share price movements.
- For large-scale increases in share price, dividends are indeed revised upwards.

Suppose we were to translate this into dividend *yield* space. For a constant dividend D, we would simply have for the yield $q_i = D/S(T_i^-)$. In terms of the dynamics, $\log(q_i)$ would be perfectly anticorrelated with $\log(S)$, and indeed have the same volatility. If we were to plot a scatter of the increments of $\log(q_i)$ vs the corresponding increments of $\log(S)$, we would then expect the points to fall predominantly on the line $y = -x$. This is shown in Figure 3.4 for the same data set.

The only exception to this behaviour is of course when the dividend is revised, as can be seen in the two outlying points above the $y = -x$ line. Figure 3.5 shows the combined scatter for the 500 underlying stocks of the

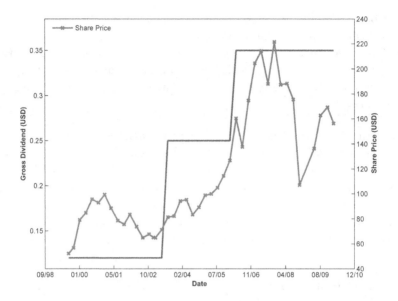

Fig. 3.3   Dividend vs stock history for a sample US stock, 2000–2010.

S&P500 over the same 10-year period.

The data is surprisingly scattered. The bulk of the data points are indeed scattered around the 'fixed dividend line' (shown in bold), but dividend revisions do account for a noticeable number of outliers. Interestingly, whilst a poor stock performance does indeed seem to correlate well with a dividend downgrade, the converse does not appear to be true. That being said, for moderate stock returns, the density of dividend yield returns tends to be focussed above the fixed dividend line, suggesting that moderate dividend upgrades occur more than downgrades during normal market conditions. Returning to the sample stock, the time series for the dividend yield is shown in Figure 3.6.

Comparing with Figure 3.4, we can see that, in spite of the doubling of the share price over the last decade, the dividend yield actually oscillated around a flat level. Such behaviour is characteristic of a *mean reverting* process. We will look into these in more detail in Chapter 4, but it's useful to describe their properties briefly here. The simplest type is referred to as an *Ornstein–Uhlenbeck* process, and can be written as follows:

$$dy_t = -\kappa(y_t - \bar{y})dt + \sigma dW_t$$

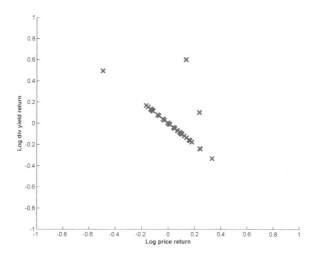

Fig. 3.4 Scatter of increment in log dividend yield vs increments in log stock for a sample US stock, 2000–2010.

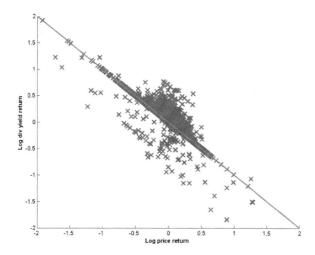

Fig. 3.5 Combined scatter of increment in log dividend yield vs increments in log stock for the 500 stocks of the S&P500, 2000–2010.

where dW_t is a standard Brownian motion $\sim \mathcal{N}(0, dt)$. Assuming that the mean reversion speed κ is positive, this process effectively penalises deviations from the long-term level $\bar{y}$, so that, over time, the average of y_t tends to the long-term level, with the variance tending to a constant $\sigma^2/2\kappa$.

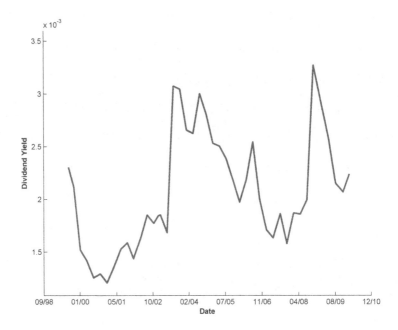

Fig. 3.6   Dividend yield time series for a sample US stock, 2000–2010.

Sample processes for a 10Y daily sampled window, with $\sigma = 10\%$, $\bar{y} = 0$ and $y_0 = -0.1$ are shown in Figures 3.7 and 3.8 for $\kappa = 1$ and $\kappa = 10$ respectively.

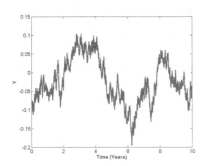
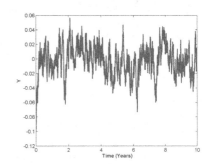

Fig. 3.7   Sample OU process, $\kappa = 1$, $\sigma = 10\%$, $\bar{y} = 0$ and $y_0 = -0.1$.

Fig. 3.8   Sample OU process, $\kappa = 10$, $\sigma = 10\%$, $\bar{y} = 0$ and $y_0 = -0.1$.

The corresponding distributions of the terminal value of y_t at 10Y are shown in Figures 3.9 and 3.10 respectively.

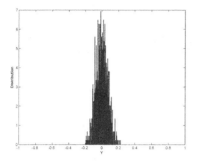

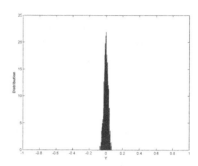

Fig. 3.9   Sample OU distribution, $\kappa = 1$, $\sigma = 10\%$, $\bar{y} = 0$ and $y_0 = -0.1$.

Fig. 3.10   Sample OU process, $\kappa = 10$, $\sigma = 10\%$, $\bar{y} = 0$ and $y_0 = -0.1$.

Now, a dividend yield should be bound by the constraint $0 \leq q \leq 1$, the lower bound eliminating the possibility of the shareholder reimbursing the company for holding stock (much though the company might want this), and the upper bound eliminating the possibility of the share price falling below zero on the ex-date. Any continuous mapping from the domain $[-\infty, \infty]$ to the domain $[0, 1]$ on the simple OU process would suffice. One possibility might be:

$$Q(T_i, T_{i+1}) = 1 - f(y_{i+1})$$
$$f(x) = \frac{e^x}{2}\mathbf{1}(-x) + \left(1 - \frac{e^{-x}}{2}\right)\mathbf{1}(x)$$

where y_t follows the simple OU process described above, with long-term yield a function of time such that $E_{\mathbb{Q}}\left[\prod_{0 \leq i \leq j} Q(T_i, T_{i+1})\right] = F(T_j)Df(t_0, T_j)/S_0$. Buehler *et al.* consider the simple OU process directly [Buehler *et al.* (2010)] to enable analytic tractability in the case of flat implied volatility. At the time of writing, work on a properly bounded process has yet to be published. Such a model would have interesting properties:

- As the dividend yield is bounded above by unity, the issue of negative stock price would automatically be resolved. Assuming that the dividend yield is perfectly negatively correlated with the stock, and assumes the same volatility, the effective dividend on any given ex-date would be constant for stock prices above the level at the previous ex-date, and then smoothly fall to zero below this point.

- The distribution of short-term dividend yields would be the mirror image of the corresponding stock distribution, in keeping with the fixed dividend model, whilst long-term yields would tend to a fixed long-term distribution with fixed variance. By contrast, the distribution of the long-term stock level has a variance proportional to maturity, causing the dividend behaviour to tend to a purely proportional dividend model with volatility tending to zero. The speed at which this change in behaviour would occur could be controlled through the mean reversion.
- The change in dividend behaviour from fixed to proportional would move forward with time, so that a 1Y forward starting option (for example) would be fixed dividend dominated *regardless of the start point.*

In effect, we can regard the simpler mixed dividend model as a proxy for actual dividend dynamics. When we discuss the effects of moving from fixed dividends to proportional dividends via a time dependent mixing function, we are effectively discussing the impact of changing dividend yield mean reversion. Sadly, the stochastic dividend yield model is hard to calibrate to spot starting implied volatility, and we shall use the mixed dividend model detailed in the last section as the method for approaching this effect tractably.

3.3   The mixed dividend model

We will base the remainder of this chapter on the processes given by (3.8) and (3.9). In fact, for the purposes of clarity, we'll make the assumption that dividends are purely cash up to some cut-off date, and fully proportional thereafter. The purpose of this book is not, after all, to provide a full trading model, but rather to focus on specific assumptions in our existing Dupire model framework which impact on the pricing of exotics. In this case we will focus purely on the impact of moving from fully proportional dividends to fully cash. Before we elaborate on local vol re-calibration however, it's instructive to see how this model behaves in the *absence* of calibration. Two representative 5Y vol slices for an annual 2% dividend are shown in Figure 3.11.

In this example, spot has been taken as unity, with dividends of 0.02 paid on an annual basis. The horizon date has been set at 10Y. The higher vol slice is given by a fully proportional dividend model, the upper one

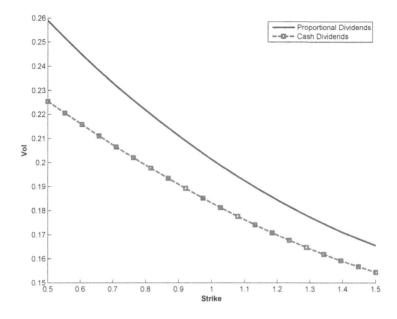

Fig. 3.11   The effect of cash dividends on implied volatility - dividend addition.

by taking the same expected dividend stream to be cash. The lowering effect on implied volatility from cash dividends from an additive model is a common, albeit somewhat un-intuitive feature. Recall that the spot of the dividend-free process at start date will always be below the actual spot. The growth is, however, the same. If we consider a path which has risen above initial spot in a proportional dividend model then, until the next div, the corresponding path on the cash dividend model will have risen less due to the lower start position on the dividend-free process. This is illustrated in Figure 3.12.

The converse is true for paths which have fallen below the initial spot. We would thus expect out of the money calls to be cheaper in a cash dividend model, and the same for out of the money puts. Given that it is these instruments used for deriving the implied volatility surface, and that the forwards between the two models will always agree, the vol surface is driven downwards, as seen. Note that the reverse is true in the subtraction dividend model (3.8). In this case the stock and dividend-free processes start from *the same* point, so that a given upside path on the stock would be expected to be driven down more by the proportional dividend at an ex-

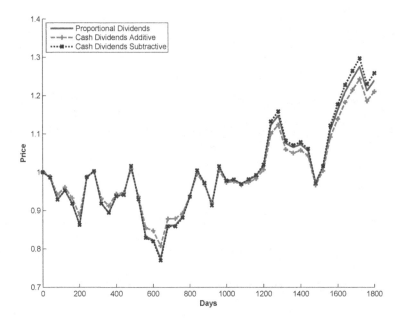

Fig. 3.12   The effect of cash dividends on path realisation.

date, and to change by the same amount between ex-dates. The converse is true for a downside path. This has the effect of raising the price of both calls and puts, as shown in Figure 3.13.

Let's look at this mathematically: the undiscounted expected value of a call, under the additive model, can be written:

$$\begin{aligned} C(F_S(T), K, \sigma_S(K), T) &= E_{\mathbb{Q}}[(S_T - K, 0)^+] \\ &= E_{\mathbb{Q}}[((X_T + D(T))Q(T) - K, 0)^+] \\ &= Q(T)C(F_X(T), \widetilde{K}, \sigma_X(K), T) \\ \widetilde{K} &= \frac{K}{Q(T)} - D(T) \end{aligned} \tag{3.10}$$

where we have dropped the tilde on D for simplicity. We have also:

$$F_S(T) = Q(T)\left[F_X(T) + D(T)\right]$$

so that we can rewrite (3.10) as:

$$C(F_S(T), K, \sigma_S(K), T) = C(F_S(T) - D(T)Q(T), K - D(T)Q(T), \sigma_X(\widetilde{K}), T) \tag{3.11}$$

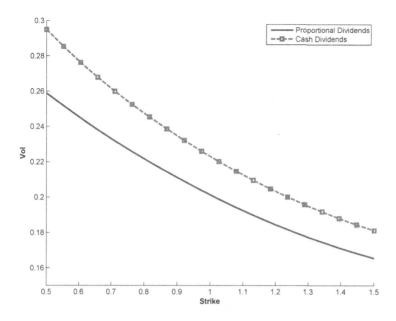

Fig. 3.13 The effect of cash dividends on implied volatility – dividend subtraction.

Writing in terms of $\widetilde{K}$, this gives us the relationship between the implied vol surface corresponding to the process on $X(T)$, and the resultant implied vol on the stock:

$$C(F_S(T), Q(T)(\widetilde{K} + D(T)), \sigma_S(Q(T)(\widetilde{K} + D(T))), T) =$$
$$C(F_S(T) - D(T)Q(T), Q(T)\widetilde{K}, \sigma_X(\widetilde{K}), T) \qquad (3.12)$$

There are a number of points to note about (3.12):

(1) For a pure proportional dividend model, we simply have:

$$C(F_S(T), Q(T)\widetilde{K}, \sigma_S(Q(T)\widetilde{K}), T) = C(F_S(T), Q(T)\widetilde{K}, \sigma_X(\widetilde{K}), T) \qquad (3.13)$$

so that the two implied vol surfaces are related by $\sigma_S(Q(T)K, T) = \sigma_X(K, T)$. Given that $X(T)$ is a continuous process, we must have that the implied vol surface be continuous likewise, which means that $\sigma_S(K, T_i^-) = \sigma_S(K(1 - q_i), T_i^+)$. Putting this another way, the volatility for constant $z = \log(K/F)$ should be continuous. But that's exactly in accordance with our original local volatility formulation, where we transformed the Dupire equation from one over K to one over z. Written as a function of moneyness, the implied vol surface on X is identical to the one on S. By deriving the local volatility from such a surface for S, originally with the assumption of continuously compounded dividends, we have in fact ended up deriving the local volatility 'properly' from an implied vol surface on a continuous process related to the stock through discrete proportional dividends. Putting it another way: *the Dupire formalism is unaffected by the discrete nature of dividends provided they're proportional.*

(2) As you might expect, we're not so fortunate when dividends are not proportional. Supposing we generate an implied vol surface on stock from a flat vol on $X(t)$. We have to first order from (3.11):

$$C(F_S(T), K, \sigma_S(K), T) = -D(T)Q(T)\left[N(d_1) - N(d_2)\right]$$

where $d_1 = \log(F_S(T)/K)/\sigma_X\sqrt{T} + \sigma_X\sqrt{T}/2$, and $d_2 = d_1 - \sigma_X\sqrt{T}$. This is always negative, in accordance with our result that cash dividends always push down the stock's implied volatility.

(3) For a continuous volatility surface on $X(T)$ the same will not be true of the implied volatility surface on stock. We have already seen this for the case of pure proportional dividends. A similarly instructive expression can be derived for pure cash. As $\sigma_X(K, T)$ is continuous as well as the forward on $X(T)$, (3.12) gives across a dividend ex-date:

$$C(F_S(T_i^-), K + D(T_i^-), \sigma_S(K + D(T_i^-)), T_i^-) =$$
$$C(F_S(T_i^+), K + D(T_i^+), \sigma_S(K + D(T_i^+)), T_i^+)$$

But given $D(T_i^+) = D(T_i^-) - div_i$, we have:

$$C(F_S(T_i^-), K + div_i, \sigma_S(K + div_i), T_i^-) = C(F_S(T_i^+), K, \sigma_S(K), T_i^+)$$

In other words, the option value with expiry immediately after the dividend goes ex must be equal to the value of the option with expiry just prior with strike adjusted up by the dividend amount, as discussed in the context of the spot model.

(4) A solution for $\sigma_X(K)$ always exists (provided $X_0 > 0$). This is in contrast to the subtraction method, where for strikes below the forward value of divs to that maturity, no solution exists. This is equivalent to

there being a minimum stock level below which propagation is no longer possible due to the dividend taking the stock below zero. Like this, in the subtraction method, we would not be able to derive a complete volatility surface for $X(T)$, and hence the implied probability distribution will not integrate to one. No such problems exist in the additive model.

(5) The corollary to the cash dividends pushing down the stock implied volatility is that an implied vol surface on $X(T)$ will always be higher than a target calibration implied vol surface from the market. Whilst this is obvious, it is nonetheless important. We might imagine, for example, that an up and out barrier option would be consistently more expensive for the cash dividend model due to the corresponding stock paths being lower. We also have, however, that the local volatility on such a process will be higher than in the proportional case, making the chances of getting to within a dividend payment of the barrier *higher*. We will look at this in detail later in the chapter.

Figures 3.14 and 3.15 illustrate this final point clearly. In this exercise we have applied (3.12) across the entire implied volatility surface of our test stock out to 5Y, and used the resultant implied vol surface on $X(T)$ to derive a local volatility via standard Dupire. The agreement between the resultant integrated implied vol surface and the input surface is clearly excellent, as seen in Figure 3.14. The enhancement of the calibrated local vol surface compared to the proportional dividend case is also clear.

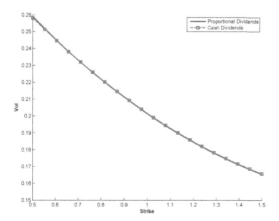

Fig. 3.14   Implied volatility slice at 5Y for an additive cash dividend process, post-calibration.

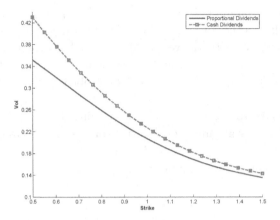

Fig. 3.15   Local volatility slice at 5Y for an additive cash dividend process, post-calibration.

3.4   Barrier options and lookbacks

Looking again at Figure 3.12, an obvious product to look at in terms of the effect of switching from a proportional to a cash dividend model would be a barrier option. There are essentially four basic forms these can take:

- **Up and Out (UO)**: the option pays out provided a barrier greater than the initial spot level has *not* been breached.
- **Up and In (UI)**: the option pays out provided a barrier greater than the initial spot level *has* been breached.
- **Down and Out (DO)**: the option pays out provided a barrier less than the initial spot level has *not* been breached.
- **Down and In (DI)**: the option pays out provided a barrier less than the initial spot level *has* been breached.

This provides the basic structure. On top of this are a large number of variants, for example:

- Double barrier options, where the spot has to trade inside (double no-touch) or outside (double one-touch) a window. Such options are popular in the foreign exchange market.
- Parisian/parasian barrier options, where the spot has to trade above or below a barrier for a specified number of days, consecutively (parisian)

or otherwise (parasian). Such options are used for managing the high
gamma risk in the vicinity of the barrier more efficiently.

- Timer options, where the option is triggered by the realised variance,
  rather than the spot of the asset. Such options are used to guard against
  high stock volatility, and reduce vega exposure on regular Europeans.
- Worst-of/Best-of autocallables, where the best/worst performer from
  a basket needs to hit a barrier to trigger the knock-out or knock-in
  condition. Such options are essentially bets on correlation. The simpler,
  European variant, will be looked at in detail in Chapter 8.

On the whole, simple barriers are used to cheapen a conventional option
(e.g. a regular call), due to the extra risk involved of the option expiring
worthless. Knock-out options tend to be used when speculating on small
moves, whilst the converse is true for knock-in options. An excellent introduction to further business rationale behind barrier option trading is
provided by Derman [Derman and Kani (1996)].

A close cousin of the barrier option is the lookback. These come in two
basic flavours:

- **Fixed Strike**: Like a regular call or put, except that the investor gets
  to execute at the *maximum* realised price over the life of the trade (in
  the case of a call), or the *minimum* price, in the case of a put. These
  options are sometimes referred to as insurance against regret, i.e. the
  regret of not having executed at the best possible price.
- **Floating Strike**: In this case, it is the strike which gets adjusted by
  the lookback strategy, as well as the spot. A floating strike lookback
  call would pay the difference between the maximum realised price and
  the minimum realised price, with the converse true for a floating strike
  lookback put. Such options are clearly more expensive than their fixed
  strike counterparts.

In this section, we will confine our attentions to barrier options, but will
use the concepts underlying the pricing of lookbacks to guide our intuition
with respect to dividend model risk. To begin, let's have a look at some
Black–Scholes barrier and lookback pricing.

3.4.1 *Basic barrier and lookback valuation*

Much of this presentation is based on West [West (2009)], who has provided
a highly clear and informative introduction to exotic options.

We will begin by assuming a simple arithmetic Brownian motion with zero drift and unit volatility:

$$dX_t = dW_t$$

Such a process has an extremely convenient characteristic, namely that, for any given move dX_t, the probability of a corresponding *reflected* move $-dX_t$ is identical, from the symmetry of the Gaussian distribution of $dW_t \sim \mathcal{N}(0, dt)$. Correspondingly, for any given *path* $\{0, W_1, \ldots W_n\}$, the corresponding reflected path $\{0, -W_1, \ldots - W_n\}$ should occur with equal probability. Armed with this fact, let's consider a digital barrier, which pays one for $X_T > K$ iff $m_T(X) < b < K$, where $m_T(X) = \min\limits_{0 < s \leq T} X(s)$ and $b < X_0$. Consider a path which starts from $X_0 = 0$ and evolves to the barrier b. Now, for the subsequent realisation of this path, construct the same path, reflected in the barrier. This is demonstrated in Figure 3.16.

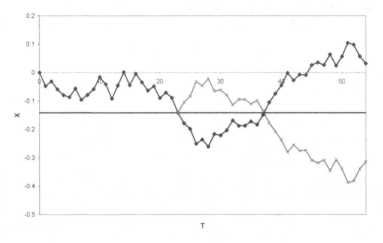

Fig. 3.16   Reflection principle for a simple barrier option.

Let's assume the strike were at $X = 0$. By construction, we can see that for every original path which ends up above the strike, the corresponding reflected path would end up below $2b$. In general, for every original path which ends up above $X = K$, the reflected path would end up below $b - (K - b) = 2b - K$. As these paths occur with equal probability, the price of the digital barrier paying one if the terminal spot ends up above the strike if the minimum falls below the barrier should be identical to a simple digital put with strike $K' = 2b - K$. Mathematically:

$$\mathbb{P}(X_T > K \cap m_T(X) < b) = \mathbb{P}(X_T < 2b - K) = N\left(\frac{2b - K}{\sqrt{t}}\right) \qquad (3.14)$$

where $N(x) = \frac{1}{\sqrt{2\pi}} \int_{-\infty}^{x} e^{-x'^2/2} dx'$.

This is a remarkable result. In spite of the fact that the digital barrier is fundamentally a path dependent option, the price can be exactly replicated by a non-path dependent digital put. Moreover, (3.14) allows us to derive an expression for the joint distribution of the minimum and the terminal spot. For an up and out option, we might be more interested in looking at the corresponding distribution for the maximum $M_T(X) = \max_{0<s\leq T} X(s)$. A corresponding argument for a digital put, up and in barrier with $b > K$, $b > X_0$ gives:

$$\mathbb{P}(X_T < K \cap M_T(X) > b) = \mathbb{P}(X_T > 2b - K) = 1 - N\left(\frac{2b - K}{\sqrt{t}}\right) \qquad (3.15)$$

Writing $f(X_T, M_T)$ for the joint distribution of X_T and M_T, we can rewrite (3.15) as:

$$\int_b^\infty \int_{-\infty}^K f(X_T, M_T) dX_T dM_T = 1 - N\left(\frac{2b - K}{\sqrt{t}}\right)$$

so that differentiating with respect to both b and K we arrive at:

$$f(K, b) = \frac{2(2b - K)}{\sqrt{2\pi t^3}} \exp\left(-\frac{(2b - K)^2}{2t}\right) = f(X_T, M_T)|_{X_T = K, M_T = b} \qquad (3.16)$$

A similar derivation can be seen in Shreve [Shreve (2004)]. Knowing the joint distribution of the terminal spot and the max, we can now derive barrier and lookback prices easily. Actually, we're not quite done, as for this to be useful we'd need to relate it to an actual stock process. For constant drift μ and volatility σ, we can write:

$$\log(S_t/S_0) = (\mu - \sigma^2/2)t + \sigma X_t$$

We can also transform a process on a driftless Brownian motion, to one with drift α, $Y_t = \alpha t + X_t$, via a change of measure. If Y has drift α under measure $\mathbb{P}$, then under measure $\mathbb{Q}$ given by the Radon–Nikodym derivative

$\frac{dQ}{d\mathbb{P}} = \exp(\frac{1}{2}\alpha^2 t - \alpha Y_t)$, Y_t will be driftless. Its joint distribution with the max will then be given by (3.16). Transforming back to $\mathbb{P}$, we then have:

$$f(Y, M, t) = \exp(-\frac{1}{2}\alpha^2 t + \alpha Y_t)\frac{2(2M - Y)}{\sqrt{2\pi t^3}}\exp\left(-\frac{(2M - Y)^2}{2t}\right) \quad (3.17)$$

Finally, taking $\alpha = (\mu - \sigma^2/2)\frac{1}{\sigma}$ we have the simple relation $S_t = S_0 e^{\sigma Y_t}$ which we can use with (3.17) for option pricing. For example: for an up and out call, with $S_0 < K < B$, the price is given by:

$$V(T) = e^{-rT}\int_k^b\int_y^b (S_0 e^{\sigma Y} - K)f(Y, M, T)dM dY$$

where $b = \frac{1}{\sigma}\log(B/S_0)$, $k = \frac{1}{\sigma}\log(K/S_0)$. After a bit of algebra this works out to be:

$$V(T) = S[N(d_1(S/K)) - N(d_1(S/B))] - e^{-rT}K[N(d_2(S/K)) - N(d_2(S/B))]$$
$$- B\left(\frac{S}{B}\right)^{-2r/\sigma^2}[N(d_1(B^2/KS)) - N(d_1(B/S))]$$
$$+ e^{-rT}K\left(\frac{S}{B}\right)^{-2r/\sigma^2 + 1}[N(d_2(B^2/KS)) - N(d_2(B/S))] \quad (3.18)$$

with

$$d_{1,2}(x) = \frac{\log x + (r \pm \sigma^2/2)T}{\sigma\sqrt{T}}$$

We can likewise derive expressions for options on the max/min (lookbacks) and the other flavours of barrier options. In all cases, however, by construction, the value will only depend on the barrier and strike levels, and the *terminal* distribution of the spot. This last observation will turn out to be important in our analysis of the dividend model risk of barriers. In the 'real' world of term structure and volatility skew, the elegant arguments based on the symmetry of the log spot process will fail. Simple European option replication, as suggested by (3.18) will likewise break down, but how badly? We might be forgiven for guessing that, provided we calibrate our models to a given option expiry, such that the terminal distributions at this expiry are identical, then the prices of barriers with the *same* expiry should at least be very similar. Let's find out.

3.4.2 *Barrier options priced with different dividend models*

Before we consider the calibrated case, let us return to the mental picture
we had of the different dividend processes shown in Figure 3.12. By construction, the additive cash dividend model is consistently lower than the
proportional dividend model on the upside and higher on the downside,
whilst the opposite is true of the subtractive model. We might then expect
that the probability of breaching an upside barrier should be lower for the
additive model, and higher for the subtractive model, with the reverse true
for a downside barrier. This turns out to be exactly right, as shown by
the distribution of the maximum and minimum over a 5Y period for the
models constructed earlier in the chapter (Figures 3.17, 3.18 respectively).

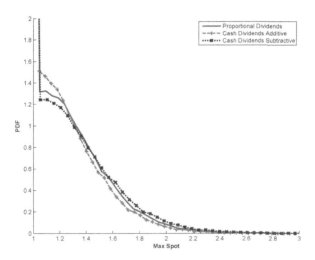

Fig. 3.17   Distribution of the maximum, 5Y window, pre-calibration.

The distribution of the maximum is shifted to higher spot levels for the
subtractive model, and to lower spot levels for the additive model, with the
reverse true for the minimum. We would then expect that an up and out
barrier would be more likely to knock out early for the subtractive model,
and less likely for the additive model. Recall that, for the same reason
(consistently higher spot paths for the subtractive model), the regular call
option price is expected to be higher for the subtractive model, and lower
for the additive. Like this, an up and out call on the subtractive model
should be suppressed for barrier levels close to spot, where the probability
of knockout is appreciable, and enhanced for barrier levels further away,

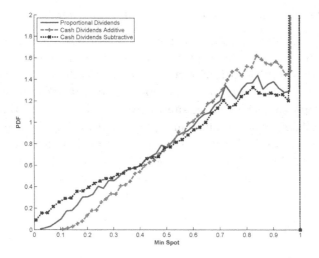

Fig. 3.18   Distribution of the minimum, 5Y window, pre-calibration.

with the reverse true for the additive model. This is indeed the case, as shown in Figure 3.19.

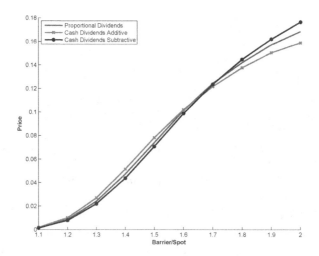

Fig. 3.19   Price of a 5Y up and out call barrier, unit strike, at different barrier levels, pre-calibration.

The arguments apply equally for the down and out put: the subtractive model is less expensive for nearby barriers, and less so for further away barriers (Figure 3.20).

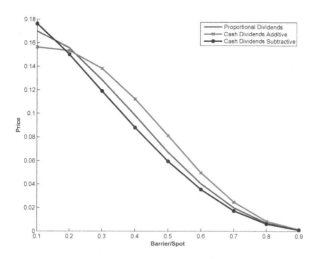

Fig. 3.20   Price of a 5Y down and out put barrier, unit strike, at different barrier levels, pre-calibration.

So far so good, our intuition seems fine. Note that all three models give identical forwards. Nonetheless, in the absence of a calibration to European option prices, the differences in price on barrier options is significant. What now happens, however, if we *do* calibrate? The prices for an up and out 5Y call are shown in Figure 3.21, and those for a down and out put in Figure 3.22.

The results are extraordinary: calibration to European options at 5Y has essentially eliminated dividend model risk on 5Y barriers. Intuitively what's happened is that the lower local volatility for the subtractive model has raised the survival probability for near-spot barriers, and vice versa for the additive model. For more deeply OTM barriers, the option becomes like a regular European, to which the prices are identical by calibration. The fact that the vol change almost exactly compensates the knockout probability, however, suggests that, even though we now have volatility skew and non-symmetrical log spot distributions, replication through European options at 5Y is *still* a good strategy. Note that this is not some trivial effect of the knockout probability being so low that the option is basically European. We can see this directly by looking at the so-called 'first passage time', i.e. the expected time at which spot crosses the barrier. The results on the upside, pre-calibration, are shown in Figure 3.23, the results post-calibration in Figure 3.24.

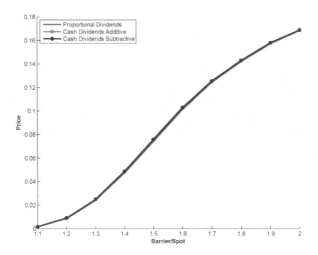

Fig. 3.21   Price of a 5Y up and out call barrier, unit strike, at different barrier levels, post-calibration.

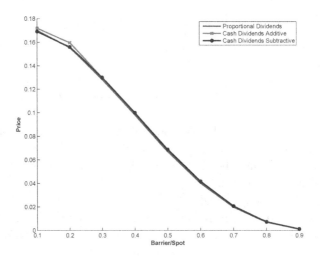

Fig. 3.22   Price of a 5Y down and out put barrier, unit strike, at different barrier levels, post-calibration.

For barriers up to 150% of spot, the first passage time is noticeably less than 5Y, and indeed calibration brings the curves more or less on top of each other. We should note in passing that there is essentially no difference between the results of the additive and subtractive models. In spite of their

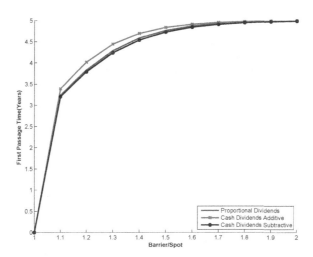

Fig. 3.23   First passage times for a 5Y upside barrier, at different barrier levels, pre-calibration.

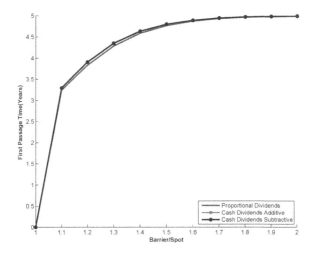

Fig. 3.24   First passage times for a 5Y upside barrier, at different barrier levels, post-calibration.

different flaws, the end results are nearly identical.

So much for 5Y barriers. What happens if we look at shorter dated options? Perhaps as we approach the 3Y dividend point a larger difference between the models might come up. The results, post-calibration are shown in Figure 3.25.

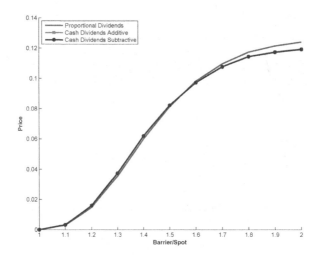

Fig. 3.25   Price of a 3Y up and out call barrier, unit strike, at different barrier levels, post-calibration.

Indeed, whilst small, we do now see a small difference open up for near the money barrier levels. It would seem that both additive and subtractive cash dividend models end up being slightly more expensive, implying that the knockout probability near the dividend point is lower. To understand why, it's helpful to look at the implied volatility surface at 3Y, *post*-calibration. The results for the subtractive model are shown in Figure 3.26, with the results from the additive model shown in Figure 3.27.

The slices are essentially identical. The point here is that we only calibrate to the *five* year vols. This tends to over-suppress vols occurring before the last div in the case of the subtractive model, and under-enhance for the additive model. The proof of this is left as an exercise at the end of this chapter. Like this, the probability of knockout up to the 3Y dividend point is suppressed in both cases, and a small enhancement in knockout price is seen. Conversely, for high barriers, where the probability of knockout is essentially zero, the higher implied volatility of the proportional dividend model takes over, raising the price over the cash dividend models.

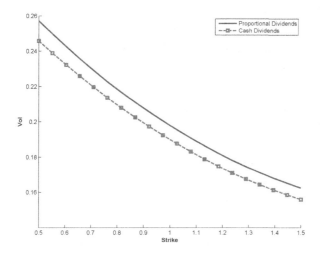

Fig. 3.26   3Y implied volatility slice, subtractive cash dividend model, post-calibration.

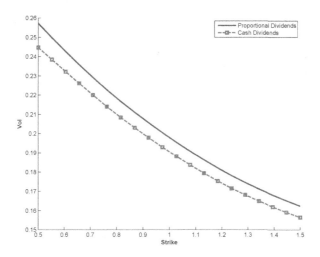

Fig. 3.27   3Y implied volatility slice, additive cash dividend model, post-calibration.

3.4.3   *What have we learned?*

The discussion of barrier options priced under different dividend models is by no means intended to be a definitive view on the subject. After all, the underlying market data is made up, only one volatility slice iscalibrated, and only barriers up to 5Y have been considered. A full investigation of this subject would require application of the above techniques to a real trading portfolio. Nonetheless, this exercise has demonstrated a couple of generic essentials, which we will revisit repeatedly in subsequent chapters:

- Pre-calibration to vanilla options, our intuition on the behaviour of different models tends to be correct. Likewise, the impact of different models can be profound in such simulations.
- Post-calibration to vanilla options, our intuition on the behaviour of different models tends, at best, to be naive. In some cases, such as the one examined in this chapter, calibration to the vanilla market can all but eliminate model risk in the exotic market, with any residual model risk the result of calibration artefact.

The second statement is extremely important. First, it is never sufficient to estimate the impact of different models on the price of exotics from qualitative argument. Ultimately, there simply is no substitute to applying the models directly and seeing how they actually behave. Second, *more is less*. The larger a vanilla market we have, the more transparent and restrictive their prices will be, and the lower our exposure should be to model choice in the exotics market. We will discuss this in more detail in the final chapter of this book.

3.5   Conclusions

In this chapter we have derived a couple of different models for modelling dividends, and looked at the impact of choosing one over another in the barrier options market. Whilst the market data was chosen to make this analysis as clear as possible, the results were no less surprising. Calibration to vanilla options was shown to be the critical factor in reducing dividend model risk on barrier options, with any residual model risk due to calibration artefact rather than deeper process differences. In the next chapter we will extend our investigation beyond stock growth, to stock volatility, and see how, even with a full market in vanillas, risk to different volatility model parameters is still a major source of price uncertainty in the exotics space.

3.6 Exercises

(1) Derive the expression for implied volatility under the subtractive dividend model, and demonstrate that a solution exists only for strikes above the forward value of cash dividends up to the expiry of the option in question.

(2) Demonstrate, for a flat volatility surface σ with a single cash dividend at time T_1 size D, that the subtractive dividend model correction to the implied volatility is to first order independent of maturity for $T > T_1$. Derive an expression for the size of the volatility shift.

(3) For the underlyer used in question 1, demonstrate, for a model calibrated at time $T > T_1$, that the implied volatility of options priced for $T < T_1$ will be less than σ regardless of whether a subtractive or additive dividend model is used.

(4) Consider the 'spot dividend' model, for which the partial differential equation on a call price $C(S_t, t, T)$, for a single dividend going ex at time τ is given by:

$$\frac{\partial C}{\partial t} + (rS - \Delta\delta(t - \tau))\frac{\partial C}{\partial S} + \frac{1}{2}\sigma^2 S^2 \frac{\partial^2 C}{\partial S^2} - rC = 0$$

Show, to first order in the dividend Δ, that an approximate solution for $t < \tau$ is given by $C(S, t, T) = C_0(S - X_n(t, T), K + X_f(t, T)\exp(r(T - t)), t, T)$, where:

$$C_0(S, K, t, T) = SN(d_1) - Ke^{-r(T-t)}N(d_2)$$

$$d_{1,2} = \frac{\log(Se^{r(T-t)}/K)}{\sigma\sqrt{T-t}} \pm \frac{\sigma\sqrt{T-t}}{2}$$

and

$$X_n(t, T) = \frac{T - \tau}{T - t}\Delta\exp(-r(\tau - t))$$

$$X_f(t, T) = \left(1 - \frac{T - \tau}{T - t}\right)\Delta\exp(-r(\tau - t))$$

$$(3.19)$$

This approximation is sometimes referred to as the 'split dividend model', and can be used as a short cut for approximating calibration of the spot dividend model to European options.

Chapter 4

Volatility

In the previous chapter we investigated the implications of different models for the first moment of the stock process, namely the growth, through different choices of dividend dynamics. In this chapter we will go on to consider the effects of different models for the second moment, through the stock's volatility. Recall from Chapter 2 that central to the local volatility model was the idea that a stock's instantaneous volatility was a *deterministic* function of the spot price. We saw that such an assumption, whilst mathematically convenient, resulted in unrealistic dynamics for the implied volatility surface, as seen today, and unrealistic shapes for the implied volatility of options striking in the future. We also saw, however, that the local volatility model could be considered as an *effective* model for richer processes which, provided that their expected local variance were equal to the Dupire local variance, would calibrate equally to European option prices. The aim of this chapter will be to use this last result to come up with a more realistic dynamic for the stock's volatility, whilst preserving calibration to the vanilla market. In this way, in the same spirit indeed as our comparison between proportional dividend and cash dividend models from the previous chapter, we would hope to be able to derive some intuition for the effect of richer volatility dynamics on the exotic equity derivatives market *alone*. Before we launch into the model itself, let's take a step back and look at how local volatility actually evolves over time.

4.1   Historical analysis of realised volatility

Instantaneous local volatility, much like instantaneous forward rates in the interest rate market, is a concept which, though highly convenient from a modelling standpoint, is essentially unobservable.

One approach for estimating parameters for a volatility process is 'GARCH' (Generalized Auto-Regressive Conditional Heteroskedasticity) [Engle (1982); Bollerslev (1986)]. In general, a GARCH(p,q) process on a discrete process y_n $(n \geq 0$ integer) can be written:

$$y_n = a_0 + \sum_{i=1}^{q} a_i y_{n-i} + \epsilon_n; \; n > 0$$

where the *residual* ϵ_n is given by $\epsilon_n = \sigma_n z_n$ with $z_n \sim \mathcal{N}(0,1)$, and

$$\sigma_n{}^2 = \alpha_0 + \sum_{i=1}^{q} \alpha_i \epsilon_{n-i}^2 + \sum_{i=1}^{p} \beta_i \sigma_{n-i}^2; \; n > 0$$

Note that in financial mathematics anything above $p = 1$ and $q = 1$ would break the Markovian constraint, though such models tend to be used more in econometrics when longer spans of data (e.g. decades of daily data) [Engle and Lee (1999)] might be used. It can shown [Javaheri (2005)], that in the continuous time limit, GARCH(1,1) reduces to:

$$\frac{dS_t}{S_t} = \mu' dt + \sqrt{v_t} dW_t$$

$$dv_t = (\omega - \theta v_t)dt + \xi v_t dZ_t$$

on the variance $v_t = \sigma_t^2$ where:

$$\omega = \frac{\alpha_0}{dt^2}$$

$$\theta = \frac{1 - \alpha_1 - \beta_1}{dt}$$

$$\xi = \alpha_1 \sqrt{\frac{\kappa - 1}{dt}}$$

and κ corresponds to the Pearson kurtosis of the mean adjusted log returns u_n:

$$u_n = \log\left(\frac{S_n}{S_{n-1}}\right) - \left(\mu - \frac{1}{2}v_n\right) = \sqrt{v_n} B_n$$

and $\mu' = \mu/dt$, $B_n \sim \mathcal{N}(0,1)$. Another popular variant on GARCH is so-called NGARCH (non-linear GARCH), first introduced by Engle [Engle and Ng (1993)], where:

$$v_{n+1} = \alpha_0 + \beta_1 v_n + \alpha_1(\epsilon_n - c\sqrt{v_n})$$

Heston and Nandi showed that, in the continuous limit, this process reduces to the square root, or Cox–Ingersoll–Ross (CIR) process on variance [Heston and Nandi (1997)]:

$$dv_t = (\omega - \theta v_t)dt + \xi\sqrt{v_t}dZ_t$$

The idea of these approaches is then to estimate the parameters of the continuous (unobservable) variance process by finding best fit solutions from GARCH(1,1) (or NGARCH) to the observable stock price data. Needless to say, this is far from trivial, and a discussion of the various techniques available would form a book in its own right (an excellent reference can be found in Javaheri [Javaheri (2005)]). For the purposes of illustration we will consider a somewhat more elementary approach, namely to look at realised volatility over short time windows. The art is to make the window long enough to be meaningful (a two day window, for example, would have an unusably large estimation error), whilst short enough to provide enough data points. We could, for example, choose a year window, which would indeed have the advantage of a low estimation error, but would require at least ten years worth of data to provide enough data points for any sensible analysis. Much longer than this, and in all likelihood the economics of the stock in question simply wouldn't be comparable over the life of the data set (for example, were we to be running the analysis on the S&P500, the constituents over ten years ago would be significantly different from those today). Moreover, a year sampling window would hardly be representative of an instantaneous process. Note also that we can't simply consider overlapping windows. The idea is to find a sequence of data points with a minimal amount of correlation in their increments. As discussed in Chapter 1, central to the idea of a derivative price is the concept that the price is given by a self-financing strategy and crucially, is *unique*. Models with correlated returns models result in a process where the value today is a function of its past history, at variance with most derivative pricing models. In Figure 4.1, we show the 10-day realised volatility on the S&P500 over the last decade.

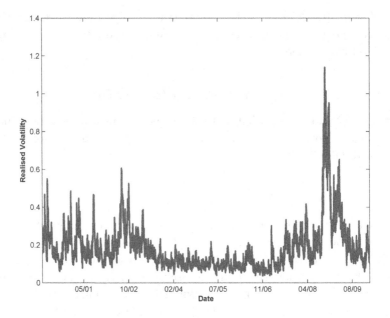

Fig. 4.1   10-day realised volatility on the S&P500, 2000–2010.

Note that we have used overlapping windows here for the purposes of illustration, though our analysis will sample every ten days, as discussed. The realised volatility has been calculated using a three day decay designed to weight the volatility calculation towards the most recent returns. Notice the prominent spike in volatility at the end of 2008. The corresponding stock price history is shown in Figure 4.2.

There were two notable bear markets. The end of the dot com bubble in 2001, and the credit crisis of 2008. Whilst the former is less obviously signalled in realised volatility, the latter is clearly negatively correlated. This is indeed what we pick up in the local volatility model: for a negatively skewed volatility surface the local vol rises as stock falls. If the model were a good reflection of reality we would expect to see a near perfect correlation between the return on volatility over a series of dates, and the return on stock. Let us define the normalised returns on stock and vol as:

$$u_n = \frac{\log(S_n/S_{n-1}) - \mu_S}{\Sigma_S}; \ v_n = \frac{\log(\sigma_n/\sigma_{n-1}) - \mu_\sigma}{\Sigma_\sigma}$$

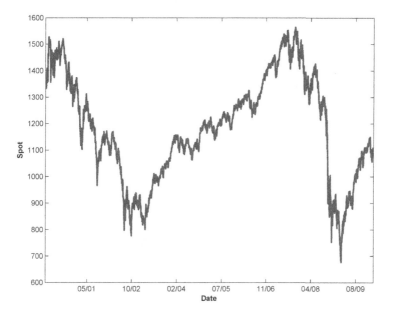

Fig. 4.2 Stock price history on the S&P500, 2000–2010.

$$\mu_S = \frac{1}{N} \sum_{n=1}^{N} \log(S_n/S_{n-1}); \; \mu_\sigma = \frac{1}{N} \sum_{n=1}^{N} \log(\sigma_n/\sigma_{n-1})$$

$$\Sigma_S^2 = \frac{1}{N-1} \sum_{n=1}^{N} [\log(S_n/S_{n-1}) - \mu_S]^2$$

$$\Sigma_\sigma^2 = \frac{1}{N-1} \sum_{n=1}^{N} [\log(\sigma_n/\sigma_{n-1}) - \mu_\sigma]^2$$

By construction both sets of returns have zero mean and unit variance, allowing a clearer picture of their covariation to be displayed. Sampling only every ten days, the corresponding scatter plot is shown in Figure 4.3.

A clear negative correlation between spot and vol returns is indeed seen, but unsurprisingly, it's far from perfect. For small deviations in spot, realised vol looks essentially uncorrelated, whilst more extreme moves, notably on the downside, do show a pronounced negative correlation. If we bucket normalised spot moves from -2 to -1, for downside moves, -1 to 1 for

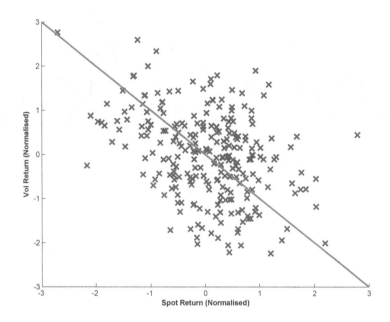

Fig. 4.3   Normalised returns on 10-day realised vol and stock on the S&P500, 2000–2010.

'standard' moves and 1 to 2 for upside moves, we find the volatility return distributions given in Figures 4.4 to 4.6.

Our suspicions about the negative correlation between spot and vol movements appear to be justified. For downside spot moves, the realised volatility distribution is shifted to the right and vice versa, with apparently little correlation for standard moves. We can actually package this result into an effective local vol profile, plotting the average normalised vol return against average normalised spot return for the different spot movement buckets. The result is shown in Figure 4.7.

Though the standard deviation on the normalised vol return is considerable, the average vol return for downside spot returns is statistically significantly different from zero – realised vol really does move up as spot moves down.

4.2   Historical analysis of implied volatility

The preceding analysis gives us some confidence in both the local volatility model, where local vol moves against spot, and the statement that

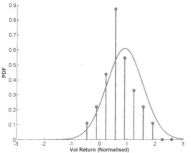

Fig. 4.4 Normalised vol return distribution on 10-day realised vol on the S&P500, 2000–2010, -2 to -1 spot return stdev.

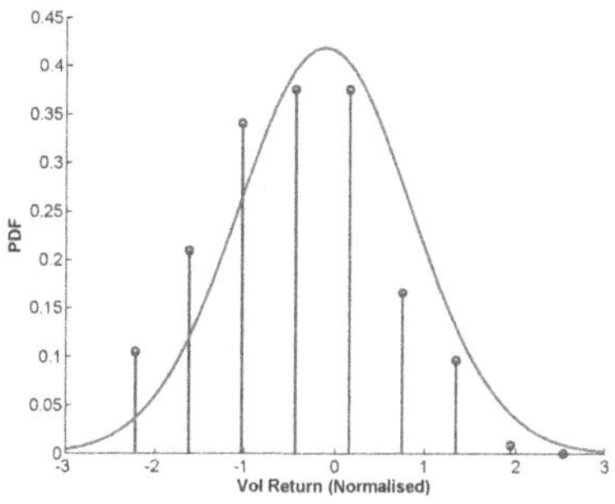

Fig. 4.5 Normalised vol return distribution on 10-day realised vol on the S&P500, 2000–2010, -1 to 1 spot return stdev.

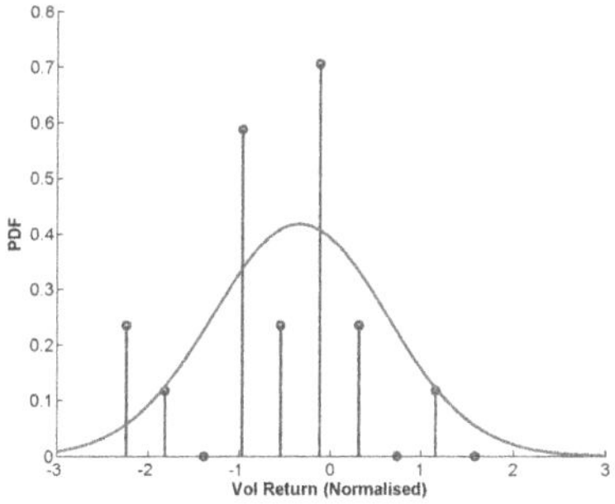

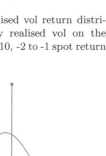

Fig. 4.6 Normalised vol return distribution on 10-day realised vol on the S&P500, 2000–2010, 1 to 2 spot return stdev.

such a model needs to be augmented by a degree of idiosyncracy in the local vol level. Nonetheless, the constraint of non-overlapping windows, and the consequently parsimonious data set, suggests that an alternative scheme for measuring local volatility dynamics would be helpful. Remember also that today's local volatility is essentially the *implied* volatility for a very short-dated option priced today. Some product approximating to this (non-existent) option might then be a more direct measure. Moreover, if such a product does exist, we can look at daily returns on its implied volatility against daily returns on spot, without the need to worry about auto-correlation effects.

A product which has gained significant popularity since its instantiation in 1993 is the VIX index, defined as the square root of the par rate for a 30-day variance swap initiated today. We will devote a section of this chapter both to the variance swap, and options on it, but suffice to say that, whilst

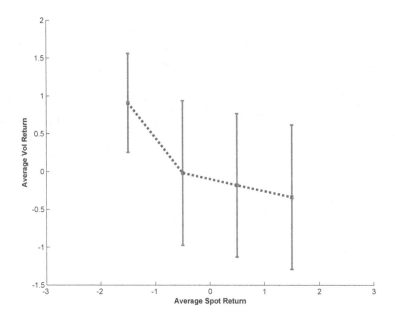

Fig. 4.7   Average normalised returns on 10-day vol for different average normalised spot returns on the S&P500, 2000–2010.

this product's price depends on the structure of the entire 30-day volatility surface, the price is dominated by the level of the ATM volatility. If we assume that the 30-day ATM volatility is closely correlated to today's local volatility, then by extension, the par rate for the 30-day VIX should be a good measure similarly. Again, let's look historically. Figure 4.8 shows the movement of the VIX vol vs 30-day realised vol.

Perhaps unsurprisingly, the two track each other very closely. Exactly as realised vol showed a negative correlation to spot, we might expect the same behaviour for VIX vols. A scatter plot for normalised log returns on the VIX vs normalised log returns on the S&P500 is shown in Figure 4.9.

Now of course, we have the benefit of many more data points. Our tentative conclusions on the negative correlation between spot and local vol are emphatically supported by this new data, and indeed the distribution slices for normalised VIX vol returns for different spot vol return buckets show the picture that much more clearly (Figures 4.10 to 4.12). Likewise, we have a rather more detailed estimate for the local vol return profile (Figure 4.13).

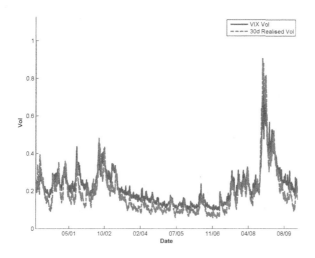

Fig. 4.8   VIX vol vs 30-day realised vol on the S&P500, 2000–2010.

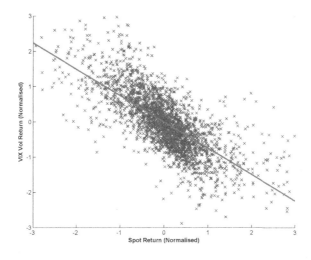

Fig. 4.9   VIX vol returns vs S&P500 spot returns, 2000–2010.

4.2.1   *Vega hedging in a volatile environment*

We have seen how both short window realised vol, and short-dated implied vol, both show considerable volatility, but also notable anti-correlation to spot movements. What does this mean in practice for a trader? For a start,

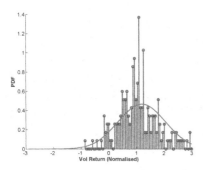

Fig. 4.10   Normalised vol return distribution on VIX vol on the S&P500, 2000–2010, -2 to -1 spot return stdev.

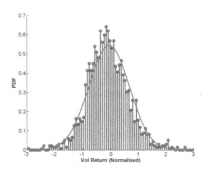

Fig. 4.11   Normalised vol return distribution on VIX vol on the S&P500, 2000–2010, 1 to 1 spot return stdev.

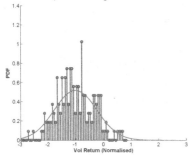

Fig. 4.12   Normalised vol return distribution on VIX vol on the S&P500, 2000–2010, 1 to 2 spot return stdev.

what can he/she say about the volatility risk (vega) of their product, which may have an expiry as long as ten years, say, given the movement of the short end of the volatility surface. As it happens, movement of the short end provides a very good measure of the movement of the *entire* surface. We can see this by looking at ATM implied volatility for one month to two year options on the S&P500 (corresponding to the liquidly exchange traded region of the surface). An historic plot for the same period 2000–2010, is shown in Figure 4.14.

Though the plot is rather messy, a clear co-movement exists between the different tenors, albeit with less movement in the long end, and more in the short, is seen (and indeed, the pattern looks similar to VIX vol, as we might expect). If we break this down into principal components, we find that the component explaining 95% of the realised variance of the data is a simple parallel shift of the curve. The second component, corresponding

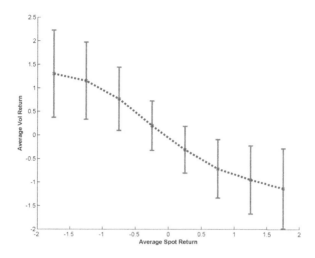

Fig. 4.13 Average normalised returns on VIX vol for different average normalised spot returns on the S&P500, 2000–2010.

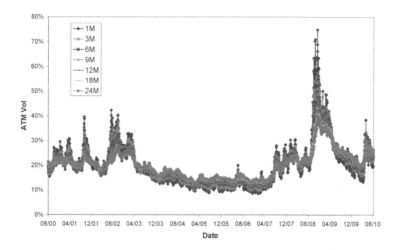

Fig. 4.14 Implied ATM volatilities for different tenors on the S&P500, 2000–2010.

to a steepening of the curve, explains 3% of the variance, with the third 'flexing' of the curve (both short and long tenor rise against the middle tenors), explaining 1%. These modes are shown in Figure 4.15.

Cont *et al.* [Cont *et al.* (2002); Cont and Fonseca (2002)] have extended this analysis to incorporate the strike dimension of the S&P500 vol surface,

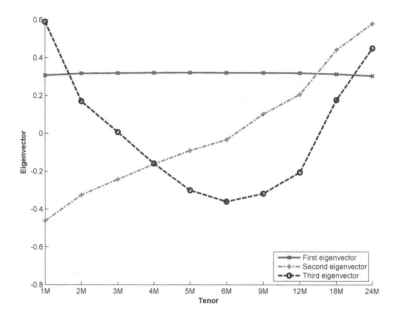

Fig. 4.15   First three eigenmodes for implied volatility returns on the S&P500, 2000–2010.

demonstrating that the bulk of the daily variance of implied volatilities is provided by a parallel shift across the *entire* surface[1].

Were a trader to hedge just to the parallel shift mode, most of the movement of the implied volatility surface, at least out to two years, would be captured. We shall concentrate the hedging argument in the next section on the parallel shift mode alone.

4.2.1.1   *Vega hedging*

Let's perform the following thought experiment. You are a trader who has sold a call, knowing that implied volatilities themselves are volatile. To hedge yourself, you offset your short vega position with a long vega position in some other options. When you come in tomorrow, implied vols have moved. The change in the vega on your option will be:

$$\delta\mathcal{V} = \frac{\partial\mathcal{V}}{\partial\sigma}\delta\sigma + \frac{\partial\mathcal{V}}{\partial S}\delta S$$

---

[1]Their analysis incorporates end of day prices for all traded European style call and put options, in the money range 0.5 to 1.5, sampled from 2/3/2000 to 2/2/2001.

where vega, and the vega of vega (a.k.a. *volga*, or *volgamma*) are calculated with respect to parallel shifts of the vol surface $\delta\sigma$. Let's consider the first term. For a call option priced with flat volatility, the vol gamma is given by:

$$\frac{\partial \mathcal{V}}{\partial \sigma} = \frac{\mathcal{V}d_1(K)d_2(K)}{\sigma}$$

The second term, commonly referred to as the *vanna* has the form:

$$\frac{\partial \mathcal{V}}{\partial S} = -\frac{\mathcal{V}d_2(K)}{S_0\sigma\sqrt{T}}$$

where the vega itself is given by:

$$\mathcal{V}(K,T) = S_0 e^{-qT} n(d_1)\sqrt{T}$$

and $n(x)$ is the standard Gaussian with $d_{1,2} = \log(F/K)/\sigma\sqrt{T} \pm \sigma\sqrt{T}/2$. Profiles for these risks vs strikes are shown in Figures 4.16 and 4.17.

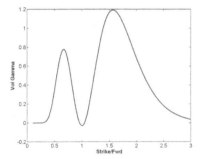

Fig. 4.16 Typical vol gamma profile, flat implied vol.

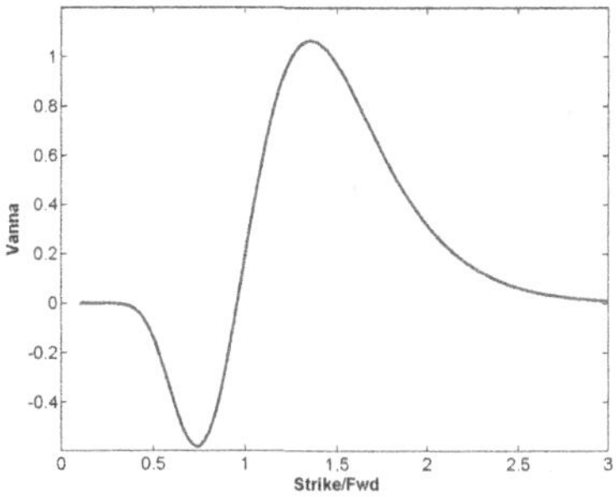

Fig. 4.17 Typical vanna profile, flat implied vol.

Suppose that the option we've sold is an ITM call ($K < F$). First, consider the effect of a rise in implied vols. The vol gamma is positive, so the vega of our option will go up. This means that we'll need to buy more offsetting hedge, but in a *rising* vol market. This is going to cost us money, and should be factored into the price of our option. If vols decrease, we end up selling into a falling market, again incurring a cost. In other words, the vol gamma of this position should incur a positive hedging cost, resulting in a higher option price the higher the vol gamma. The same would be true for an OTM call, so, in the absence of a correlated spot move, we would expect the vega hedging to increase the cost of both OTM and ITM calls. The more volatile implied vol, the higher the expected cost should be. Translated back into the implied vol itself, volatility of implied volatility should result in a volatility *smile*.

Notice, however, that there's another factor to be considered, namely the movement of the spot. Let's go back to our ITM call and assume spot moves are anticorrelated with vol moves. The vanna is negative for these options, so in addition to the vega being increased through the vol gamma, it would be *further* raised through an anticorrelated spot move, and vice versa for a fall in vol. Negative spot-vol correlation should thus make ITM calls even more expensive. For OTM calls, however, the vanna is positive, and the reverse is true: negative spot-vol correlation cheapens our hedging cost through reducing the increase in vega from increasing vol. Like this, negative spot-vol correlation should increase the implied vol of ITM calls, and decrease that of OTM calls, in a fair trade where the cost of an option is consistent with its hedging costs. Spot-vol correlation results in volatility *skew*.

The above argument considered making our option neutral with respect to first order spot and volatility moves. In practice traders also try to hedge themselves against the second-order vega risks. An example is given by Wystup [Wystup (2008)], and runs as follows. Consider the pricing of a simple knockout barrier. Conventionally, as pointed out by Castagna and Mercurio [Castagna and Mercurio (2007)], forex traders, for example, would value and hedge the option according to a Black–Scholes flat smile model, with the ATM volatility being continuously updated to the actual market level. The contract would be delta hedged through spot, and vega hedged through an ATM option of the maturity of the contract, with the change in vega with spot moves hedged through *risk reversals*, and the change in vega through vol moves hedged with *butterflies*. The contracts are defined as follows:

$$RR(\Delta, T) = Call(\Delta, T) - Put(\Delta, T)$$
$$BF(\Delta, T) = \frac{[Call(\Delta, T) + Put(\Delta, T)]}{2} - \frac{[Call(\Delta_0, T) + Put(\Delta_0, T)]}{2}$$

where Δ_0 corresponds to the ATM point, typically 50%. Conventionally, the Δ of the risk reversal and butterfly contracts would be taken from the most liquidly traded options, commonly $|\Delta| = 25\%$ (a.k.a 25Δ) in the forex market. These contracts have the advantage that both have very little vega, and orthogonal second-order risks, i.e. the risk reversal has very little vol gamma, whilst the butterfly has very little vanna, through the symmetry of the risk profiles shown in Figures 4.16 and 4.17. The approach taken is to factor the cost of hedging the vol gamma and vanna into the price of the exotic.

Let us posit for the barrier price B:

$$B = B^0 + \alpha(RR - RR^0) + \beta(BF - BF^0) \qquad (4.1)$$

where superscript zero denotes pricing Black–Scholes with the ATM vol. We have for the vanna-volga sensitive part of the portfolio:

$$\Pi = B - \alpha RR - \beta BF = B^0 - \alpha RR^0 - \beta BF^0 \qquad (4.2)$$

As only B_0 and RR_0 are vanna sensitive, and only B_0 and BF_0 vol gamma sensitive, we can achieve vanna and vol gamma neutrality through the weightings:

$$\alpha = \frac{\partial^2 B^0/\partial S \partial \sigma_0}{\partial^2 RR^0/\partial S \partial \sigma_0}$$

$$\beta = \frac{\partial^2 B^0/\partial \sigma_0^2}{\partial^2 BF^0/\partial \sigma_0^2}$$

Combining with (4.1) gives the approximation for the barrier price:

$$B = B^0 + [\text{cost of vanna} + \text{cost of volgamma}]$$

where

$$\text{cost of vanna} = \frac{\partial^2 B^0/\partial S \partial \sigma_0}{\partial^2 RR^0/\partial S \partial \sigma_0}[RR - RR^0]$$

$$\text{cost of volgamma} = \frac{\partial^2 B^0/\partial \sigma_0^2}{\partial^2 BF^0/\partial \sigma_0^2}[BF - BF^0]$$

Actually, this would overestimate the cost of implied volatility dynamics. The problem with such a strategy is that is assumes continuous diffusion. If the spot suddenly jumps below the barrier (in the case of a down and out, for example), the barrier option would become worthless, but we'd be left holding the hedge, with a net unwind cost of $\alpha(RR - RR^0) + \beta(BF - $

BF^0). Assuming that this occurs with probability p, we should subtract the expected cost from the value of our barrier, giving:

$$B = B^0 + (1 - p)[\text{cost of vanna} + \text{cost of volgamma}]$$

Of course, this method of valuation is at best heuristic, though it does at least encompass the main vega hedging considerations of the trade. In practice, the risk reversals do have residual vol gamma, and the butterflies residual vanna. The estimation of p depends very much on the product being traded [Wystup (2008)], though the one-touch probability in the case of forex knockouts, and 0.5 in the case of double no-touches [Lipton and McGhee (2002)] seems to be a common practice. One tantalising aspect of the approach is that, through the relatively high flow in the forex barriers (so-called *flow-exotics*), a *market* in p actually exists, to which we can calibrate fully fledged microscopic models. Sadly, this market is not yet sufficiently developed for equities, but we will at least compare the results from our calibrated stochastic volatility model for simple barriers with those from the 'trader model' and discuss how well these rules of thumb might work in practice.[2]

4.3   Stochastic volatility modelling

The previous section discussed attempts to hedge stochastic *implied* volatility. To build a microscopic model, however, we need to consider the general problem of hedging *local* volatility movements. Assuming a pure diffusion on the stock process, we can write:

$$\frac{dS_t}{S_t} = \mu_t^S dt + \sigma_t dW_t^S \tag{4.3}$$

$$\frac{d\sigma_t}{\sigma_t} = \mu_t^\sigma dt + \xi_t dW_t^\sigma \tag{4.4}$$

---

[2]There is a large body of literature on the problem of hedging barrier options. We refer the reader to [Poulsen (2006)], [Derman *et al.* (1994)], [Carr and Chou (1997)] for the problem of static hedging, and [Wystup (2002)] for the problem of dynamic hedging and overhedging.

The hedging strategy now runs as follows. Construct a delta hedged portfolio in the usual way, but now include another option to hedge the stochastic volatility σ, i.e.:

$$\Pi_t = V_t + \alpha_t S_t + \beta_t B_t + \gamma V_t'$$

Assuming no dividend reinvestment we then have:

$$d\Pi_t = dV_t + \alpha_t dS_t + \beta_t dB_t + \gamma dV_t'$$

and

$$dB_t = r_t B_t dt \tag{4.5}$$

$$dV_t = \frac{\partial V}{\partial t} dt + \frac{\partial V}{\partial S} dS_t + \frac{\partial V}{\partial \sigma} d\sigma_t$$
$$+ \frac{1}{2} \left[\frac{\partial^2 V}{\partial S^2} dS_t^2 + 2 \frac{\partial^2 V}{\partial S \partial \sigma} dS_t d\sigma_t + \frac{\partial^2 V}{\partial \sigma^2} d\sigma_t^2 \right] \tag{4.6}$$

$$dV_t' = \frac{\partial V'}{\partial t} dt + \frac{\partial V'}{\partial S} dS_t + \frac{\partial V'}{\partial \sigma} d\sigma_t$$
$$+ \frac{1}{2} \left[\frac{\partial^2 V'}{\partial S^2} dS_t^2 + 2 \frac{\partial^2 V'}{\partial S \partial \sigma} dS_t d\sigma_t + \frac{\partial^2 V'}{\partial \sigma^2} d\sigma_t^2 \right] \tag{4.7}$$

The self-financing condition then reads:

$$\Pi_0 = 0$$
$$d\Pi_t = 0$$

giving us:

$$\beta_t B_t = -(V_t + \alpha_t S_t t + \gamma V_t')$$
$$\Rightarrow (dV_t - r_t V_t dt) + \alpha_t (dS_t - r_t S_t dt) = -\gamma (dV_t' - r_t V_t' dt) \tag{4.8}$$

Substituting (4.6) and (4.7) into (4.8), we get:

$$\frac{\partial V}{\partial t}dt + dS_t\left(\frac{\partial V}{\partial S} + \alpha_t\right) + \frac{\partial V}{\partial \sigma}d\sigma_t$$

$$+\frac{1}{2}\left[\frac{\partial^2 V}{\partial S^2}dS_t^2 + 2\frac{\partial^2 V}{\partial S\partial\sigma}dS_t d\sigma_t + \frac{\partial^2 V}{\partial\sigma^2}d\sigma_t^2\right]$$

$$+\gamma\left(\frac{\partial V'}{\partial t}dt + \frac{\partial V'}{\partial S}dS_t + \frac{\partial V'}{\partial \sigma}d\sigma_t\right.$$

$$\left.+\frac{1}{2}\left[\frac{\partial^2 V'}{\partial S^2}dS_t^2 + 2\frac{\partial^2 V'}{\partial S\partial\sigma}dS_t d\sigma_t + \frac{\partial^2 V'}{\partial\sigma^2}d\sigma_t^2\right]\right)$$

$$= r_t dt(V_t + \alpha_t S_t + \gamma V_t') \tag{4.9}$$

If we now set the pre-factors of dW_t^S and dW_t^σ to zero, we have for the hedge parameters α and γ:

$$\frac{\partial V}{\partial S} + \alpha_t + \gamma\frac{\partial V'}{\partial S} = 0$$

$$\frac{\partial V}{\partial \sigma} + \gamma\frac{\partial V'}{\partial \sigma} = 0$$

giving:

$$\gamma_t = -\frac{\frac{\partial V}{\partial \sigma}}{\frac{\partial V'}{\partial \sigma}}$$

$$\alpha_t = -\frac{\partial V}{\partial S} - \frac{\partial V'}{\partial S}\gamma_t$$

Substituting back into (4.9), and using $dS_t^2 \to S_t^2\sigma_t^2 dt$, $d\sigma_t^2 \to \sigma_t^2\xi_t^2 dt$, $dS_t d\sigma_t \to \xi_t\sigma_t^2 S_t\rho dt$, in the limit $dt \to 0$:

$$\frac{\frac{\partial V}{\partial t} + \frac{1}{2}\left[\frac{\partial^2 V}{\partial S^2}\sigma_t^2 S_t^2 + 2\frac{\partial^2 V}{\partial S\partial\sigma}S_t\sigma_t^2\rho\xi_t + \frac{\partial^2 V}{\partial\sigma^2}\xi_t^2\sigma_t^2\right] - r_t(V_t - S_t\frac{\partial V}{\partial S})}{\frac{\partial V}{\partial \sigma}}$$

$$= \frac{\frac{\partial V'}{\partial t} + \frac{1}{2}\left[\frac{\partial^2 V'}{\partial S^2}\sigma_t^2 S_t^2 + 2\frac{\partial^2 V'}{\partial S\partial\sigma}S_t\sigma_t^2\rho\xi_t + \frac{\partial^2 V'}{\partial\sigma^2}\xi_t^2\sigma_t^2\right] - r_t(V_t' - S_t\frac{\partial V'}{\partial S})}{\frac{\partial V'}{\partial \sigma}}$$

Without loss of generality, we can simply equate both sides of this equation to $-g_t\sigma_t$, where g_t is arbitrary. We then have the final result:

$$\frac{\partial V}{\partial t} + r_t S_t\frac{\partial V}{\partial S} + g_t\sigma_t\frac{\partial V}{\partial \sigma} + \frac{1}{2}\left[\frac{\partial^2 V}{\partial S^2}\sigma_t^2 S_t^2 + 2\frac{\partial^2 V}{\partial S\partial\sigma}S_t\sigma_t^2\rho\xi_t + \frac{\partial^2 V}{\partial\sigma^2}\xi_t^2\sigma_t^2\right] = r_t V_t$$

$$\tag{4.10}$$

for either the option or its hedging option. This is a somewhat surprising result, namely that, for *any* growth used on the local volatility σ_t, the portfolio is fully delta and vega hedged provided that it is itself completed by another option whose price obeys (4.10). Contrast this with the risk-neutral growth on the stock of r_t, which came about because, unlike the volatility, the stock is itself a *tradable* instrument in which we can hedge directly (recall the discussion from Chapter 1). So, given that there is no unique specification of the risk-neutral drift of volatility, how should we specify it? Essentially, by calibration to market data. Though an option priced under (4.10) will be properly hedged if completed by another option priced similarly, the price may not agree with the market. If then, we were pricing some exotic, and vega hedging with options based on market prices, the implied volatility growth on the hedge options and our exotic would disagree, resulting in PL leakage.

The problem then, is that there are a multitude of possible dynamics for the volatility process which can reproduce vanilla option prices. Until recently, a popular choice was the Heston model mentioned briefly above. The model evolves the variance $v_t = \sigma_t^2$ rather than the volatility, in the spirit of GARCH:

$$\frac{dS_t}{S_t} = \mu(t)dt + \sqrt{v_t}dW_t^S$$
$$dv_t = -\kappa(v_t - \bar{v}) + \xi\sqrt{v_t}dW_t^v$$
$$E[dW_t^S dW_t^v] = \rho dt$$

This model has the significant advantage that closed-form solutions exist for European options. Also, as we saw above, the model parameters can be obtained through fitting of non-linear GARCH to observable market data. One of the major drawbacks, however, is that the maximum volatility skew that can be achieved for short-dated options tends to $\rho\xi/2$ as the maturity of the option tends to zero [Gatheral (2006)]. Another significant problem is that, unless the *Feller condition*, namely $2\kappa\bar{v} > \xi^2$ is satisfied, the variance is not guaranteed to be positive, making propagation unstable. This tends to limit the applicability of what is admittedly a rather elegant model. Technical discussions of the procedures for implementing and calibrating the model can be found in Mikhailov and Noegel [Mikhailov and Noegel (2003)] and Andersen [Andersen (2007)].

An alternative model one might consider is an extension to the *constant elasticity of variance* model (CEV), first suggested by Cox [Cox (1996)]. In this model, the local volatility is modelled simply as:

$$\sigma(S, t) = CS_t^\lambda$$

where λ is referred to as the elasticity of local volatility [Davydov and Linetsky (2001)], related to Cox's original elasticity of variance θ through $\lambda + 1 = \theta/2$. We can see immediately that

$$\frac{d\sigma_t}{\sigma_t} = \lambda \frac{dS_t}{S_t} + \text{higher order terms}$$

λ can be thought of as a regression coefficient between the return on stock and the return on vol. In the light of our results on VIX volatility, this is an extremely useful property. Let's consider a small extension:

$$\sigma(S, t) = CS_t^\lambda e^{\alpha_t} \qquad (4.11)$$

where α_t is some purely idiosyncratic stochastic parameter. We then have, from Itō:

$$\frac{d\sigma_t}{\sigma_t} = \lambda \frac{dS_t}{S_t} + d\alpha_t + \text{higher order terms}$$

Thus, by regressing returns on stock vs returns on short-dated volatility, we might be able to come up with some parameters for the idiosyncratic component of local volatility α_t through analysis of the residuals.

Figure 4.18 shows the regression of un-normalised returns on the VIX vs un-normalised returns on the S&P500. Though there is considerable scatter around the best fit linear regression, we can see that, looking over the last decade, vols tended to react about 3 times more strongly than spots, and in the opposite direction.

Whilst this may appear high, it is actually lower than the findings of other researchers [Jackworth and Rubinstein (2001, 2003)] who find that fits to 6M options on the S&P500 suggest an elasticity of volatility in the region of -5 (they use $\sigma(S, t) = \sigma' S_t^{\rho-1}$ and find good fits to implied distributions with $\rho = -4$). It is tantalising to reflect that the same authors observe that in the period 2nd April 1986 to 16th October 1987 (Black Monday), good fits to 6M S&P500 options could be obtained with the classical *restricted* CEV model, where $-1 < \lambda < 0$, whilst post-crash options suggest a much lower value for λ. This is mathematically significant, as the probability

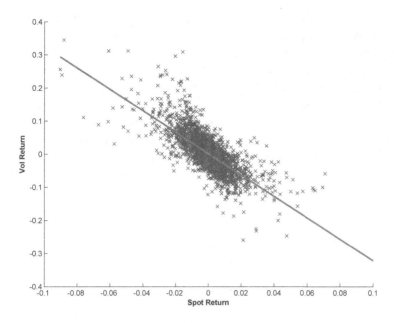

Fig. 4.18   Un-normalised vix vol returns vs spot returns on the S&P500, 2000–2010.

of the index reaching zero becomes finite for $\lambda < -1/2$ [Davydov and Linetsky (2001)]. Like this, our fit of VIX volatilities to the CEV model suggests a finite probability of *index* bankruptcy, in strong opposition to the arguments of Bates [Bates (1996b)] that a stock market index can never go bankrupt. On the contrary, Jackworth and Rubinstein suggest that their fit to 6M options suggests a probability of bankruptcy of the S&P500 over a 4 to 7 month horizon of up to 3%. In the light of the events of 2008, this may no longer seem so economically unreasonable, but more importantly suggests that the index has taken on significant *non-diffusive* jump characteristics since 1987, resulting in an *effective* elasticity parameter of -3 ± 0.5. Note, however, a strong caveat here: we have assumed a zero correlation between the idiosyncratic term $d\alpha_t$ and the stock process dS_t. We could equally well have assumed $\lambda = 0$, giving us a 'pure' stochastic volatility model. The joint distribution of returns could then have been picked up through negative correlation between α_t and S_t, with a high volatility on the former. As per the Heston model, such an approach would probably not be able to fit the high implied volatility skew for short-dated options. The reality is somewhere in between these two extremes. We need stochastic volatility to model the dispersion of volatility observed, but we equally well require jumps on the stock process to account for short-dated skew. Merely looking historically at joint spot and vol data is in fact insufficiently constrained. A better posed problem would be to fit to *both* historical and implied volatility data, but this lies outside the scope of this chapter. For illustration, we will continue with the simple model of an uncorrelated idiosyncratic vol parameter, and investigate the effect of the volatility and mean reversion of this parameter on exotics.

Completing our analysis, if we now assume that $d\alpha_t \sim \mathcal{N}(0, \xi^2 dt)$, the distribution of residuals can be used to compute a volatility of alpha, given by:

$$\xi^2 = AF \times \frac{1}{N-1} \sum_{i=1}^{N} [d\alpha_i - \mu_\alpha]^2$$

$$\mu_\alpha = \frac{1}{N} \sum_{i=1}^{N} d\alpha_i$$

Again, we conduct this exercise for a range of sampling windows, to give the picture shown in Figure 4.19.[3]

The results are quite encouraging. In spite of the complexity of the data set, the volatility of the residuals appears quite stable over increasingly long sampling windows. It would be tempting then to try and model option prices entirely with this model with $\lambda = -3$ and $\xi = 70\%$. This might serve some use for relative value purposes (i.e. developing statistical arbitrage strategies where we buy if the market option price falls below the price predicted by this model and vice versa) but the goal of this chapter is not to come up with trading strategies. Our purpose is to maintain *exact* fits to the vanilla option market whilst stressing our model assumptions and investigating the reaction of exotics. This approach has allowed us to come up with a good starting point for inputting stochastic volatility parameters, but we still need to address the fit to vanillas. One such model is *Stochastic Local Volatility* (SLV), which we will discuss in the next section, and apply to a set of volatility sensitive exotics in the rest of this chapter.

---

[3]We have used the assumption that variance of n i.i.d. variables y_i is distributed with mean $\sigma^2 = \text{Var}[y_i]$ and variance $\sigma^4 \left(\frac{2}{n-1} + \frac{\kappa}{n}\right)$ where κ is the fourth standardised moment of y_i. This is reflected in the error bars of Figure 4.19.

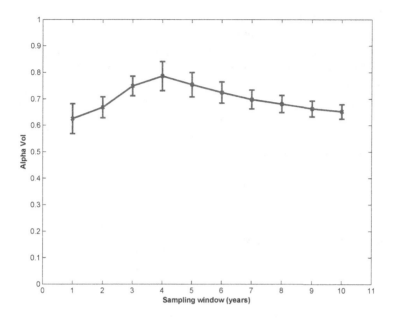

Fig. 4.19   Alpha volatility for the S&P500, 2000–2010, varying sampling windows.

4.4   Stochastic Local Volatility

Our approach will follow the work of Madan *et al* closely [Madan *et al.* (2007)], and follows a technique suggested by Lipton [Lipton (2002b)] in his paper on approaches to volatility smile modelling. In essence, we'd like to generalise the approach of the previous section to a local volatility function, to be determined, which *exactly* fits the European options market. The CEV process, whilst appealing from the point of view of statistical fitting, is observably too constrained to fit option prices exactly [Jackworth and Rubinstein (2001)]. We will extend (4.11) as follows:

$$\sigma(S,t) = \tilde{\sigma}(S,t)e^{\alpha_t}$$

where

$$\frac{dS_t}{S_t} = \mu(t)dt + \sigma(S,t)dW_t^S$$
$$d\alpha_t = -\kappa(\alpha_t - \theta(t))dt + \xi dW_t^\alpha \tag{4.12}$$
$$E[dW_t^S dW_t^\alpha] = \rho dt$$

Before we proceed, some points to note:

- We have included mean reversion in line with other models of stochastic volatility. On the whole it is deemed conceptually reasonable that volatility should not be allowed to drift upwards indefinitely, necessitating that a drag term which increases with departure from some mean reverting level $\theta(t)$ should be present (c.f. the Heston model earlier). In practice, as we shall see, this simply imposes a term structure on implied volatility, which we're going to pick up through local vol calibration. From a calibration point of view, the term is not really essential for this model, though it does have an impact on exotics. We will thus leave it in as a source of potential model risk.

- The mean reversion level $\theta(t)$ can be set arbitrarily, but for the purposes of simplification we will adopt the approach of Madan *et al* that $E[e^{2\alpha_t}|t = 0] = 1$, with a view to interpreting $\widetilde{\sigma}^2(S, t)$ as the average local variance. This gives:

$$\theta(t) = -\frac{\xi^2}{2\kappa}\left(1 + e^{-2\kappa t}\right)$$

- Whilst, in principle, we can use a non-zero correlation between the stock and residual Wiener terms, in the spirit of the previous sections analysis we will assume it to be zero for model risk analysis, though the derivation of the pricing methodology will treat the term generally.[4]

Conditional on the stock being at height S at time t, we can use Itō's lemma to write for the evolution of the stochastic volatility:

$$\frac{d\sigma_t}{\sigma_t} = [-\kappa(\alpha_t - \theta(t)) + \frac{1}{2}\xi^2]dt + \xi dW_t^\alpha$$

Noting further that:

$$\frac{\partial}{\partial\sigma} = \frac{1}{\sigma}\frac{\partial}{\partial\alpha} \tag{4.13}$$

$$\frac{\partial^2}{\partial\sigma^2} = \frac{1}{\sigma^2}\left[-\frac{\partial}{\partial\alpha} + \frac{\partial^2}{\partial\alpha^2}\right]$$

---

[4]This assumption is really driven by the desire for clarity. Whilst indeed the recalibration of the local volatility surface will recover the vanilla smile, so that, unlike a Heston based approach for example, stock-vol correlation is not required for matching the vanilla market, a non-zero correlation can have a profound effect on the persistence of *forward* skew for long-dated exotics (notably cliquets and barriers). In this chapter we will only really be looking at the effect of volatility of volatility on the forward *smile*, though the effects on skew through non-zero correlation are no less important.

we can rewrite (4.10) as:

$$\frac{\partial V}{\partial t} + \mu(t)S_t\frac{\partial V}{\partial S} - \kappa(\alpha_t - \theta(t))\frac{\partial V}{\partial \alpha}$$
$$+ \frac{1}{2}\left[\frac{\partial^2 V}{\partial S^2}\widetilde{\sigma}(S,t)^2 S_t^2 e^{2\alpha_t} + 2\frac{\partial^2 V}{\partial S\partial\alpha}S_t\widetilde{\sigma}(S,t)e^{\alpha_t}\rho\xi + \frac{\partial^2 V}{\partial\alpha^2}\xi^2\right] = r_t V_t$$

(4.14)

Now, recall, from Gyöngy's theorem, that, provided the conditional expectation of the local variance matches the Dupire variance, the terminal distributions of the stochastic volatility process will match those driven by Dupire, and hence calibration to European options will be exact (subject to the implied volatility surface being non-arbitrageable). Mathematically, for spot price K at time T, we need:

$$E[\sigma(S,T)^2|S=K] = \widehat{\sigma}^2(K,T)$$

where we denote $\widehat{\sigma}$ to refer to the Dupire local volatility. This gives:

$$\widetilde{\sigma}(K,T)^2 = \frac{\widehat{\sigma}^2(K,T)}{\psi(K,T)}$$

where

$$\psi(K,T) = \frac{\int_{-\infty}^{\infty} e^{2\alpha}\phi(K,\alpha,T)d\alpha}{\int_{-\infty}^{\infty} \phi(K,\alpha,T)d\alpha}$$

(4.15)

So now we need a PDE for the evolution of the joint density $\phi(S,\alpha,T)$. Recall from Chapter 2, however, the elegant relationship between the backward and forward Kolmogorov equations for probability density:

$$\frac{\partial G(x,t;x',t')}{\partial t} + \mathfrak{L}_{x,t}G(x,t;x',t') = 0$$

and

$$-\frac{\partial G(x,t;x',t')}{\partial t'} + \mathfrak{L}^*_{x',t'}G(x,t;x',t') = 0$$

(4.16)

respectively. In general, x can be an n-dimensional vector state, and in this case we have $x = (S,\alpha)$. For ease of construction going forward, it's actually helpful to re-express (4.14) in terms of $z = \log(S/S_0)$, and to consider the forward valued option $\widetilde{V}_t = V_t/Df(0,t)$. This gives

$$\frac{\partial \widetilde{V}}{\partial t} + \mathfrak{L}_{z,\alpha,t}\widetilde{V}(z,\alpha,t) = 0$$

where

$$\mathfrak{L}_{z,\alpha,t} = \left(\mu(t) - \frac{1}{2}\widetilde{\sigma}(z,t)^2 e^{2\alpha_t}\right)\frac{\partial}{\partial z} - \kappa(\alpha_t - \theta(t))\frac{\partial}{\partial \alpha}$$
$$+ \frac{1}{2}\left[\frac{\partial^2}{\partial z^2}\widetilde{\sigma}(z,t)^2 e^{2\alpha_t} + 2\frac{\partial^2}{\partial z \partial \alpha}\widetilde{\sigma}(z,t)e^{\alpha_t}\rho\xi + \frac{\partial^2}{\partial \alpha^2}\xi^2\right]$$

Following the same procedure of integration by parts as in Chapter 2, and maintaining the assumption that the value of G and the x' derivatives of G vanish as $x' \to \pm\infty$, we can write for the adjoint operator:

$$\mathfrak{L}^*_{z',\alpha',t'}G(x,t;x',t') =$$
$$-\frac{\partial}{\partial z'}\left[\left(\mu(t) - \frac{1}{2}\widetilde{\sigma}(z',t')^2 e^{2\alpha'_t}\right)G(x,t;x',t')\right]$$
$$+ \frac{\partial}{\partial \alpha'}\left[\kappa(\alpha'_t - \theta(t))G(x,t;x',t')\right]$$
$$+ \frac{1}{2}\left[\frac{\partial^2}{\partial z'^2}\left(\widetilde{\sigma}(z',t')^2 e^{2\alpha'_t}G(x,t;x',t')\right)\right.$$
$$\left. + 2\frac{\partial^2}{\partial z'\partial \alpha'}\left(\widetilde{\sigma}(z',t')e^{\alpha'_t}\rho\xi G(x,t;x',t')\right) + \frac{\partial^2}{\partial \alpha'^2}\xi^2 G(x,t;x',t')\right] \quad (4.17)$$

where $G(x,t;x',t') = G(z,\alpha,t;z',\alpha',t')$. So, denoting $\phi(z,\alpha,T) = G(0,0,0;z,\alpha,T)$, (4.17) can be inserted into (4.16) to complete the PDE for the evolution of the joint probability distribution from the initial state $\phi(z,\alpha,0) = \delta(z)\delta(\alpha)$.

A simplifying transformation is given by $\widetilde{z} = \log[S/F(0,t)]$ and $\widetilde{\alpha} = \alpha - \widehat{\alpha}$ where $d\widehat{\alpha} = -\kappa(\widehat{\alpha} - \theta(t))dt$ and $\widehat{\alpha}(0) = 0$. Using (4.16) and (4.17), we arrive at the simpler expression for the evolution of the forward density $\phi(\widetilde{z},\widetilde{\alpha},T)$:

$$-\frac{\partial}{\partial T}\phi(\widetilde{z},\widetilde{\alpha},T)$$
$$+ \frac{1}{2}\frac{\partial}{\partial \widetilde{z}}\left[\left(\widetilde{\sigma}(z,T)^2 e^{2(\widetilde{\alpha}+\widehat{\alpha}(T))}\right)\phi(\widetilde{z},\widetilde{\alpha},T)\right] + \frac{\partial}{\partial \widetilde{\alpha}}\left[\kappa\widetilde{\alpha}\phi(\widetilde{z},\widetilde{\alpha},T)\right]$$
$$+ \frac{1}{2}\left[\frac{\partial^2}{\partial \widetilde{z}^2}\left(\widetilde{\sigma}(\widetilde{z},T)^2 e^{2(\widetilde{\alpha}+\widehat{\alpha}(T))}\phi(\widetilde{z},\widetilde{\alpha},T)\right) + \frac{\partial^2}{\partial \widetilde{\alpha}^2}\xi^2\phi(\widetilde{z},\widetilde{\alpha},T) + \right.$$
$$\left. 2\frac{\partial^2}{\partial \widetilde{z}\partial \widetilde{\alpha}}\left(\widetilde{\sigma}(\widetilde{z},T)e^{(\widetilde{\alpha}+\widehat{\alpha}(T))}\rho\xi\phi(\widetilde{z},\widetilde{\alpha},T)\right)\right] = 0 \quad (4.18)$$

We can then solve (4.18) recursively with (4.15) as outlined by Madan *et al.* [Madan *et al.* (2007)]. In other words, starting from the initial condition $\phi(\tilde{z}, \tilde{\alpha}, 0) = \delta(\tilde{z})\delta(\tilde{\alpha})$, and the volatility at time $t_0 = 0$ given by the Dupire vol $\hat{\sigma}(0, 0)$, we can find $\phi(\tilde{z}, \tilde{\alpha}, t_1)$ at the next time-step on a two-dimensional finite difference grid from (4.18), which we can then apply to (4.15) to find $\tilde{\sigma}(\tilde{z}, t_1)$ and so on up to the option's expiry. It turns out to be efficient, particularly if we're allowed to assume zero correlation between $\tilde{z}$ and $\tilde{\alpha}$, to apply an alternating direction implicit methodology, where we divide each time interval into two half intervals, solving implicitly in one variable and explicitly on the other for the first half interval, then vice versa for the second. An excellent reference is given in the first volume of Andersen and Piterbarg [Andersen and Piterbarg (2010)].

4.4.1 *Initial observations*

To begin, let's try and gain some intuition for how stochastic volatility is going to affect our exotics by looking at its effect on vanillas. As discussed in the previous section on vega hedging, we might expect that increased volatility of volatility would generate an increased implied volatility smile, whilst a negative equity-vol correlation would result in increased implied volatility skew. For ease of analysis, we'll construct a representative 5Y vol surface on an asset with unit spot and no dividends. The effects of vol of vol and equity-vol correlation are shown in Figures 4.20 and 4.21, assuming zero mean reversion.

Note that, in addition to raising the wings of the implied volatility surface, vol of alpha also lowers the ATM vol. To understand why, consider the price of a European call when volatility and stock are uncorrelated[5]. The out-turn spot level at time T is given by:

$$S_T = S_0 \exp\left[\int_0^T \sigma_t dW_t - \frac{1}{2}\int_0^T \sigma_t^2 dt + \int_0^T \mu(t)dt\right]$$

---

[5]The argument follows Hull and White [Hull and White (1987)], but an extension to the case of non-zero correlation between stock and vol is provided as an exercise at the end of this chapter.

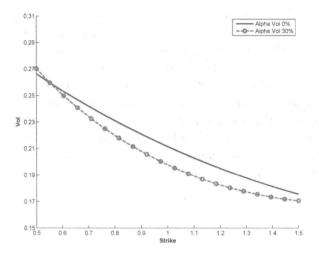

Fig. 4.20   The effect of increased vol of vol on an example 5Y implied volatility slice, zero equity-alpha correlation.

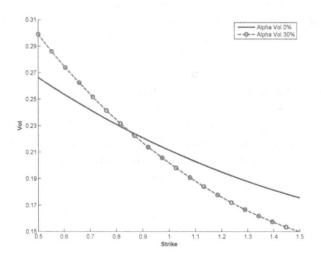

Fig. 4.21   The effect of negative equity-vol correlation on an example 5Y implied volatility slice, equity-alpha correlation -50%.

But, *conditional* on the realisation of some set of spot volatilities $\{\sigma_t\}$, $\log(S_T/F_T)$ is normally distributed $\sim \mathcal{N}(-\Sigma_T^2/2, \Sigma_T^2 T)$ where $\Sigma_T = \sqrt{(1/T)\int_0^T \sigma_t^2 dt}$. The forward valued call option price for such a distribution is just $\widetilde{C}(F_T, \Sigma_T, K, T) = F_T N(d_1) - KN(d_2)$ where $d_{1,2} = \log(F_T/K)/\Sigma\sqrt{T} \pm \Sigma\sqrt{T}/2$. We can thus write for the full option price:

$$C(F_T, K, T) = \int \widetilde{C}(F_T, \Sigma_T, K, T)\psi(\Sigma_T, T)d\Sigma_T$$

If we now Taylor expand around $\overline{\Sigma}(T) = E[\Sigma_T]$ we can write:

$$C(F_T, K, T) = \widetilde{C}(F_T, \overline{\Sigma}(T), K, T) + \frac{1}{2}\frac{\partial^2}{\partial\Sigma^2}\widetilde{C}(F_T, \Sigma_T, K, T)|_{\Sigma_T = \overline{\Sigma}(T)} Var[\Sigma_T]$$

$$(4.19)$$

as we've assumed zero correlation between the volatility and spot processes. Recalling the form of vol gamma in Figure 4.16, we can see that the variance of the square root of the realised variance drives up the implied volatility for both calls and puts, as discussed qualitatively earlier. Now, we have for our process:

$$\alpha_t = -\frac{\xi^2}{2\kappa}\left(1 - e^{-2\kappa t}\right) + \int_0^t \xi e^{\kappa(s-t)}dW_s$$

(see exercise). This gives for the mean and variance of α:

$$E[\alpha_T] = -\frac{\xi^2}{2\kappa}\left[1 - e^{-2\kappa T}\right]$$

$$Var[\alpha_T] = \frac{\xi^2}{2\kappa}\left[1 - e^{-2\kappa T}\right]$$

giving an effective vol of alpha of:

$$\widetilde{\xi} = \xi\sqrt{\frac{1 - e^{-2\kappa T}}{2\kappa T}}$$

By construction, as $E[e^{2\alpha_t}] = 1$, then for a flat $\widetilde{\sigma}(S, t) = \sigma_0$, we would have $E[\Sigma_T^2] = E[V_T] = \sigma_0^2$. However, it can be shown (see exercise), that to second order $E[\Sigma_T] = \overline{\Sigma}(T) = \sqrt{E[\Sigma_T^2]}\exp[-\Xi^2/8]$, where $\Xi = Var[\log(V_T/E[V_T])]$. So, we have a so-called convexity correction for the expectation of the square root of the realised variance which drags down $\overline{\Sigma}(T)$, and hence the ATM volatility (from 4.19).

A curve of the vol of alpha is shown in Figure 4.22.

Note that as we increase the level of mean reversion, we drive down the effective vol of alpha. Whilst a full derivation is somewhat tedious, it should be clear that a decreased vol of alpha will result in a decreased vol of variance. By construction, however, the expectation of the variance will be unaltered, so we would expect mean reversion to *raise* the ATM vol level, and decrease the implied volatility smile. This is shown in Figure 4.23.

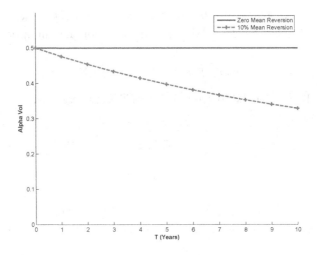

Fig. 4.22   The effect of mean reversion on the effective vol of α.

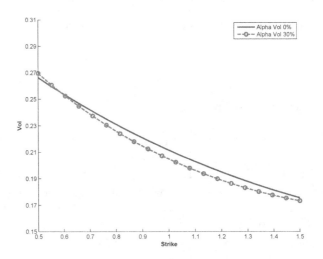

Fig. 4.23   The effect of increased mean reversion of vol on an example 5Y implied volatility slice, mean reversion 30%, zero equity-alpha correlation.

As per our investigation into dividends in the last chapter, we might expect that once we've calibrated to the market implied vol surface, the effective local vol $\tilde{\sigma}$ will have to move in opposition to the implied vol pre-calibration. In other words, vol of vol should make the local vol surface more concave and higher than the Dupire surface, whilst these effects should be lessened by mean reversion. This is illustrated in Figure 4.24 for zero correlation.

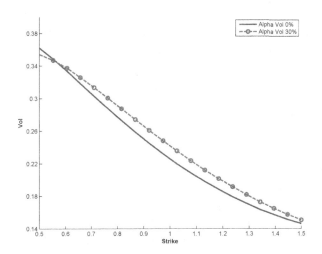

Fig. 4.24 The effect of vol of vol and mean reversion of vol on 5Y local volatility, post-calibration, mean reversion 30%.

A check of the implied vol calibration is shown in Figure 4.25.

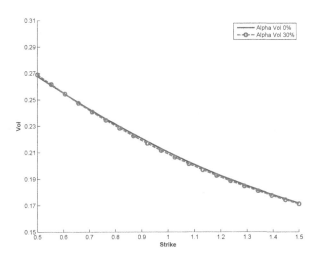

Fig. 4.25 Post-calibration 5Y implied volatility, mean reversion 30%.

These post-calibration effects on local volatility will be crucial to our understanding of the behaviour of exotics under different stochastic volatility regimes. The point to bear in mind at this stage is that stochastic volatility introduces two separate phenomena:

- Changes to price from first-order local volatility effects;
- Changes to price from second-order vega effects.

How exactly the exotic reacts turns out to be a subtle interplay of the two. To begin, let's look at one of the simplest (and popularly traded) products on volatility, the variance swap.

4.5   Trading realised volatility: Variance swaps

In the previous section, we discussed how one might go about hedging vega through a dynamic hedge in European options. However, such a strategy tends to be quite costly due to transaction costs involved. An area which has become increasingly popular is static, or at least semi-static hedging. In the former, as per a forward contract for example, one simply puts the hedge on at the start of the trade and leaves it untouched until the end. In the latter, the hedge is designed to be static with respect to the movement of one variable (spot, for example), though needs to be re-weighted as other variables (notably implied vols) move around. Good examples are provided in Derman [Derman *et al.* (1994)] and Carr and Chou [Carr and Chou (1997)]. As it happens, one non-trivial option with a purely static hedge is provided by the variance swap.

4.5.1   *Definition and trading rationale*

The variance swap pays the holder the difference between the realised variance on a stock and some strike, referred to as the *fair variance*. We can write the payoff as:

$$P = \sigma_R^2 - K_{var}$$

where

$$\sigma_R^2 = \frac{B}{N} \sum_{i=1}^{N} \log \left(\frac{S_i}{S_{i-1}} \right)^2 \tag{4.20}$$

B the annualisation factor. Those familiar with statistics will quickly notice that this is not the un-biased estimate of the stock's variance. For that we'd need to subtract off the realised mean of the log returns from the individual log returns, and divide by $N - 1$ rather than N. Whilst these variants do exist, the pricing difference tends to be small. Those who recall the last chapter will also notice that the above would be affected by dividends. Indeed, if we were to assume proportional dividends, (4.20) would introduce a dividend variance given by:

$$\sigma^2_{div} = \frac{B}{N} \sum_{t_1 \leq t_j \leq t_N} \log(1 - q_j)^2$$

To avoid this, the log returns are sometimes corrected for dividends, i.e. we consider $\log^2[(S_i + div_i)/S_{i-1}]$ when t_i falls on an ex-date. This tends to be the norm for single stock variance swaps paying sizeable dividends at relatively widely dispersed intervals (e.g. quarterly), rather than indices which effectively pay small dividends frequently. For the purposes of clarity, we will assume a non-dividend paying stock in this section.

For a start, why would you trade such an instrument? First, because it provides 'pure' exposure to realised volatility. As we shall see, the contract's value is unaffected by movements in spot. Whilst someone hedging vega in the regular options market would have to rebalance their option hedge every time spot moves, the holder of a variance swap need only worry about changes to the implied vol surface. Of course, given that, as we saw in Chapter 2, movements in implied vol are closely correlated with spot moves, this statement isn't quite true, but in practice the delta of a variance swap is substantially lower than an ATM option. Other reasons you might buy a variance swap are [Derman (1999a)]:

- *Realised volatility speculation*: for example, someone betting on the decline in stock market volatility following a period of economic turmoil.
- *Relative value trading* between implied and realised volatility: the fair variance is based on the former, the payoff on the latter. Proprietary traders who believe that implied vols look cheap relative to realised might go long a variance swap and profit if realised variance continues at historic levels (and vice versa).

Another major application of variance swaps is actually correlation trading. If we go long the realised variance of an index, and short the appropriately weighted variance swaps on the underlyers (generally weighted to make the enter strategy vega-neutral with respect to each component), a change in the value of such a product will be generated by a change in implied correlation. Such strategies are referred to as *dispersion variance swaps* and will be discussed in more detail in Chapter 8.

4.5.2   *Pricing*

There are actually numerous factors which influence the value of a variance swap. In addition to dividends we need to worry about jumps in the stock price (Chapter 6), stochastic rates (Chapter 7), sampling frequency, and the volatility of volatility itself. To begin, however, let us assume a purely diffusive, deterministic rate process with no dividends. Using the expression for stochastic stock evolution we can re-write (4.20) as:

$$\sigma_R^2 = \frac{B}{N} \sum_{i=1}^{N} \left(\left[\mu_{i-1} - \frac{\sigma_i^2}{2} \right] (t_i - t_{i-1}) + \sigma_i(W_i - W_{i-1}) \right)^2$$

The value of the contract is given by:

$$E_{\mathbb{Q}}[\sigma_R^2] = \frac{B}{N} E_{\mathbb{Q}} \left[\sum_{i=1}^{N} \left[\mu_{i-1} - \frac{\sigma_i^2}{2} \right]^2 (t_i - t_{i-1})^2 + \sigma_i^2(t_i - t_{i-1}) \right]$$

If we assume for simplicity equal time interval Δt, then:

$$E_{\mathbb{Q}}[\sigma_R^2] = B E_{\mathbb{Q}} \left[\left\langle \left(\mu - \frac{\sigma^2}{2} \right)^2 \right\rangle \Delta t^2 + \langle \sigma^2 \rangle \Delta t \right]$$

where we use the mean squared notation: $\langle x^2 \rangle = (1/N) \sum_i x_i^2$. As we take $\Delta t \to 0$, the first of these terms (the mean correction) will disappear, leaving us with the pure realised variance term. As, for maturity T, $\Delta t = T/N$ and $BT = N$, this term is of the order of T/N. Provided that the number of samples per year is large the effect of this term tends to be negligible. For certain contracts which sample weekly, however, some care needs to be applied.

Let us assume that we are in the continuous limit. We then have:

$$E_{\mathbb{Q}}[\sigma_R^2] = \langle \sigma^2 \rangle = \frac{1}{T} \int_0^T E_{\mathbb{Q}}[\sigma_t^2] dt$$

Now we find something quite surprising. Even though this contract is manifestly path generated, it turns out *not* to be path dependent. To see this consider Itō's lemma:

$$\frac{dS_t}{S_t} = \mu(t)dt + \sigma_t dW_t$$

$$d\log S_t = [\mu(t) - \sigma_t^2/2]dt + \sigma_t dW_t$$

giving:

$$\sigma_t^2 dt = 2\left[\frac{dS_t}{S_t} - d\log S_t\right]$$

Integrating up and taking risk-neutral expectations we get:

$$
\begin{aligned}
E_{\mathbb{Q}}[\sigma_R^2] &= \frac{2}{T}\int_0^T E_{\mathbb{Q}}\left[\frac{dS_t}{S_t} - d\log S_t\right] \\
&= \frac{2}{T}\int_0^T \mu(t)dt - E_{\mathbb{Q}}\left[\log\left(\frac{S_T}{S_0}\right)\right] \\
&= \frac{2}{T}E_{\mathbb{Q}}\left[\log\left(\frac{F_T}{S_T}\right)\right]
\end{aligned}
$$

But this is just a payoff at expiry. Indeed, if we just add to this log contract the future contract $(F_T - S_T)/F_T$, it can be shown (see exercise) that the variance swap reduces to a weighted sum of calls and puts:

$$E_{\mathbb{Q}}[\sigma_R^2] = \frac{2}{T}\left[\int_0^{F_T}\frac{1}{K^2}P(K,T)dK + \int_{F_T}^{\infty}\frac{1}{K^2}C(K,T)dK\right] \qquad (4.21)$$

This result has major implications. First, if we write $C(K,T) = K[e^z N(d_1) - N(d_2)]$ and $P(K,T) = K[N(-d_2) - e^z N(-d_1)]$ where $d_{1,2} = z/\sigma(z,T)\sqrt{T} \pm \sigma(z,T)\sqrt{T}/2$ and $z = \log(F/K)$, we can re-write:

$$E_{\mathbb{Q}}[\sigma_R^2] = \frac{2}{T}\left[\int_{-\infty}^0 dz\,\widetilde{c}(z,T) + \int_0^{\infty} dz\,\widetilde{p}(z,T)\right] \qquad (4.22)$$

$$\widetilde{c}(z,T) = e^z N(d_1) - N(d_2)$$

$$\widetilde{p}(z,T) = N(-d_2) - e^z N(-d_1)$$

So that if indeed $\sigma(z, T)$ is constant for changes in spot, the variance swap will have no delta at instantiation.[6] Such a model for implied volatility is sometimes called *sticky delta* in that, for a surface which is frozen as a function of *moneyness* $\log(K/F)$, the surface is also frozen as a function of Δ (see exercise). Like this, the cost of hedging vega through var swaps should be cheaper than hedging via regular options, as stated earlier.

The second implication is highly germane to this book. If a variance swap can be replicated via European options, it should in principle have no model risk. Actually, this is an over-statement. First, our derivation assumed no discontinuities in the process. Were we to put back dividends or jumps, the exact nature of those discontinuities can have profound effects on the value of the swap. Second, the variance swap is on the realised variance of the *spot*, whilst European options trade on the realised variance of the *forward*. We will discuss this in detail in the chapter on stochastic rates, but suffice to say for now that the issue only becomes relevant for the more long-dated contracts.

Jumps and rates aside, why do we care about these products in this chapter? The issue lies in the way these contracts are modified. Suppose you sell a variance swap on a stock. What happens if the stock defaults? The stock price drops to zero and the realised variance becomes unbounded, bankrupting us instantly. To protect against this eventuality, most single stock variance swaps come with a protective cap, i.e. we pay $P = \min(Cap, \sigma_R^2) - K_{var}$. Notice, however, that this can be re-written: $P = \sigma_R^2 - K_{var} - \max(\sigma_R^2 - Cap, 0)$. In other words, we have an embedded short *call* on variance, which evidently is going to be sensitive to our stochastic volatility model. In general, these caps are taken deeply out of the money, commonly 6.25 times fair variance, and for a long time they were either not priced in at all, or just priced at intrinsic. That, however, was before 2008. Figure 4.26 shows what would have happened to a variance swap struck on the 3rd January 2007 with a three year maturity.

What we've done in this figure is to break out the historically accrued variance from the forward fair variance (FFV), i.e. we can write for the value of a variance swap during the life:

$$Var = \frac{B}{N}[HistVar + FutVar]$$

---

[6] As we progress through the life of the swap, the last historic fixing does in fact generate some delta to the next unset fixing, albeit small.

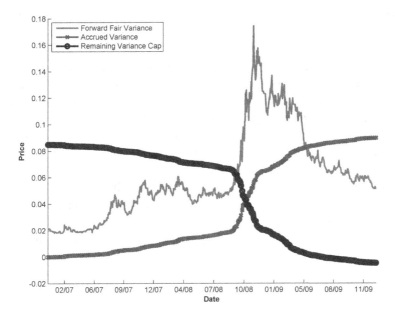

Fig. 4.26   3-year variance swap on the S&P500, struck on 3/1/2007, cap at 400% initial
FFV.

$$HistVar = \sum_{i=1}^{i=j} \log\left(\frac{S_i}{S_{i-1}}\right)^2$$

$$FutVar = \sum_{i=j+1}^{i=N} \log\left(\frac{S_i}{S_{i-1}}\right)^2 = \frac{N-j}{B}FFV$$

where $0 \le j \le N$. We then have for a variance capped swap:

$$P = Var - \max(Var - Cap, 0) = Var - \max\left(\frac{B}{N}FutVar - \widetilde{Cap}, 0\right)$$

$$= Var - \max\left(\frac{N-j}{N}FFV - \widetilde{Cap}, 0\right)$$

where

$$\widetilde{Cap} = Cap - \frac{B}{N}HistVar$$

We refer to $\widetilde{Cap}$ as the *remaining cap*. There were then two effects of
the crash of 2008 on variance swaps (in this context). First, the spiking

of implied vols drove up the forward fair variance. Second, the remaining cap was strongly suppressed by the sudden increase in accrued variance. The overall effect was to drive the *effective* cap deep into the money. Indeed, had we struck the cap originally at 400% at the start of 2007 (quite common for index variance swaps where the problem of jumps is considered more benign than with stocks), the effective cap would actually have gone negative. Suddenly, products which had hitherto been considered model risk-free suddenly became exquisitely sensitive to the assumptions on volatility dynamics. To see how sensitive, let's apply our SLV model to a 5-year variance swap on the dividend-free stock made up in the previous section. To begin, we'll pull out the embedded call on variance and see the effect of vol of α and mean reversion of α on the value of a call struck at FFV (i.e. at the money in the context of an option on variance). The undiscounted price, post-calibration to the vol surface, is shown in Figure 4.27.

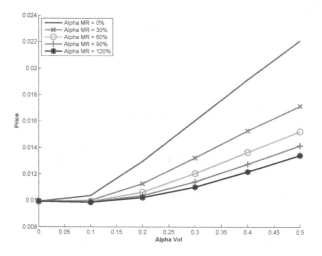

Fig. 4.27   5-year variance option, struck at 100% FFV.

This is in line with our expectations from the previous section. Unsurprisingly, an increase in vol of α causes an increase in the volatility of realised variance, as discussed. To an extent, we have compensated by decreasing local volatility to match the out-turn European option surface, but not enough to mitigate the effect of increased vol of α altogether.

We also see that the dampening effect of mean reversion on the effective vol of α works back into the price of the variance cap, in the same way that it reduced the effects of vol of α on the implied volatility surface. What is striking is that, even for fairly modest levels of stochastic volatility, the price of an ATM variance option can easily be doubled, assuming low levels of mean reversion of α. As one might expect, the proportional effect on out of the money options is even greater, as shown in Figure 4.28 (post-calibration).

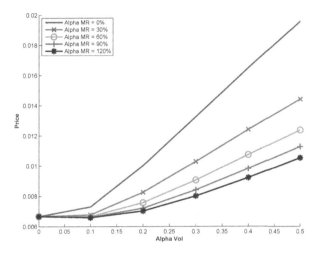

Fig. 4.28   5-year variance option, struck at 120% FFV.

Note also that for zero vol of α the variance option still has some value. This is unsurprising given that the implied vol surface is non-flat, and that the corresponding dependance of spot on vol in the local vol limit is non-zero. This point is actually quite important in practice. As the market for variance options develops, the temptation might be to dissociate the vol of variance from the vol on spot. Clearly though, if European options on spot exhibit vol skew, there cannot be an *arbitrarily* low level for implied vol of variance. The demonstration of this lower bound (and also an upper bound) for implied vol of variance under the assumption of diffusion is discussed by Carr and Lee [Carr and Lee (2010)]. In the examples shown, the forward fair variance for the swap was 0.05, so that volatility of volatility could have extracted as much as 50% of value.

Those familiar with the Heston model might be used to seeing substantially higher values for mean reversion, typically of the order of 1–5

[Javaheri (2005); Gatheral (2006)]. It should be noted though that such estimates are based on calibration of the Heston model to the market implied vol surface. In this model, however, *any* value of mean reversion could (subject to numerical difficulty) calibrate to market implied vols, so these numbers are not really comparable. By virtue of the greater flexibility of this model, we'd need to look at the exotics space to get some more colour on reasonable inputs for this number. One possibility, as pointed out by Madan *et al.* [Madan *et al.* (2007)], would be to look at the term structure of implied volatility of variance. Representative curves for 1Y to 5Y ATM variance options are shown in Figure 4.29 for vol of α of 30%.

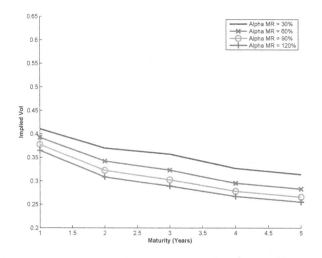

Fig. 4.29   ATM implied vol of variance curves, 30% vol of α.

As you might expect, there is a general augmentation of these curves for higher vol of α (Figure 4.30).

Given a liquid market in variance options, or at least in embedded variance options via variance swaps, it might be possible to fit vol of α and mean reversion of α to implied volatility of variance. An example implied volatility curve for ATM variance options on the EuroSTOXX50E (.STOXX50E) is shown in Figure 4.31.

Two features are immediately apparent:

- The short-dated implied vol of variance implies a very high vol of vol for short-dated options;

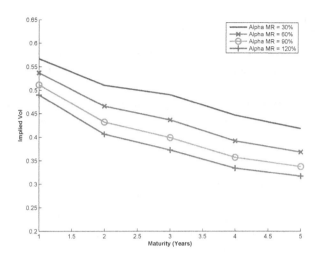

Fig. 4.30   ATM implied vol of variance curves, 50% vol of α.

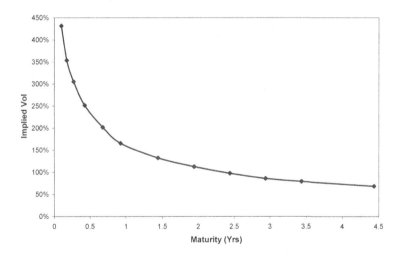

Fig. 4.31   ATM implied vol for .STOXX50E options on variance (as of 15/7/2011).

- The decay in implied vol of variance implies a rapid mean reversion of vol in the short end, settling down to a slower longer term level.

We have not attempted to fit this model to the data shown, though at the very least, we believe that such behaviour would require either a term structure of mean reversion or, perhaps more elegantly, *two* idiosyncratic stochastic drivers for local volatility, one with high mean reversion speed and volatility, one with lower mean reversion speed and volatility. For the purposes of illustration, however, we will stay with the more modest range of vol and mean reversion of alpha, in keeping with longer dated products, but leave this example data on variance options to suggest areas for further development. With this in mind, let us now move from products on *realised* volatility to those on *implied* volatility, more commonly known as *cliquets*.

4.6   Trading implied volatility: Cliquets

The first cliquet options to be traded were S&P500 bear market warrants with a periodic reset [Shparber and Resheff (2004)], traded on the Chicago Board of Options Exchange in 1996. In these structures, the investor was essentially long a put struck at the stock level at a reset date, and the level at expiry, conditional on the reset level being less than a pre-determined strike level X. In the case where the reset level turned out to be above X, the investor received a regular put at expiry struck at X. One can think of the contract as a standard protection against downside moves, cheapened by the possibility of the guaranteed amount resetting downwards if the stock ends up below the strike at the reset date. Such a structure, however, is somewhat atypical. The more common 'vanilla' cliquet is the *ratchet* option, given by:

$$\sum_{i=1}^{N} \max(S_i/S_{i-1} - 1, 0)$$

where the sum may be paid out periodically or as a lump sum at maturity. An investor buying such a product would tend to combine the structure with a regular bond (e.g. a US government bond), using the floored return on the associated index (S&P500 in this case) to augment the potential yield on the equity linked structure without any downside risk. Naturally, there's a premium for the upside, which, provided we assume proportional dividends, giving the undiscounted value[7]:

---

[7]For ease of illustration, we will take all values in this section as undiscounted.

$$V = \sum_{i=1}^{N} F(i-1,i)N(d_1) - N(d_2) \qquad (4.23)$$

$$F(i-1,i) = F(i)/F(i-1)$$

$$d_{1,2} = \frac{\log(F(i-1,i))}{\sigma(i-1,i)\sqrt{T_i - T_{i-1}}} \pm \frac{\sigma(i-1,i)\sqrt{T_i - T_{i-1}}}{2}$$

In the above $\sigma(i-1,i)$ refers to the implied *forward* volatility of the *clicklet* option $\max(S_i/S_{i-1}-1, 0)$. Such a structure is likely to be quite expensive. A more common structure [Wilmott (1998)] would be to cap and floor each clicklet at LC and LF respectively:

$$\sum_{i=1}^{N} \min(\max(S_i/S_{i-1}, LF), LC)$$

This effectively reduces each clicklet to a call spread between the *LocalFloor* and the *LocalCap* plus a coupon equal to the *LocalFloor*, which may well be negative. To further cheapen the structure, the entire sum might be capped and floored at GC and GF respectively, resulting in the following:

$$\min(\max(GF, \sum_{i=1}^{N} \min(\max(S_i/S_{i-1}, LF), LC)), GC)$$

A common structure would be the *minimum coupon cliquet*, where only the global floor is applied. This is sometimes referred to as the *accumulator* [Bergomi (2005)].

Such structures could be referred to as 'bearish', as they would tend to be popular with investors looking for protection against downside moves. An investor who, on the other hand, is confident that the market is going to keep rising, and that implied volatilities are over-priced relative to historics, might be attracted by the reverse versions of the above, where the cliquet explicitly pays *less* if the market falls. If implied volatilities (or more accurately forward implied volatilities) are high, the value of the embedded puts will significantly reduce the price of the note to which they're attached. Provided that the market keeps on rising, the investor has effectively bought a regular note cheaply by virtue of what he/she perceives to be over-priced option volatility. Two popular versions of this 'bullish' structure are the *reverse cliquet* and the Napoleon[8]:

---

[8]The payoff shown here is a for a single Napoleon coupon. Commonly several of these

$$\text{ReverseCliquet} = \max\left(0, C + \sum_{i=1}^{N} \min(0, r_i)\right)$$

$$\text{Napoleon} = \max\left[0, C + \min_i(r_i)\right]$$

$$r_i = \frac{S_i}{S_{i-1}} - 1$$

As we shall see, these last two structures turn out to be strongly sensitive to stochastic volatility parameters. To begin to understand how they work, let's backtrack to the simple ratchet. For convenience, we shall considered the somewhat contrived example of the ratchet whose local floor equals the forward-forward $F(i-1, i)$ and whose local cap is infinite. The value of the embedded calls is given by:

$$V = \sum_{i=1}^{N} F(i-1, i) \left[N\left(\frac{\sigma(i-1,i)\sqrt{T_i - T_{i-1}}}{2}\right) - N\left(-\frac{\sigma(i-1,i)\sqrt{T_i - T_{i-1}}}{2}\right) \right]$$

Expanding to second order this is just given by:

$$V \simeq \sum_{i=1}^{N} F(i-1, i) \frac{\sigma(i-1,i)\sqrt{T_i - T_{i-1}}}{\sqrt{2\pi}}$$

as $n'(0) = 0$ for $n(x) = e^{-x^2/2}/\sqrt{2\pi}$. So the (truly) ATM ratchet is effectively a basket of ATM forward starting implied volatilities, weighted by the corresponding forward forwards divided by $\sqrt{2\pi}$. Like this, when we enter into a cliquet contract, we can think of ourselves entering into an option on forward implied volatility. Whilst this notion shouldn't be taken too literally, it does provide a powerful intuitive tool in understanding how different models for spot and volatility propagation, of which SLV is only one of many, impact on the price of this class of exotics. To see this, let's begin by comparing a ratchet with a globally capped ratchet. By Jensen's

---

will be paid (e.g. five yearly coupons based on monthly returns), where payment is immediate, or summed at expiry. We will focus on a single coupon with annual sampling for ease of comparison.

inequality, we can write:

$$V_{cappedRatchet} = E\left[\min\left(GC, \sum_{i=1}^{N}\max\left(\frac{S_i}{S_{i-1}} - \frac{F_i}{F_{i-1}}, 0\right)\right)\right]$$

$$< \min\left[GC, E\left[\sum_{i=1}^{N}\max\left(\frac{S_i}{S_{i-1}} - \frac{F_i}{F_{i-1}}, 0\right)\right]\right]$$

$$= \min\left[GC, \sum_{i=1}^{N}F(i-1, i)\frac{\sigma(i-1, i)\sqrt{T_i - T_{i-1}}}{\sqrt{2\pi}}\right]$$

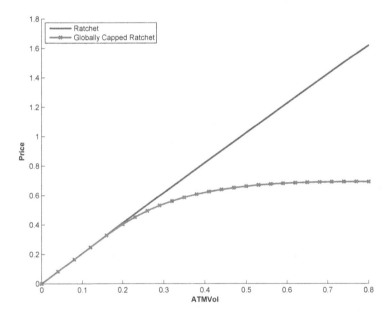

Fig. 4.32   5Y yearly sampled ratchet vs capped ratchet (100% cap).

Analogously to a capped basket option, we might expect then that if we plot the price of the ratchet and capped ratchet vs implied volatility, that the two should track each other closely for low vol, but then diverge at higher vol as the cap on the capped ratchet kicks in. Figure 4.32 shows this for the particularly simple case of deterministic flat volatility (20%) on 5Y, yearly resetting cliquets.

It seems that the intuition of thinking about cliquets as options on implied volatility is valuable, at least in this case. Crucial to our understanding of how these products behave with stochastic volatility is vol gamma. Figure 4.33 shows the corresponding vega profiles vs vol for these products[9]:

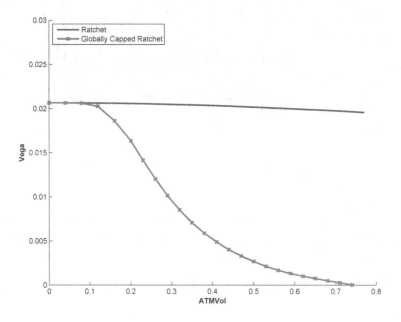

Fig. 4.33   Vega for 5Y yearly sampled ratchet vs capped ratchet (100% cap).

As expected, the vega on the vanilla ratchet is essentially flat. The vega for the capped ratchet, however, is monotonically decreasing vs vol (c.f. delta on a capped basket vs basket spot), making the product short vol gamma. As discussed in the section on the influence of vol gamma on hedging costs, this is problematic for the holder of such an option. The vega is positive, necessitating that we short options to vega hedge. If vols rally, we have to short fewer options, as the vega has dropped, requiring that we buy back options in a rising market. As per barriers and vanilla options discussed above, this is going to subtract a hedging cost from the option. A similar problem is seen for the *issuer* of a Napoleon or reverse cliquet. Price profiles vs vol are shown in Figures 4.34 and 4.35 respectively.

The corresponding vega profiles are shown in Figures 4.36 and 4.37 respectively.

In the same way that we thought of the capped ratchet as a covered call on vol, we can think of the reverse cliquet as a put on vol. Correspondingly,

---

[9]Using the market convention of vega as change in value per 1% move in the vol.

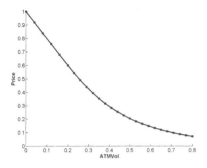

Fig. 4.34 Price vs vol for a 5Y yearly sampled reverse cliquet, 100% base coupon.

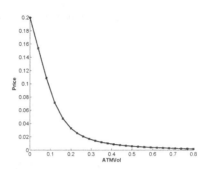

Fig. 4.35 Price vs vol for a 5Y yearly sampled Napoleon, 20% base coupon.

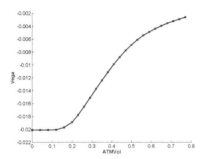

Fig. 4.36 Vega vs vol for a 5Y yearly sampled reverse cliquet, 100% base coupon.

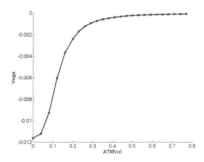

Fig. 4.37 Vega vs vol for a 5Y yearly sampled Napoleon, 20% base coupon.

the vega profiles are mirror images of each other, switching the vol gamma problem to the issuer side.

Let's try and express this more rigorously. We can write in general for the price of a cliquet:

$$V = \int P(r_1, \ldots, r_n) \phi(r_1, \ldots, r_n) dr_1 \ldots dr_n$$

where $r_n = \log(S_n/S_{n-1})$. To make life easier at this stage, we will approximate $r_n = S_{n-1} \exp\left([\mu_{n-1} - \sigma_{n-1}^2/2](t_n - t_{n-1}) + \sigma_{n-1}(W_n - W_{n-1})\right)$. This is effectively the local log-normal assumption, valid in the limit of small $t_n - t_{n-1}$. We can then write:

$$V = \int P \left[(\mu_0 - \sigma_0^2/2)(t_1 - t_0) + \sigma_0(W_1 - W_0), \right.$$

$$\left. \ldots, (\mu_{n-1} - \sigma_{n-1}^2/2)(t_{n-1} - t_n) + \sigma_{n-1}(W_n - W_{n-1}) \right]$$

$$\times \phi(W_1, \ldots, W_n | \sigma_1 \ldots \sigma_{n-1}) \Phi(\sigma_1, \ldots, \sigma_{n-1})$$

$$dW_1 \ldots dW_n d\sigma_1 \ldots d\sigma_{n-1}$$

But $W_1 \ldots W_n$ are independent increments, so this just reduces to:

$$V = \int \tilde{V}(\sigma_0, \ldots, \sigma_{n-1}) \Phi(\sigma_1, \ldots, \sigma_{n-1}) d\sigma_1 \ldots d\sigma_{n-1}$$

This is a powerful result. First, it further justifies our original statement that, by virtue of cliquets being options on *returns*, the product ends up being an option on sequential forward volatilities. Second, it affords us a Taylor expansion:

$$V \simeq \tilde{V}(\bar{\sigma}_0, \ldots, \bar{\sigma}_{n-1}) + \frac{1}{2} \sum_{i=1}^{n-1} \sum_{j=1}^{n-1} \frac{\partial^2 V}{\partial \sigma_i \sigma_j} E[(\sigma_i - \bar{\sigma}_i)(\sigma_j - \bar{\sigma}_j)] \qquad (4.24)$$

neatly summarising the vol gamma problem. Negative vol gamma will reduce the price of a cliquet, in line with our arguments on the cost of adverse hedging[10]. An issuer will demand more for hedging the risk, a holder would demand to pay less likewise. Note, however, that we've introduced another level of complexity. Not only do we need to worry about the variance of volatility, we also need to worry about *serial covariance*. It happens that this is directly related to mean reversion. For our exponential OU process $x = e^\alpha$, we can write for the serial covariance:

---

[10]It should be noted that the expression for $\tilde{V}(\bar{\sigma}_0, \ldots, \bar{\sigma}_{n-1})$ is considerably complicated by non-zero stock-vol correlation. In the examples considered in this chapter, we will continue with the simplification of zero correlation, for illustration, allowing $\tilde{V}(\bar{\sigma}_0, \ldots, \bar{\sigma}_{n-1})$ to be taken as the value of the cliquet itself for *given* $\{\bar{\sigma}_0, \ldots, \bar{\sigma}_{n-1}\}$.

$$\langle (x_i - \bar{x}_i)(x_j - \bar{x}_j) \rangle = \exp\left[-2\beta \left(2 - e^{-2\kappa t_i} - e^{-2\kappa t_j}\right)\right]$$

$$\times \exp\left[\beta \left[1 + e^{-\kappa(t_j - t_i)}\right]^2 \left(1 - e^{-2\kappa t_i}\right)\right.$$

$$\left. + \beta(1 - e^{-2\kappa(t_j - t_i)})\right]$$

$$- \exp\left[-\beta \left(2 - e^{-2\kappa t_i} - e^{-2\kappa t_j}\right)\right]$$

where $\beta = \xi^2/4\kappa$ and $t_j \geq t_i$. (The proof is left as an exercise). A plot of this function is shown in Figure 4.38.

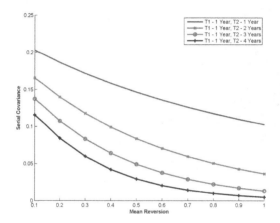

Fig. 4.38   Serial covariance of an exponential OU process $\xi = 50\%$.

This behaviour is a common feature of mean reversion, namely that the higher the mean reversion, the lower the serial covariance, and the wider the interval between time points, the lower likewise. The intuition is simple. For high mean reversion, whatever the process might be doing at an earlier time, mean reversion will dampen its effect by the time we get to the later time, reducing the correlation between the two measurements. Of course, variance is just a special case of serial covariance between identical times (top curve), so for a given *cross vol gamma* matrix $\partial V/\partial \sigma_i \partial \sigma_j$, then provided the entries have the same sign, we would expect mean reversion to reduce the effects of stochastic volatility uniformly. The cross vol gammas for the three cliquets in question are shown in Figures 4.39, 4.40 and 4.41.

For this vol, the sign is indeed predominantly uniform across the matrix, which should make the analysis of mean reverse somewhat easier.

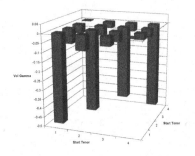

Fig. 4.39   Cross vol gamma for a 5Y yearly sampled capped ratchet, 100% cap.

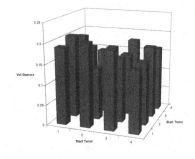

Fig. 4.40   Cross vol gamma for a 5Y yearly sampled reverse cliquet, 100% base coupon.

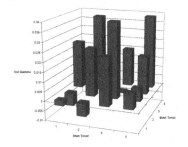

Fig. 4.41   Cross vol gamma for a 5Y yearly sampled Napoleon, 20% base coupon.

Before we get onto the analysis of the effects of stochastic volatility on the three cliquets themselves, let's pause to think about the meaning of $\overline{\sigma}_i$ in (4.24). Imagine we traded a simple ATM forward starting option, starting at t_{i-1} and ending at t_i. As discussed, the value is closely approximated by $F(i-1,i)\frac{\sigma(i-1,i)\sqrt{T_i-T_{i-1}}}{\sqrt{2\pi}}$. But as the vol gamma is zero, with the locally log-normal approximation we have $\overline{\sigma}_{i-1} \simeq \sigma(i-1,i)$. The average volatility for the interval $[t_{i-1}, t_i]$ is then roughly the implied ATM forward volatility of the corresponding forward starting option. Had we considered an OTM forward starting call, or a corresponding OTM put, the positive vol gamma would have pushed up the wings, according to the degree of variance of vol. But recall from Chapter 2 that the local volatility model predicted decreasing forward skew, for a given tenor, the further out the start date. Stochastic volatility manifestly *persists the skew through the idiosyncratic component of volatility*. A graph of forward starting vol surfaces for different levels of vol of α is shown in Figure 4.42.

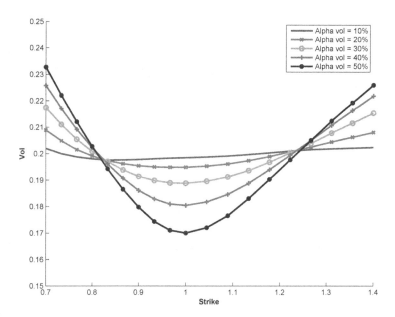

Fig. 4.42   Representative forward implied vol surfaces, 1Y into 2Y, zero vol mean reversion.

Going back to (4.24) we would thus expect two dominant effects of stochastic volatility on cliquets:

- A vega impact from the reduction of forward ATM vol;
- A vol gamma impact from the increase of variance of volatility.

For the capped ratchet and reverse cliquet, these effects should be complementary. The capped ratchet is positive vega and negative vol gamma. Both the fall in ATM forward vol and the increase in variance of vol should push up the price of the reverse cliquet, and drive down the price of the capped ratchet. As the vega profile is similar, the Napoleon should show similar behaviour to the reverse cliquet. The results for increased vol of vol, at zero mean reversion, are shown in Figures 4.43, 4.44 and 4.45, for 40% base vol.

Following our earlier reasoning, we should also see the effects of vol of vol decrease uniformly the higher the mean reversion. This is shown in Figures 4.46, 4.47 and 4.48 at 40% vol for different levels of mean reversion.

So far so good, but what about calibration? To compare apples for apples, let's turn this on for *flat* implied vol initially. Results are shown in Figures 4.49, 4.50 and 4.51.

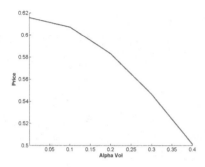

Fig. 4.43   Volatility of volatility behaviour for 5Y yearly sampled capped
ratchet, 100% cap, 40% vol.

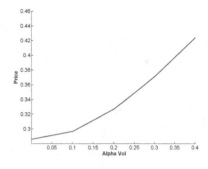

Fig. 4.44   Volatility of volatility behaviour for 5Y yearly sampled reverse
cliquet, 100% base coupon, 40% vol.

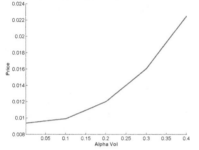

Fig. 4.45   Volatility of volatility behaviour for 5Y yearly sampled Napoleon, 20% base
coupon, 40% vol.

Qualitatively, the picture is much the same. All that's happened is that
calibration has pushed up the ATM fwd vol, and pushed down the effective
variance of volatility, as shown in a representative 1Y to 2Y vol surface
(Figure 4.52).

Contrast this to dividend model risk discussed in the previous chapter.
There, calibration to the implied vol surface all but removed model risk
on barriers. For stochastic volatility modelling however, strong model risk
is still observed on cliquets (and indeed barriers, as we shall see in the
next section) even after calibration. Whilst the risk is reduced, it is by
no means eliminated. Of course, if we actually knew the price of forward
starting options at a reasonable range of strikes, maturity and tenor, we
could in principle constrain vol of vol and vol of mean reversion so tightly
that the model risk on cliquet exotics might become negligible. Once again,
more is less. The deeper a market in simple instruments we have, the more
comfortably we can trade exotics.

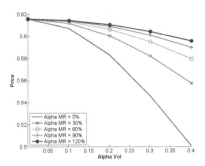

Fig. 4.46 Volatility of volatility behaviour for 5Y yearly sampled capped ratchet, 100% cap, 40% vol, increasing vol mean reversion.

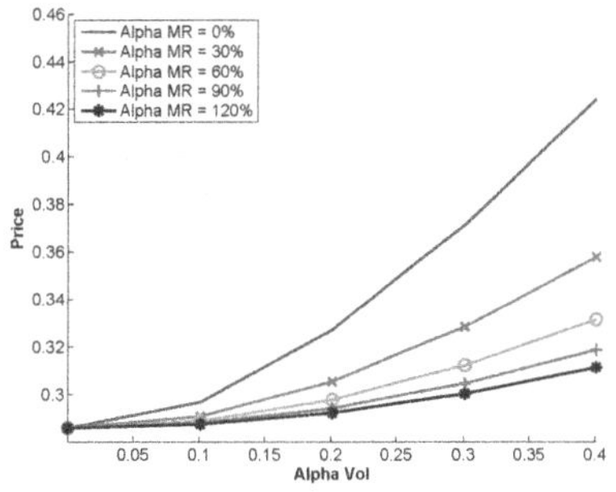

Fig. 4.47 Volatility of volatility behaviour for 5Y yearly sampled reverse cliquet, 100% base coupon, 40% vol, increasing vol mean reversion

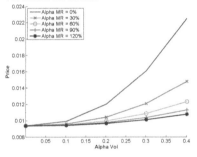

Fig. 4.48 Volatility of volatility behaviour for 5Y yearly sampled Napoleon, 20% base coupon, 40% vol, increasing vol mean reversion.

To close this section on cliquets, what about skew? Calibrated results for the three cliquets for the skewed surface used on variance swaps earlier are shown in Figures 4.53, 4.54 and 4.55.

We might naively expect the capped ratchet and reverse cliquet to show little difference, given that the embedded ratchets are strips of at the money options. We would, however, be wrong, and the effect is yet another subtlety of these products. Although the embedded vanilla is at the money, the global floor acts as an OTM long put on the payoff. The higher the implied vol, or the lower the base coupon, the stronger the effect of this put, so that negative implied vol skew drives up the price of the reverse cliquet. Likewise, the global cap on the capped ratchet acts as a short OTM call, also raising value for negative skew. The Napoleon once again shows similar behaviour to the reverse cliquet.

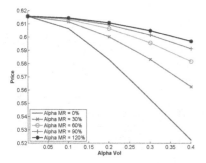

Fig. 4.49 Volatility of volatility behaviour for 5Y yearly sampled capped ratchet, 100% cap, 40% vol, increasing vol mean reversion, calibrated.

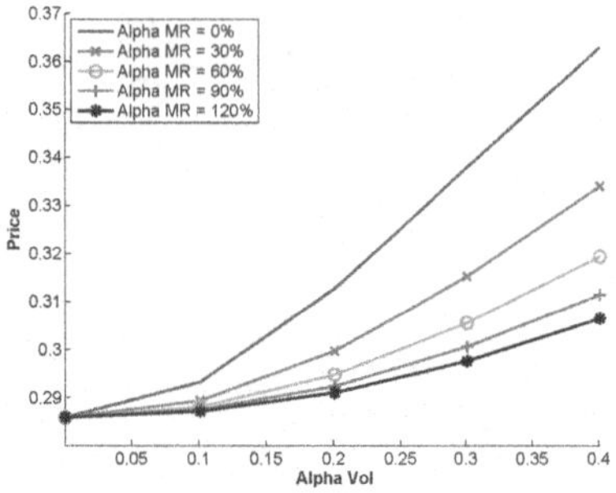

Fig. 4.50 Volatility of volatility behaviour for 5Y yearly sampled reverse cliquet, 100% base coupon, 40% vol, increasing vol mean reversion, calibrated.

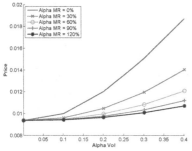

Fig. 4.51   Volatility of volatility behaviour for 5Y yearly sampled Napoleon, 20% base coupon, 40% vol, increasing vol mean reversion, calibrated.

Historically, the influence of local volatility on Napoleons and reverse cliquets has been crucial. Until 2002, a popular model for cliquets, was the *independent returns model*, where, not only are returns taken to be (necessarily) uncorrelated, but actually *independent*. The model was believed to be a more realistic means for capturing the preservation of forward skew, and also allowed independent setting of vol of vol. Such models tended to underprice the embedded long puts, though for that very reason, most of the business was won as a result. This effectively resulted in certain firms building up substantial short exposure to local volatility related model risk. The correction of the assumption of independent returns resulted in a significant negative remarking of the cliquet positions. A summary of the period is provided by Christopher Jeffery [Jeffery (2004)]. The lesson was clear, model risk should not be taken lightly.

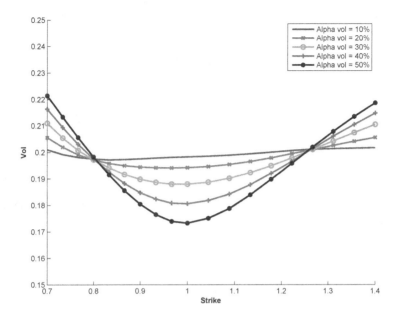

Fig. 4.52   Representative forward implied vol surfaces, 1Y into 2Y, calibrated to 20% vol.

4.7   Barriers revisited

We have looked at two product classes with strong sensitivity to stochastic volatility modelling, one on realised variance, one on implied forward variance. By way of completeness, let's revisit the barrier options from Chapter 3, which showed such low sensitivity to dividend modelling once calibration to Europeans had been sorted out. To begin, let's consider a simple 150% one-touch 5Y barrier. Some price curves at different levels of volatility of α and zero mean reversion, for a flat 20% local vol surface, are shown in Figure 4.56.

It may come as no surprise, but increasing the level of vol of vol decreases the one-touch probability. One way to think about this is that the vol of vol increases the kurtosis of the spot distribution, pulling the distribution of the maximum towards the forward, away from the upside barrier. Let's consider what's going on more rigorously. Consider the case of a barrier option with two observations T_1, T_2 with $T_2 > T_1 > T_0$. We can write for the KO probability $p(B)$:

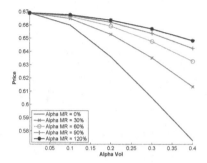

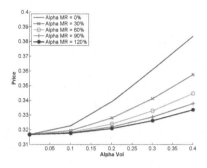

Fig. 4.53 Volatility of volatility behaviour for 5Y yearly sampled capped
ratchet, 100% cap, skewed surface, increasing vol mean reversion, calibrated.

Fig. 4.54 Volatility of volatility behaviour for 5Y yearly sampled reverse
cliquet, 100% base coupon, skewed surface, increasing vol mean reversion, calibrated.

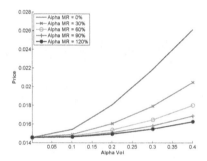

Fig. 4.55 Volatility of volatility behaviour for 5Y yearly sampled Napoleon, 20% base
coupon, skewed surface, increasing vol mean reversion, calibrated.

$$p(B) = p(S(T_1) > B \cup S(T_2) > B)$$
$$= p(S(T_1) > B) + p(S(T_2) > B) - p(S(T_1) > B \cap S(T_2) > B)$$

$$(4.25)$$

It is clear then, that to hedge this option *perfectly*, we'd need a European
option expiring at T_1 and T_2, but also a forward starting option from T_1
to T_2. Before we calibrate the vol surface, most of the effect of vol of vol
is picked up by the option with the largest vol gamma, namely the longest
dated European. We might then expect that, pre-calibration, the behaviour
of the KO probability with vol gamma should be closely related to the shape
of the vol surface at the maturity of the barrier. For a digital, we just have:

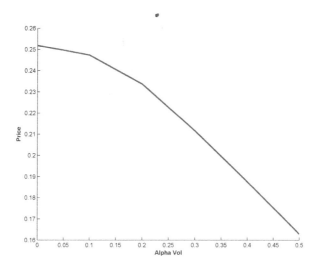

Fig. 4.56   150% 5Y one-touch prices as a function of α volatility.

$$p(S_T > K) = \int_K^\infty \phi(S_T)dS_T = -\frac{\partial C}{\partial K}$$
$$= -\left.\frac{\partial C}{\partial K}\right|_\sigma - \left.\frac{\partial C}{\partial \sigma}\right|_K \frac{\partial \sigma}{\partial K}$$

Now, as we raise the vol of vol we add positive curvature to the vol surface. The increased vol at the barrier raises the value of the first derivative $= N(d_2)$, but the positive gradient of the vol surface at the barrier increases the *negative* contribution of the second term. For barriers sufficiently close to the money, it's the second term that dominates, lowering the KO probability. As we shall see shortly, the effect of skew switches sign as we increase the barrier level.

Now let's consider what happens when we calibrate. The first two terms of (4.25) will be unaffected by vol of vol, leaving the difference in KO probability only to the third, conditional piece. So now we have two things to consider. First, vol of vol will curve the vol surface of forward starting options, as we saw for cliquets. In the same way that up and out barriers are short skew, down and outs are long, so we would expect forward starting vol curvature to increase the probability of knockout at t_2 *given* we're above the barrier at T_1. We might then expect that the probability of staying above the barrier would be reduced by vol of vol, increasing the overall KO probability. Life is not so simple of course. In order to calibrate, the local vol for out of the money levels needed to be suppressed, which in turn would increase the probability of staying above the barrier. It turns out that the latter effect wins in this case as we can see in Figure 4.57.

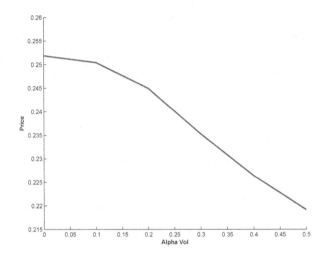

Fig. 4.57   150% 5Y one-touch prices as a function of α volatility, post-calibration.

Notice though that the effect of vol of vol is very much suppressed: the dominant effect on one-touch probabilities was indeed coming from spot starting vol surface curvature.

Now let's see how this works with skew. The uncalibrated curves for the difference between the price of an up and out barrier priced with SLV on a skewed surface with time invariant ATM vol of 20%, and a barrier priced with the same ATM vol but no skew (TV), are shown in Figure 4.58. Zero mean reversion of α has been assumed.

Notice the non-trivial effect of skew in the zero α vol line. For barriers close to the money, the negative slope of our surface increases the probability of KO, reducing the barrier price, whilst for deeply OTM barriers, the lower vol at the barrier decreases the KO probability, increasing the price. Negative vol skew is *not* always favourable to up and out no-touches. As we increase vol of vol, as we might expect from the one-touch curves, the probability of KO is reduced, increasing the value of the option. The post-calibration case is shown in Figure 4.59.

Again, as per the one-touch analysis the effect of calibration is to reduce the positive price impact of vol of vol, but by no means to zero, in contrast

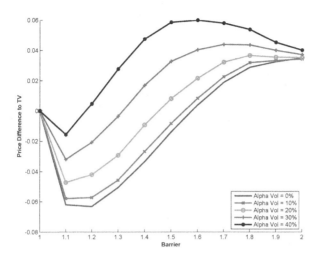

Fig. 4.58 5Y no-touch price differences to TV as a function of α volatility and barrier level, pre-calibration.

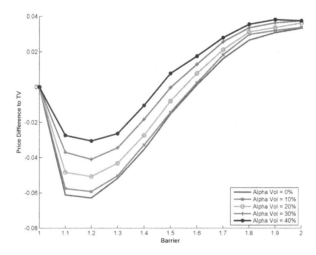

Fig. 4.59 5Y no-touch price differences to TV as a function of α volatility and barrier level, post-calibration.

with our experiments on dividend modelling. By way of interest, what would the 'rule of thumb' have given us? The vega, vol gamma and vanna profiles for the Black–Scholes barrier, are shown in Figures 4.60, 4.61 and 4.62 respectively.

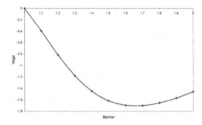

Fig. 4.60 Vega of a 5Y no-touch barrier, 20% vol, vs barrier level.

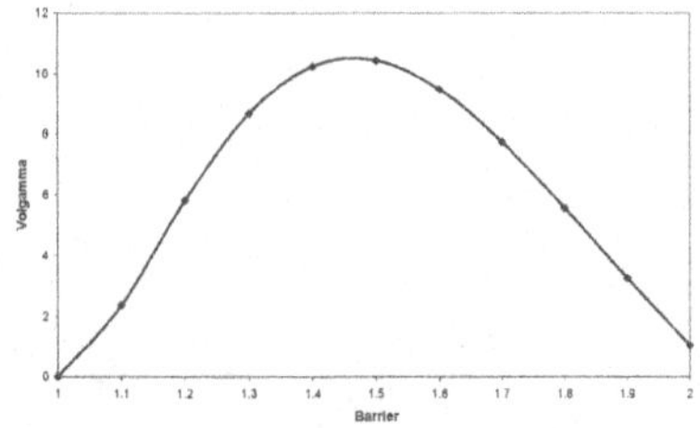

Fig. 4.61 Volgamma of a 5Y no-touch barrier, 20% vol, vs barrier level.

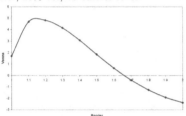

Fig. 4.62 Vanna of a 5Y no-touch barrier, 20% vol, vs barrier level.

For this surface, the effect of skew is mostly from the gradient, leaving little price impact from the butterfly premium. If we weight the risk reversal cost by $1 - p$, where p is the Black–Scholes probability of KO, we arrive at the price difference curve shown in Figure 4.63.

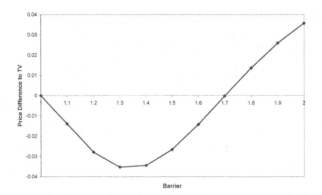

Fig. 4.63 5Y no-touch price differences to TV as a function of α volatility and barrier level, post-calibration.

The rule of thumb seems to perform quite well, though it noticeably over-estimates the no-touch price relative to local vol for close to the money barriers. Such a discrepancy is well-known, and has been commented on for other popular FX barriers such as double no-touches (DNT) [Lipton and McGhee (2002)]. Another way of putting this is to say that traders are pricing in an additional vol of vol charge over and above local vol. This is actually quite tantalising, as comparison with Figure 4.59 would suggest that the SLV model could be calibrated quite successfully to barrier prices, assuming that such a rule of thumb had been used to come up with those prices in the first place. This is indeed what is done in the forex market, where simple barrier options on actively traded currency pairs (e.g. USD/JPY) are liquid enough to provide a sound basis for stochastic vol calibration [Jex *et al.* (1999)]. At the time of writing, however, the market in simple equity barriers is not yet deep enough to perform this calibration reliably.

4.8 But does it make sense?

We have seen how three significant exotic product areas react to model assumptions on volatility, but is the approach in fact consistent? Recall, from the analysis of historical data on the S&P500 and VIX that a local vol surface constructed along the lines of the CEV model with a strongly negative exponent, together with a further stochastic factor for modelling the residuals around this, appeared to be a good representation of reality. Inspired by this, we refined the approach to calibrate a local vol surface together with an idiosyncratic factor α to European vol surfaces exactly. Note though that there's a problem here. The CEV process predicted a finite probability of the S&P500 hitting zero. Our model is inherently a locally log-normal *diffusion*, and so should always have identically *zero* probability of hitting zero. We propose, and will investigate further in Chapter 6, that our historical data was not in fact purely diffusive, but contained a strong jump element which gave an *effective* local vol with a CEV exponent of around -3. Another possible indication that this might be the case comes from revisiting the problem of implied volatility dynamics, discussed in Chapter 2. Supposing we adopt the same exercise for SLV. The results for a 5Y implied volatility slice for 10% up move in spot, whilst preserving the original calibrated local volatility surface with 30% vol of α and zero mean reversion, are shown in Figure 4.64.

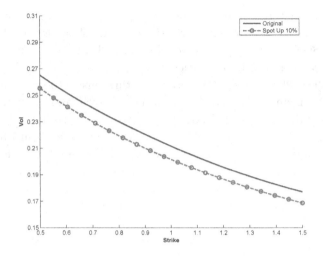

Fig. 4.64   5Y implied vol surface, original vs 10% spot move, 30% α vol.

The results are qualitatively similar to regular local volatility. This has been commented on in the literature [Dupire (2005); Bergomi (2004, 2009)], and essentially derives from the fact that we've calibrated to the Dupire local volatility surface[11]. Whilst the dynamics of forward skew are indeed very different between local volatility and SLV, the dynamics of spot skew, for a diffusion, are driven by the expectation of the local variance conditional on spot realisation, i.e. the Dupire local variance. If we want to get anything more like the market observed implied volatility dynamics, it would appear that we're going to need a non-diffusive approach.

4.9   Conclusions

In this chapter we looked at the behaviour of local and implied volatilities, and attempted to derive a model which captured some of those dynamics. In the process, we were able to quantify the effect of volatility modelling assumptions on three products of interest: options on realised volatility, options on implied volatility (cliquets) and one-touch and no-touch bar-

---

[11]Strictly speaking, the implied volatility dynamics of local and stochastic volatility models calibrated to the same implied volatility surface become *identical* in the limit of short maturity (compared to the inverse of the volatility mean reversion rate) and low skew [Bergomi (2004)]. The example here is for a rather long maturity, by conventional standards, but illustrates the point nonetheless.

rier options. Whilst this enabled us to develop some intuition as to where volatility modelling can be important, and why, it threw up a whole new problem: is diffusion sufficient as a model for the equity derivatives market? In the next section we'll look at the coarsest deviation from diffusive behaviour: default.

4.10 Exercises

(1) Show, that for a log-normal process X_T whose mean is $\overline{X}_T$, and whose log variance is Ξ_T^2 that the expectation of $\sqrt{X_T}$ is given by:
$$E[\sqrt{X_T}] = \overline{X}_T^{1/2} \exp[-\Xi_T^2/8]$$

(2) Demonstrate, for the Ornstein–Uhlenbeck process in (4.12), whose initial value is zero, that α_t is given by:

$$\alpha(t) = -\frac{\xi^2}{2\kappa}\left(1 - e^{-2\kappa t}\right) + \int_0^t \xi e^{\kappa(s-t)} dW_s$$

Use this result to show that the serial covariance between $x_i = e^{\alpha(t_i)}$ and $x_j = e^{\alpha(t_j)}$ is given by:

$$
\begin{aligned}
\langle (x_i - \bar{x}_i)(x_j - \bar{x}_j) \rangle &= \exp\left[-2\beta\left(2 - e^{-2\kappa t_i} - e^{-2\kappa t_j}\right)\right] \\
&\quad \times \exp\left[\beta\left[1 + e^{-\kappa(t_j - t_i)}\right]^2\left(1 - e^{-2\kappa t_i}\right)\right. \\
&\qquad \left. + 1 - e^{-2\kappa(t_j - t_i)}\right] \\
&\quad - \exp\left[-\beta\left(2 - e^{-2\kappa t_i} - e^{-2\kappa t_j}\right)\right]
\end{aligned}
$$

with $\beta = \xi^2/4\kappa$.

(3) Consider the Hull–White volatility process:

$$\frac{dS_t}{S_t} = \mu dt + \sigma_t dW_t^S$$

$$\frac{dV_t}{V_t} = \lambda dt + \xi dW_t^V$$

$$V_t = \sigma_t^2$$

In the chapter, we worked under the simplifying assumption (as per Hull and White's original paper), that the variance and stock processes were uncorrelated. Now consider the more general case $E[dW_t^S dW_t^V] = \rho dt$.

Derive an integral expression for the undiscounted price of a call by considering the distribution of the stock conditional on realised variance.

(4) Using a change of order of integration between strike and spot, demonstrate that the expectation of the variance swap log payoff $V = \log(F(T)/S_T) + \frac{S_T - F_T}{F_T}$ reduces to the $1/K^2$ weighted replication formula given in (4.21). By substituting $z = \log(F/K)$ derive (4.23), and hence demonstrate that the delta of a variance swap at instantiation will be identically zero if and only if the vol surface is fixed in z space (sticky-delta move). Demonstrate that this is equivalent to the surface being fixed as a function of Δ.

(5) Show that, for constant drift μ and volatility σ, and zero discount rate, that the price of an up and in one-touch option, barrier height $B \geq S$, maturity T is given by:

$$1 - N(-d_2) + \left(\frac{B}{S}\right)^{(2\mu/\sigma^2 - 1)} N(d_1')$$

where

$$d_1' = \frac{\log(S/B) - \mu T}{\sigma\sqrt{T}} + \frac{\sigma\sqrt{T}}{2}$$

$$d_2 = \frac{\log(S/B) + \mu T}{\sigma\sqrt{T}} - \frac{\sigma\sqrt{T}}{2}$$

(Use (3.17) for the joint density of the terminal spot for a constant drift Brownian motion and its maximum over the interval of the trade.) Show that the vega of this option is given by:

$$\mathcal{V} = -\frac{n(d_2)d_1}{\sigma} - \frac{n(d_1')d_2'}{\sigma}\left(\frac{B}{S}\right)^{(2\mu/\sigma^2 - 1)}$$
$$- \frac{4\mu}{\sigma^3}\log\left(\frac{B}{S}\right)\left(\frac{B}{S}\right)^{(2\mu/\sigma^2 - 1)} N(d_1')$$

where

$$d_2' = \frac{\log(S/B) - \mu T}{\sigma\sqrt{T}} - \frac{\sigma\sqrt{T}}{2}$$

$$d_1 = \frac{\log(S/B) + \mu T}{\sigma\sqrt{T}} + \frac{\sigma\sqrt{T}}{2}$$

Chapter 5

Default

Up until now, our discussion of model risk has been built on the premise that the dynamics of equity are diffusive, or at best a displaced diffusion (in the case of dividend modelling). This turns out to be a considerable over-simplification. In this chapter, we will look at the simplest deviation away from diffusion, namely jump to zero. Such behaviour is characteristic of stocks on companies which have, for one reason or another, defaulted on their debt obligations. The wave of bankruptcies in the credit crisis of 2008, and the following year, is well-known, but default is by no means a recent phenomenon. Figure 5.1 shows the global default rate, and relative default rates of investment grade and speculative grade companies globally. Speculative grade is defined as any company with a Standard & Poors credit rating of BB+ or below [Global Fixed Income Research (2010)].

In Figure 5.1, default is defined as:

- Missed interest or principal payments;
- Distressed exchange (the debt issuer offer bondholders a new security or package of securities amounting to a diminished financial obligation [Moody's (2000)]);
- Chapter 11 filings (federal bankruptcy in which the debtor remains in control of the business, subject to court oversight);
- Receivership;
- Debt re-organisation.

As we might expect, the correlation between default and economic recession (the 1987 crash, the 2001 dot-com crash and the 2008 credit crisis) is manifest. What was notable about the crisis of 2008, however, was the *level* of default. Figure 5.2 shows the total amount of debt defaulting over the same time period.

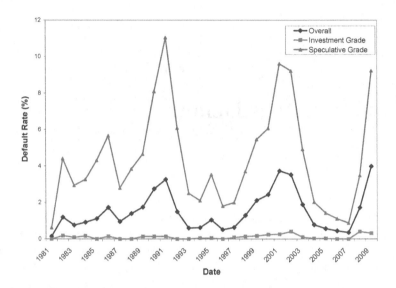

Fig. 5.1   Global default rate from 1981–2010.

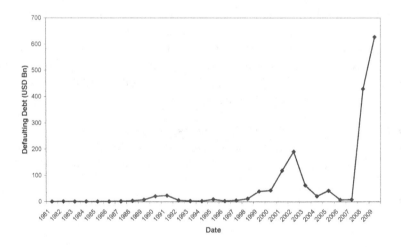

Fig. 5.2   Global amount of defaulting debt from 1981–2010.

Though the actual frequency of defaults during the 2008 crisis was not markedly different from 2001, the amount defaulting was around *three times* higher. One of the principal reasons for this was the explosion of activity in the credit derivatives market over the 2000–2008 period. For now let's take it as read that no company lasts for ever. Indeed, the lower rated the company, the longer the expected survival time, as shown in Figure 5.3 [Global Fixed Income Research (2010)].

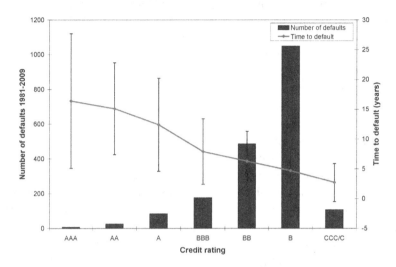

Fig. 5.3   Time to default and number of defaults vs S&P credit rating, 1981–2009.

This raises a number of critical questions, from a modelling standpoint:

- How should we model default?
- How can we hedge default?
- What impact does default have on the price of exotics, subject to option prices quoted in the vanilla market?

We will address each of these questions in turn.

5.1   How to model default

The problem of modelling default of a company essentially boils down to the following question: do we want to *explain* how and why default happens, or do we want to *price* it whilst calibrating as closely as possible to the price of observable market instruments? The first option lends itself to a class of models referred to as *structural models*, whilst the second is generally addressed with a *reduced form* model. In the former, a *mechanism* for the debt default of a firm is postulated, and that process fitted to market observables. In the second, the explanation of why the company has defaulted is put to one side, and a *process* for the default itself, wherever it may come from, is postulated and fitted to market observables. The problem with the first approach is that, whilst a consistent mechanism for default might, in principle, give us considerable predictive power for the price of debt over a wide variety of instruments of a given firm, in practice the degree of complexity required to match a relatively reduced set of market observables is considerable. Whilst a fit to the vanilla credit market is a reasonable proposition, a combined fit to the equity and credit markets is all but impossible. In contrast, as we are no longer bound by the framework of a structural mechanism in a reduced form model, the form of the drivers of the equity and credit processes can be as ugly as we like, provided they calibrate to vanillas. Of course, what we gain through calibration accuracy, we lose in explanatory power. Such a model might be a poor choice for a relative value arbitrageur, for example, attempting to determine if a particular bond is 'cheap' or 'expensive' relative to other bonds on the same company. The same model is exactly what we might need if our aim is to look at the model risk impact of default, *per se*, on the value of exotic equity, subject to our usual constraints of close calibration to the vanilla market. We will thus opt for the latter approach for the majority of this chapter, but will take a moment to summarise, albeit briefly, the development of structural models.

5.1.1   *Structural models of default*

In his seminal 1974 paper [Merton (1974)], Merton proposed the following. Let us consider the value of a firm's assets $V = E + B$, where E is the value of the firm's equity and B the value of its debt. Let us assume further that:

- The assets evolve according to a geometric Brownian motion at the risk-free rate;
- The firm can default only at a pre-determined horizon T given by the maturity of its debt obligations;
- The firm's debt pays no coupons;
- The liabilities outstanding are worth D today, and remain so through the life of the firm;
- Interest rates are deterministic.

These are some fairly heavy assumptions, but they have the huge advantage of quantitative tractability. Key to the model is the ansatz that, at maturity of the bonds T, their value will either be D, if the assets of the firm cover the payment, or simply V_T, corresponding to the break up value of the company upon bankruptcy. Correspondingly, the equity value of the firm must either be $V_T - D$, if the firm is still solvent, or zero. We thus have for the terminal value of the bond and equity:

$$B(T) = \min(V_T, D) \tag{5.1}$$
$$E(T) = \max(0, V_T - D) \tag{5.2}$$

This is quite powerful. If we can somehow calibrate the dynamics of the unobservable asset level V_t to the observable equity dynamics, given the current leverage ratio $L = D/V$ and the maturity of the firm's liabilities, then we should be able to predict the price of those liabilities today, together with their relation to the current equity level of the firm. Given the assumptions above, we can write for the asset dynamics:

$$\frac{dV_t}{V_t} = r(t)dt + \sigma_V dW_t^V$$

Then, from (5.2) we have:

$$E(0) = V(0)N(d_1) - De^{-\bar{r}T}N(d_2) \tag{5.3}$$
$$\bar{r} = \frac{1}{T}\int_0^T r(t)dt$$

But, from Itō's lemma we have:

$$dE = \left[\frac{\partial E}{\partial t} + \frac{1}{2}\frac{\partial^2 E}{\partial V^2}V^2\sigma_V(t)^2 + \frac{\partial E}{\partial V}Vr(t)\right]dt + \frac{\partial E}{\partial V}V\sigma_V(t)dW_t^V$$
$$= E\left[\mu_t^E dt + \sigma_E(t)dW_t^E\right]$$

So that by inspection of the Wiener term we can see that (a) the equity and the assets are perfectly correlated, and that (b) the asset volatility is given by:

$$\sigma_V = \sigma_E \frac{E(V)}{V\partial E/\partial V} = \sigma_E \frac{E}{VN(d_1)} \tag{5.4}$$

So, indeed, given the observed equity volatility σ_E, the equity level today E, and the level of debt of the firm D, we can simultaneously solve (5.3) and (5.4) to give V and σ_V, whence we can compute the value of the bonds of the firm from:

$$B(0) = V(0) - E(0)$$

Expressing this in yield terms $B(0) = \exp[-(\bar{r} + s)T]$ gives us an expression for the effective credit spread s through $s = -\log[B(0)]/T - \bar{r}$. Note also that the above assumed a flat equity volatility. This is not in fact essential, though it does obviously greatly ease calibration. The model is clearly a huge simplification of reality, but does come with the nice qualitative feature that the probability of default and the level of equity are inversely related. This is easy to see. If, for a given calibrated asset volatility, we raise the asset level, then the value of the embedded call against D will rise correspondingly. The probability of the firm's assets ending up below the strike will decrease and the value of the bond will rise also, lowering the effective credit spread. The converse is equally true. Whilst the qualitative features are encouraging, the quantitative results are less so. The assumption of default only at bond expiry is a powerful simplification. It effectively means that, for short-dated bonds where the firm is *de facto* still solvent, the probability of default tends to zero as the bond approaches zero maturity. Like this, the Merton model tends to underestimate credit spreads of shorter dated bonds [Altman *et al.* (2002); Eom *et al.* (2004)]. The first solution to this problem was to introduce the concept of a *default barrier*, allowing the firm to default if the assets fell below some barrier level at *any* point in the life of the bonds. Such approaches can be seen in the work of Hull and White [Hull and White (1995)], Kim, Ramaswamy and Sundaresen [Kim *et al.* (1993)] and Longstaff and Schwartz [Longstaff and Schwartz (1995)]. The original idea was proposed by Black and Cox [Black and Cox (1976)], with the work of Longstaff and Schwartz, and Kim, Ramaswamy and Sundaresen extending the approach to incorporate stochastic interest rates. In all of these approaches, the default barrier is taken to be *exogenous*, in that it is defined as a model input rather than derived intrinsically. Leland and Toft [Leland and Toft (1996)] proposed an *endogenous* model for the default barrier where (a) the firm is assumed to issue (continuous) coupon bearing debt at a continuous rate such that the outstanding debt at any one time is constant (the amount issued exactly compensating the amount retired) and (b) the bankruptcy trigger is determined as the point at which the change in the equity price over a time interval $[t, t + dt]$ just equals the additional cash flow that must be provided by equity holders to keep the firm solvent. In contrast to the Merton model, the Leland and Toft model tends to overpredict credit spreads, largely due to the assumption of a continuous coupon [Eom *et al.* (2004)]. The *CreditGrades* model of Finkelstein [Finkelstein (2002)] and Lardy [Lardy (2002)], relax the assumption of determinism of barrier, allowing it to take a log-normal distribution around some mean $\overline{L}$ with standard deviation λ. Such a model tends to do a better job of predicting short-dated credit spreads, as they allow the default barrier to take a level close to the value of the firm's assets at time zero with some non-zero probability. The other possible way of resolving the short-dated credit spread problem is to incorporate jumps on the asset [Lipton (2002a); Sepp (2006)].

Eventually, with enough parameters, we can do a pretty good job of matching the vanilla credit market. But what about the equity market? Calibration to equity *price* is of course given, but an equity option effectively becomes a *compound* option on the firm's assets, i.e. $E[(S_T - K, 0)^+] = E[(E[(V'_T - D, 0)^+|T] - K, 0)^+]$ with $T' > T$. The problem is that, once we've gone through the involved process of calibrating our structural model to the credit market, the implied volatility of equity options is uniquely determined. We can of course introduce more parameters to try and accommodate this [Chen and Kou (2009); Lipton and Sepp (2009); Lipton and Rennie (2011)], but the increase in complexity tends to diminish the explanatory *raise d'être* of the model. Where a close fit to the equity implied vol surface is required for model risk analysis, it would seem that a different approach is needed.

5.1.2 *Reduced form models of default*

A reduced form model of default is essentially an approach which models the default event *directly*, rather than attempting to derive it from some mechanism on the firm. Numerous examples from the world of credit derivatives exist in the literature, notably Litterman and Iben [Litterman and Iben (1991)], Madan and Unal [Madan and Unal (1996)], Jarrow, Lando and Turnbull [Jarrow *et al.* (1997)] and Duffie and Singleton [Duffie and Singleton (1999)]. Most of these models take as model inputs: default-free interest rates, the recovery rate of bonds at default and a process for the probability of default. In the case of Jarrow, Lando and Turnbull, the latter is inferred from a Markov chain, defining the transition probabilities between different credit ratings, and the default state itself, created from a combination of ratings agency actuarial data (e.g. Moody's) and calibration to risky zero coupon bonds spanning the credit ratings underlying the Markov chain. Duffie and Singleton propose a continuous time process linking the default-free short rate process, and the product of the hazard rate and the loss fraction (a.k.a the *short spread*). The model is then fitted to corporate bond prices. Stochastic hazard rates, whilst undeniably of importance to equity modelling (e.g. [Overhaus *et al.* (2007)]), will not form the basis of discussion in this chapter. We will rather take one step back and address the question of the importance of default *at all*. To begin, let's define some basic credit concepts.

5.1.2.1   *Survival probability, hazard rates and basic credit instruments*

Credit modelling, as we have seen already, fundamentally addresses the problem of the effect of a company not surviving until the maturity of the instruments it issues. Let us define the probability of survival from time $t = 0$ to $t = \tau$ as $Q(\tau)$. Let us also define a *Poisson process* λ_τ, characterised by a *hazard rate* (a.k.a *default intensity*) according to the relation:

$$Q(\tau + d\tau) = Q(\tau)(1 - \lambda_\tau d\tau) \qquad (5.5)$$

In other words, the hazard rate at time τ, multiplied by a *small* time interval, gives us the probability of defaulting *given* survival up to time τ. The relation is in fact the small time limit of the probability of one Poisson distributed event occurring over the interval $[\tau, \tau + d\tau]$. In general, for a piecewise flat intensity λ over the interval $[t_i, t_{i+1}]$, the probability of n such events occurring over the period is given by:

$$p_n(t_i, t_{i+1}) = \frac{\lambda^n (t_{i+1} - t_i)^n}{n!} e^{-\lambda(t_{i+1} - t_i)}$$

(which can be proven from the property that each event is independent and identically distributed (i.i.d), and that the expected number of events over the interval is $\lambda(t_{i+1} - t_i)$ (see exercise)). Clearly, in the limit of small $\Delta t = t_{i+1} - t_i$, the probability of all but one event becomes negligible, with the latter reducing to $\lambda \Delta t$. Equation (5.5) gives:

$$\lambda_\tau = -\frac{\partial}{\partial \tau} \log[Q(\tau)]$$

Trivially, as $0 \leq Q(\tau) \leq 1 \ \forall \ \tau$, $\lambda_\tau \geq 0$, $\forall \ \tau$: a strong no arbitrage constraint for any reduced form credit model incorporating stochastic hazard rates. To say something about the default process, we need to be able to measure a survival probability curve. There are as many ways of doing this as there are vanilla credit instruments. One might, for example use:

- Risky zero coupon bonds, valued at $\tilde{P}(T) = P(T)Q(T)$, where $P(T)$ corresponds to the risk-free bond;
- Asset swaps;
- Credit default swaps;

and numerous other instruments. In an asset swap, a bond is exchanged for a floating interest rate leg (London Interbank Offered Rate (Libor) + spread on the coupon dates in question), plus unity at strike date. Whilst not a credit derivative in the strict sense of an instrument whose payoff is linked to default events, it does serve as a means of replacing pre-default payoff streams with a uniform Libor stream. The seller of the swap bears full default risk. In the event of default the swap will either have to be serviced at a loss, or unwound at market value. As the spread is set to ensure that the package has an initial value of one (so that the whole swap is entered into at zero cost), the resultant asset swap spread is given by [Schönbucher (2003)]:

$$s^A(T) = \frac{P(T) - \tilde{P}(T)}{dv01(T)}$$

$$dv01(T) = \sum_{i=1}^{N} dcf(t_{i-1}, t_i)P(t_i); \ t_N = T$$

Like this, the survival probability curve can be backed out from the asset swap spread curve as:

$$Q(T) = 1 - \frac{s^A(T)dv01(T)}{P(T)}$$

Unlike the asset swap, a credit default swap (CDS) *can* be used to hedge out default risk. The structure is as follows. At the start of the swap, no notionals are exchanged. Subsequently, at a regular set of coupon dates (typically semi-annually), one party, known as the protection buyer, pays a fixed coupon to the protection seller. The protection seller pays nothing until a default event occurs, at which point, two things can happen. If the CDS is physically settled, the protection buyer delivers bonds to the protection seller at their market value, in return for the *full* notional on the bond. If the swap is cash settled, a group of dealers are asked to provide quotes for the bond of the defaulted obligor, and an average taken after eliminating the outliers. The difference between notional and this averaged market value is then paid by the protection seller. A minor complication to this procedure is that, in addition, the protection buyer is required to pay the accrued coupon from the last fixing to the default date. Let us refer to the market value of the bond as the recovery value R, the coupon S and assume a series of n coupon dates $\{t_i\}$, $1 \le i \le n$, with t_0 denoting the valuation date. The value of the coupon stream (a.k.a the *premium leg*) is given by:

$$V_{premium} = S \sum_{i=1}^{N} dcf(t_{i-1}, t_i) Df(t_0, t_i) Q(t_i)$$

$$+ S \sum_{i=1}^{N} \int_{t_{i-1}}^{t_i} dcf(t_{i-1}, s) Df(t_0, s) Q(s) \lambda(s) ds \qquad (5.6)$$

where the first term corresponds to the payment conditional on survival, and the second the accrued payment conditional on default. $Df(t, t')$ refers to the discount factor between t and t'.

The value of the recovery payment (a.k.a *protection leg*) is given by:

$$V_{protection} = (1 - R) \int_{t_0}^{t_N} Df(t_0, s) Q(s) \lambda(s) ds \qquad (5.7)$$

Now, if we actually *know* what R is, and we have a traded coupons S in the market for a set of CDS contracts of increasing maturity (e.g. 1Y, 3Y, 5Y, 7Y, 10Y), then we can in principle bootstrap a survival probability curve to match those spreads, given that the par spread is that which makes $V_{premium} = V_{protection}$. Actually, the form of (5.6) and (5.7) is somewhat cumbersome. O'Kane and Turnbull [O'Kane and Turnbull (2003)] use the approximations:

$$V_{premium} = S \times RPV01$$

$$RPV01 = \sum_{i=1}^{N} dcf(t_{i-1}, t_i) Df(t_0, t_i) \times \left[Q(t_i) + \frac{1_{PA}}{2} (Q(t_{i-1}) - Q(t_i)) \right]$$

where 1_{PA} is 1 if the contract specifies that the accrued is to be paid on default and zero otherwise. They also approximate $V_{protection}$ as:

$$V_{protection} = (1 - R) \sum_{i=1}^{N} Df(t_0, t_i) [Q(t_{i-1}) - Q(t_i)]$$

Giving us the somewhat more tractable expression for the par spread:

$$S = \frac{(1-R)\sum_{i=1}^{N} Df(t_0,t_i)\,[Q(t_{i-1})-Q(t_i)]}{RPV01} \tag{5.8}$$

A distribution of typical par spreads is shown in Figure 5.4.

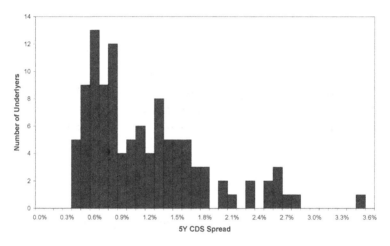

Fig. 5.4 Distribution of par spreads amongst investment grade US corporates (CDX.NS.IG), September 2010.

So this is great: we have an instrument we can use, very cleanly, to hedge against default, and that same instrument can supply us with the information we need to build a *market implied* survival curve, on which we can then build a reduced form default model. The problem of course is that we don't know what the recovery rate is. In practice most dealers use rating agency recovery rate data as a guideline, with the caveat that these rates [O'Kane and Turnbull (2003)] (a) do not view restructuring as a default event (unlike a CDS), (b) are heavily biased towards US corporates, where most of the data originates, (c) are based on historical analysis, and (d) are not name or sector specific. One way to get round this is to trade a *recovery swap*, which swaps the real recovery on the underlyer with a rate agreed today. Assuming that recovery and default are uncorrelated (a common, albeit unrealistic assumption), we can replace R in (5.8) with this agreed rate (effectively the *recovery forward*). At the time of writing, however, the market for these instruments is still dwarfed by the market for credit default swaps. The other solution to the problem of course is to trade a fixed recovery CDS. Again though, these tend to be the exception rather than the norm [Whetten (2006)].

Before we leave the discussion, a quick observation. If we assume that the coupon on the CDS is paid *continuously* at a rate s, and that hazard rates are flat, (5.6) and (5.7) greatly simplify:

$$V_{premium} = s \int_0^T e^{-(\lambda + \bar{r}(t))t} dt$$

$$V_{protection} = \lambda(1 - R) \int_0^T e^{-(\lambda + \bar{r}(t))t} dt$$

whence we arrive at the simple relation $s = \lambda(1 - R)$. We will return to this expression in the next section, when we come to look at the observed correlation between hazard rates and equity, implied by the correlation between CDS spreads and the latter.

5.2   The Andersen–Buffum model

Armed with the machinery to compute default probabilities from the credit market, let us now proceed to develop a reduced form model for equity subject to default. We will consider a very simple extension to the local volatility model:

$$\frac{dS_t}{S_t} = \mu(t)dt + \sigma(S,t)dW_t - dN_t$$

where dN_t can take a value of zero or one over the interval $[t, t+dt]$ according to a Poisson distribution with mean and variance $\lambda_t dt$, and is independent of dW_t. Before we discuss the form the hazard rate λ_t can take, let us first consider how to value options in this paradigm. Unlike a Merton jump process where the magnitude of the jump size itself takes on a continuous distribution (see Chapter 6), a jump to zero process has the great advantage that it can, in principal, be hedged perfectly. The argument follows the same pattern of reasoning used for stochastic volatility in the previous chapter, except that in this case, the second stochastic driver that we need to hedge against is non-diffusive. As before, consider constructing a portfolio $\Pi_t = V_t + \alpha S_t + \beta V_t' + \gamma B_t$ from a position in stock S_t, bond B_t and another option V_t'. For simplicity, we will assume zero dividends. We have for the evolution of the portfolio:

$$dΠ_t = dΠ_t|_{survival}(1 - dN_t) + dΠ_t|_{default}dN_t$$

where $dΠ_t|_{survival}$ denotes the change in the value of the portfolio conditional on survival and $dΠ_t|_{default}$ the change conditional on default. The first term is given by:

$$dΠ_t|_{survival} = \frac{\partial V}{\partial t}dt + \frac{\partial V}{\partial S}dS_t + \frac{1}{2}\frac{\partial^2 V}{\partial S^2}dS_t^2 +$$
$$αdS_t + β\left[\frac{\partial V'}{\partial t}dt + \frac{\partial V'}{\partial S}dS_t + \frac{1}{2}\frac{\partial^2 V'}{\partial S^2}dS_t^2\right] +$$
$$γdB_t \tag{5.9}$$

Taking the portfolio to be entered into at zero cost, and remain at zero value through self-financing gives $γB_t = -(V_t + αS_t + βV_t')$. Elimination of the Wiener term dW_t then gives:

$$\frac{\partial V}{\partial S} + β\frac{\partial V'}{\partial S} = -α \tag{5.10}$$

This still leaves the default term. We have:

$$dΠ_t|_{default} = V_t^{def} - V_t + β\left(V_t'^{def} - V_t'\right) - αS_t$$

where the last term follows from the assumption that the stock jumps to zero on default. As $dt \to 0$, $E[dΠ_t|_{survival}dN_t] \sim O(dt^2)$, and hence can be ignored in the limit. To eliminate the risk from the Poisson jump term dN_t we simply require $dΠ_t|_{default} = 0$, giving:

$$β = \frac{-(V_t^{def} - V_t) + αS_t}{V_t'^{def} - V_t'} \tag{5.11}$$

Combining with (5.10), this gives for $β$:

$$β = -\frac{V_t^{def} - V_t + \frac{\partial V}{\partial S}S_t}{V_t'^{def} - V_t' + \frac{\partial V'}{\partial S}S_t} \tag{5.12}$$

Using the self-financing condition $d\Pi_t = 0$, and using $dW_t^2 \to dt$ in the limit of small dt, together with the expressions for α and γ, we can rearrange (5.9) to give:

$$\frac{\partial V}{\partial t} + \frac{1}{2}\frac{\partial^2 V}{\partial S^2} S^2 \sigma^2(S,t) - r(t)\left(V_t - \frac{\partial V}{\partial S}S_t\right) =$$
$$- \beta \left[\frac{\partial V'}{\partial t} + \frac{1}{2}\frac{\partial^2 V'}{\partial S^2} S^2 \sigma^2(S,t) - r(t)\left(V_t' - \frac{\partial V'}{\partial S}S_t\right)\right]$$

So that, combining finally with (5.12), as per stochastic volatility, we arrive at a consistent option hedging expression:

$$\frac{\frac{\partial V}{\partial t} + \frac{1}{2}\frac{\partial^2 V}{\partial S^2} S^2 \sigma^2(S,t) - r(t)(V_t - \frac{\partial V}{\partial S}S_t)}{V_t^{def} - V_t + \frac{\partial V}{\partial S}S_t} =$$
$$\frac{\left[\frac{\partial V'}{\partial t} + \frac{1}{2}\frac{\partial^2 V'}{\partial S^2} S^2 \sigma^2(S,t) - r(t)(V_t' - \frac{\partial V'}{\partial S}S_t)\right]}{V_t'^{def} - V_t' + \frac{\partial V'}{\partial S}S_t}$$

Again, we can re-write this in terms of some arbitrary parameter, $g(S_t, t)$:

$$\frac{\partial V}{\partial t} + \frac{1}{2}\frac{\partial^2 V}{\partial S^2} S^2 \sigma^2(S,t) - r(t)\left(V_t - \frac{\partial V}{\partial S}S_t\right) = g(S_t, t)\left[V_t^{def} - V_t + \frac{\partial V}{\partial S}S_t\right]$$
$$(5.13)$$

But now of course we have an instrument whose value we know from the survival probability, namely a risky zero coupon bond paying zero on default. Assuming a deterministic process for both rate and hazard rate, the value of the risky bond is just given by:

$$\tilde{P}(t,T) = \exp\left[-\int_t^T [\lambda(s) + r(s)]ds\right]$$

Inserting this into (5.13), using $P^{def}(t,T) = 0$, gives:

$$\lambda(t) = -g(S_t, t)$$

Unlike stochastic volatility, where we had infinite freedom to choose the volatility growth term consistently with a perfectly hedged portfolio, this is not true in the case of jump to default. We could happily extend the definition of the hazard rate to incorporate state dependence, but its functional form would need to be calibrated to the survival curve, as per the deterministic case. The corresponding backward equation for $g(S_t, t) = -\lambda(S_t, t)$ is given by:

$$\frac{\partial V}{\partial t} + \frac{1}{2}\frac{\partial^2 V}{\partial S^2}S^2\sigma^2(S, t) + [\mu(t) + \lambda(S_t, t)]\frac{\partial V}{\partial S}S_t =$$
$$[r(t) + \lambda(S_t, t)]V_t - \lambda(S_t, t)V_t^{def} \tag{5.14}$$

where we have generalised the riskless forward growth to $\mu(t)$. Before we move onto the problem of calibrating this model to European implied volatilities, let's pause for a few remarks:

(1) It is often said that jumps are 'unhedgeable'. When the magnitude of a jump, and the probability of its occurring, are known with certainty, this is clearly not true. Any option can be used to hedge the jumps consistently on the other option. Indeed, that option could simply be a risky bond. Consider the case of a simple call option. Suppose that, rather than investing the cash from the net proceeds of delta hedging the option and buying the option itself in a riskless bond, we had instead invested in a bond on the same company. In the absence of default, the accrual on our option + delta hedge would be exactly matched by the accrual on the bond. In the event of default, the entire portfolio would sum to zero. In either event then, the portfolio is self-financing. Jumps are technically unhedgeable when their magnitude is *uncertain*. In the case of a continuum of possible jump sizes, it turns out that the portfolio is hedgeable only in the limit of an *infinite* number of offsetting option hedges. We will explore this case in more detail in Chapter 6.

(2) European options still obey regular put-call parity. Reverting back to deterministic hazard rates for illustration, by simple change of discounting $r(t) \to r(t) + \lambda(t)$ we can see that the value of a call at $t = 0$ is given by:

$$C(K, T) = Q(T)Df(T)\widetilde{C}(K, T) \tag{5.15}$$

where

$$\widetilde{C}(K, T) = \widetilde{F}N(d_1) - KN(d_2)$$
$$\widetilde{F} = F/Q(T)$$

and $Q(T) = \exp\left[-\int_0^T \lambda(s)ds\right]$ is the survival probability to expiry, with $Df(T) = \exp\left[-\int_0^T r(s)ds\right]$, the corresponding riskless discount factor. Puts are slightly complicated by the fact that their recovery value is just strike discounted to the default time τ. We have the modified expression:

$$P(K,T) = Q(T)\widetilde{P}(K,T) + [1 - Q(T)]KDf(T) \qquad (5.16)$$

Combining with (5.15), this gives:

$$\begin{aligned}
C(K,T) - P(K,T) &= Q(T)Df(T)\left[\widetilde{C}(K,T) - \widetilde{P}(K,T)\right] \\
&\quad - (1 - Q(T))KDf(T) \\
&= Q(T)Df(T)[\widetilde{F} - K] - [1 - Q(T)]KDf(T) \\
&= Df(T)[F - K]
\end{aligned}$$

Thus, the non-zero default value of the put restores put-call parity[1]. The forward is unaffected, which is again clear by considering the hedge. Suppose we enter into a forward contract on a dividend-free risky asset. As before, we short the stock, but this time invest the proceeds in a riskless bond. Whether the stock defaults or not, we still have to buy it back at the forward price at expiry, ending in a net zero stock and cash position as normal. The fair price is transparently still Se^{rT}. Like that, if we back out implied volatilities from options on risky assets, we can still apply the regular Black–Scholes pricing formula off the riskless forward and obtain the *same* implied volatility for both calls and puts at the same level of moneyness (see exercise).

With respect to the second point, what would a surface driven by jump to zero look like? Let us consider the extreme example where the diffusion volatility is zero, and hazard rates are flat. Our equation for implied volatility would then read:

$$FN(d_1(\widehat{\sigma})) - KN(d_2(\widehat{\sigma})) = F - Ke^{-\lambda T}$$

For an ATM call, this would give us an effective ATM vol of $\widehat{\sigma}_0 = \lambda\sqrt{2\pi T}$. A forward valued deeply out of the money put, however, would be valued as

---

[1]The result continues to hold for spot dependent hazard rates, though the survival probability needs to be included in integral expressions for the call and put.

$K(1 - e^{-\lambda T})$. For that to be true, however, we'd need $d_2 \to N^{-1}(1 - e^{-\lambda T})$ as $K \to 0$, in which case the implied volatility would need to rise to infinity as $\sqrt{\log(F/K)}$ (see exercise). A representative surface is shown in Figure 5.5.

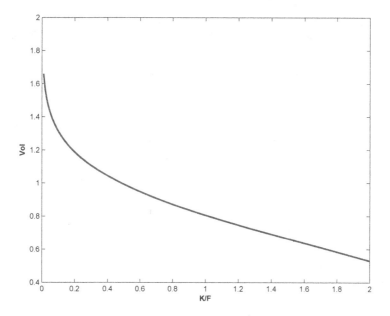

Fig. 5.5   Representative implied volatility surface from a pure jump to zero process.

Whilst the example is somewhat contrived, the interpretation is no less profound.

- Jump to zero generates its own volatility surface. As we introduce a non-zero probability of default, the overall level of the implied volatility surface should rise correspondingly, though in the limit of zero maturity, implied volatility should follow the diffusion vol (the ATM vol shift going as $\sim \sqrt{T}$).
- Jump to zero generates its own skew. Unsurprisingly, the effect enhances the implied volatility on the downside, and vice versa. Note, however, that the implied volatility of such a process, even with a non-zero diffusion vol, will *always* go to infinity as strike goes to zero. There is thus no way that a finite zero strike implied volatility extrapolation can be valid. Such a surface implies a zero probability of the stock ever

reaching zero, and can be immediately arbitraged through the credit market [Gatheral (2006)]. One simply needs to go long a regular put and short an equal amount of a bond paying the same strike in the event of default. If the put vol is below the minimum vol that can be obtained assuming zero diffusion vol, one would end up net long cash, the put having been sold too cheaply. In the event of default, the bond and put would exactly offset, leaving one still cash positive. There is, however, a caveat. Such strategies tend to look attractive based on the mid vol (generally the average of bid and ask vols, or the implied vol for the average of the bid and ask price). When the actual ask vol is used, though, the arbitrage may have vanished. Note also that the arbitrage is conditioned on knowing the survival probability to expiry. As remarked above, this is conditional on knowledge of the recovery of the associated credit instrument (commonly a CDS), which again is rarely true in practice.

The second point, however, is key to our understanding of how default impacts on model risk. In the previous chapters we were able to calibrate near perfectly to the entire volatility surface, assumed finite for all strikes. That very assumption (which incidentally is almost always used in the market) will limit the range of strikes over which we can actually calibrate our jump to zero process. Indeed, the higher the hazard rate, the worse that calibration will become. As we will see for the equity default swap market, such an effect can cause our intuition on the effect of jumps to zero on exotics to be badly wrong.

5.2.1   *Calibration*

Following the same methodology as Chapter 2, we have for the Green's function corresponding to (5.14) *conditional on survival*, that

$$
\begin{aligned}
\frac{\partial G(S_t, t; S_T, T)}{\partial T} = &-\frac{\partial}{\partial S_T}[(\mu(T) + \lambda(S_T, T))S_T G(S_t, t; S_T, T)] \\
&+\frac{1}{2}\frac{\partial^2}{\partial S_T^2}[\sigma^2(S_T, T)S_T^2 G(S_t, t; S_T, T)] \\
&-\lambda(S_T, T)G(S_t, t; S_T, T)
\end{aligned} \tag{5.17}
$$

(see exercise). Using:

$$\widetilde{C}(t, S_t; K, T) = \int (S_T - K)^+ G(S_t, t; S_T, T) dS_T$$

for the undiscounted risky call price, differentiating w.r.t T, and combining with (5.17):

$$\frac{\partial}{\partial T} \widetilde{C}(t, S_t; K, T) = \int -\lambda(S_T, T)(S_T - K)^+ G(S_t, t; S_T, T) dS_T$$

$$+ \int dS_T (S_T - K)^+ \left[-\frac{\partial}{\partial S_T} [(\mu(T) + \lambda(S_T, T)) S_T G(S_t, t; S_T, T)] \right.$$

$$\left. + \frac{1}{2} \frac{\partial^2}{\partial S_T^2} [\sigma^2(S_T, T) S_T^2 G(S_t, t; S_T, T)] \right]$$

(5.18)

Again, integrating by parts, the first derivative wrt S becomes:

$$- \int dS_T (S_T - K)^+ \frac{\partial}{\partial S_T} [(\mu(T) + \lambda(S_T, T)) S_T G(S_t, t; S_T, T)]$$

$$= \int dS_T \mathbf{1}(S_T - K)(\mu(T) + \lambda(S_T, T)) S_T G(S_t, t; S_T, T)$$

$$= \mu(T)\widetilde{C} - K\mu(T) \frac{\partial \widetilde{C}}{\partial K} + \int_K^\infty dS_T \lambda(S_T, T)(S - K) G(S_t, t; S_T, T)$$

$$+ K \int_K^\infty dS_T \lambda(S_T, T) G(S_t, t; S_T, T)$$

(5.19)

The second derivative becomes:

$$\frac{1}{2} \int dS_T (S_T - K)^+ \frac{\partial^2}{\partial S_T^2} [\sigma^2(S_T, T) S_T^2 G(S_t, t; S_T, T)] = \frac{1}{2} K^2 \sigma^2(K, T) \frac{\partial^2 \widetilde{C}}{\partial K^2}$$

(5.20)

where in (5.19) and (5.20) we have used:

$$\frac{\partial \widetilde{C}}{\partial K} = - \int_K^\infty G(S_t, t; S_T, T)$$

$$\frac{\partial^2 \widetilde{C}}{\partial K^2} = G(S_t, t; K, T)$$

Inserting (5.19) and (5.20) into (5.18) gives:

$$\frac{\partial}{\partial T}\widetilde{C}(t, S_t; K, T) = \mu(T)\widetilde{C} - K\mu(T)\frac{\partial \widetilde{C}}{\partial K} + \frac{1}{2}K^2\sigma^2(K, T)\frac{\partial^2 \widetilde{C}}{\partial K^2}$$
$$+ K \int_K^\infty dk\lambda(k, T)\frac{\partial^2 \widetilde{C}(t, S_t; k, T)}{\partial k^2}$$

So, the effect of jumps on local volatility calibration is essentially to add an extra term. Rearranging, we arrive at:

$$\sigma^2(K, T) = \sigma^2_{Dupire}(K, T) - \frac{2\int_K^\infty dk\lambda(k, T)\frac{\partial^2 \widetilde{C}(t, S_t; k, T)}{\partial k^2}}{K\frac{\partial^2 \widetilde{C}}{\partial K^2}} \qquad (5.21)$$
$$= \sigma^2_{Dupire}(K, T) - \Lambda(K, T)$$

Whilst the modification may seem trivial, its effect is profound. Though we may have started with a perfectly well-defined Dupire model, assuming no jump to default, the effect of jumps is to remove variance, until the revised local variance $\sigma^2(K, T)$ ultimately hits zero. This will always happen at sufficiently low strike, and is equivalent to the observation earlier that jump to zero will always result in infinite implied vol as strike goes to zero. Practically, all we can do to make the model work is floor the local volatility at zero, so that the process for spot lower than this boundary will be purely driven by default. When integrated back up, the effect on implied volatilities is to make them 'peel away' from the target implied vol surface, with the point of departure moving upwards with increasing hazard rate. This is shown in Figure 5.6.

Before we delve further into the effect of such behaviour on exotics, a brief comment on the form of the hazard rate function. In (5.21) we have employed a general, albeit deterministic relation between the hazard rate and spot. From the earlier discussion on structural models, we might expect that some sort of inverse relation between the two might be appropriate, and indeed, such a relationship is clearly seen in practice. Figure 5.7 shows the history of par spreads on Ford Motor Company (F.N) vs price, over the last decade. Both in the downturn of 2001, and the credit crisis of 2008, a clear inverse relationship is observed.

This is perhaps hardly surprising. As companies run into financial difficulty, in all likelihood the market will sell the stock, whilst the cost of borrowing for the company in question will rise as default is perceived by lenders as becoming more likely. That being said, such relationships tend

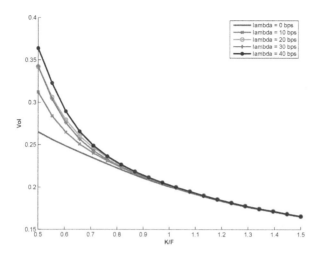

Fig. 5.6   The effect of hazard rates on calibrated implied volatility, 1Y expiry.

to be characteristic of distressed market conditions. A scatter of the normalised weekly log returns on 5Y CDS spreads vs normalised log returns
on stock is shown, again for Ford, in Figure 5.8[2].

Whilst there is a clear negative correlation, the scatter is still quite
wide. Nonetheless, users of Andersen–Buffum style jump to zero model
tend to allow for an inverse relationship between hazard rate and spot. For
example:

$$\lambda(S, t) = a + b/S^p \tag{5.22}$$

$$\lambda(S, t) = c - d \log S \tag{5.23}$$

$$\lambda(S, t) = e + f \exp(-gS) \tag{5.24}$$

$$\lambda(S, t) = c \left(\frac{S_0}{S} \right)^p \tag{5.25}$$

(5.22) is due to Takahashi *et al.* [Takahashi *et al.* (2001)], (5.23) is due to
Davis and Lischka [Davis and Lischka (1999)], (5.24) is due to Arvanitis and
Gregory [Arvanitis and Gregory (2003)], whilst (5.25) is due to Andersen
and Buffum [Andersen and Buffum (2002)]. In our initial investigations,

---

[2]Credit spreads tend to be quite 'sticky', holding at fixed levels for a small number of
business days. Like this, extending the sampling interval from daily to around a week
tends to be useful in reducing the de-correlating effect of constant spreads vs dynamic
spot movement. In effect, we have attempted to separate the jump component of credit
spreads from the diffusive part.

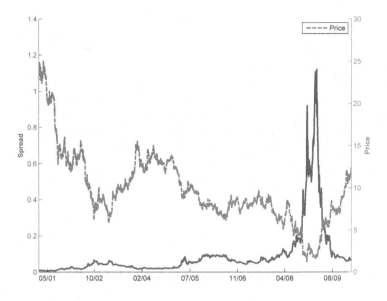

Fig. 5.7   5Y CDS spreads vs spot for F.N, 2000–2010.

we will take the hazard rate as being a function of time only. This is, first, to simplify analysis, but second, as noted earlier, because incorporation of spot dependence on the hazard rate requires an iterative procedure to correctly recover risky zero coupon bond prices subject to calibration to the equity implied volatility surface. We will revisit the issue in our analysis of convertible bonds (for which such a model was originally designed). To begin, however, let us consider one of the simplest products for which the effect of jump to zero is profound: the equity default swap.

5.3   Equity Default Swaps

Following the huge success of the credit default swap, an equity based variant, the equity default swap (EDS) was launched by JP Morgan in May 2005. Whilst the structure is formally similar to a CDS, namely periodic coupons until default, with recovery payment minus accrued coupon on default, the default event is quite different. Typically, an EDS treats default as occurring when the equity falls below 30% of its initial level. Unlike a CDS, the recovery level is also fixed, generally to 50% of notional. Like this, they remove both the ambiguity of default definition inherent in a

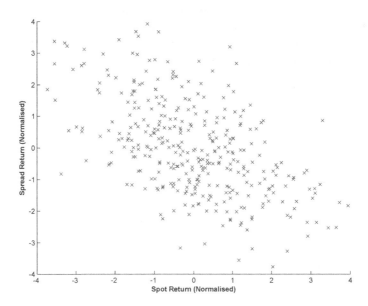

Fig. 5.8 Normalised weekly log returns for 5Y CDS spreads vs spot for F.N, 2000–2010.

CDS, and the problem of unknown recovery rates. Furthermore, as a drop of 70% in the stock price is a more likely, albeit drastic, event than the complete default of a company, EDS tend to command higher spreads than CDS. If, on the other hand, the EDS default event is concomitant with the CDS event, the discrepancy in spread provides a source of relative value arbitrage. An investor, for example, could sell EDS protection and buy CDS protection on the same name. In the case of no default, the investor would gain from the net positive coupon. In the case of default, provided the CDS recovery were less than 50% the investor would still make money. The risk, in such a strategy, is that the equity default is not in fact accompanied by a credit default, or that the events occur together, but CDS recovery is greater than 50%.

A significant amount of work was published on the pricing of such an instrument, notably by Albanese and Chen [Albanese and Chen (2005)]. In their paper, the authors compare the pricing of an EDS from a jump model of credit quality, with a purely diffusive CEV process (see Chapter 4), both calibrated to the credit market. They demonstrate that the pure diffusion, CEV model tends to result in the sorts of high ratios of EDS spread to CDS spread seen in the market, whilst the credit quality model (referred to as the 'credit barrier model') results in ratios of at most 2:1. On this basis they conclude that, at the time of writing (2005), the market was still pricing the EDS from simple local volatility models. The data set on which they based this conclusion is shown in Figure 5.9[3].

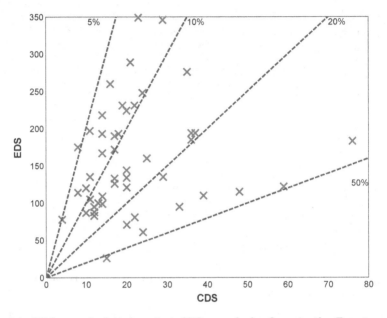

Fig. 5.9   EDS spread plotted against CDS spreads for firms in the Eurostoxx 50, 4th August 2004. Dotted lines show lines of constant EDS to CDS spread ratio.

Let's see how the extension to jump to zero affects the value of an EDS. For simplicity, we will focus first on the value of the protection leg. Our intuition on this might be quite simple. Surely, as we increase the probability of jump to zero, the value of this leg should increase correspondingly. Indeed, *before calibration* to the implied volatility surface, this is the case, as shown in Figure 5.10, for a semi-annual EDS on a stock with no dividends and constant vol skew corresponding to Figure 5.6.

Post-calibration, however, life is not so simple. The price for the protection leg, as we increase hazard rates is shown in Figure 5.11.

Surprisingly, the value of the protection leg actually goes *down* for low hazard rates, and then indeed starts rising for higher hazard rates. The way to understand this is to refer back to the conditional probability arguments

---

[3]Reprinted with kind permission of the author.

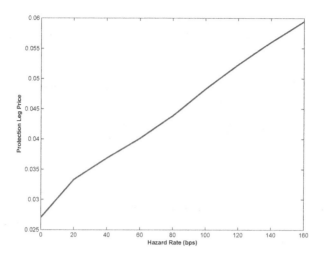

Fig. 5.10 5Y EDS protection leg, vs hazard rate, constant vol skew, no dividends, pre-calibration.

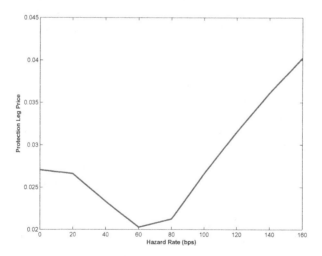

Fig. 5.11 5Y EDS protection leg, vs hazard rate, constant vol skew, no dividends, post-calibration.

for barriers used in Chapter 4. Suppose we again consider the simple two fixing barrier. We have for the down and out knock-in probability:

$$p(KO) = p(S(T_1) < B \cup S(T_2) < B) =$$
$$p(S(T_2) < B) + p(S(T_2) < B) - p(S(T_1) < B \cap S(T_2) < B)$$
$$(5.26)$$

Now, for sufficiently low hazard rates, the vol surface should be well calibrated down to the barrier level, so that the first two terms are unchanged. On the other hand, we know from (5.21) that the local volatility for low spot levels must be suppressed by the effects of default. Like this, the probability of the stock falling below the barrier *and staying below the barrier*, should be enhanced, thereby subtracting from the KO probability $p(KO)$ and reducing the price of the protection leg. Conversely, when hazard rates are sufficiently high, the 'peeling away' effect on the vol surface at low strikes kicks in, increasing the value of digital puts struck at these deeply out of the money levels. Meanwhile, the last term tends to unity, as local volatility below the barrier tends to zero, so that knockout probability increases consistently with the increase in the first two terms, both of which tends to unity themselves, taking the overall knockout probability itself to unity. Of course, our expectation that jump to zero would have a profound effect, given the low probability of the simple diffusion breaching the 30% barrier, was correct, but exactly where the effect kicks in has proven to be more subtle. Whilst these products did not in fact meet with the popularity expected at the time of their invention, they do serve as a nice example of the sometimes counter-intuitive nature of model risk.

Putting back in the premium leg, we can solve for the coupon which results in zero cost, a.k.a 'par spread'. We can solve similarly for the corresponding CDS, using (5.8), allowing us to plot one spread vs the other. As discussed, given that a jump to zero will necessarily include a jump through the 30% barrier, but not vice versa, we would always expect the EDS par spread to exceed that of the CDS. For the uncalibrated case, this is manifestly true, as shown in Figure 5.12.

The ratio of EDS par spread to CDS par spread goes from infinite, at zero hazard rate, to around 2:1, for hazard rates of around 160 bps. When we introduce calibration to implied vols, however, the EDS par spreads are suppressed in keeping with the initial reduced probability of knock-out for low CDS spreads, and then increase as we might have expected for high CDS spreads (Figure 5.13).

There is an interesting observation to be made here. For the calibrated model, the suppression of local volatility to zero for spots around the knock-out barrier suggests that the dynamics of down and out knockout are almost

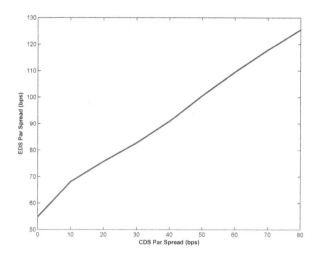

Fig. 5.12 5Y EDS par spread vs 5Y CDS par spread, constant vol skew, no dividends, pre-calibration.

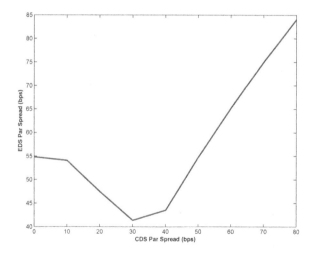

Fig. 5.13 5Y EDS par spread vs 5Y CDS par spread, constant vol skew, no dividends, post-calibration.

exclusively driven by jump to zero. Like this, the EDS par spread should quickly tend to the CDS par spread, as indeed in Figure 5.13. Referring back to the market picture from 2004 in Figure 5.9, however, it seems that, at the time these products went to market, the ratio of spreads was bounded below by 2:1, in line with Figure 5.12. Had the market not priced in default at all for the EDS, one might have expected a wide distribution of EDS spreads at *any* CDS spread level, upwards of the 2:1 ratio. It appears, however, that spreads were in fact drawn to this ratio for high spread stocks. Had the market *calibrated* a jump to default model to the implied volatility surface, we might have expected the ratio be drawn to 1:1, rather than 2:1. Like this, it seems reasonable to infer that, whether directly through a jump to zero process, or indirectly via CEV, or structural models, EDS on high spread stocks were pricing in jump to zero, but not consistently with the implied volatility market.

5.4   Convertible Bonds

The previous discussion on equity default swaps could be considered as an example of *implicit* hybrid model risk, namely model risk to a market different to the market of the underlyer, credit in this case, where the payoff has no explicit dependance on that market. In this section we will consider *explicit* hybrid model risk to credit on a product where the payoff is a function both of a credit instrument, namely a risky corporate bond, and an equity one, namely the equity of the company in question. A convertible bond, fundamentally, consists of a regular corporate bond which can be converted into a certain number of shares, depending on the performance of the equity. In its simplest form, where conversion is only possible at expiration, and the bond pays only face value F at expiry, the product can be considered to be a combination of a bond and a regular call option on the equity:

$$P = \max(nS, F) = n \max(S - F/n, 0) + F \qquad (5.27)$$

Why would these products trade? A nice description of the rationale is provided by Derman [Derman (1994)]. From the point of view of the issuer, the bond provided a cheap source of debt financing. In effect, the company is selling call options on its own equity in exchange for a lower cost of debt. When the market levels and volatilities are high, the value of the embedded call illustrated in (5.27), and the corresponding reduction in the par coupon, can be substantial. The other commonly cited reason for issuing convertibles is as a means for delaying the issuance of actual equity, reducing dilution effects and circumventing regulatory hindrances [Nyborg (1996); Davis and Lischka (1999)]. From the holders point of view, the option has the same characteristics as a capital guarantee structure. The investor essentially pays a premium for protection against downside movements in the equity.

Equation (5.27), whilst useful as a limiting check of any given convertible bond model, is rather too simplistic in practice. In general, the bond is coupon bearing, and the conversion possible at *any* time during the life, i.e. its conversion is 'American', in the option sense of the word. A common further complication is that the bond can be called by the issuer, at some predefined level, or sold back ('put') by the holder, at another level. The former will always cheapen the bond, whilst the latter will always make it more expensive. In practice, the issuer is generally prevented from calling the bond until a prespecified period has elapsed. Such bonds are said to be 'call-protected'. Further variants again include, amongst many others, bonds where:

- Conversion is mandatory at expiry.
- The conversion ratio can be reset during the life, based on the performance of the equity (a.k.a. *resettables*). Such structures have seen marked popularity in Japan.
- The bond can only be called by the issuer if the stock trades above some level, a.k.a 'contingent calls'. In a further variant, the stock may have to remain above this level for a predefined number of days (a.k.a. *soft calls*).
- The conversion ratio can be reset according to the difference between a pre-agreed dividend amount, and the realised dividend or the difference passed through to the convertible bond holder. Such agreements are designed to mitigate dividend risk.
- Any unrealised coupons on the bond are paid to the issuer on conversion (a.k.a *make wholes*).
- The bond is issued by a third party, rather than the company itself. Such bonds, known as *exchangeables*, have the advantage that the payout is guaranteed by the third party, and hence tend to depend predominantly on the credit quality of the latter, rather than the company itself. As the third party tends to be of a higher credit quality than the underlyer, such bonds also tend to be more expensive. A full discussion of the product, along with an appropriate modelling approach is given by Overhaus *et al.* [Overhaus *et al.* (2007)].

For this section, we will limit our attention to the simple non-coupon bearing, American convertible bond, issued by the underlying company.

Before we apply the model used in the previous section, however, it's instructive to review the various approaches to convertible bond modelling which preceded it.

5.4.1 *A brief history of conversion*

Theoretical pricing models for convertible bonds first appeared in the 1960's [Ingersoll (1977)]. The general procedure was to set the payoff of the CB to be the maximum of the regular bond and common stock times the conversion ratio at some point in the future, and then discount back this value to the present. For examples, see Poensgen [Poensgen (1965)], Baumol, Malkiel and Quandt [Baumol *et al.* (1966)], Weil, Segal and Green [Weil *et al.* (1968)]. Such an approach, however, clearly fails to value the premium for being able to convert at *any* point in the life of the bond, and tends to undervalue the option. One of the first attempts at factoring in the American exercise condition, and also incidentally the callability by the issuer, was given by Ingersoll [Ingersoll (1977)]. In his approach, and similarly in the approach of Brennan and Schwartz [Brennan and Schwartz (1977)], the CB is considered as an option of the *assets* of the firm, rather than the equity directly, in keeping with the Merton structural model of default described earlier. However, as with other structural models, such an approach suffers from the problem that the firm value itself is not tradable, so that its dynamics have to be inferred from the observable dynamics of the derived equity and bond prices. Second, as pointed out by Jarrow and Turnbull [Jarrow and Turnbull (1995)], all corporate liabilities senior to the convertible at hand need to be valued at the same time. Such problems have made structural approaches inapplicable to the pricing of CBs in practice.

So began a series of papers attacking the problem of CB valuation from reduced form approaches. Essentially, the idea is to treat the option as a security contingent on stock price and interest rates. This is not without its difficulties. One of the first problems one hits in such an approach is *which* interest rate to use. Supposing that the equity has performed badly, so that the CB is almost certain to remain a bond. In this circumstance, the appropriate discount rate to apply to the option is clearly the risk-free rate plus the credit spread of the underlying bond. On the other hand, supposing the equity has performed well. In this circumstance the firm can always issue a share which can then be sold and the proceeds invested risk-free. The appropriate discount rate in the case of guaranteed conversion would then appear to be the risk-*free* rate. Derman [Derman (1994)] was one of the first to model this effect directly, referring to it as the *credit-adjusted discount rate*. The idea is simple, and lends itself immediately to the Cox–Ross–Rubinstein binomial tree method in vogue at the time. Suppose that, at a given node, the probability of conversion is P. We then define the credit-adjusted discount rate to be $y = Pr + (1 - P)(r + s)$, where r is the risk-free rate and s the credit spread. The algorithm then proceeds as follows:

(1) Build an N step binomial tree out to the maturity of the option that matches the conditional expectation of the stock process from time t_i to t_{i+1}, and the corresponding conditional volatility. The paper assumes state independent local volatility, though this is not in fact essential.

(2) Set the boundary condition of the CB at maturity t_N as $\max(nS, F)$, as per (5.27), and define the probability of conversion at node $S_{N,j}$ as $P_{N,j} = \mathbf{1}(S_{N,j} > F/n)$.

(3) Move backwards down the tree, slice by slice, using the backward induction relation for the conversion probability:

$$P_{i,j} = p_i P_{i+1,j+1} + (1 - p_i) P_{i+1,j}$$

for a probability p_i of an up move $S_{i,j} \to S_{i+1,j+1}$ designed to satisfy the conditional expectation and variance of the stock price according to the standard binomial construction [Hull (2008)]. *The stock process is assumed to evolve according to the risk-free rate.*

(4) With the new set of conversion probabilities, compute the credit-adjusted discount factor at each node on the given time slice t_i, and compute the value of the convert at each node $S_{i,j}$ as the sum of cash flows occurring over $(t_i, t_{i+1}]$ and the probability weighted sum of the two nodes at $S_{i+1,j+1}$ and $S_{i+1,j}$, discounted by the computed discount rate at $S_{i,j}$.

(5) Compare the computed value against the value on conversion $nS_{i,j}$. If lower, replace with $nS_{i,j}$ and set the conversion probability $P_{i,j}$ to unity.

The scheme can readily be extended to callability and puttability, by ensuring further that the value of the convert $V_{i,j} \geq P$ for the put price P and $V_{i,j} \leq C$ for the call price (the holder will wish to maximise value, selling the bond for the pre-determined put price if the bond value falls below this level. The issuer will want, conversely, to minimise the payment to the holder, calling the bond if the value rises above the call level). If the holder has the choice of exercising on being called, the second condition would be modified to $V_{i,j} \leq \max(C, nS)$. If the bond is put, the conversion probability is set to zero, and likewise if on being called conversion is sub-optimal.

A different, but related approach was adopted by Tsiveriotis and Fernandes in 1998 [Tsiveriotis and Fernandes (1998)]. Maintaining the idea that the equity upside component of the convert has zero default risk, whilst the downside cash component should be discounted at the risky rate appropriate to the credit risk of the debt, they split the bond into an equity and cash only component, with different discount rates. Calling the convert u, and the 'cash only convertible bond' v, we have, from this argument (adding in a coupon stream $\{c_i\}$ on the cash piece):

$$\frac{\partial}{\partial t}(u - v) + \frac{\sigma^2 S^2}{2} \frac{\partial^2}{\partial S^2}(u - v) + (r - q)S \frac{\partial}{\partial S}(u - v) = r(u - v) \tag{5.28}$$

$$\frac{\partial v}{\partial t}v + \frac{\sigma^2 S^2}{2} \frac{\partial^2 v}{\partial S^2} + (r - q)S \frac{\partial v}{\partial S} - f(t) = (r + s)v \tag{5.29}$$

$$f(t) = \sum_i c_i \delta(t - t_i)$$

Adding (5.29) to (5.28) gives:

$$\frac{\partial u}{\partial t} + \frac{1}{2}\sigma^2 S^2 \frac{\partial^2 u}{\partial S^2} + (r - q)S \frac{\partial u}{\partial S} - f(t) = r(u - v) + (r + s)v$$

$$\frac{\partial v}{\partial t} + \frac{1}{2}\sigma^2 S^2 \frac{\partial^2 v}{\partial S^2} + (r - q)S \frac{\partial v}{\partial S} - f(t) = (r + s)v$$

$$f(t) = \sum c_i \delta(t - t_i)$$

Effectively forming a set of coupled PDEs in u and v. In the spirit of v being cash *only*, the terminal boundary condition is then specified as:

$$u(S, T) = \begin{cases} aS & S \geq F/n \\ F & otherwise \end{cases}$$

and

$$v(S, T) = \begin{cases} 0 & S \geq F/n \\ F & otherwise \end{cases}$$

During the life $0 \leq t < T$, we have further for conversion:

$$u \geq nS$$
$$v = 0 \text{ if } u < nS$$

Upside constraints for callability at B_c over $T_c \leq t < T$, where it is assumed that the holder will convert at the maximum of B_c and nS:

$$u \leq \max(B_c, nS)$$
$$v = 0 \text{ if } u \geq B_c$$

and downside constraints for puttability at B_p over $T_p \leq t < T$

$$u \geq B_p$$
$$v = B_p \text{ if } u \leq B_p$$

where it assumed that cash only is transferred when the holder puts back the option.

Owing to its relative simplicity, and ability to incorporate the main characteristics of convertibles for which market data might be limited, the Tsiveriotis–Fernandes model (which we shall refer to as the TF model) became a popular choice amongst banks and several software vendors. However, whilst conceptually simple, the model is internally inconsistent. Ayache *et al.* [Ayache *et al.* (2003)] demonstrate that a hedge portfolio constructed along the lines of (5.9) cannot in fact be simultaneously self-financing and risk-neutral. The corollary of this, which the authors also demonstrate, is that the expected losses on the convertible due to default in the TF model are not compensated by the expected gains without default. The reason is essentially that the TF model simply sets out to model the expected characteristics of default, rather than address them through a first principles hedging model. One of the first attempts at constructing an internally consistent approach to default was presented by Takahashi *et al.* [Takahashi *et al.* (2001)], inspired by the Duffie–Singleton reduced form approach to credit derivatives. In their model, they assume (a) constant local volatility, (b) a state dependent hazard rate, and (c) a recovery value for the convert proportional to the pre-default value, and (d) a jump to zero of the stock in the event of default, giving:

$$\frac{\partial V}{\partial t} + [\alpha(S,t) + \lambda(S,t)]\, S \frac{\partial V}{\partial S} + \frac{1}{2}\sigma^2 S^2 \frac{\partial^2 V}{\partial S^2} + f(t) = [r(t) + L\lambda(S,t)]\, V$$

with $\alpha(S,t)$ corresponding to the local risk-free spot growth, L the loss given default, and $f(t)$ the term due to coupons, as per the TF model. They employ a hazard rate function:

$$\lambda(S,t) = \theta + \frac{c}{S^b}$$

and attempt to calibrate the exponent b by matching market prices of regular bonds, assuming levels for L, θ and c. Such an approach includes the modification to the stock growth $\lambda(S,t)$ given by risk-neutral self-financing portfolio construction, but suffers from the constant volatility assumption. Where European single stock option data is lacking (as indeed is the case in Japan), so much so that the implied option volatility is effectively driven by the convertible market rather than the options market, such an approach is not without its merits. However, it is not a reasonable approach for model risk analysis where European option data is assumed. The solution to this problem is given by allowing the local volatility to become state dependent, as per the Andersen–Buffum model of 2002 described in detail in Section 5.2.

So, after around thirty years of model development, we find ourselves in a position to calculate the price of convertibles consistently with both the well developed equity and credit markets. Before we illustrate the effects of the Andersen–Buffum model on a variety of different convertibles, a note about recovery and jump to zero.

Ayache *et al.* [Ayache *et al.* (2003)] derive a more general PDE for the valuation of a convertible on a stock whose post-default level $S^+ = S^-(1-\eta)$ and where the holder has the option to convert on default as:

$$\mathcal{MV} = -\lambda \max(nS(1-\eta), RX)$$

where

$$\mathcal{MV} = V_t + \frac{\sigma^2}{2}S^2 V_{SS} + (r(t) - q(t) + \lambda\eta)SV_S - (r(t) + \lambda)V$$

using the shorthand notation V_x to denote $\partial V/\partial x$. Their formulation assumes constant volatility and hazard rate, but the expression generalises immediately to spot and time dependence. A jump to a non-zero value of default can also easily be incorporated into the Andersen–Buffum framework, but will form part of the generalisation to uncertain jump size in the next chapter. The question of recovery RX, however, is interesting in the context of this chapter. The simplest approach is to assume, as per Duffie and Singleton, that $RX = (1 - L)V$ (referred to a *recovery of market value* by Overhaus *et al.* [Overhaus *et al.* (2007)]). In the absence of conversion on default, this allows us to write:

$$\mathcal{M}'V = 0$$

where

$$\mathcal{M}'V = V_t + \frac{\sigma^2}{2}S^2 V_{SS} + (r(t) - q(t) + \lambda\eta)SV_S - (r(t) + \lambda L)V$$

Such an approach has the advantage of mathematical elegance, but appears not to be consistent with bankruptcy proceedings [Andersen and Buffum (2002)]. Another reasonably simple alternative is recovery of face value, which we can solve for by introducing a simple 'source term' $-\lambda\max(nS(1 - \eta), RF)$ into a one-dimensional PDE solver. The more complicated assumption we can make is that the recovery is proportional to the pre-default *bond component* of the convertible B. Such an approach leads to the equity-bond decoupling scheme seen in the TF model. Writing the convertible value V as the sum of the equity value C and the bond value B, Ayache *et al.* demonstrate that such a scheme can be solved using the coupled PDEs:

$$\mathcal{M}C + \lambda\max(nS(1 - \eta) - RB, 0) = 0$$

subject to the constraints:

$$B + C \leq \max(B_c, nS)$$
$$B + C \geq nS$$

and

$$\mathcal{M}B + \lambda RB = 0$$

subject to the constraints:

$$B \leq B_c$$
$$B + C \geq B_p$$

(where in their paper they also assume callability and puttability over the life of the option). As pointed out by Overhaus *et al.* [Overhaus *et al.* (2007)], the choice as to which approach to adopt depends on one's assumptions of what actually happens in the event of default. If the assumption is that default will result in a renegotiation of debts, a model based on the prevailing value of the convertible, or the embedded bond, might seem more appropriate. If on the other hand the assumption is that default corresponds to an actual bankruptcy, recovery on face value of the bond might be a more realistic model. As mentioned earlier in our discussion on credit default swaps, the actual level of recovery is in practice unknown, and a model which incorporates idiosyncratic recovery correlated with stock and hazard rate might be equally valid. Certainly, the impact of different recovery assumptions on the price of a convertible will be significant, but will be left as outside the scope of this chapter. For ease of illustration, we will make the simple assumption of zero recovery of notional, with no option to convert, and confine our attention to the impact of hazard rates alone, pre- and post-calibration, for a range of convertible bond settings. Face value and parity will be taken as 100.

5.4.2   *The impact of state independent hazard rates*

Before we address the effect of consistent hazard rate modelling on converts *per se*, it's useful to take a step back and establish a few preliminaries about converts themselves. For a start, how important are dividends to conversion? Do we convert in the absence of them in a riskless model, and if not, does the possibility of default somehow encourage conversion through reduction of the underlying bond value? The answer to these questions are: (a) vital, (b) no and (c) no again. We can understand this by first considering a dividend-free riskless convert. At expiry we simply have the payoff $\max(N_0, nS)$ (using N_0 for face value, for reasons that will become apparent). The Black–Scholes equation for the evolution *backwards* in time can be written:

$$\frac{\partial V}{\partial \tau} = r(\tau)\left[S\frac{\partial V}{\partial S} - V\right] + \frac{1}{2}S^2\sigma_\tau^2\frac{\partial^2 V}{\partial S^2} \tag{5.30}$$

where $\tau = T - t$ with $V(0) = \max(N_0, nS)$. It will be convenient to apply the transformations $F = e^{\bar{r}(\tau)\tau}S$ and $\tilde{V} = e^{\bar{r}(\tau)\tau}V$ with $\bar{r}(\tau)\tau = \int_0^\tau r(s)ds$. This reduces (5.30) to the somewhat simpler:

$$\frac{\partial \tilde{V}}{\partial \tau} = \frac{1}{2}F^2\sigma_\tau^2\frac{\partial^2 \tilde{V}}{\partial F^2}$$

We now solve for $\widetilde{V}(F, \tau)$ subject to the boundary condition $\widetilde{V}(F, 0) = \max(N_0, nF)$. As the payoff is manifestly convex, we must have, at time $d\tau$, $\widetilde{V}(d\tau, F) \geq \widetilde{V}(0, F)$. But $\widetilde{V}(0, F) \geq nF$, so $\widetilde{V}(d\tau, F) \geq nF$, i.e. $V(d\tau, S) \geq nS$, demonstrating that early exercise is not optimal at this point. We can then validly write $\widetilde{V}(d\tau, F) = nFN(d_1) - N_0(N(d_2) - 1)$. But this function is also manifestly convex, so $\widetilde{V}(2d\tau, F) \geq \widetilde{V}(d\tau, F) \geq nF$ and so on back to $\tau = T$. At all times $0 \leq \tau \leq T$ we thus have $V(\tau, S) \geq nS$, demonstrating that, in the absence of dividends, it is *never* optimal to exercise early.

What happens to this picture when we introduce hazard rates? The surprising answer is: not much. The reason is simple: *both* the default-free risk-neutral stock drift *and* the discount factor change from $r(t) \to r(t) + \lambda(t)$, so the logic from the default-free picture simply carries over. Although it is indeed the case that the embedded bond value is reduced by the survival probability up to expiry, the stock forward conditional on survival is enhanced correspondingly, maintaining the positive optionality over immediate conversion.

So, in the absence of dividends, whether we have a non-zero default probability or not, the value of the simple American convert should equal the European. A demonstration of this is shown in the schematic continuation value plots in Figure 5.14.

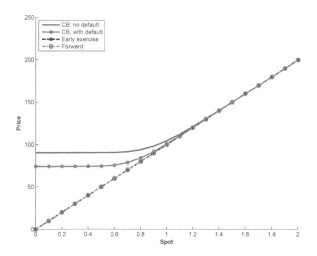

Fig. 5.14   Schematic early exercise vs continuation value for a convert, no dividends.

Though, as can be seen in the continuation profile with default, the bond floor is dragged down by the positive hazard rate, the value tends asymptotically to the early exercise value, which happens to be the conversion number multiplied by the discounted forward in this case. In both the riskless and defaulting cases, early exercise is clearly non-optimal.

Now for non-zero dividends. In the riskless case, the European convert tends to the discounted forward level, but this will now be *below* the early exercise value from just before the ex-dividend date back to today. This is shown schematically in Figure 5.15.

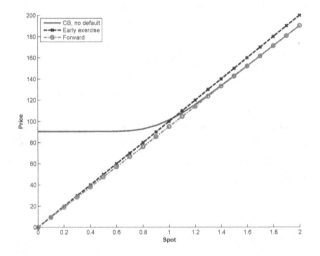

Fig. 5.15   Schematic early exercise vs continuation value for a convert, proportional dividends.

Note that this case corresponds to the one being modelled, where dividends vary in proportion to the stock level at the ex-div date (recall Chapter 3). For the case of cash dividends the discounted forward line is just parallel shifted down by the dividend amount. In either case, the continuation value must now cut the early exercise line, making it optimal to exercise at stock levels above this point. What about just before this early exercise point? Now we again have a dividend-free process, with a payoff function roughly equal to the European value up to early exercise, and the conversion number time stock above it. In fact, to avoid arbitrage the curve needs to be differentiable to second order, so that we must have $\partial V/\partial S = 1$ at this point. We can, however, just treat the ex-div date as a new expiry, with the boundary condition given by the early exercise profile. As this function, again, is convex, by the same logic as the dividend-free case we must have that $\widetilde{V}(\tau, F)$ is monotonically increasing, though F is now defined for expiry equal to ex-div date. Transforming back to present value, as before, we maintain the relationship $V(\tau, S) \geq nS$ back until the next ex-div date. It is thus *only* optimal to exercise just before the ex-div date, for any positive dividend. This observation was first made by Brennan and Schwartz [Brennan and Schwartz (1977)], on the back of earlier work done by Merton on American warrants [Merton (1973)]. As a corollary, a continuous early exercise boundary will exist for a continuous dividend yield. Though this is unrealistic for dividends *per se*, it is a reasonable model for borrow costs, but will be ignored for the remainder of this chapter.

What happens when we *now* introduce default? As before, the bond floor gets dragged down, but the continuation value tends towards the discounted riskless forward. This *does* affect where the continuation value crosses the early exercise line, as shown in Figure 5.16.

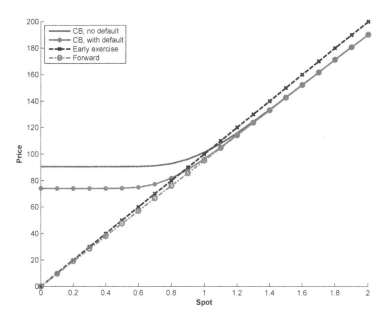

Fig. 5.16 Schematic early exercise vs continuation value for a convert, proportional dividends, with default.

The upshot is that we'd expect to exercise just before the ex-div date at lower spot levels. Note, however, that the effect on valuation is not

trivial. Whilst the payoff at the early exercise point is lower, driving down
the value of the product, recall that the hazard rate itself introduced extra
volatility to the problem. This of course will drive *up* the value of the
embedded option. However, the effective strike of this option is around the
early expiry boundary, which is being driven down by hazard rates, forcing
the option towards a zero strike call, i.e. forcing the convert value to par.
It might be the case then that, as per the equity default swap, the price
of a convert might not in fact be a simple monotonic function of hazard
rates. In practice, however, we found this not to be the case. Figure 5.17
demonstrates this both for the case calibrated to European options, and the
uncalibrated case. In the calibrated case, the local vol is consistently lower,
as discussed, which both lowers the early exercise point and the value of
the corresponding payoff. The effect of calibration is twofold. The example
shown is for a five-year convert with 10% dividends at 1Y and 3Y, parity
100.

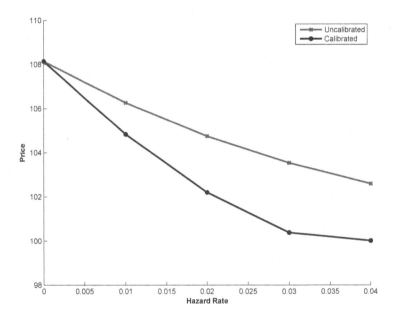

Fig. 5.17   Schematic behaviour of a convertible vs hazard rates, pre- and post-implied
vol calibration.

The example shown is also for zero coupon. As one might expect, the
effect of a coupon, apart from causing price jumps at each coupon date, is

to raise the early exercise boundary, and the value of the option. We can likewise mitigate some of the effect of hazard rates by introducing a call by the issuer. This will simply drive the value of the convert down overall, as the issuer has the right to call back the bond when its price exceeds the call level. This is shown in Figure 5.18, for a call level of 110 (no right to convert).

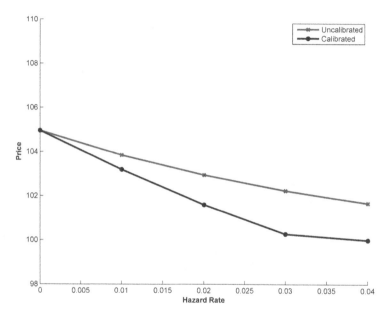

Fig. 5.18 Schematic behaviour of a convertible vs hazard rates, pre- and post-implied vol calibration, call at 110.

5.4.3 *The impact of state dependent hazard rates*

Whilst the previous discussion was interesting from the point of view of the impact of implied vol calibration on simple convert price, it perhaps misses one of the key concerns behind credit model risk for these products. Aside from the uncertainty on recovery, hazard rates are not really parameters one can sensibly 'turn off' when valuing a convert. The credit risk on the bond is *de facto* indicated by the credit spread on the simpler debt instruments of the firm. What we do *not* know, however, is the extent to which credit spreads are dependent, or at least correlated, with equity levels. Earlier structural model work [Brennan and Schwartz (1977); Ingersoll (1977)] naturally imply that, as the firm heads towards bankruptcy, the value of the convertible bond should 'collapse' correspondingly. Translating to a reduced form model, this would imply that the effective hazard rate should rise to infinity as the spot falls to zero. We have in our model an easy way of simulating this. Recall (5.25):

$$\lambda(S,t) = c \left(\frac{S_0}{S} \right)^p$$

If we simply set $p > 0$, we should get exactly the effect on the bond floor of low equity levels that we're looking for. To be somewhat more general, we will employ the following form:

$$\lambda(S,t) = \lambda_0(t) \left(\frac{\kappa F(t)}{S} \right)^\alpha$$

This format allows us to remove the effect of dividends from the hazard rate, provided dividends are assumed to be proportional. Were we not to scale the effective 'crash strike' $K_c = \kappa F(t)$ by the forward, the fall in the stock price over a dividend payment would cause an anomalous spiking of the hazard rate. Applying (5.21) we can simply integrate the implied distribution over this state dependent function to derive a new local volatility which matches, as closely as possible, the implied vol surface. The results are shown in Figure 5.19 for various levels of α (1Y expiry, λ_0 =20 bps).

As can be seen, post-calibration, the difference between the integrated vol surfaces for different alpha is actually quite small. We should thus be able to confine our attention to the basic effect of the state dependence on the bond floor without worrying unduly about non-equivalent implied volatilities.

Note that Figure 5.19 uses values of α from 1.0 to 5.0. The estimation of this parameter is a problem in itself. Andersen and Buffum make the observation that α is effectively the ratio of equity to credit spread volatility, as can be seen by applying Itō's lemma to λ:

$$\frac{d\lambda}{\lambda} = \left[\frac{1}{\lambda_0(t)} \frac{\partial \lambda}{\partial t} - \alpha\lambda + \frac{1}{2}\alpha(\alpha+1)\sigma^2(S,t) \right] dt - \alpha\sigma(S,t)dW$$

In a study of Japanese companies, Muromachi [Muromachi (1999)] estimates α to be in the range 1.2 to 2.0 on this basis. Andersen and Buffum themselves takes values in the range 0.0 to 2.0. One small caveat

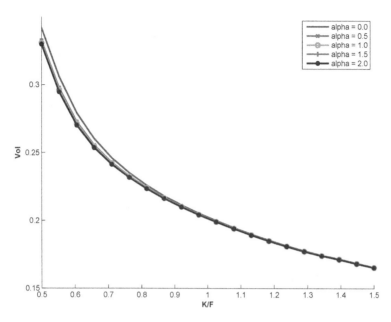

Fig. 5.19   The effect of the hazard rate exponent alpha on calibrated implied volatility, 1Y expiry.

in the usage of this function: the integrated survival probability using $\lambda_0(t) = -\frac{\partial}{\partial t} \log Q(t)$ will no longer be equal to the input survival probability $Q(t)$. As mentioned, some care is needed to calibrate $\lambda_0(t)$ to the risky zero coupon price consistent with the local volatility given by (5.21). In practice the adjustment tends to be small.

We are now in a position to look at the effect of state dependent hazard rates on the value of a convertible, consistent with the vanilla credit and equity markets. A sample plot of the price vs spot of a non-callable, non-puttable 5Y convert, for α in the range 0.0 to 1.5, is shown in Figure 5.20. κ is taken as unity in this example. The credit spread is taken flat at 2%, for illustration.

This is indeed the famous 'collapse of the bond floor', discussed earlier in the context of structural models of default. As spot falls below the forward, in this case, hazard rates start to rise appreciably, with the effect more pronounced for higher α. For $\alpha = 1.5$, and spot at 20% of today's level, as much as half the value of the bond is wiped out. This alone is reason enough to take hazard rate-spot dependence seriously, but what about the risk management? Though this book deals primarily with the

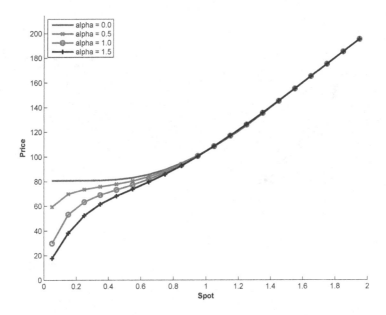

Fig. 5.20   The effect of the hazard rate exponent alpha on the value of a convert, 5Y expiry.

effect of different model assumptions on value rather than risk, in this case it is worthwhile looking at what happens to the delta of the option. This is shown in Figure 5.21.

The effect is striking. Where, for a state independent hazard rate, the delta smoothly fell to zero as spot fell to zero, state dependence has introduced delta which rises to infinity as spot goes to zero. Worse still, the gamma switches from being long gamma everywhere, to short gamma for spot below around 50%. If we were trying to hedge this position with stock, we'd suddenly find ourselves selling large quantities of stock in a falling market, reminiscent of the short vol gamma problem in the vega hedging of cliquets in Chapter 4. If we didn't attempt to hedge this effect at all, the fall in the price of the convert for falling stock would be horribly unmatched by the under-short stock position. One way or the other, the link between credit and equity is a significant hedging problem for convertibles, and possibly the most significant of all model uncertainties in bearish periods.

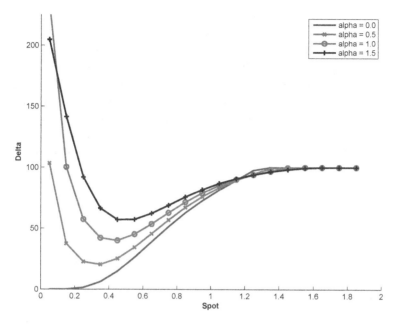

Fig. 5.21   The effect of the hazard rate exponent alpha on the delta of a convert, 5Y expiry.

5.5   Conclusions

In this chapter we have the collapse of the stock to zero in the wake of a credit event. We have attempted to calibrate as closely as possible to the given equity options market, but in addition have faced the added challenge of simultaneous calibration to the credit market, on which the estimation of the probability of these events is based. The effect of default have been investigated on two credit-linked instruments: equity default swaps and convertible bonds. In both cases the importance of credit based model risk on both price and risk was manifest, both from the market implied default probability itself, but also the linkage between equity and credit in the instantaneous probability of default. In the next chapter we will relax the departure from diffusion somewhat, and attack the more complex problem of stock *survival* following a jump.

5.6   Exercises

(1) Demonstrate, for a call price C and put price P, that if the forward given by put-call parity $F = (C - P)e^{rT} + K$ is the same for all K, then if this forward is used to back out an implied volatility from C, the same implied volatility must also be obtained from P. Explain why, on this basis, we would expect the implied volatility surface backed out from the riskless forward to be continuous, regardless of default.

(2) Prove that, for a Poisson arrival process where n arrivals over a fixed time period are independent and identically distributed (i.i.d) with expectation λ, that, in the limit of large n the probability of k arrivals over the same period is given by:

$$P(X = k) = \frac{\lambda^k}{k!}e^{-\lambda}$$

Demonstrate that the moment generating function for this process is given by:

$$E\left[e^{tX}\right] = e^{\lambda(e^t - 1)}$$

By differentiation, use the previous expression to demonstrate that both the mean and variance of the Poisson distribution are given by λ. (We will be using these results in the following chapter).

(3) Derive an approximate expression (to $O(\sqrt{T})$) for the implied ATM volatility on a stock entirely driven by jump to zero (i.e. zero diffusion vol). Discuss how one might exploit an implied volatility quote below this level.

(4) Demonstrate that, in the case where the $x(K) \to 0$ linearly with strike, the implied volatility must necessarily rise asymptotically to infinity. On this basis, explain why any implied volatility surface which remains finite as $K \to 0$ must always underprice puts for a positive expectation of a stock jump to zero.

(5) Following the same methodology as Chapter 2, derive the modified Fokker–Planck equation for the evolution of the risk-neutral stock price density, as written in (5.17).

(6) Derive an expression for a dividend-free, zero coupon European convert, for conversion ration n, initial stock price S_0, face value N_0 risk-free

rate r, flat volatility σ and flat hazard rate λ. Demonstrate that this must always be above the immediate conversion price S_t for any time $0 \leq t \leq T$.

Chapter 6

Jumps

In the previous chapter, we looked in some detail into the problem of *fatal* jumps in the stock price to zero. Such a picture of the world, whilst perhaps appropriate to single stocks, is not representative of stock indices, whose basket construction (and reweighting by market capitalisation) tends to absorb the effect of a default on one or more of the underlyers. Indeed, the market itself does appear to jump in response to global events (changes in fiscal policy, interest rates, wars, natural disasters etc) though the size of the jump and its frequency is unknown. In this chapter we will extend the framework of the previous one and look at the effect of non-fatal jumps whose magnitude, as well as their incidence, is sampled randomly.

6.1 Historical and market inference

One of the common reasons given in support of index jumps is the non-normal behaviour of log returns. A simple histogram of the log returns on the S&P500 does indeed support the idea of non-normality, as shown in Figure 6.1 for a 10-year daily sampled period.

Two features are immediately apparent from this plot:

- The distribution is *leptokurtic*, more commonly known as 'fat-tailed', i.e. the density in the wings appears to be enhanced at the expense of the central density.
- The distribution is skewed to the downside.

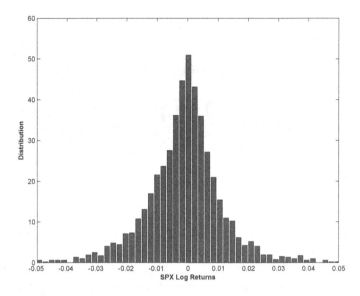

Fig. 6.1   Distribution of log returns on the S&P500, 2000–2010.

In his seminal paper, *Option pricing when underlying stock returns are discontinuous*, Merton comments [Merton (1976)]

> *Indeed, since empirical studies of stock price series tend to show far too many outliers for a simple, constant-variance log-normal distribution, there is a prima facie case for the existence of such jumps.*

A seemingly promising approach to fitting to such a distribution is to look at the *cumulants* κ_n of the sample, defined as:

$$\kappa_n = \left.\frac{\partial^n}{\partial t^n}\right|_{t=0} \log\left[E\left(e^{tX}\right)\right]$$

A simple application to the normal distribution (see exercise) $n(X) = e^{-(X-\mu)^2/2\sigma^2}$ gives $\kappa_1 = \mu$, $\kappa_2 = \sigma^2$ and $\kappa_n = 0 \ \forall \ n > 2$. On the other hand, consider a jump model defined by:

$$S(t) = S(0)e^{(\mu - \sigma^2/2)t + \sigma W_t} \prod_{k=1}^{N_t} J_k$$

where the jump sizes J_k over the interval $[0, t]$ are independent and log-normal with mean $\mu_J - \delta^2/2$ and standard deviation δ, and where, further,

N_t is an independent Poisson point process with hazard rate λ_t (this is in fact the Merton model for jump-diffusion). We will show below that the distribution of stock returns in this model is given by:

$$\phi(r) = \sum_{k=0}^{\infty} n\left(r; \mu\Delta t + k(\mu_J - \delta^2/2); \sigma^2\Delta t + k\delta^2\right) e^{-\lambda\Delta t} \frac{(\lambda\Delta t)^k}{k!}$$

where Δt is the interval corresponding to the return, and $n(x, \mu, \sigma^2)$ the Gaussian density at x of a variable distributed $\sim \mathcal{N}(\mu, \sigma^2)$. The cumulants for a weighted sum of normal distributions do not cut off at 2, i.e. a weighted sum of normals is not itself normal, so in principle such a model might allow us to recover the observed skewed, fat-tailed distribution shown in Figure 6.1. Such an approach can be seen in the work of Press [Press (1967)] and Beckers [Beckers (1981)], but make simplifying assumptions on the jump distribution (Press assumes zero log drift, Beckers assumes zero log jump mean) and moreover contained instances of negative variance, both in σ^2 and δ^2. A more sophisticated approach is to use *maximum likelihood* estimates. The technique is well documented, but we summarise here for illustration. Assume we have a sample $x_1, \ldots, x_n$ of n i.i.d observations, sampled from some (to be determined) distribution $f(\theta_0)$, where θ_0 is the set of parameters defining the 'true' distribution (e.g. (μ, σ) for the normal distribution). As our samples are i.i.d., we can write for the joint density of the observations

$$f(x_1, \ldots, x_n, \theta_0) = \prod_{i=1}^{n} f(x_i, \theta_0)$$

The problem though is that we don't know, *a priori* what this θ_0 is. The idea of maximum likelihood then is to postulate some guess θ, and then adjust until the joint distribution, or so-called 'likelihood function' is maximised. In practice, it turns out to be more convenient to work with the log-likelihood function given by:

$$\ell(\theta) = \frac{1}{n} \sum_{i=1}^{n} \log\left[f(x_i, \theta)\right]$$

The maximum likelihood estimate $\ell(\hat{\theta})$ is then given by:

$$\ell(\hat{\theta}) = \sup_{\theta=\hat{\theta}} \ell(\theta)$$

$$\hat{\theta} = \mathrm{argmax}_\theta \ell(\theta)$$

For the simple normal distribution, the solution to the joint equations $\frac{\partial \ell}{\partial \mu} = 0$ and $\frac{\partial \ell}{\partial \sigma} = 0$ is the well-known estimate of mean and variance $\hat{\mu} = \frac{1}{n}\sum_i x_i$ and $\hat{\sigma}^2 = \frac{1}{n}\sum_i (x_i - \hat{\mu})^2$. For Merton jump-diffusion, our likelihood vector is now five-dimensional $\theta = (\mu, \sigma^2, \mu_J, \delta^2, \lambda)$ and the problem correspondingly more involved. Examples in the literature can be seen in Ball and Torous [Ball and Torous (1985)], Akgiray and Booth [Akgiray and Booth (1986)], Pickard, Kempthorne and Zakaria [Pickard *et al.* (1986)] and Duncan, Randal and Thomson [Duncan *et al.* (2009)]. The latter two papers develop an extension to maximum likelihood known as *Expectation Maximisation* [Dempster *et al.* (1977)], where the problem is transformed to a recursion whereby the distributional parameters at the next step are expressed, via maximum likelihood, in terms of the expectations of the stochastic drivers (in this case the Brownian and Poisson processes), conditional on the observed stock returns, with these expectations themselves dependent on the distributional parameters at the previous step. Whilst the authors claim better convergence over standard maximum likelihood multi-dimensional optimisation, it is unclear that the procedure does a better job of robust *global* minimisation of the log-likelihood function. The essential difficulty with historical inference of jump-diffusion parameters is that the problem is near degenerate, i.e. the distribution given by a zero jump standard deviation and zero jump mean is almost identical to one with a non-zero jump standard deviation, zero jump mean and a reduced log-normal variance, for example. Convergence to the wrong extremum is thus a common problem in these estimations.

Faced with the poorly posed problem of historical inference, inference from market data, either on a given day [Andersen and Andreasen (2000); He *et al.* (2005)] or averaged over a period [Bakshi *et al.* (1997); Bates (1996b)] has been a popular alternative for estimation of jump-diffusion parameters. The problem then of course is that the parameters one ends up with are very much a function of the model one's fitting to. For example, Bakshi, Cao and Chen consider a fit of short-dated (< 60 days to maturity), medium dated (60–180 days) and long-dated (≥ 180 days) implied volatility on the S&P500, but on a stochastic volatility plus jumps model (SVJ) given by:

$$\frac{dS_t}{S_t} = (\mu(t) - \lambda\mu_J)dt + \sqrt{\nu_t}\,dW_t^S + J(t)dN_t$$
$$d\nu_t = -\kappa(\nu_t - \bar{\nu})dt + \xi\sqrt{\nu_t}\,dW_t^\nu$$

Table 6.1 Market inferred Merton jump parameters for the S&P500 from three different models.

Authors	λ	μ_J	δ
Andersen, Andreasen	8.9%	-88.98%	45.05%
He, Kennedy *et al.*	10%	-92%	42.5%
Bakshi, Cao, Chen	61%	-9%	14%

where the options are fitted daily from June 1988 through to May 1991, and the fitted parameters averaged. The model was a popular response, at the time, to the problem of fitting both the strong negative skew for short-dated options, and the vol surface curvature for long-dated options, the former being generated by the jump process, the latter by the stochastic volatility. Andersen and Andreasen, by contrast, consider direct fitting of the Merton model to a set of options from 1M expiry to 10Y expiry, as of April 1999. Kennedy *et al.* attempt to add in some non-flat local volatility in line with the actual model proposed by Andersen and Andreasen (see Section 6.3), but end up with similar results. The resultant fitted parameters are shown in Table 6.1.

Interestingly, Eraker *et al.* [Eraker *et al.* (2000)] estimate λ as 6.6%, μ_J as -175% and δ as 288% for the same SVJ model used by Bakshi *et al.*, but based on historical returns from 1980–1999. Clearly, a) our choice of volatility process is essential to the results of market inference and b) the results of historical inference on stock returns can be significantly different to market inference from options data, even for the same model. We might then be forgiven for making the observation that neither historical return series nor vanilla option data is particularly useful in pinning down parameters for index jump processes. So where do we go from here? Well, happily this book is devoted to the impact of model risk on exotics, not vanillas. However we choose the jump-diffusion model, and the parameters which go into it, there are four areas where jump processes *do* clearly delineate from pure diffusions:

(1) **Realised variance**. The seemingly innocent looking variance swap introduced in Chapter 4 can be acutely sensitive to jumps, provided the jumps are large enough. Discrepancies between prices from the log contract and market traded prices, can, in principle, be used to infer jump parameters.

(2) **Investment strategies**. So-called *dynamic allocation strategies*, notably *Constant Proportion Portfolio Insurance* (CPPI), are guaranteed

never to fall below a certain level (commonly a bond floor), in the limit
of a continuously sampled diffusion. Jumps on the underlying 'risky
asset' can cause this floor to be breached, providing value to puts on
the strategy if, *and only if*, jumps are introduced to the underlyer.

(3) **Forward skew.** Products whose value is strongly linked to the forward
starting marginal distribution of the stock, such as cliquets or barrier
options, may show strong sensitivity to jumps, depending on the exact
structure of the payoff.

(4) **Smile dynamics.** Recall the result from Chapter 4 that, post-
calibration, stochastic volatility did nothing to alleviate the unrealistic
dynamics of the implied volatility surface under spot bumping. Jumps
have the effect of absorbing some of the skew generation of implied
volatility surfaces, and in turn suppress the gradient of the calibrated
local volatility surface. In this way we end up being able to recover
observed implied volatility surface movement with spot only by incorporating jumps.

These four areas will be examined in some detail in the remainder of
this chapter via application of the Andersen–Andreasen model. Before we
describe how this model works, and how we calibrate from it, let's take a
step back and consider whether we can even talk about risk-neutrality at
all under a continuous spectrum of jump sizes.

6.2   How to hedge a continuum of jumps

The short answer to this problem is that you can't, at least not perfectly,
for the simple reason that a *continuum* of stochastic drivers requires a
continuum of hedges. To derive this rigorously, let's extend the hedging
argument developed for a single jump in Chapter 5. Formally, our stock
evolves according to the following process:

$$\frac{dS_t}{S_t} = \mu_t dt + \sigma_t dW_t + \sum_{i=1,n} (J_i - 1) dN_t^i$$

where we have n possible jump sizes J_i with Poisson indicators dN_t^i, which
are one for a jump to state $J_i S_t$ and zero otherwise. Over a given time
interval $[t, t + dt]$ no more than one of dN_t^i can be one (i.e. the jump states
are mutually exclusive). Let us now consider constructing the following
portfolio:

$$\Pi = V_0 + \alpha S + \sum_{j=1,n} \beta_j V_j + \phi B$$

As always, the idea is to come up with hedging weights α, β_j so as to ensure the portfolio is self-financing in all states of the world. For simplicity we will take dividends to be zero. We then have:

$$d\Pi = \frac{\partial V_0}{\partial t} dt + \frac{\partial V_0}{\partial S} S(\mu_t dt + \sigma_t dW_t) + \frac{1}{2}\sigma^2 S^2 \frac{\partial^2 V_0}{\partial S^2} dt$$

$$+ \sum_i [V_0(J_i S) - V_0(S)] dN_t^i + \alpha S[\mu_t dt + \sigma_t dW_t + \sum_i (J_i - 1) dN_t^i]$$

$$+ \sum_j \beta_j \left[\frac{\partial V_j}{\partial t} dt + \frac{\partial V_j}{\partial S} S(\mu_t dt + \sigma_t dW_t) + \frac{1}{2}\sigma^2 S^2 \frac{\partial^2 V_j}{\partial S^2} dt \right.$$

$$\left. + \sum_i [V_j(J_i S) - V_j(S)] dN_t^i \right] + \phi B r_t dt = 0 \qquad (6.1)$$

So, taking the portfolio to be costless, we have:

$$\phi = -\frac{(V_0 + \alpha S + \sum_j \beta_j V_j)}{B}$$

Taking the net change due to dW_t to be zero gives:

$$\alpha = -\frac{\partial V_0}{\partial S} - \sum_j \beta_j \frac{\partial V_j}{\partial S}$$

And taking the net change due to dN_t^i to be zero gives:

$$[V_0(J_i S) - V_0(S)] + \alpha S(J_i - 1) + \sum_j [V_j(J_i S) - V_j(S)] = 0 \qquad (6.2)$$

Putting this together, we find for (6.1):

$$\frac{\partial V_0}{\partial t} + \frac{1}{2}\sigma_t^2 S^2 \frac{\partial^2 V_0}{\partial S^2} + \sum_j \beta_j \left[\frac{\partial V_j}{\partial t} + \frac{1}{2}\sigma_t^2 S^2 \frac{\partial^2 V_j}{\partial S^2} \right] =$$

$$r_t \left[V_0 - \left(\frac{\partial V_0}{\partial S} + \sum_j \beta_j \frac{\partial V_j}{\partial S} \right) S + \sum_j \beta_j V_j \right]$$

We can write this more succinctly as:

$$\sum_{j=0,n} \beta_j d\Pi_j = 0 \tag{6.3}$$

where $\beta_0 = 1$ and

$$d\Pi_j = \frac{\partial V_j}{\partial t} + \frac{1}{2}\sigma_t^2 S^2 \frac{\partial^2 V_j}{\partial S^2} - r_t \left(V_j - S\frac{\partial V_j}{\partial S} \right) \tag{6.4}$$

Similarly, we can rewrite (6.2) as:

$$M_{i0} + \sum_{j=1,n} M_{ij}\beta_j = 0 \tag{6.5}$$

where

$$M_{ij} = V_j(J_i S) - V_j(S) - \frac{\partial V_j}{\partial S} S(J_i - 1) \tag{6.6}$$

Combining (6.3) and (6.5) gives:

$$d\Pi_0 = \sum_j \sum_i \widehat{M}_{ji} M_{i0} d\Pi_j \tag{6.7}$$

Denoting $\widehat{M} = M^{-1}$, a self-consistent solution to (6.3) and (6.5) is given by:

$$d\Pi_j = g(t) \sum_{i=1,n} \pi_i M_{ij} \ \forall \, j \in 0, n$$

as:

$$\sum_{j=1,n} \beta_j d\Pi_j = -\sum_{j=1,n} \sum_{i=1,n} \widehat{M}_{ji} M_{i0} \left(g(t) \sum_{k=1,n} \pi_k M_{kj} \right)$$

$$= -g(t) \sum_{i=1,n} \sum_{k=1,n} \delta_{ik} \pi_k M_{i0}$$

$$= -g(t) \sum_{i=1,n} \pi_i M_{i0}$$

$$= -d\Pi_0$$

as required by (6.3). Note that this holds for *any* $g(t)$ and π_j. Substituting back into (6.4) gives:

$$\frac{\partial V_j}{\partial t} + \frac{1}{2}\sigma_t^2 S^2 \frac{\partial^2 V_j}{\partial S^2} - r_t\left(V_j - S\frac{\partial V_j}{\partial S}\right)$$
$$= g(t)\sum_j \pi_i\left[V_j(J_i S) - V_j(S) - \frac{\partial V_j}{\partial S}S(J_i - 1)\right]$$

As per Chapter 5, if we now consider a zero coupon bond which pays zero in the case of *any* jump, then we have:

$$g(t)\sum_i \pi_i = -\lambda(t)$$

where $\lambda(t)dt$ denoted the probability of a jump over the interval $[t, t+dt]$. This gives finally:

$$\frac{\partial V_j}{\partial t} + \frac{1}{2}\sigma_t^2 S^2 \frac{\partial^2 V_j}{\partial S^2} - r_t\left(V_j - S\frac{\partial V_j}{\partial S}\right)$$
$$= -\lambda(t)\sum_i \widetilde{\pi}_i\left[V_j(J_i S) - V_j(S) - \frac{\partial V_j}{\partial S}S(J_i - 1)\right]$$

where $\widetilde{\pi}_i = \pi_i/\sum_k \pi_k$ and hence, by construction $\sum_i \widetilde{\pi}_i = 1$. This constraint allows us to interpret the weights $\widetilde{\pi}_i$ as probabilities, allowing for the more familiar representation:

$$\frac{\partial V_j}{\partial t} + (r_t - \lambda(t)(E_J[J] - 1))S\frac{\partial V_j}{\partial S} + \frac{1}{2}\sigma_t^2 S^2 \frac{\partial^2 V_j}{\partial S^2}$$
$$= (r_t + \lambda(t))V_j(S) - \lambda(t)E_J[V_j(JS)] \tag{6.8}$$

where $E_J(f(J)) = \sum_i \widetilde{\pi}_i f(J_i)$. In the limit of an infinite number of possible jump sizes, this reduces exactly to Merton's original formulation. Interestingly, Merton himself derived the equation on the basis of the Capital Asset Pricing Model [Merton (1976)]:

> Inspection of the return dynamics ... shows that the only source of uncertainty in the return is the jump component of the stock. But by hypothesis, such components represent only non-systematic risk, and therefore the beta of this portfolio is zero. If the Capital Asset Pricing Model holds, then the expected return on all zero-beta securities must equal the riskless rate.

The equivalence of this statement to (6.8) can be seen trivially by taking the expected change in a purely delta hedged portfolio over jumps to be zero (see exercise). Notice a couple of points arising from this analysis:

- As stated initially, a continuum of jumps requires a continuum of option hedges to be risk-neutral. In practice, hedging through a small finite set (~ 10), with weights given by the density of the jump sizes in the physical measure turns out to be a good hedge for vanilla strategies at least [Andersen and Andreasen (2000); He *et al.* (2005)].
- The hedging strategy is valid for *any* distribution of jump sizes, analogous to the way that the stochastic volatility hedging strategy was valid for any volatility growth parameter (see Chapter 4). The choice of distribution, however, obviously does impact on the price of the instrument. Provided though that we hedge with instruments according to (6.5) and (6.6) consistently, the strategy will be risk-neutral. Ultimately though, the distribution of jump sizes applicable to pricing is that of the risk-neutral, rather than the physical measure. Whilst the standard deviation of jump sizes might be expected to be the same between both measures, this will not be true of the mean, as discussed by Naik and Lee [Naik and Lee (1990)]. Marking of jump size distribution parameters from market rather than historical return inference would therefore seem more consistent for modelling.

6.3   The Andersen–Andreasen model

In spite of the problems around imperfect hedging, we will work under the idealised assumption that we have enough options at our disposal to hedge a continuum of jumps near perfectly. As in previous chapters, however, we still have some work to do before we can start applying the model to exotics. Jumps themselves introduce considerable distortions to the implied volatility surface. The presence of a negative jump mean introduces downward implied volatility skew. The presence of a non-zero jump standard deviation introduces implied volatility smile. *Both* jump mean and jump standard deviation introduce an upward shift to the volatility surface, with the effect becoming more pronounced the higher the hazard rate. To maintain calibration to observed vanilla option prices, we have to introduce some dynamics to the diffusion volatility. In the spirit of earlier chapters, we will follow the method of Andersen and Andreasen [Andersen and Andreasen (2000)] and develop a modified Dupire framework to address this problem. To begin, however, let's consider some basic results coming out of the original Merton formulation.

6.3.1 *The Merton model*

One of the obvious complexities of the Merton equation (6.8) is the inclusion of the integral term $\lambda(t)E_J[V_i(JS)]$. Such partial *integro* differential equations can be solved by use of Fourier analysis, provided the advection and diffusion coefficients are constant. In the more general case where the terms are spatially and time varying, a stepwise approach combining finite differences and Fourier transforms may be employed [Andersen and Andreasen (2000)]. In this section we will focus on the simpler Merton problem.

Recall the integral expression for a call option (Chapter 2):

$$C(S,t;K,T) = P(t,T) \int_0^\infty (S_T - K, 0)^+ G(S_t,t;S_T,T)dS_T \qquad (6.9)$$

where $G(S,t;S_T,T)$ is the transition density (Green's function) from state (S_t,t) to (S_T,T). Transforming to $z = \log(S_T/F(t,T))$ and $k = \log(K/F(t,T))$ with $c(k,t,T) = C(S,t;K,T)/(P(t,T)F(t,T))$. We have:

$$c(k,t,T) = e^k \int_{-\infty}^\infty (e^{z-k} - 1, 0)G(0,t;z,T)dz \qquad (6.10)$$

As we shall see below, the Green's function for the Merton equation is both spatially and time homogenous, allowing us to write $G(z,t;z',t') = G(z'-z,t'-t)$, simplifying (6.10) to:

$$c(k,\tau) = e^k \int_{-\infty}^\infty (e^{z-k} - 1, 0)G(z,\tau)dz \qquad (6.11)$$

where $\tau = T - t$. Writing $f(z) = (e^z - 1, 0)^+$, we employ the Fourier transform:

$$\hat{f}(\xi) = \int_{-\infty}^\infty e^{i\xi z} f(z)dz$$

with the inverse transform:

$$f(z) = \frac{1}{2\pi} \int_{-\infty+i\gamma}^{\infty+i\gamma} e^{-i\xi z} \hat{f}(\xi)d\xi$$

where $\gamma \in [\alpha, \beta]$ defines a *strip of regularity* for which the original Fourier transform exists. Using the result $\int_{-\infty}^{\infty} e^{iz(\xi - \xi')} dz = 2\pi\delta(\xi - \xi')$, we arrive at:

$$c(k, T) = \frac{e^k}{2\pi} \int_{-\infty+i\gamma}^{\infty+i\gamma} e^{-i\xi k} \hat{f}(-\xi) \widehat{G}(\xi, \tau) d\xi \qquad (6.12)$$

It can be shown (see exercise and [Lipton (2000); Lewis (2001); Lipton (2002b); Gatheral (2006)]) that (6.12) can be used to write the call price as:

$$C(K, \tau) = P(t, T) \left[F - \sqrt{FK} \frac{1}{\pi} \int_0^\infty \frac{d\xi}{\xi^2 + \frac{1}{4}} \Re\left[e^{-ik\xi} \widehat{G}(\xi - i/2, \tau) \right] \right]$$
$$(6.13)$$

This formula, first derived independently by Alan Lewis and Alex Lipton, is a useful device for calibrating to option prices from models where the characteristic function can be expressed analytically. For more information on the application of this expression, see Lipton [Lipton (2002b)].

To solve for the call price deriving from the Merton equation, we simply have to solve for the characteristic function $\widehat{G}(\xi, \tau)$ and insert into (6.13). As per Chapter 2, we start from the backward equation applied to the option price $V(t)$ given by:

$$\left[\frac{\partial}{\partial t} + \mathfrak{L} \right] V(t) = 0$$

As the option is a martingale under the risk-neutral measure (assuming deterministic rates), we have:

$$V(x, t) = P(t, T) \int V(z, T) G(x, t; z, T) dz$$

Hence:

$$0 = -r(T) \int V(z, T) G(x, t; z, T) dz + \int \frac{\partial V}{\partial T} G(x, t; z, T) + V(z, T) \frac{\partial G}{\partial T}$$

giving

$$\left[-\frac{\partial}{\partial T} + \mathfrak{L}^* + r(T) \right] G(x, t; z, T) = 0 \qquad (6.14)$$

where $\mathfrak{L}^*$ is the adjoint operator to $\mathfrak{L}$ defined by:

$$\int G(x,t;z,T)\mathfrak{L}V(z,T)dz = \int V(z,T)\mathfrak{L}^*G(x,t;z,T)dz \qquad (6.15)$$

For the Merton equation, $\mathfrak{L}$ is given by:

$$\mathfrak{L}V(S,t) = [g(t) - \lambda(E_J[J] - 1)]\,S\frac{\partial V}{\partial S}$$
$$+ \frac{1}{2}\frac{\partial^2 V}{\partial S^2}S^2\sigma^2(t) - (r(t) + \lambda)V(S,t) + \lambda E_J\left[V(JS,t)\right]$$

where $g(t)$ corresponds to the growth of the forward. Re-expressing in terms of $x = \log(S)$ and $J' = \log(J)$:

$$\mathfrak{L}V(x,t) = \left(g(t) - \frac{\sigma^2(t)}{2} - \lambda(E_{J'}[e^{J'}] - 1)\right)\frac{\partial V}{\partial x} +$$
$$\frac{1}{2}\frac{\partial^2 V}{\partial x^2}\sigma^2(t) - (r(t) + \lambda)V(x,t) + \lambda E_{J'}\left[V(x + J',t)\right] \quad (6.16)$$

So that integrating by parts we have:

$$\int \mathfrak{L}V(z,T)G(x,t;z,T)dz =$$

$$\int dz V(z,T)\left(-\frac{\partial}{\partial z}(\mu(T)G(x,t;z,T)) + \frac{1}{2}\frac{\partial^2}{\partial z^2}(\sigma^2(T)G(x,t;z,T))\right.$$

$$\left. -(r(T) + \lambda)G(x,t;z,T) + \lambda E_{J'}[G(x,t;z - J',T)]\right)$$

where

$$\mu(t) = g(t) - \frac{\sigma^2(t)}{2} - \lambda(E_{J'}[e^{J'}] - 1)$$

Combining with (6.14) and using the definition (6.15), we end up with the forward equation for the Green's function of the Merton model:

$$-\frac{\partial G(x,t;z,T)}{\partial T} - \frac{\partial}{\partial z}(\mu(T)G(x,t;z,T)) + \frac{1}{2}\frac{\partial^2}{\partial z^2}(\sigma^2(T)G(x,t;z,T))$$
$$- \lambda G(x,t;z,T) + \lambda E_{J'}[G(x,t;z - J',T)] = 0 \qquad (6.17)$$

By inspection of (6.16), we can see that the process corresponding to x is simply:

$$dx_t = \mu(t)dt + \sigma(t)dW_t + J'dN_t \qquad (6.18)$$

(this may also be derived directly from Itō's lemma, see exercise). Now, let us assume, as per Merton's original paper [Merton (1976)], that μ and σ are time invariant. It is then transparent that the increment in x_t is independent of the start point, both in space and time. We can thus see that the transition density corresponding to x_t must itself be spatially and time homogeneous, allowing us to write $G(x, t; z, T) = G(z - x, T - t)$. We can thus write for the characteristic function:

$$\widehat{G}(\xi, t, T) = \widehat{G}(\xi, \tau) = \int_{-\infty}^{\infty} G(u, \tau)e^{i\xi u}du \qquad (6.19)$$

where $\tau = T - t$ and $u = z - x$.

To see the point of all this formalism, look at the last integral term in (6.17). This is nothing other than a convolution of the Green's function over the jump size density $\omega(J')$:

$$E_{J'}[G(x, t; z - J', T)] = \int G(x, t; z - J', T)\omega(J')dJ'$$

So that substituting the Fourier transform into (6.17), and equating the integrand to zero:

$$-\frac{\partial \widehat{G}(\xi, \tau)}{\partial \tau} + \widehat{G}(\xi, \tau)[i\xi\mu - \xi^2\sigma^2 - \lambda + \lambda\widehat{\omega}(\xi)] = 0 \qquad (6.20)$$

Noticing further that the initial density in u is just the delta function, we have $G(\xi, 0) = 1$, enabling us to solve (6.20) as:

$$\widehat{G}(\xi, \tau) = \exp\left[\left(i\xi\mu - \frac{1}{2}\xi^2\sigma^2 + \lambda(\widehat{\omega}(\xi) - 1)\right)\tau\right] \qquad (6.21)$$

The above is a special case of the *Lévy–Khintchine formula*, which states that for a Lévy process with continuous triple (μ, σ^2, ν) defining the drift and variance of the diffusion, and the Lévy measure of jumps, respectively, the characteristic function $\phi(\xi)$ can be written:

$$\phi(\xi, \tau) = \exp\left[\Psi(\xi)\tau\right]$$

where the characteristic exponent $\Psi(\xi)$ is given as:

$$\Psi(\xi) = i\xi\mu - \frac{1}{2}\xi^2\sigma^2 + \int \left[e^{i\xi\chi} - 1 - \mathbf{1}_{|\chi|<1}i\xi\chi\right]\nu(d\chi) \qquad (6.22)$$

The Lévy measure is defined formally as:

$$\nu[A] := E[\#t \leq 1 : \Delta_t X \in A]$$

i.e. the expected number of jumps up to $t = 1$ with a size belonging to the set A. A Lévy process itself is defined as:

Definition 6.1. A Lévy process X_t is defined to be a càdlàg[1] process, which:

(1) Has independent and stationary increments;
(2) Is *stochastic continuous*, i.e. the probability of a jump at some fixed time is zero. Formally, $\lim_{h\to 0} P[|X_{t+h} - X_t| \geq \epsilon] = 0 \, \forall \, 0 < \epsilon < 1$.

By independent increments, we mean that for $s > t$, $u > v$ and $[s,t]$, $[u,v]$ non-overlapping, $X_s - X_t$ is independent of $X_u - X_v$. By stationary increments, we mean that the distribution of $X_s - X_t$ depends only on $s - t$. Both Brownian motions $X_s - X_t \sim \mathcal{N}(0, s-t)$ and Poisson processes $X_s - X_t \sim \mathcal{P}(\lambda(s-t), \lambda(s-t))$ are examples of Lévy processes.

Note that, associated with the Lévy measure is the intensity measure defined as:

$$\mu[(a,b] \times \tilde{A}] = \lambda \int_a^b \nu(\tilde{A})dt$$

This measure need not be finite. Those which are (e.g. Brownian motion, Poisson point process), are referred to as finite *activity*. Other processes, such as variance gamma or CGMY [Kyprianou *et al.* (2005); Carr *et al.* (2002)] have infinite activity, requiring special treatment for stable numerical simulation. Note that where the process is finite activity, the last term in (6.22) can simply be absorbed into the drift term, reducing the characteristic exponent to the simpler form we see in (6.21).

We will return to some of the desirable properties of Lévy processes on option valuation later in the chapter, but for the moment, let's return to our expression in (6.21). Expanding the jump contribution gives:

---

[1] *continu à droite, limites à gauche*: right continuous with left limits defined everywhere.

$$\widehat{G}(\xi, \tau) = \exp\left[\left(i\xi\mu - \frac{1}{2}\xi^2\sigma^2\right)\tau\right]\left(\sum_{n=0}^{\infty} e^{-\lambda\tau}\frac{(\lambda\tau)^n}{n!}\widehat{\omega}(\xi)^n\right) \qquad (6.23)$$

where

$$\widehat{\omega}(\xi) = \exp\left[i\xi\left(\mu_J - \frac{\delta^2}{2} + i\frac{\delta^2\xi}{2}\right)\right] \qquad (6.24)$$

Combining with (6.23) gives:

$$\widehat{G}(\xi, \tau) = \sum_{n=0}^{\infty} e^{-\lambda\tau}\frac{(\lambda\tau)^n}{n!}\widehat{G}_n(\xi, \tau)$$

where

$$\widehat{G}_n(\xi, \tau) = \exp\left[\left(i\xi(g - \lambda(e^{\mu_J} - 1) + n\mu_J/\tau - \Sigma_n^2/2) - \frac{1}{2}\xi^2\Sigma_n^2\right)\tau\right]$$

where $\Sigma_n^2 = \sigma^2 + n\delta^2/\tau$. Applying this to (6.12), we can see that the solution to the call price from the Merton equation is given by:

$$C(K, \tau) = \sum_{n=0}^{\infty} e^{-\lambda\tau}\frac{(\lambda\tau)^n}{n!}C(F_n(\tau), \Sigma_n(\tau), \tau) \qquad (6.25)$$

where:

$$F_n(\tau) = F(\tau)e^{n\mu_J}\exp\left[\lambda\tau(1 - e^{\mu_J})\right]$$

6.3.1.1   *Volatility surfaces in the Merton model*

Armed with the expression for the call in (6.25), we're now in a position to investigate the effect of jump dynamics on implied volatility. As before, this will be essential for understanding the modifications to local volatility post-calibration, and thence the effects of implied volatility calibration on exotics.

Figures 6.2 and 6.3 show the impact of non-zero jump mean μ_J (for zero jump stdev) and non-zero jump stdev δ (for zero jump mean) respectively. The forward is taken flat at unity, diffusion vol 20%, hazard rate 3%.

Intuitively, these pictures are quite easy to understand. A negative jump mean clearly increases the likelihood of lower stock prices, with a corresponding increase in the value of downside puts and implied volatility.

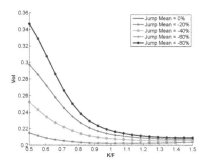
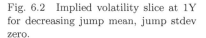
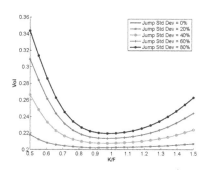

Fig. 6.2 Implied volatility slice at 1Y
for decreasing jump mean, jump stdev
zero.

Fig. 6.3 Implied volatility slice at 1Y
for increasing jump stdev, jump mean
zero.

A non-zero jump standard deviation increases the likelihood both of higher
and lower stock prices, with a corresponding increase in call and put prices
respectively, generating a volatility 'smile'. The addition of a jump process
also adds to the variance of the stock price (see later), with a corresponding
increase in the overall volatility level.

Such vol surface shapes were initially very attractive from the point of
view of an explanation of quoted option prices through a fundamental model
[Bates (1991)]. There are (at least) a couple of drawbacks in attempting to
explain the market through jumps alone:

- The volatility skew and curvature due to jumps decays quickly with
  maturity due to the damping by the hazard rate. The corresponding
  picture for a 5Y slice is shown in Figures 6.4 and 6.5 respectively.
- Such approaches yield insufficient volatility of volatility to price instruments with strong exposure to vol gamma (e.g. cliquets, barriers,
  variance options (see Chapter 4)).

Ultimately, some dynamics on the volatility itself is required for market
consistency. These broadly divide into two camps:

(1) Augmentation of a parsimonious stochastic volatility model with a
    jump process as per Bates [Bates (1996a)] or Bakshi, Cao and Chen
    [Bakshi *et al.* (1997)] and an optimised, rather than exact fit to vanilla
    market prices.
(2) An exact fit to vanilla market prices through local volatility calibration.

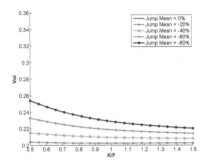

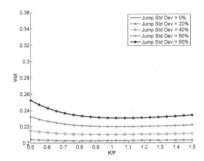

Fig. 6.4   Implied volatility slice at 5Y for decreasing jump mean, jump stdev zero.

Fig. 6.5   Implied volatility slice at 5Y for increasing jump stdev, jump mean zero.

The argument in favour of the first approach is that it provides greater explanatory power, doesn't suffer from the 'bad vol surface' problems of local vol models and provides for more stable hedging, provided the underlying model parameters are stable. The argument in favour of the second approach is that it allows us to investigate the effects of jumps on exotics on a like-for-like basis with non-jump models which also exactly fit the implied vol surface. As this second argument drives the model risk approach of this book, we will adopt the second method. Happily, the seminal work on local vol adaptation to jump processes was published by Andersen and Andreasen in 2000 [Andersen and Andreasen (2000)], which we will now describe in detail.

6.3.2   *Local volatility in the presence of jumps*

We consider the following process:

$$\frac{dS_t}{S_t} = (g(t) - \lambda(E[e^J] - 1))dt + \sigma(S_t, t)dW_t + (e^J - 1)dN_t$$

where $J \sim \mathcal{N}(\mu_J - \delta^2/2, \delta^2)$. Applying (6.17) to (6.9), and integrating by parts (see exercise), Andersen and Andreasen derived the extension to the Dupire equation:

$$-\frac{\partial \widetilde{c}}{\partial T} + (\lambda' - \lambda)k\frac{\partial \widetilde{c}}{\partial k} + \frac{1}{2}\sigma^2(T, k)k^2\frac{\partial^2 \widetilde{c}}{\partial k^2}$$
$$+ \lambda'\left(\int_{-\infty}^{\infty} \widetilde{c}(t, T, ke^{-\mu_J + \delta^2/2 - \delta z})\phi(z - \delta)dz - \widetilde{c}\right) = 0 \quad (6.26)$$

where $\lambda' = \lambda e^{\mu_J}$, $\phi(z)$ is a standard normal distribution, $\tilde{c}(t,T,k)$ the undiscounted call price divided by the forward, with $k = K/F(t,T)$. In the cases where a volatility surface is supplied, (6.26) can be applied directly to compute an autocalibrating local vol. Andersen and Andreasen, however, considered the fitting of this model directly to *market* quoted prices. Rather than attempt to create a second-order differentiable surface fitting Black–Scholes implied volatilities, they considered rather converting the option prices to *Merton volatilities* defined by:

$$M(t,T,k,\hat{\sigma}(k,T)) = \tilde{c}(t,T,k)$$

where

$$M(t,T,k,\hat{\sigma}(k,T)) = \sum_{n=0}^{\infty} A(n)N(d_n) - k\sum_{n=0}^{\infty} B(n)N(d_n - \nu_n)$$

$$A(n) = \frac{e^{-\lambda'(T-t)}[\lambda'(T-t)]^n}{n!}$$

$$B(n) = \frac{e^{-\lambda(T-t)}[\lambda(T-t)]^n}{n!}$$

$$\nu_n = \sqrt{\hat{\sigma}^2(k,T)(T-t) + n\delta^2}$$

$$d_n = \frac{-\log k + (\lambda - \lambda')(T-t) + n\mu_J}{\nu_n} + \frac{\nu_n}{2}$$

and using these to construct a volatility surface for local vol calculation. The approach lends itself to better behaved local volatility profiles than would be obtained through fitting to Black–Scholes vols (recall the collapse of local volatility for deep OTM puts in the Andersen–Buffum model of Chapter 5).

Andersen and Andreasen's approach now was effectively to try to back out the local volatility from the diffusive contribution to the vol surface. Like this, in the case where the vol surface happened to be exactly that implied by the Merton model, the local volatility would automatically come out flat. After a certain amount of algebra, we arrive at:

$$\sigma(k,T) = \sqrt{num/den} \tag{6.27}$$

with

$$num = \sqrt{T-t}\sum_{n=0}^{\infty} \sqrt{\alpha_n}A(n)\phi(d_n)\left[\frac{\hat{\sigma}}{2(T-t)} + (\lambda - \lambda')k\hat{\sigma}_k + \hat{\sigma}_T\right]$$

$$+ \lambda'M\left(t,T,ke^{-\mu_J}, \sqrt{\hat{\sigma}(k,T)^2 + \delta^2/(T-t)}\right)$$

$$- \lambda E_J[JM(t,T,k/J,\hat{\sigma}(k/J,T))] \tag{6.28}$$

and

$$den = \frac{k^2}{2}\sqrt{T-t}\sum_{n=0}^{\infty}A(n)\phi(d_n)\sqrt{\alpha_n}$$

$$\times\left[\widehat{\sigma}_{kk} + \widehat{\sigma}_k^2\left(\frac{1-\alpha_n}{\widehat{\sigma}} - d_n\sqrt{\alpha_n(T-t)}\right)\right.$$

$$\left.+\frac{1}{\widehat{\sigma}}\left(\alpha_n d_n\widehat{\sigma}_k + \frac{1}{k\sqrt{T-t}}\right)^2\right] \qquad (6.29)$$

with

$$A(n) = \frac{e^{-\lambda'(T-t)}[\lambda'(T-t)]^n}{n!}$$

$$\alpha_n = \left(1 + \frac{n\delta^2}{\widehat{\sigma}^2(k,T)(T-t)}\right)$$

For conciseness, we have employed the underscore convention $f_y = \partial f/\partial y$, $f_{yy} = \partial^2 f/\partial y^2$ to denote differentiation.

In the case where $\widehat{\sigma}(k,T)$ is flat, it can easily be verified that

$$\lambda'M\left(t,T,ke^{-\mu_J},\sqrt{\widehat{\sigma}(k,T)^2 + \delta^2/(T-t)}\right) = \lambda E_J[JM(t,T,k/J,\widehat{\sigma}(k/J,T))]$$

reducing the local vol to $\sigma(k,T) = \widehat{\sigma}$, as required. The only remaining complexity is to deal with the convolution term. In practice, the most efficient approach is to apply a fast Fourier transform to compute the transform of the Merton call function, multiply by the transform of the Gaussian distribution characterising the log jump size (see (6.24)), and Fourier transform back.

6.3.2.1   *Calibrated local vol profiles in the Andersen–Andreasen model*

One of the key features of jump incorporation with local volatility is the effect such incorporation has on the local volatility surface post-calibration to European options. As per earlier chapters, we will find that the local volatility will respond to the new model parameters in the opposite direction to implied volatility, but for jump modelling this effect has profound consequences. Recall, for example, the flattening of implied volatility skew on forward starting options, reviewed in Chapter 2. Imagine that the post-calibrated local vol surface were perfectly flat. In this case our jump model would reduce to a Lévy process with *stationary* increments. The resultant implied volatility surface would look *the same* for any future start point, exactly the effect that traders are keen to capture when pricing cliquets, for example. Recall, likewise, the 'overshoot' problem in the movement of implied volatility with spot for frozen local vol. This problem was unaffected by the addition of stochastic local vol, as the implied volatility of short-term options for a given spot level simply depended on the local variance conditional on being at that point, which by calibration was simply equal to the Dupire variance. When we include jumps, however, our effective Dupire variance flattens, with jumps 'taking up the slack' on the implied volatility skew. In the case where Dupire variance actually flattens completely, the implied vol surface at a higher spot level just shifts to the right with the ATM vol unaltered. This 'sticky delta' model of implied vol surface movement, whilst extremely useful for large shock risk management purposes (see exercise), is in practice rather idealised. The actual vol surface movement tends to be one where the ATM vol moves according to the implied volatility skew. Notice, however, that we can control how much local vol flattening we're going to get with our jump mean and standard deviation. In turn, we can control how the implied vol surface moves for static local vol, calibrating, not only to implied volatility itself, but actual implied volatility *dynamics*. We will illustrate both of these effects in the next section. For the moment though, Figures 6.6 and 6.7 show the effect of jumps on the 1Y to 5Y local vol surface of the S&P500.

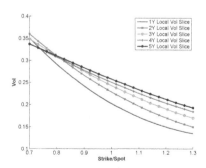 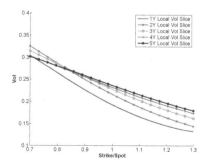

Fig. 6.6 1Y to 5Y local vol slices, S&P500, no jumps.

Fig. 6.7 1Y to 5Y local vol slices, S&P500, jump mean -150%, jumps stdev 80%, hazard rate 1%.

The effect is indeed as we might expect from the simple implied volatility analysis of the previous section. As we introduce jumps, both the local volatility level decreases, as does the slope, and to a lesser extent curvature. Note, incidentally, that non-zero jumps suffer from the same problems as jump to zero. As jumps themselves introduce their own volatility and skew, if the implied vol we're trying to calibrate to is insufficiently high, the resultant calibrated local variance can fall below zero. There is thus a limit to how negative our jump mean can be, and how high our jump standard deviation similarly, given a target vol surface and trial hazard rate. Following Andersen and Andreasen, we will use the range 0 to -100% for jump means, and 0 to 80% for jump standard deviation, though this does necessitate a somewhat lower hazard rate of 3% (Andersen and Andreasen use 10% with a lower jump mean) to enable calibration of the S&P500 vol surface (as of 1st March 2010) up to 5Y.

6.4   The effects of jumps on equity exotics

As outlined in Section 6.1, neither historical analysis nor vanilla option market inference is particularly effective in determining the appropriate model parameters for a jump process added to a local volatility diffusion. As per stochastic volatility modelling, however, the exotics market may be able to provide some guidance. We will begin with that seeming innocuous product, the variance swap, introduced in Chapter 4, and demonstrate that our assumption that this trade is model independent is based strongly on the idea that the underlying process is purely diffusive. (In the next chapter we will also demonstrate that the assumption of deterministic rates is also vital.)

6.4.1   *Variance swaps*

To begin, let's consider the situation before calibration. In the limit of continuous sampling, we have that the variance swap is the difference between the *quadratic variation* of the log stock price and a fair strike, where the former is given by:

$$[\log S]_T = \lim_{\|P\| \to 0} \sum_{i=1}^{n} \log^2 \left(\frac{S(t_k)}{S(t_{k-1})} \right)$$

where P ranges over the partitions of the interval $[0, t]$ and $\|P\|$ denotes the norm of P^2. In the case of equally spaced partitions we can write this in the more familiar form:

$$[\log S]_T = \lim_{\Delta t \to 0} \sum_{i=1}^{n} \log^2 \left(\frac{S_i}{S_{i-1}} \right)$$

where $t_i - t_{i-1} = \Delta t \ \forall \ 1 \le i \le n$. Applying (6.18), and recalling that the Brownian motion, Poisson process and jump size are all independent, allows us to write:

$$[\log S]_T = \int_0^T \sigma_t^2 dt + \int_0^T J_t^2 \lambda(t) dt$$

giving us for the undiscounted value of the variance swap:

$$V = \frac{1}{T} E_{\mathbb{Q}} \left([\log S]_T \right) = E_{\mathbb{Q}} \left[\int_0^T \sigma_t^2 dt \right] + \int_0^T E_{\mathbb{Q}}[J_t^2] \lambda(t) dt$$

Thus, for the Merton model, writing $\mu'_J = E[J] = \mu_J - \delta^2/2$, we have:

$$V = \sigma^2 + \lambda(\mu'^2_J + \delta^2) \tag{6.30}$$

We would thus expect the variance swap to exhibit a quadratic dependence both on jump mean and jump standard deviation. This is demonstrated for a 5Y variance swap with a diffusive vol of 20%, and a hazard rate of jumps of 1% in Figure 6.8.

Perhaps unsurprisingly, jumps do add a considerable amount of value to the variance swap. Note that the effect is always positive, in line with our observation that jumps always add to implied volatility. What about the calibrated case? Gatheral [Gatheral (1999)] provides an elegant derivation of the effect using the characteristic function formalism described in Section 6.3.1. Consider the log contract used for replicating variance swaps in Chapter 4. From the definition of the characteristic function (6.19) we can write:

$$E_{\mathbb{Q}}[\log(S_T/F(T))] = -i \left. \frac{\partial \widetilde{G}(\xi)}{\partial \xi} \right|_{\xi=0}$$

---

[2]The partition of an interval $[a, b]$ on the real line is a finite sequence $x_0, \ldots, x_n$ where $x_i > x_{i-1}$, $x_0 = a$, and $x_n = b$. The norm of the partition denotes the longest of the associated subintervals, i.e. $\|P\| = \max_{i=1,\ldots,n}(|x_i - x_{i-1}|)$.

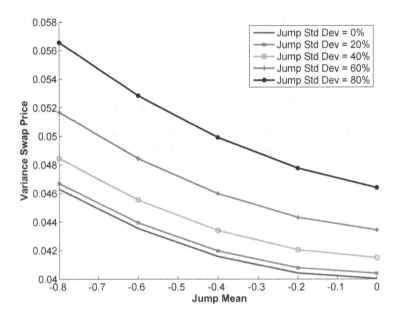

Fig. 6.8   Dependence of variance swap price on jump mean and standard deviation, hazard rate 1%.

where (taking $\tau = T$ for illustration):

$$\widetilde{G}(\xi) = \exp\left[\left(-i\xi\sigma^2/2 - \frac{1}{2}\xi^2\sigma^2\right)T\right]\left[e^{\lambda T(\widehat{\omega}(\xi)-1)}e^{-i\xi\lambda T(e^{\mu_J}-1)}\right]$$

We thus get:

$$E_{\mathbb{Q}}[\log(S_T/F(T))] = -\sigma^2 T/2 + \lambda T\left(-i\frac{\partial\widehat{\omega}(\xi)}{\partial\xi}\big|_{\xi=0} - (e^{\mu_J}-1)\right)$$

$$= -\sigma^2 T/2 + \lambda T\int_{-\infty}^{\infty}(1+J-e^J)\omega(J)dJ$$

Combining with (6.30) this then gives the rather nice relation:

$$V = \frac{2}{T}E_{\mathbb{Q}}[\log(F(T)/S_T)] + 2\lambda\int_{-\infty}^{\infty}\left(1+J+\frac{J^2}{2}-e^J\right)\omega(J)dJ$$

Now, *post-calibration*, the first term will be unaltered, depending only on the volatility surface and forward at time T. Expanding the integrand of the second term gives:

$$\int_{-\infty}^{\infty}\left(1+J+\frac{J^2}{2}-e^J\right)\omega(J)dJ = \int_{-\infty}^{\infty}-\frac{J^3}{6}\omega(J)dJ + \text{higher order terms}$$

In other words, the effect of jumps, post-calibration, goes approximately as the third moment of the jump distribution. For the Gaussian distribution (see exercise), this gives:

$$V = V_0 - \frac{1}{3}\lambda\mu'_J(\mu'^2_J + 3\delta^2)$$

This is shown in Figure 6.9 for the same flat implied volatility surface.

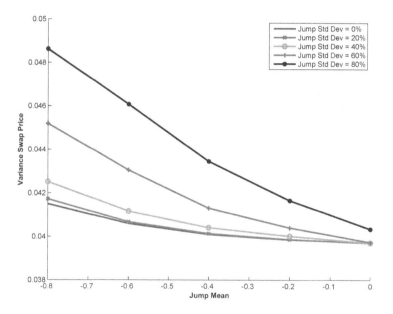

Fig. 6.9 Dependence of variance swap price on jump mean and standard deviation, hazard rate 1%, calibrated.

So, as we might expect, the effect of jumps on variance swaps post-calibration is reduced, but by no means insubstantial. Note also that for jump means less than -0.3 (assuming $\delta = 0$), jumps will actually become *more* significant post-calibration, assuming that implied volatility remains calibrated. In fact, for jump means of this magnitude, calibration will tend to break down, causing the vol surface to 'peel away' as per Chapter 5, further increasing their effect on the variance swap price. Variance swaps may also help to distinguish between models of high frequency, small jumps and low frequency, large jumps. If we take, for example, $\lambda\mu'_J = const$, the post-calibrated effect of jumps will grow as μ'^2_J, even though the expected log jump size is constant. It is tempting to postulate that the recently observed expensiveness of variance swaps on indices relative to the log contract may, at least in part, be due to an increase in the jump mean [Crosby (2011)].

6.4.2   *Investment strategies*

Over the course of the last decade, so-called 'dynamically rebalanced portfolio' strategies, where the client holds a portfolio of fixed income and equity instruments with weights determined *formulaically*, became popular as investment products. The essential idea is to reduce the investor's exposure to the equity market in times of market fall, and increase it during market rallies. Of the many variants available, one of the most well-known is the Constant Proportion Portfolio Insurance (CPPI) product. The strategy works as follows [Overhaus *et al.* (2007)]. At every fixing date t_i, we compute the level of the strategy $F(t_i)$ based on the level at the previous fixing $F(t_{i-1})$ according to the following formula:

$$F(t_i) = F(t_{i-1})\left[1 + L(t_{i-1})\left(\frac{S(t_i)}{S(t_{i-1})} - 1\right)\right.$$

$$\left. + (1 - L(t_{i-1}))\left(\frac{P(t_i)}{P(t_{i-1})} - 1\right)\right] \tag{6.31}$$

where $P(t_i)$ represents the value of the fixed income portfolio at time t_i and $S(t_i)$ the value of the corresponding equity portfolio. The investment level $L(t_i)$ is given by:

$$L(t_i) = m\frac{F(t_i) - P(t_i)}{F(t_i)}$$

where m is referred to as the multiplier. In the 'classical' CPPI strategy, the *bond floor* $P(t_i)$ is taken to be a zero coupon bond, no restriction is imposed on the investment level, no fees are taken out of the CPPI index, and no ratcheting is applied to the bond floor. This strategy is obviously idealised, but provides an excellent example of an asset whose optionality is *entirely* dominated by jumps. To see this, let's consider the limiting case of continuous sampling on a stock diffusion with flat model parameters, including the short rate. (The following derivation is due to Overhaus *et al.* [Overhaus *et al.* (2007)]). Denoting the CPPI 'cushion' $C_t = F_t - P_t$, we have for the dynamics of the strategy:

$$dF_t = (F_t - L(t))\frac{dP_t}{P_t} + L(t)\frac{dS_t}{S_t}$$

where $L(t) = mC_t$.
The corresponding dynamics of the cushion are then:

$$
\begin{aligned}
dC_t &= dF_t - dP_t \\
&= (C_t + P_t - mC_t)rdt + mC_t\left[\mu dt + \sigma dW_t\right] - dP_t \\
&= C_t[(1-m)r + \mu m]dt + mC_t\sigma dW_t
\end{aligned}
$$

using $dP_t = rP_t dt$ for the zero coupon bond. Solving for C_t gives:

$$
\begin{aligned}
C_t &= C_0 \exp\left[\left((1-m)r + \mu m - \frac{m^2\sigma^2}{2}\right)t\right]\exp\left[m\sigma W_t\right] \\
&= \alpha_t S_t^m \\
\alpha_t &= \frac{C_0}{S_0^m}\exp\left[\left(r - m\left(r - \frac{\sigma^2}{2}\right) - \frac{m^2\sigma^2}{2}\right)t\right]
\end{aligned}
$$

Thus the CPPI strategy is simply $F_t = \alpha_t S_t^m + P_t$, which is transparently bounded below by the bond floor P_t. A put option on F_t struck at unity would, therefore, have identically zero value if the stock is purely diffusive (in the continuous limit at least). The distribution for a 5Y strategy with multiplier 2, 20% vol, is shown in Figure 6.10.

Now let's consider what happens when we introduce jumps. In the continuous time limit, one can show easily (see exercise), that if the stock falls by more than $1/m$ of its current level over the interval $[t, t+dt]$, then the strategy will breach the bond floor. Such a *finite* move in stock over an infinitesimal time period can only be achieved through a jump. The distribution of CPPI spots, again at 5Y for 20% vol, but now with a jump mean of -100% and zero jump standard deviation, 1% hazard rate is shown in Figure 6.11.

Indeed we have a small, but finite, probability that the terminal CPPI spot is below the bond floor. An ATM put option on this structure should clearly now have value. The higher the standard deviation of jumps, the more likely the $1/m$ fall becomes, and the higher the value of this option.

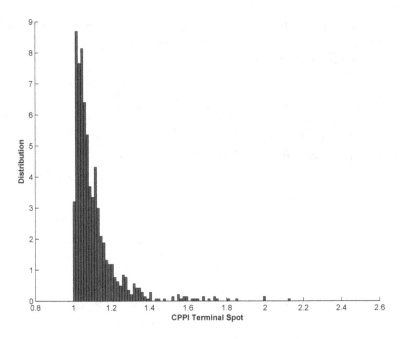

Fig. 6.10   Distribution of CPPI terminal spots, 20% vol, 5Y, no jumps.

The behaviour against jump mean and standard deviation is shown in Figure 6.12.

We might expect, as diffusion has no impact on the optionality of this product, that the results post-calibration to the vol surface should look much the same, and indeed this is the case, as shown in Figure 6.13.

Interestingly, calibration does appear to push the value of the option up slightly. This is presumably an effect of the reduction in the downside local volatility. As we increase volatility *on top* of a jump process, the distribution of the strategy spreads out, but as per Figure 6.10, biased to the right of both the zero vol state conditional on no jumps (unity) and that conditional on having jumped. This then lowers the expected payoff of the put option, making the put short vega, assuming the existence of jumps. Either way, whether we calibrate to implied volatility or not, we have in this product an example of a trade whose value is entirely dependent on the departure from diffusive behaviour. The strong sensitivity to the price of puts on this strategy again suggests a method for market inference of the actual jump parameters, but sadly such classical CPPI strategies almost never trade, in addition to which the options traded tend to be calls rather

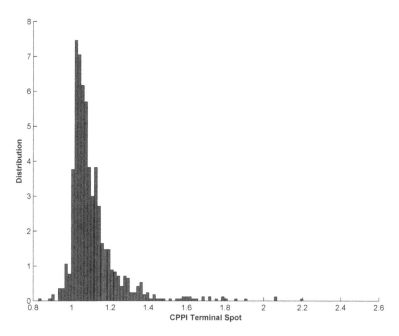

Fig. 6.11   Distribution of CPPI terminal spots, 20% vol, 5Y, jump mean -100%, jump stdev 0%, 1% hazard rate.

than puts. That being said, these products almost always incorporate some hedge for the downside jump behaviour, of which knockout OTM cliquet puts (a.k.a *stability notes*) are popular. These products pay out a series of cliquet put spreads on the equity component with a reset frequency equal to the CPPI. We will look at the effect of jumps on cliquets in the next section.

6.4.3   *Forward skew*

Recall our earlier discussion of the stationary increment properties of Lévy processes. In the light of the local vol flattening demonstrated in Section 6.3.2.1, we might imagine that, as we increase the impact of jumps and flatten the local volatility profile accordingly, our process should begin to resemble the pure Merton process described in Section 6.3.1. In other words, if we look at the forward starting option $[(S(t_i)/S(t_{i-1}) - \kappa, 0]^+$ introduced in Chapter 2, we should see the implied volatility skew profile (as a function of κ) tend to the same curve (the implied volatility level of course will continue to be a function of the spot starting implied volatility surface

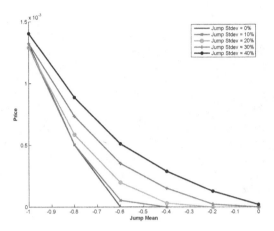

Fig. 6.12   5Y ATM put option on CPPI, 20% vol, against different jump means for increasing jump stdev, 1% hazard rate.

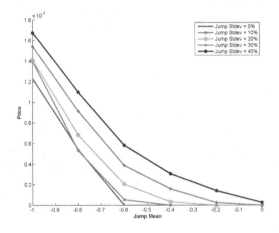

Fig. 6.13   5Y ATM put option on CPPI, 20% implied vol, against different jump means for increasing jump stdev, 1% hazard rate, calibrated.

term structure). This is indeed the case, as can be seen by comparing Figure 6.14, for the 1Y tenor forward starting call on the S&P500 with no jumps, with Figure 6.15, corresponding to the same option but with jump mean -100%, jump standard deviation 50% and hazard rate 3%.

Jumps then seem to have 'come to the rescue' on the forward skew problem introduced in Chapter 2. Options with a strong long sensitivity to the

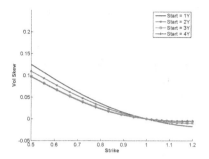

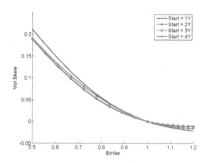

Fig. 6.14   1Y tenor forward starting vol slice, S&P500, no jumps.

Fig. 6.15   1Y tenor forward starting vol slice, S&P500, jumps mean -100%, jump stdev 50%, jump hazard rate 3%.

forward skew profile, such as Napoleon and reverse cliquets, will arguably be more realistically priced relative to their Dupire model priced counterparts. Indeed, should a liquid market for these products exist, here too we might find an exotic inroad for calibrating jump model parameters. Figures 6.16 and 6.17 show the behaviour of the reverse cliquet and Napoleon introduced in Chapter 4 against jump mean and standard deviation, post-calibration to the S&P500 vol surface.

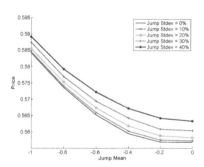

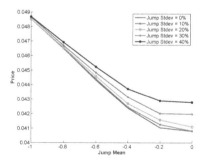

Fig. 6.16   Price vs jump mean for a 5Y yearly sampled reverse cliquet, 100% base coupon, increasing jump stdev.

Fig. 6.17   Price vs jump mean for a 5Y yearly sampled Napoleon cliquet, 20% base coupon, increasing jump stdev.

The behaviour of the two products is qualitatively similar. There are actually two effects going on. The first is the reduction in the level of local volatility as jump standard deviation is increased, increasing the value of these short vega products. The second is the impact of the global floor, which as discussed in Chapter 4, serves as a deep OTM put on the structure.

As forward skew is increased with more negative jump mean, the long put position causes the product to increase in value. Interestingly, the Napoleon looks more like a 'pure skew' product than the reverse cliquet for strongly negative jump mean. The overall shift of the forward starting vol surface caused by the increase in jump standard deviation seems to have a decreasing impact on what is effectively a put spread on the worst performer, the more negative the jump mean becomes.

6.4.4 *Smile dynamics*

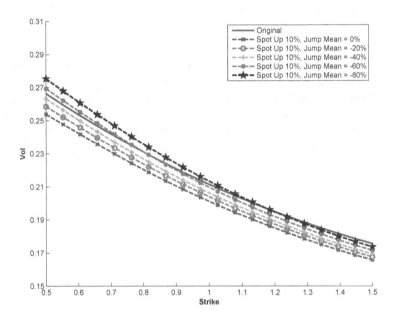

Fig. 6.18   5Y maturity vol slice moves vs spot, jump stdev 40%, hazard rate 3%.

It turns out that, not only do jumps appear to address the forward smile problem, but they also appear to address the problem of the dynamics of the spot starting volatility surface. As discussed, the addition of a stochastic component on top of the local volatility function does little, post-calibration, to alleviate the overshoot problem derived by Hagan *et al.* [Hagan *et al.* (2002)]. On the other hand, we know that the Merton model will give a pure 'sticky delta' move of the vol surface for spot moves. It would seem reasonable that, for some intermediate state between pure

Dupire and pure Merton, we might be able to recover an implied volatility movement which agrees at least with market practice. This appears to be true, as shown in Figure 6.18 for the simplified vol surface used in Chapter 4, assuming a jump standard deviation of 40% and a hazard rate of 3%.

This is quite striking. For a jump mean of -80% (in this example), we actually get a move very similar to market, where the ATM vol moves down the original smile to the level at 110% of spot. Some sort of joint calibration to both implied volatilities, and implied volatility dynamics, might well prove useful as a means of inferring suitable levels for these jump parameters, though as far as we know this research has yet to be done.

6.5 Conclusions

In this chapter we relaxed the 'jump to ruin' assumption of the previous chapter and explored the impact of jumps of *indeterminate* size on the price of various exotic instruments. In the process, we have demonstrated that jump modelling is as elusive as it is essential. The fact that jumps in index prices do exist is strongly suggested by the implied volatility dynamics, over and above earlier work around the distribution of historic returns, or attempts to fit the implied volatility surface from idealised stochastic vol with jump models. Certain instruments, such as options on investment strategies, *must* be hedged for jumps, given that their entire value derives from non-diffusive behaviour. Other instruments, such as cliquets, depend on the modelling of forward volatility skew, which in turn depends critically on jump processes. We can therefore not ignore jumps. Determining exactly how to model them, however, is hampered by the lack of transparency on the relevant exotics. Like this, jump modelling can be considered one of the principal model risks underlying the valuation of equity derivatives. At best, we can try to establish reasonable bounds on what the jump parameters might be, and reserve accordingly.

6.6 Exercises

(1) Demonstrate, for the normal distribution $n(X) = e^{-(X-\mu)^2/2\sigma^2}$ that the cumulants $\kappa_1 = \mu$, $\kappa_2 = \sigma^2$ and $\kappa_n = 0 \ \forall \ n > 2$, where the cumulant κ_n is defined by:

$$\kappa_n = \left. \frac{\partial^n}{\partial t^n} \right|_{t=0} \log \left[E \left(e^{tX} \right) \right]$$

(2) For the Merton process:

$$\frac{dS_t}{S_t} = \mu dt + \sigma dW_t + (e^J - 1)dN_t$$

demonstrate that we can recover the Merton equation from the expression:

$$E_{\mathbb{Q}}[d\Pi_t] = 0$$

where

$$\Pi_t = V_t - \Delta S_t + B_t$$

and the expectation takes into account the behaviour of the portfolio conditional on a jump, and conditional on no jumps. (This is effectively the original CAPM based argument used by Merton.)

(3) Demonstrate that the solution to:

$$c(k, T) = \frac{e^k}{2\pi} \int_{-\infty+i\gamma}^{\infty+i\gamma} e^{-i\xi k} \hat{f}(-\xi) \widehat{G}(\xi, \tau) d\xi$$

is given by:

$$c(k, \tau) = 1 - e^{k/2} \frac{1}{\pi} \int_0^\infty \frac{d\xi}{\xi^2 + \frac{1}{4}} \Re \left[e^{-ik\xi} \widehat{G}(\xi - i/2, \tau) \right]$$

(Hint: re-express the call price in terms of stock and a *covered call* $\min(S, K)$. Show that the Fourier transform of the latter exists only in the domain $0 < \gamma < 1$ and choose an appropriate contour in this region to complete the continuation from the integral along the real line.)

(4) For a jump process X_t given by:

$$X_t = X_t^c + J_t = X_0 + \int_0^t \sigma_s dW_s + \int_0^t \mu_s ds + J_t$$

where J_t denotes the cumulative effect of jumps over the interval $[0, t]$, and X_t^c the diffusive part of the process, the Itō integral for the function $f(X_t)$ is given by [Privault (2009)]:

$$f(X_t) = f(X_0) + \int_0^t f'(X_s)dX_s^c + \frac{1}{2}\int_0^t f''(X_s)\sigma_s^2 ds$$
$$+ \sum_{0 < s \le t} [f(X_s) - f(X_{s^-})]$$

where s^- denotes the time just prior to s. Use this result to show that, for the process given in question 2, the process for $\log(S_t)$ is given by:

$$d\log(S_t) = (\mu_S - \sigma_S^2/2)dt + \sigma_S dW_t + J dN_t$$

(5) Show, by applying (6.17) for the evolution of the probability density of the stock price under Merton jump-diffusion, to the integral (6.9) for the call price, that

$$-\frac{\partial \tilde{c}}{\partial T} + (\lambda' - \lambda)k\frac{\partial \tilde{c}}{\partial k} + \frac{1}{2}\sigma^2(T,k)k^2\frac{\partial^2 \tilde{c}}{\partial k^2}$$
$$+ \lambda'\left(\int_{-\infty}^{\infty} \tilde{c}(t,T,ke^{-\mu_J + \delta^2/2 - \delta z})\phi(z - \delta)dz - \tilde{c}\right) = 0$$

where $\lambda' = \lambda e^{\mu_J}$, $\phi(z)$ is a standard normal distribution, $\tilde{c}(t,T,k)$ the undiscounted call price divided by the forward, with $k = K/F(t,T)$.

(6) Demonstrate, that for a volatility surface $\hat{\sigma}(K,T)$ which is non-arbitrageable everywhere according to a proportional dividend model, that the 'sticky delta' transformation:

$$\hat{\sigma}'(K,T) = \hat{\sigma}(KS/S',T)$$

under spot shock $\Delta S = S' - S$ will preserve the no arbitrage conditions for arbitrary spot shock. (Hint: consider the Dupire local vol formula.)

(7) For the log jump size J distributed $\sim \mathcal{N}(\mu'_J, \delta)$, show that:

$$\int_{-\infty}^{\infty} J^3 \omega(J)dJ = \mu'_J(\mu'^2_J + 3\delta^2)$$

(8) For the CPPI formula (6.31), demonstrate that the strategy will breach the bond floor if $S(t_i)/S(t_{i-1}) - 1 < -1/m$. Derive the value of an ATM put on such a strategy if $m = 1$.

Chapter 7

Rates

Up until now our analysis of model risk has been predicated on the assumption that the cost of funding our option position is deterministic. Such an assumption greatly simplifies analysis, allowing us, at worst, simply to take the discount factor to a particular payoff outside the risk-neutral expectation. Is, however, the assumption of deterministic interest rates reasonable? What do we observe historically? What does the market tell us? Can we model stochastic rates effectively, and if so, can we incorporate them in the vanilla equity options market consistently? What sort of exotics are likely to respond most strongly to interest rate volatility, and why? In this chapter we will attempt to address each of these questions, ultimately deriving an intuition for what is perhaps the most un-intuitive of model risks.

7.1 Historical analysis

By now it should come as no surprise to us that every time we look historically at some model variable of interest, that variable, or at least the nearest approximation to it, turns out to be stochastic. Interest rates are of course no exception, though the drivers on their evolution are somewhat different from volatility or jumps, for example. Figure 7.1 shows a set of curves for 1M, 6M and 12M implied Libor rates for USD, over the period 2005–2010.

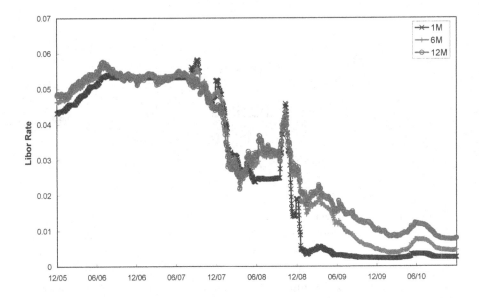

Fig. 7.1   USD Libor evolution, 2005–2010.

We can see two distinct features:

- Jumps: rates tend to remain stable over relatively long periods (order of a year), and then switch to a new level in response to government base rate changes designed to stabilise the national economy.
- Diffusion: in between base rate changes, high volume trading activity in government issued debt leads to a natural stochasticity around the new base rate level.

Already then, we can see that interest rates demonstrate rich dynamics. Note that we refer to implied Libor[1] rates, given by the relation:

$$Df(T_0, T_i) = \frac{1}{1 + L_i \tau(T_0, T_i)}$$

where $\tau(t_1, t_2)$ corresponds to the effective accrual period corresponding to the calendar interval $[t_1, t_2]$ calculated according to the currency's *day count convention*. These go under a variety of different names, e.g.

---

[1] The London Interbank Offered Rate: a daily reference rate based on interest rates at which banks borrow unsecured funds from other banks in the London wholesale money market.

- *Act/365*: actual number of days between t_1 and t_2 divided by 365.
- *Act/360*: actual number of days between t_1 and t_2 divided by 360.
- *30/360*: number of days between t_1 and t_2 divided by 360, adjusting the start or end date such that, if it falls at the end of the month, and that month is not of length 30 days, the date is made to be the 30th of that month. Various methods exist according to whether the month in question is February and if both t_1 and t_2 fall at the end of a non-30-day month (30/360 US, 30E/360, 30/360 ISDA). [Mayle (1993); Christie (2002)].
- *Act/Act*: accounts for leap years, i.e. days not in leap year/365 + days in leap year/366. This is actually the *Actual/Actual ISDA* convention, distinct from *Actual/Actual ICMA*, specific to US Treasury bonds [Mayle (1993)], or Act/Act AFB, which uses either 365 or 366 depending on whether the calculation period involves the 29th February or not [ISDA (1998)].

For the remainder of this chapter, we will use the simplest day count convention *Act/365*. It is perhaps obvious, but the *instantaneous* short rate r_t which has hitherto been taken for granted in our modelling approaches, is not directly observable, but rather corresponds to a zero coupon bond entered into at time t and expiring at $t + dt$ as $dt \to 0$. As with local volatility, such a rate needs to be imputed from actual traded instruments making up the full discount curve. Common products include:

- *Money market instruments*: short-term loans of one year maturity or less (typically), e.g. Treasury bills, commercial paper, certificates of deposit;
- *Interest rate futures*: e.g. Treasury bill futures, Eurodollar futures: essentially a contract allowing the buyer to lock in a future investment rate (e.g. 1M Libor);
- *Forward rate agreements* (FRAs): a forward contract where one party agrees to pay a fixed interest rate over a single period and receive a floating rate. In practice, only the differential is paid at expiry. Similar conceptually to an interest rate future, except that the latter is generally margin called on exchange, whilst an FRA is an OTC transaction paying only at maturity.
- *Interest rate swaps*: a contract to swap floating coupons for fixed coupons. The fixed coupon which values the contract at zero is referred to as the par spread (see next section). The swap can easily be seen to be nothing more than a combination of FRAs.

Once one has built up the discounting curve in such a way that all of the associated interest rate instruments are priced with minimal arbitrage opportunity between them [Lesniewksi (2008)], one effectively has a *continuum* of short rates $r(t)$ rather than, say, the growth curve for a single tradable interest rate underlyer. This distinction with, say, a stock or fx, is important. When we construct a dynamic interest rate model, we are not describing a portfolio where we short the underlyer against an option and accrue interest on the cash balance (a so-called 'cash-and-carry' strategy). What we are in fact doing is attempting to hold a portfolio of instruments designed to hedge out the movements to principal components of the rate curve. Just how complicated we make this depends on how sensitive the instrument is to the higher principal components. This will be explored in more detail in the next section, but for the moment, what do these components look like? Figure 7.2 shows the first three principal components, for the period December 2005 to December 2010, based on sequential 3M FRA rates, up to 10Y.

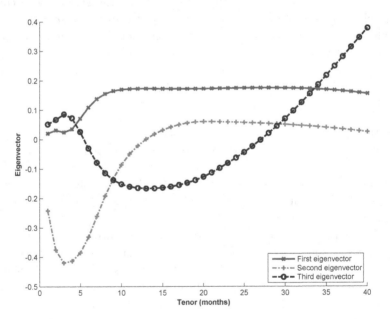

Fig. 7.2   USD rate curve principal components, based on daily 3M FRA returns from December 2005 to December 2010.

The picture is not dissimilar to implied volatility movement, namely that the bulk of rate curve movement (80 % of realised variance) is given by a parallel shift to longer dated 3M FRA rates, the next largest contributor (14%) by curve steepening of short-dated FRAs, and the third component (4%) by curve flexing. This is an important observation. If we design an interest rate model where the discount curve is driven entirely off one Brownian short rate process, such a model will in fact capture much of the observed curve movement. If, on the other hand, we hold a contract exposed directly to a higher principal component (e.g. a spread between constant maturity swap (CMS) rates[2]), such a model will clearly be insufficient to capture the key dynamics and hedges underlying the contract. This chapter will limit our attention to short rate models, but we will describe more general approaches in the next section.

So much for the idiosyncratic movements of the rate curve. What about their relation to equity? A common view is that people tend to 'fly to Treasuries' in times of market distress. One might imagine then that correlation to equity movements and zero coupon bonds should be negative in bearish periods. Conversely, we might expect that equity and Libor should become positively correlated in such periods. A picture for the 3M correlation between the returns on the first principal component of the rate curve and the log returns on the S&P500 over the period April 2006 to September 2010, is shown in Figure 7.3.

Our intuition appears to be correct. Whilst the data is quite noisy, correlation does appear to become noticeably positive in the run up to the 2008 crisis and subsequently. Corresponding pictures for EUR vs .STOXX50E, and JPY vs .NK225 are shown in Figures 7.4 and 7.5 respectively.

Correlation between equity and interest rates then, clearly cannot be ignored. Even if we took the view that it averaged out around zero and priced accordingly, such a view could leave us significantly misvalued in times of distress. Ultimately, it comes down to another model risk, with our view on how to set this parameter guided principally by the sensitivity of our trade to it. This will be explored in detail through the examples given in the rest of this chapter.

---

[2]An interest rate swap exchanging a floating rate for a fixed maturity par swap rate, reset at the start of each coupon. The floating rate is generally Libor corresponding to the tenor of the swap, but may be another par swap rate.

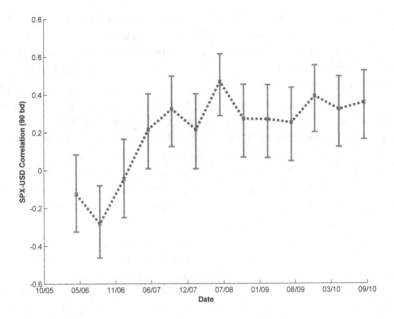

Fig. 7.3   3M rolling correlation between S&P500 and USD first principal component.

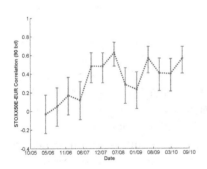

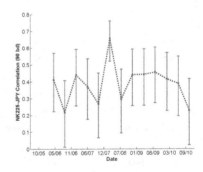

Fig. 7.4   3M rolling correlation between .STOXX50E and EUR first principal component.

Fig. 7.5   3M rolling correlation between .NK225 and JPY first principal component.

7.2   Market analysis

We have seen that, viewed historically, interest rates are far from deterministic. The market of course takes the same view, with a plethora of options on interest rate products giving direct calibration targets for whatever interest rate model we might choose to come up with. Indeed, whilst one of the challenges in equity derivatives is to deal with the *lack* of information coming from the market, a big challenge in interest rate derivatives is to deal with too *much* information. Consider, for example, one of the most commonly traded interest rate options, the *swaption*. This is a contract providing the holder with the right, but not the obligation, to enter into an interest rate swap, of a given tenor and maturity, at a given rate at a given time in the future. For a *payer* swaption, we can write the payoff V at expiry T formally as follows:

$$V = [DV01(S_T - K, 0)]^+$$

where

$$DV01 = \sum_{i=1,n} \tau(T_{i-1}, T_i) P(T_0, T_i)$$

with $T_0 = T$, and $P(T_0, T_i)$ the value of a zero coupon bond entered into at T_0 and paying unity at T_i. (The *receiver* swaption takes the form of a put on the par spread.) By definition of the par spread rate, we have:

$$S_T DV01 = \sum_{i=1,n} L_{i-1} \tau(T_{i-1}, T_i) P(T_0, T_i) = 1 - P(T_0, T_n) \qquad (7.1)$$

using the relation between the discount factor and Libors:

$$P(T_0, T_i) = \prod_{j=1,i} \frac{1}{1 + L_{j-1} \tau(T_{j-1}, T_j)}$$

(see exercise). So, collecting terms, we arrive at:

$$V = \left[1 - P(T_0, T_n) - K \sum_{i=1,n} \tau(T_{i-1}, T_i) P(T_0, T_i), 0 \right]^+ = f(L_0, \dots, L_{n-1})$$

The value of this contract at time $t \leq T_0$ is then given by:

$$E_{\mathbb{Q}}[V] = E_{\mathbb{Q}} \left[\left(P(t, T_0) - P(t, T_n) - K \sum_{i=1,n} \tau(T_{i-1}, T_i) P(t, T_i), 0 \right)^+ \right]$$
$$(7.2)$$

which by a change of measure (see Section 7.3.1) we can write as:

$$P(t, T_0) E_{T_0} [f(L_0, \ldots, L_{n-1})]^+$$

where the *T-forward measure* is defined by:

$$\frac{X_t}{P(t, T)} = E_T [X_T | \mathcal{F}_t]$$

(c.f. the risk-neutral measure $\mathbb{Q}$ given by:

$$\frac{X_t}{B(t)} = E_{\mathbb{Q}} \left[\frac{X_T}{B(T)} \middle| \mathcal{F}_t \right]$$

for $B(t) = \exp \left[\int_0^t r(s)ds \right]$). We can equally employ a change of measure to the DV01 or *annuity* measure, to simplify (7.2) as:

$$E_{\mathbb{Q}}[V] = P(t, T_0)DV01 E_{\mathrm{DV01}} \left[(S_T - K, 0)^+ \right]$$
$$= P(t, T_0)DV01 \left[FN(d_1) - KN(d_2) \right] \tag{7.3}$$

allowing us to write the value of the option in a more familiar Black–Scholes format. The forward swap rate F is known, as:

$$F \times P(t, T_0)DV01 = P(t, T_0) - P(t, T_n)$$

(from (7.1)), allowing us to map observed swaption prices to implied vols. Note that the structure of the implied vol data is potentially one dimension more complex than an equity implied vol surface, as the underlying swap is defined by tenor and maturity. A model which matches the interest rate swaptions market alone then, potentially has to model the correlated marginal distributions of all associated Libors, under all the associated *T*-forward measures of the corresponding swaption maturities. Even if we confine our attention to at the money USD swaptions on 1Y swap tenors, a typical swaption vol grid (by swaption maturity and underlying swap maturity) would be represented well by Figure 7.6. Fitting exactly to all of these points is clearly going to require a high factor model, some of which will be discussed briefly in the next section. The market for interest rate volatility is large. As of the end of 2010, over USD 40 trillion notional outstanding on swaptions, and their simpler counterparts, caps and floors (put and calls on a single Libor payment), were reported in the TriOptima Rates Repository [ISDA (2010)], compared with around USD 10 trillion for all of equity derivatives. Interest rate dynamics are far from under-specified. As far as equity derivatives are concerned, the real model risks are (a) in the choice of interest rate model and (b) the equity-rate correlation, for which a transparent market has indeed yet to be formed. We will approach (a) in a somewhat crude manner, namely looking at the effect of applying one stochastic interest rate model vs not applying one at all. Within this context, we will then look at the effect of stressing our equity-rate correlation assumptions. It should be emphasised though that the model chosen is only one of many, and is selected primarily to allow us to develop a clearer intuition than might be afforded by more complex models which might provide a closer fit to the actual interest rate options market.

	1Y	2Y	3Y	4Y	5Y	6Y	7Y	8Y	9Y	10Y	12Y	15Y	20Y	25Y	30Y
1M	123.77%	98.19%	82.16%	66.81%	58.56%	50.38%	44.98%	37.83%	35.48%	35.70%	33.65%	29.35%	30.15%	27.30%	28.93%
3M	97.75%	80.95%	64.63%	55.75%	51.28%	44.78%	40.38%	36.25%	34.40%	34.23%	32.90%	28.38%	27.45%	25.63%	25.68%
6M	82.77%	72.24%	58.61%	50.40%	46.18%	40.88%	37.60%	34.60%	32.93%	32.35%	30.45%	27.60%	25.68%	24.95%	24.43%
9M	78.56%	66.07%	54.01%	46.83%	43.03%	38.28%	35.48%	34.00%	32.60%	31.13%	29.40%	26.85%	25.15%	24.45%	23.83%
1Y	73.81%	59.87%	49.32%	43.15%	39.75%	35.93%	33.63%	35.25%	30.88%	29.95%	29.15%	26.05%	25.08%	23.60%	23.60%
2Y	51.11%	43.11%	37.58%	34.01%	31.76%	30.18%	28.98%	27.90%	27.20%	27.03%	26.30%	24.13%	23.23%	22.45%	22.33%
3Y	36.26%	31.88%	29.88%	28.03%	27.38%	26.55%	25.83%	25.30%	24.75%	24.60%	23.55%	22.45%	21.77%	21.40%	21.05%
4Y	28.55%	26.75%	25.70%	25.05%	24.63%	24.38%	23.78%	23.20%	22.93%	22.95%	22.80%	21.35%	20.60%	20.50%	20.20%
5Y	25.35%	24.28%	23.78%	23.43%	23.10%	22.90%	22.45%	21.90%	21.60%	21.78%	21.65%	20.35%	19.70%	19.32%	19.37%
6Y	23.10%	22.80%	22.55%	22.30%	22.05%	21.85%	21.60%	21.60%	21.30%	21.10%	20.60%	19.90%	19.15%	19.05%	18.95%
7Y	21.98%	21.75%	21.25%	21.05%	20.85%	20.72%	20.42%	20.08%	19.90%	19.95%	19.75%	18.75%	18.22%	18.00%	17.80%
8Y	20.80%	20.45%	20.35%	20.15%	20.00%	20.20%	20.25%	20.05%	19.85%	19.65%	19.30%	18.75%	18.00%	17.75%	17.70%
9Y	20.05%	19.65%	19.55%	19.35%	19.30%	19.65%	19.60%	19.30%	19.05%	18.80%	18.60%	18.75%	17.55%	17.35%	17.00%
10Y	19.20%	18.97%	18.87%	18.72%	18.60%	18.55%	18.47%	18.47%	18.22%	18.02%	18.00%	18.25%	16.30%	16.25%	16.20%
12Y	18.41%	18.27%	18.18%	18.13%	18.05%	17.99%	17.96%	17.92%	17.73%	17.58%	17.52%	17.05%	15.97%	15.80%	16.14%
15Y	17.29%	17.50%	17.50%	17.50%	17.40%	17.35%	17.40%	17.30%	17.20%	17.12%	16.97%	16.86%	15.60%	15.27%	16.25%
20Y	17.10%	17.00%	16.92%	16.77%	16.90%	16.40%	16.42%	16.20%	16.07%	15.87%	15.62%	16.75%	14.35%	14.27%	14.15%
25Y	16.30%	16.20%	16.10%	16.00%	16.00%	15.90%	15.85%	15.75%	15.70%	15.65%	15.50%	15.30%	14.10%	13.90%	13.75%
30Y	15.86%	15.75%	15.70%	15.60%	15.60%	15.60%	15.45%	15.20%	15.20%	15.25%	15.40%	15.70%	13.50%	13.40%	13.35%

Fig. 7.6   Representative ATM USD swaption vol grid (semi-annual).

7.3   Interest rate models

It should be stated up front that it is not the intention of this book to provide a full presentation of this rich and complex field. Excellent references may be found in Brigo and Mercurio [Brigo and Mercurio (2006)], James and Webber [James and Webber (2000)], Rebonato [Rebonato (2002a)], and of course the recently published work by Andersen and Piterbarg [Andersen and Piterbarg (2010)]. We will provide a brief overview here, by way of illustration, and go on to discuss how to integrate one of the simplest (but nonetheless powerful) of these models into equity-rate hybrid derivative modelling.

7.3.1   *Preliminaries*

Up until now, we had been working exclusively in the risk-neutral measure. We saw, in Chapter 1, that, for any delta hedging strategy, where we replicate an option price through a weighted combination of a stock and a bond, that:

$$\frac{V_t}{B_t} = E_\mathbb{Q}\left[\frac{V_T}{B_T}\middle| \mathcal{F}_t\right] \tag{7.4}$$

Indeed, as demonstrated by Harrison and Pliska [Harrison and Pliska (1981)], the result can be generalised as follows:

Definition 7.1. A trading strategy is a (K+1-dimensional) process $\phi = \{\phi_t : 0 \le t \le T\}$ whose components $\phi^0, \phi^1, \ldots, \phi^K$ are locally bounded and predictable. The value process associated with the strategy ϕ_t is defined by:

$$V_t(\phi) = \phi_t S_t = \sum_{k=0}^{K} \phi_t^k S_t^k$$

Harrison and Pliska go on to show that the strategy ϕ is self-financing if, and only if, $V_t(\phi)/B_t = V_0(\phi) + \int_0^t \phi_u d(S_u/B_u)$, where $S_t^0 = B_t$. But, as by definition, every undiscounted (non-dividend paying) security S^k/B_t is itself a martingale under the risk-neutral measure $\mathbb{Q}$, we have $E_\mathbb{Q}[d(S_t/B_t)|\mathcal{F}_t] = 0$, and hence $E_\mathbb{Q}[V_t(\phi)/B_t|\mathcal{F}_0] = V_0(\phi)$. Starting from time t we can write equally $B_t E_\mathbb{Q}[V_T(\phi)/B_T|\mathcal{F}_t] = V_t(\phi)$, proving (7.4).

So, any undiscounted self-financing trading strategy should be a martingale under the risk-neutral measure. This measure is, however, only one possible choice for valuation. We can generalise by considering a different measure, $\mathbb{N}$ associated with the *numeraire* N such that, by definition:

$$\frac{V_t}{N_t} = E_\mathbb{N}\left[\frac{V_T}{N_T}\middle| \mathcal{F}_t\right] \tag{7.5}$$

We can relate the expectation of a stochastic variable X_t under two different probability measures via the Radon–Nikodym derivative $d\mathbb{Q}/d\mathbb{N}$, introduced in Chapter 1 as:

$$E_\mathbb{N}\left[X_t \frac{d\mathbb{Q}}{d\mathbb{N}}\right] = E_\mathbb{Q}[X_t] \tag{7.6}$$

But now we come to a crucial condition. For the absence of arbitrage, the price of a tradable security must be *unique*. The financial universe does not care, essentially, which probability measure we choose to price it in. We must therefore have:

$$V_t = N_t E_{\mathbb{N}} \left[\frac{V_T}{N_T} \bigg| \mathcal{F}_t \right] = B_t E_{\mathbb{Q}} \left[\frac{V_T}{B_T} \bigg| \mathcal{F}_t \right]$$

But, by definition (7.6), this gives:

$$V_t = N_t E_{\mathbb{Q}} \left[\frac{V_T}{N_T} \frac{d\mathbb{N}}{d\mathbb{Q}} \bigg| \mathcal{F}_t \right] = B_t E_{\mathbb{Q}} \left[\frac{V_T}{B_T} \bigg| \mathcal{F}_t \right]$$

This is satisfied, for all (t, T) if we set:

$$\frac{d\mathbb{N}}{d\mathbb{Q}} = \frac{N_T}{B_T} \frac{B_t}{N_t} \tag{7.7}$$

Thus, through a simple quotient of *numeraires*, we can easily transform from one probability measure to another. Why is this useful? Consider an option paying at time T. We have for the price $V_0 = E_{\mathbb{Q}}[V_T/B_T]$. This is fine if rates are deterministic, but if we now have that rates are *stochastic*, and presumably correlated with the underlying securities of V, this is going to be an awkward integral to calculate. But suppose we define a new measure $\mathbb{T}$, with respect to the *numeraire* $P(t, T)$ (i.e. the zero coupon bond price). Then, from (7.7), we'd have

$$\frac{d\mathbb{Q}}{d\mathbb{T}} = \frac{B_T}{P(T, T)} \frac{P(t, T)}{B_t} = \frac{B_T P(t, T)}{B_t}$$

allowing us to write:

$$V_0 = P(0, T) E_{\mathbb{T}}[V_T]$$

This is immensely powerful. All of the complexities of discounting have effectively been pulled *outside* the expectation. The cost is only that we now have to work out the distribution of the underlying instruments in the new $T - forward$ measure. We will discuss this in detail in the context of equity in the next section, but we can note a couple of points up front:

- For the simple forward contract, struck at F, we have:

$$V_0 = P(0,T)E_{\mathbb{T}}[S_T - F]$$

Regardless of dividend model, we must then have for the fair forward level $F = E_{\mathbb{T}}[S_T]$.
- For a simple call option, we have for the price:

$$C_0 = P(0,T)E_{\mathbb{T}}[(S_T - K)^+] \tag{7.8}$$

In the absence of dividends, the stock itself is a tradable, so that $S_t/P(t,T)$ should be a martingale under $\mathbb{T}$. We thus have:

$$\frac{S_t}{P(t,T)} = \frac{S_0}{P(0,T)} \exp\left[\int_0^t \sigma_F(s,T)dW_s - \frac{1}{2}\int_0^t \sigma_F^2(s,T)ds\right]$$

where $E_{\mathbb{T}}[dW_t|\mathcal{F}_t] = 0$. This allows us to return the well-known Black–Scholes formula $C_0 = P(0,T)[F(T)N(d_1) - K(d_2)]$, where:

$$d_{1,2} = \frac{\log(F(T)/K)}{\widehat{\sigma}_F(T)\sqrt{T}} \pm \frac{\widehat{\sigma}_F(T)\sqrt{T}}{2}$$

$$\widehat{\sigma}_F^2(T)T = \int_0^T \sigma_F^2(s,T)ds \tag{7.9}$$

Note though that it is now the volatility of the process $S_t/P(t,T)$, i.e. the conditional *forward*, rather than the spot, which enters the implied variance (7.9). We will return to this point in our discussion of calibration of a local volatility equity process in the presence of stochastic rates. The expression is unaffected by dividends if, and only if, the dividends are proportional (see exercise).

7.3.2   *Market models*

Change of measure, while certainly a convenience for equity modelling, is essential for a general model of interest rates. Following the spirit of the analysis of historic FRA rates in the previous section, a natural choice would be to model such rates *directly*. As we saw, the market for options on FRA (or baskets of FRA via swaptions) is very well traded. It should be possible to build an entire model of interest rates based on these market *observables*, and the correlation between them, alone. Such an approach, suggested originally by Brace, Gatarek and Musiela (BGM) [Brace *et al.* (1997)] is generally referred to as a *market model*, and has spawned a great deal of variants and approaches since its original inception in 1997, notably Miltersen, Sandmann and Sondermann [Miltersen *et al.* (1997)] and Jamshidian [Jamshidian (1997)]. The beauty of such models is that they are, notionally, model independent. Given a finite set of liquidly traded instruments, and a measurable correlation structure between them, such information is sufficient to price any derivative whose payoff is some function of the same instrument process, the price of which should be unique. We will look at similar approaches for equity in Chapter 9. Of course, life is never so simple. Whilst we may have a well traded market in at the money Libor caps and floors, for example, the same is less true of the out of the money variants. The correlation between different Libors, whilst inferable to an extent from the swaptions market, is also far from directly observable, and the approach taken to this problem alone is sufficient to generate model risk. Nonetheless, such models *do* allow us to model a very rich structure of rate curve dynamics beyond simple short rate models (see below), and can be key in making prices in instruments where the higher modes of the rate curve evolution are significant.

Let us begin by considering a forward rate agreement to fix Libor over the period (T_1, T_2). No arbitrage arguments (see exercise), give for the fair FRA rate at time $t \leq T_1 < T_2$:

$$F(t; T_1, T_2) = \frac{1}{\tau(T_1, T_2)} \left(\frac{P(t, T_1)}{P(t, T_2)} - 1 \right) \tag{7.10}$$

where $\tau(t_1, t_2)$ corresponds to the day count fraction between t_1 and t_2. Now, observe that we can rewrite (7.10) as:

$$F(t; T_1, T_2) = \frac{1}{P(t, T_2)} \frac{P(t, T_1) - P(t, T_2)}{\tau(T_1, T_2)} = \frac{V_t}{P(t, T_2)} \tag{7.11}$$

But V_t is simply the difference between two zero coupon bonds divided by the day count fraction, which is manifestly a tradable itself. We have then, by definition, that:

$$F(t; T_1, T_2) = E_{\mathbb{T}_2}[F(T_1; T_1, T_2)]$$

i.e. *all FRAs expiring at T are martingales in the associated measure* $\mathbb{T}$.

Now consider where, rather than being obliged to receive the Libor $L(T_1, T_2)$ rate over (T_1, T_2) against some strike K, settling at T_2, we had the *option* to do so. Such an option is referred to as a *caplet*, a *cap* being a basket of such options over sequential periods. (The put equivalent is referred to as a *floor*, itself comprised of *floorlets*.) The option pays out at T_2, so we can write for its present value:

$$E_{\mathbb{Q}}\left[\frac{\tau(T_1, T_2)}{B(T_2)}[L(T_1, T_2) - K, 0]^+\right] \tag{7.12}$$

But we have $F(T_1; T_1, T_2) = 1/\tau(T_1, T_2)(1/P(T_1, T_2) - 1) = L(T_1, T_2)$, so, changing measure now to $\mathbb{T}_2$ (7.12) can be rewritten as:

$$P(0, T_2)\tau(T_1, T_2)E_{\mathbb{T}_2}\left[(F(T_1; T_1, T_2) - K, 0)^+\right] \tag{7.13}$$

But as $F(t; T_1, T_2)$ is a martingale under $\mathbb{T}_2$, this simplifies again to the Black–Scholes form:

$$P(0, T_2)\tau(T_1, T_2)\left[F(0; T_1, T_2)N(d_1) - KN(d_2)\right]$$

where

$$d_{1,2} = \frac{\log(F(0; T_1, T_2)/K)}{\sigma(T_1; T_1, T_2)\sqrt{T_1}} \pm \frac{\sigma(T_1; T_1, T_2)\sqrt{T_1}}{2}$$

The result is commonly referred to as 'Black's formula', in keeping with Black's original work on interest rate options [Black (1995)]. Note of course that the process for $F(t; T_1, T_2)$ need not be log-normal, it simply has to be driftless under $\mathbb{T}_2$. We can then, without loss of generality make the implied volatility strike dependent, so that, given a liquid market in caplets at a range of strike, we can completely characterise the $\mathbb{T}_2$ distribution of FRA expiring at T_2. For the remainder of this section, we will use the shorthand $F_i(t)$ to denote $F(t; T_{i-1}, T_i)$, where i runs over the set of fixings of relevance to a given derivative. A number of models exist to capture non-log-normal dynamics, notably the stochastic alpha, beta rho (SABR) model introduced by Hagan, Kumar, Lesniewski and Woodward [Hagan *et al.* (2002)], where the FRA rate F_j is allowed to evolve under its associated measure $\mathbb{T}_j$ as:

$$dF_j(t) = V(t)F_j(t)^\beta dZ_j(t)$$
$$dV(t) = \epsilon V(t)dW_j(t)$$
$$V(0) = \alpha$$
$$dZ_j(t)dW_j(t) = \rho dt$$

The model is widely used in practice, largely due to its tractability, and its ability to derive semi-analytic approximations for implied caplet volatilities for rapid calibration. Other stochastic FRA volatility models of note include the Andersen–Brotherton-Ratcliffe model [Andersen and Brotherton-Ratcliffe (2001)], the Wu–Zhang model [Wu and Zhang (2002)] and the Piterbarg model [Piterbarg (2003)]. For an excellent summary of these models, together with a comparison of their properties, see Brigo and Mercurio [Brigo and Mercurio (2006)].

Returning to the simpler case where the FRA rate is taken as lognormal in its associated measure, how do we use this construction to price options which, in general will be a function of multiple FRA rates, paying at multiple times? The problem is that, for a given payoff time T_i, the associated $\mathbb{T}_i$-forward measure will not be the natural measure for all of the related underlying FRAs. Happily, we can transform the dynamics of a FRA whose natural measure is $\mathbb{T}_k$ to the $\mathbb{T}_i$ measure via a drift adjustment:

$$
\begin{aligned}
dF_k(t) &= \sigma_k(t)F_k(t) \sum_{j=i+1}^{k} \frac{\rho_{k,j}\tau_j\sigma_j(t)F_j(t)}{1+\tau_j F_j(t)}dt \\
&+ \sigma_k(t)F_k(t)dZ_k(t), \ i < k, t \le T_i \\
dF_k(t) &= \sigma_k(t)F_k(t)dZ_k(t), \ i = k, t \le T_{k-1} \\
dF_k(t) &= -\sigma_k(t)F_k(t) \sum_{j=k+1}^{i} \frac{\rho_{k,j}\tau_j\sigma_j(t)F_j(t)}{1+\tau_j F_j(t)}dt \\
&+ \sigma_k(t)F_k(t)dZ_k(t), \ i > k, t \le T_{k-1}
\end{aligned}
$$

(7.14)

where $\rho_{i,j}dt = \langle dZ_i(t)dZ_j(t) \rangle$ and $\tau_i = \tau(T_{i-1}, T_i)$. The proof is left as an exercise at the end of the chapter.

The complexity of this conceptually appealing model is beginning to dawn on us. To price an option with N fixings $\mathcal{E} = \{T_1, \ldots, T_N\}$, say, we need to be able to generate the N-dimensional joint distribution of the associated forward rates F_k. But to do this at a given payoff fixing T_i, we need to evolve all the relevant forward rates, in the $\mathbb{T}_i$ measure up to T_i. As there is no analytic solution for (7.14), this has to be done by time discretisation over small time steps. We cannot, for example, simply generate the marginals for an uncorrelated set of Gaussian normal variates, correlate them via a Cholesky matrix and invert to the distribution of the associated forward rate, as we might do for a basket of stocks (see

Chapter 8). Moreover, to enable us to fit to the term structure of swaptions, for example, we need each forward rate to have its own volatility term structure, and then calibrate the correlation matrix linking all the relevant rates, given that structure. To enable us to do this efficiently, some sort of parsimonious approach to both the forward rate volatilities, and the correlation matrix, needs to be employed. Whilst there is no arbitrage constraint linking the different curves, one simplifying assumption for the forward rate implied volatilities is to compute them from a *single* curve of instantaneous volatilities, where the curve is a function of the time to maturity $\tau = T_{i-1} - t$:

$$\sigma_i(t) = [a(T_{i-1} - t) + d]e^{-b(T_{i-1}-t)} + c$$

Such a structure gives a 'humped' structure of instantaneous volatilities as a function of time to maturity . It actually turns out that such a curve is insufficient for joint calibration to caps and swaptions. A slightly richer form allows the instantaneous volatilities for different forward rates to be separated by a multiple:

$$\sigma_i(t) = \Phi_i[a(T_{i-1} - t) + d]e^{-b(T_{i-1}-t)} + c \qquad (7.15)$$

The squared caplet volatility for a caplet of expiry T_i measured at time $t < T_i$ is then given by:

$$v_i^2(t) = \Phi_i^2 \int_t^{T_{i-1}} \left[[a(T_{i-1} - s) + d]e^{-b(T_{i-1}-s)} + c\right]^2 ds$$

Clearly, for constant time to maturity $\tau = T_{i-1} - t$, $\Phi_i = 1$ the caplet volatility is time homogeneous. Writing:

$$\int_0^{T_{i-1}} \left[[a(T_{i-1} - s) + d]e^{-b(T_{i-1}-s)} + c\right]^2 ds = I^2(T_{i-1})$$

we have $\Phi_i^2 = v_i^2(0)/I^2(T_{i-1})$, so that such a scheme can calibrate to an arbitrary set of caplet volatilities seen today. In this case of course, the time homogeneity of the caplet vol will be broken. In practice, however, the calibrated Φ_i tends to be close to unity [Rebonato (1999b)]. For other, piecewise flat, approaches to instantaneous forward rate volatility, see Brigo and Mercurio [Brigo and Mercurio (2006)].

So much for volatility, what about correlation? Broadly speaking, the approach can be divided between full rank, where effectively all of the possible N eigenmodes of our system $\mathcal{E}$ are considered, or reduced rank, where we concentrate on the top M eigenmodes by correlation matrix eigenvalue. Either way, the approach attempts, as per volatility, to find a parsimonious parameterisation for the correlation matrix. Typically, these parameterisations are based on the following considerations [Brigo and Mercurio (2006)]:

- We expect $\rho_{i,j} \geq 0$ for all i, j.
- We expect correlation to decrease monotonically as a function of forward rate tenor separation, i.e. the map $i \mapsto \rho_{i,j}$ is decreasing for $i \geq j$.
- When moving along the yield curve, we expect adjacent forward rates to become more correlated the further along the curve we go, i.e. the map $i \mapsto \rho_{i+p,i}$ should be increasing for fixed p.

Numerous candidates exist which satisfy all three constraints. One of the simplest is Rebonato's three parameter parameterisation [Rebonato (1999a)]:

$$\rho_{i,j} = \rho_\infty + (1 - \rho_\infty) \exp[-|i - j|(\beta - \alpha(i \wedge j - 1))]$$

Such a parameterisation, whilst attractive in terms of its simplicity, does suffer the drawback of not being automatically positive semi-definite, i.e. the eigenvalues are not necessarily all greater than or equal to zero. An alternative, somewhat more complex parameterisation was proposed by Schoenmakers and Coffey [Schoenmakers and Coffey (2000)], where $\rho_{i,j} = c_i/c_j$, $c_i < c_j$; $i < j$ and $c_i/c_{i+1} < c_{i+1}/c_{i+2} \; \forall \; 0 \leq i < N - 2$. They went on to show that c_i can always be formulated through a sequence of non-negative numbers $\Delta_1, \ldots, \Delta_N$, as:

$$c_i = \exp \left[\sum_{j=1}^{i} j\Delta_j + \sum_{j=i+1}^{N} (i - 1)\Delta_j \right]$$

A simple example of such a scheme is the exponentially decaying parameterisation:

$$\rho_{i,j} = \rho_\infty + (1 - \rho_\infty) \exp[-\beta|i - j|]$$

In the end, it comes down to a choice of an automatically semi-definite optimisation, with reduced fitting power, to a constrained optimisation with increased fitting power. The latter tends to be preferred in practice.

The full rank approach necessarily requires a parsimonious parameter-isation as dealing with all $N(N-1)/2$ entries of the full $N \times N$ matrix is going to be unfeasible for the number of forward rates involved in a typi-cal calibration (~ 20). Such parametric constraints on the matrix can be overly restrictive. An alternative approach is to allow a richer correlation structure via a reduced rank approach. This is most easily illustrated by the Rebonato angle formulation [Rebonato (1999b)].

Consider the forward rate F_t^i as being subject to M principal component shocks $\{dZ_t^k\}$ such that $E[dZ_t^k dZ_t^l] = \delta_{kl} dt$ under any measure. We can write, for the evolution of F_t^i in the $\mathbb{T}_i$ forward measure:

$$\frac{dF_t^i}{F_t^i} = \sigma^i(t) \sum_{k=1}^{M} b_t^{ik} dZ_t^k = \sigma^i(t) dW_t^i$$

From the condition for the Wiener term $(dW_t^i)^2 = dt$ and the correlation structure of $\{dZ_t^k\}$ we have:

$$\sum_{k=1}^{M} (b_t^{ik})^2 = 1$$

In other words, the components of the projection of dW_t^i onto the eigenvec-tor space $\{dZ_t^k\}$ map to the co-ordinates of an M-dimensional hypersphere of unit radius. We can represent this in polar co-ordinates as [Rebonato (1999b)]:

$$b_t^{i1} = \cos(\theta_t^{i1})$$
$$b_t^{ik} = \cos(\theta_t^{ik}) \prod_{j=1}^{k-1} \sin(\theta_t^{ij}) \quad k = 2, \ldots, M-1$$
$$b_t^{iM} = \prod_{j=1}^{M-1} \sin(\theta_t^{ij}) \tag{7.16}$$

For $M = 1$, we simply have a perfect correlation between the forward rates and the first principal component of the yield curve, i.e. a parallel shift. For $M = 2$, however, we allow ourselves exposure to the second principal com-ponent, characterised by a single vector of 'angles' θ_t^i. The resulting rank 2 correlation structure has a particularly elegant form $\rho_{i,j}(t) = \cos(\theta_i - \theta_j)$ (see exercise). If we were then to try to calibrate caplets and swaptions with a volatility structure of the form (7.15), characterised by a vector Φ_i, and a rank 2 correlation structure characterised by Rebonato's angles θ_i, the former could be calculated exactly (as correlation has no effect on caplets), whilst the latter could occur through an N- dimensional optimisation routine. A common procedure is to do just this, but fit the correlation to an approximation to implied Black swaption volatilities, also due to Rebonato [Rebonato (2002a)]:

$$\sigma_{\alpha,\beta}^2 T_\alpha = \sum_{i,j=\alpha+1}^{\beta} \frac{w_i(0)w_j(0)F_i(0)F_j(0)\rho_{i,j}}{S_{\alpha,\beta}^2(0)} \int_0^{T_\alpha} \sigma_i(t)\sigma_j(t)dt \qquad (7.17)$$

Where T_α and T_β refer to the start and end times of the underlying swap, with forward rates $\{F_{\alpha+1}(t), \ldots, F_\beta(t)\}$ spanning the swap period, whose par rate at time $t \leq T_\alpha$ is given by $S_{\alpha,\beta}(t) = \sum_{i=\alpha+1}^{\beta} w_i(t)F_i(t)$ with:

$$w_i(t) = \frac{\tau_i \prod_{j=\alpha+1}^{i} \frac{1}{1+\tau_j F_j(t)}}{\prod_{k=\alpha+1}^{\beta} \tau_k \prod_{j=\alpha+1}^{k} \frac{1}{1+\tau_j F_j(t)}}$$

(see exercise). The implied swaption volatility is extracted as per (7.3). Apart from its elegant simplicity, Rebonato's correlation formalism also ensures that the fitting correlation matrix is positive semi-definite, by construction, as the matrix itself is built from eigenmodes with positive variance.

7.3.3   *The Heath–Jarrow–Morton model*

The above discussion on the market model approach outlines one of the popular methods for modelling interest rate derivatives such that calibration to market instruments can be as close as possible. Ultimately, we saw that a concentration on the dominant principal components of the rate curve was required for the calibration to be tractable. An alternative approach, from which the original BGM model was in fact derived, is to consider a *continuum* of 'instantaneous' forward rates, rather than a discrete set of real forward rates, and limit their dynamics to a small number of Brownian shocks. Such a model was originally proposed by Heath, Jarrow and Morton [Heath *et al.* (1987)], which we will now formulate.

Define the instantaneous forward rate to be the limit of the fair strike for a forward rate agreement from T to T', paying at T', as T' tends to T from above. From (7.10) we have:

$$f(t,T) = \lim_{T' \to T+} \frac{P(t,T) - P(t,T')}{\tau(T,T')P(t,T')}$$

$$= -\frac{1}{P(t,T)} \frac{\partial P(t,T)}{\partial T}$$

$$= -\frac{\partial}{\partial T} \log[P(t,T)]$$

We immediately end up with the relationship between forward discount factor and instantaneous forward rates:

$$P(t,T) = \exp\left(-\int_t^T f(t,s)ds\right) \tag{7.18}$$

Now, let us define some diffusion for $f(t,T)$:

$$df(t,T) = \alpha(t,T)dt + \sigma(t,T)dW(t)$$

In general, $dW(t)$ can be a multi-dimensional Brownian motion, with $\sigma(t,T)$ vector valued. It turns out, however, that the requirement that zero coupon bonds (ZCB) be tradable restricts the drift on instantaneous forward rates $\alpha(t,T)$ to be a function of the volatility $\sigma(t,T)$. We can see this as follows. As the ZCB $P(t,T)$ is tradable, it must be a martingale under the risk-neutral measure. Hence $d[P(t,T)/B(t)]$ must be driftless under the risk-neutral measure. Take $X(t) = \log(P(t,T)) = -\int_t^T f(t,s)ds$. From Itō's lemma we have:

$$\frac{dP(t,T)}{P(t,T)} = dX_t + \frac{1}{2}(dX_t)^2$$

From (7.18) we have:

$$dX_t = r(t)dt - \left[\int_t^T \mu(t,s)ds\right]dt - \left[\int_t^T \sigma(t,s)ds\right]dW(t)$$

using the definition for the short rate $r(t) = f(t,t)$. (See exercise). Hence:

$$(dX_t)^2 = \left[\int_t^T \sigma(t,s)ds\right]^2 dt$$

But as $E_{\mathbb{Q}}[dW(t)] = 0$ and

$$d(P(t,T)/B(t)) = dP(t,T)/B(t) - r(t)P(t,T)/B(t)dt$$

the condition that $P(t,T)/B(t)$ be driftless under $\mathbb{Q}$ gives for the drift:

$$\int_t^T \mu(t,s)ds = \frac{1}{2}\left[\int_t^T \sigma(t,s)ds\right]^2$$

Differentiating w.r.t T gives the well-known HJM drift relation:

$$\mu(t,T) = \sigma(t,T)\int_t^T \sigma(t,s)ds$$

We thus end up with a final expression for the integrated forward rate:

$$f(t,T) = f(0,T) + \int_0^t \sigma(u,T)\int_u^T \sigma(u,s)dsdu + \int_0^t \sigma(s,T)dW(s) \quad (7.19)$$

Equivalently, we have for the short rate:

$$r(t) = f(0,t) + \int_0^t \sigma(u,t)\int_u^t \sigma(u,s)dsdu + \int_0^t \sigma(s,t)dW(s) \quad (7.20)$$

Where we allow the Brownian motion to be multi-dimensional, we should think of the product of volatilities in (7.19) and (7.20) as a dot product over the vector components. One of the great advantages of such a model is that, as the process is built around zero coupon bonds, the risk-neutral expectation of the integrated discount factor will always match today's rate curve $P(0,t)$. We can see this easily by noting that $f(0,t) = -\frac{\partial \log P(0,t)}{\partial t}$ and integrating $P(0,t) = E_{\mathbb{Q}}\left[-\int_0^t r(s)ds\right]$ (see exercise). A significant disadvantage, however, is that the past history of the instantaneous forward rate volatility now impacts on the current value of the short rate. In other words, the process is no longer Markovian. An attempt to discretise this process would result in a non-recombining tree, and indeed the number of required nodes for $r(t)$ would grow exponentially as the number of time steps. Happily, there is a subset of HJM models which *is* Markovian, as we shall see in the next section.

7.3.4   *From HJM to HW*

Generalising to a multi-dimensional Brownian motion, Carverhill [Carverhill (1994)] showed that, if each element of the forward rate volatility is decomposed as $\sigma_i(t, T) = \xi_i(t)\psi_i(T)$, where $\xi_i(t)$ and $\psi_i(t)$ are strictly positive and deterministic functions of time, then the short rate process given by (7.20) becomes Markovian. We can see this for the one-dimensional case as follows:

$$r(t) = f(0, t) + \int_0^t \xi(u)\psi(t) \int_u^t \xi(u)\psi(s)dsdu + \int_0^t \xi(s)\psi(t)dW(s)$$

$$= f(0, t) + \psi(t) \int_0^t \xi^2(u) \int_u^t \psi(s)dsdu + \psi(t) \int_0^t \xi(s)dW(s)$$

Defining:

$$A(t) := f(0, t) + \psi(t) \int_0^t \xi^2(u) \int_u^t \psi(s)dsdu$$

We have:

$$dr(t) = A'(t)dt + \psi'(t) \int_0^t \xi(s)dW(s) + \psi(t)\xi(t)dW(t)$$

$$= \left[A'(t) + \psi'(t)\frac{r(t) - A(t)}{\psi(t)} \right] dt + \psi(t)\xi(t)dW(t)$$

$$= [a(t) + b(t)r(t)]dt + c(t)dW(t)$$

Clearly, the evolution of the short rate at time t is now only dependent on its value at time t, making the process transparently Markovian. Note, however, that in introducing this simplification, we have recovered a well-known short rate model due to Hull and White [Hull and White (1990)]:

$$dr(t) = -\kappa\left[r(t) - \theta(t)\right]dt + \sigma dW(t)$$

By inspection, if we take:

$$\xi(t) = \sigma e^{\kappa t}$$
$$\psi(T) = \sigma e^{-\kappa T}$$

Then we recover the Hull–White process provided the average short rate

$\theta(t)$ satisfies:

$$\theta(t) = \frac{1}{\kappa}\left[\frac{\partial}{\partial t}f(0,t) + \kappa f(0,t) + \frac{\sigma^2}{2\kappa}(1 - e^{-2\kappa t})\right] \tag{7.21}$$

The Hull–White model in fact was a generalisation to an earlier model by Vasicek [Vasicek (1977)], where the equilibrium rate θ was taken as a constant (and hence unable to fit to general term structures of the rate curve). Other popular one-factor short rate models include:

- Cox–Ingersoll–Ross (CIR) [Cox *et al.* (1985)]:

$$dr_t = -\kappa(\theta - r_t)dt + \sigma\sqrt{r_t}dW_t$$

- Black–Karasinski (BK) [Black and Karasinski (1991)]:

$$dr_t = r_t[\eta_t - a\log r_t]dt + \sigma r_t dW_t$$

Both CIR and BK have since been extended to model the short rate with a shift φ_t such that the *shifted* process $x_t = r_t + \varphi_t$ enters the original process, rather than the short rate alone. Such shifted log-normal (for BK) or shifted non-central χ^2 distributions (for CIR) allow for some control of the volatility skew of caplets, as discussed earlier in the context of the SABR model. Both CIR and BK have the advantage over HW that interest rates are bounded below by zero (although CIR requires the Feller condition $2\kappa\theta > \xi^2$ to hold for this to be strictly true (see Chapter 4)). CIR has the advantage over BK that the conditional prices of zero coupon bonds have an analytic form. A finite difference solution is required for a solution of the ZCB in the BK model. All these models, however, suffer the drawback of being overly constrained in their dynamics. As we have seen from the derivation of the Hull–White model from multi-dimensional HJM, single factor short rate models effectively assume that the stochasticity of the rate curve is entirely driven by a parallel shift to the instantaneous forward rates. Two-factor short rate models, which attempt to address this simplification include:

- Longstaff–Schwartz (a.k.a CIR2) [Longstaff and Schwartz (1992)]:

$$dx_t = a(b - x_t)dt + \sqrt{x_t}dW_x(t)$$
$$dy_t = c(d - y_t)dt + \sqrt{y_t}dW_y(t)$$
$$r_t = \mu_x x_t + \mu_y y_t$$

- Two-factor Vasicek:

$$dx_t = k_x(\theta_x - x_t)dt + \sigma_x dW_x(t)$$
$$dY_t = k_y(\theta_y - y_t)dt + \sigma_y dW_y(t)$$
$$r_t = x_t + y_t$$

where in general the two underlying process x_t and y_t are correlated. As we have already mentioned, such approaches are useful when dealing with products with sensitivity to correlation between different forward rates, e.g. spread options between long-dated and short-dated Libor, or options involving constant maturity swap (CMS) rates (the payment of the n-year swap rate at a given time T_i involves a change of measure from the swap *numeraire* to the $\mathbb{T}_i$ *numeraire*, which itself involves the correlation between forward rates via the associated swaption volatility [Brigo and Mercurio (2006)]. A one-factor short rate model simply does not have enough degrees of freedom to calibrate to both swap rates and CMS rates). We will therefore avoid such options in the product analysis of the remainder of this chapter, and re-iterate the point that our choice of the Hull–White model as a basis for investigation of equity-rate model risk is based on the desire for clarity rather than an attempt at accurate hybrid equity-rate modelling.

7.4   Equity-rate hybrid modelling

Continuing in the spirit of previous models introduced in this book, we will once again attempt to adapt the Dupire local volatility model, this time to incorporate stochastic rates. As per stochastic volatility modelling, our portfolio for hedging the extra diffusion factor, in this case the parallel shift to the rate curve, will consist of an option, stock, bond and a hedging option. Proceeding along exactly the same lines as Chapter 4, we arrive at the backward equation:

$$\frac{\partial V}{\partial t} + r(t)S_t\frac{\partial V}{\partial S} + g(r_t, t)\frac{\partial V}{\partial r}$$
$$+ \frac{1}{2}\left[\sigma^2(S_t, t)S_t^2\frac{\partial^2 V}{\partial S^2} + 2\rho\sigma(S_t, t)\xi S_t\frac{\partial^2 V}{\partial S\partial r} + \xi^2\frac{\partial^2 V}{\partial r^2}\right] - r_t V = 0$$

$$(7.22)$$

We will assume, for the remainder of this chapter, that the short rate follows a Hull–White evolution with constant volatility:

$$dr_t = g(r_t, t)dt + \xi dW_t^r$$
$$g(r_t, t) = -\kappa(r_t - \theta(t))$$

and $E[dW_t^S dW_t^r] = \rho dt$. The equilibrium rate $\theta(t)$ is taken to match the rate curve, as per (7.21). As per Chapter 5, we now want to derive the modified evolution of the stock density at time T, but now in the $\mathbb{T}$-forward, rather than the risk-neutral measure. Recall, from (7.8) that we can write for the present value of any European payout $V(S_T, T)$:

$$V(S_0, 0) = P(0, T) \int V(S_T, T)\phi(S_T, T)dS_T \tag{7.23}$$

where $\phi(S_T, T)$ is the stock price density in the $\mathbb{T}$-forward measure. It will actually be more convenient to work in $x_t = \log(S_t)$ for the remainder of this derivation. Equation (7.22) then transforms to:

$$\frac{\partial V}{\partial t} + \left[r_t - \frac{1}{2}\sigma^2(x_t, t) \right] \frac{\partial V}{\partial x} + g(r_t, t)\frac{\partial V}{\partial r}$$
$$+ \frac{1}{2}\left[\sigma^2(x_t, t)\frac{\partial^2 V}{\partial x^2} + 2\rho\sigma(x_t, t)\xi\frac{\partial^2 V}{\partial x \partial r} + \xi^2\frac{\partial^2 V}{\partial r^2} \right] - r_t V = 0 \tag{7.24}$$

Following the derivation by Overhaus et al. [Overhaus *et al.* (2007)], we will now define the Arrow–Debreu price $\psi(x', t)$ as the present value of a derivative paying $\delta(x_T - x')$ at time T. From (7.23) we have for this price $\psi(x', T) = P(0, T)\phi(x', T)$, giving:

$$V(x_0, 0) = \int V(x_T, T)\psi(x_T, T)dx_T \tag{7.25}$$

Now, differentiating both sides of (7.25) w.r.t T and using (7.24) gives:

$$0 = \int \left[V\frac{\partial \psi}{\partial T} + \psi\left(r_t V - \mu_x \frac{\partial V}{\partial x} - \mu_r \frac{\partial V}{\partial r} - \right.\right.$$
$$\left.\left. \frac{1}{2}\left[\sigma^2(x_t, t)\frac{\partial^2 V}{\partial x^2} + 2\rho\sigma(x_t, t)\xi\frac{\partial^2 V}{\partial x \partial r} + \xi^2\frac{\partial^2 V}{\partial r^2} \right] \right) \right] dx$$

where $\mu_x = r_T - \frac{1}{2}\sigma^2(x_t, t)$ and $\mu_r = g(r_T, T)$. Integrating by parts, as per Chapter 2, gives for the evolution of the Arrow–Debreu price:

$$\frac{\partial \psi}{\partial T} + r_T \psi + \frac{\partial}{\partial x}(\mu_x \psi) + \frac{\partial}{\partial r}(\mu_r \psi) =$$
$$\frac{1}{2}\left[\frac{\partial^2}{\partial x^2}(\sigma^2(x_T, T)\psi) + 2\rho\xi\frac{\partial^2}{\partial x \partial r}(\sigma(x_T, T)\psi) + \xi^2\frac{\partial^2 \psi}{\partial r^2}\right]$$

So, using $\psi(x, T) = P(0, T)\phi(x, T)$, and the relationship $\partial P(0, T)/\partial T = -f(0, T)P(0, T)$, we arrive at the modified Fokker–Planck equation for the evolution of the $\mathbb{T}$-forward density:

$$\frac{\partial \phi}{\partial T} + (r_T - f(0, T))\phi + \frac{\partial}{\partial x}(\mu_x \phi) + \frac{\partial}{\partial r}(\mu_r \phi) =$$
$$\frac{1}{2}\left[\frac{\partial^2}{\partial x^2}(\sigma^2(x_T, T)\phi) + 2\rho\xi\frac{\partial^2}{\partial x \partial r}(\sigma(x_T, T)\phi) + \xi^2\frac{\partial^2 \phi}{\partial r^2}\right] \quad (7.26)$$

It is in fact convenient to define a new variable $y_t = r_t - f(0, t) - \bar{y}(t)$, where

$$dy_t = -\kappa y_t dt + \xi dW_t^r$$

and $\bar{y}(t)$ has been calibrated to fit the yield curve.

Likewise, if we define another variable $z_t = \log(S_t/F(T))$ where $F(T) = S(0)/P(0, T)$ for a dividend-free process, we can further rewrite (7.26) as:

$$\frac{\partial \phi}{\partial T} + (y_T + \bar{y}(T))\left(\phi + \frac{\partial \phi}{\partial z}\right) - \frac{1}{2}\frac{\partial}{\partial z}(\sigma^2(z_T, T)\phi) - \frac{\partial}{\partial y}(\kappa y_T \phi) =$$
$$\frac{1}{2}\left[\frac{\partial^2}{\partial z^2}(\sigma^2(z_T, T)\phi) + 2\rho\xi\frac{\partial^2}{\partial z \partial y}(\sigma(z_T, T)\phi) + \xi^2\frac{\partial^2 \phi}{\partial y^2}\right] \quad (7.27)$$

We are now in a position to re-derive the Dupire local variance. Writing the call option as $C(K, T) = P(0, T)F(T)c(k, T)$, and $k = \log(K/F(T))$, we have:

$$c(k, T) = \int_{-\infty}^{\infty} \int_{k}^{\infty} (e^z - e^k)\,\phi(z, y, T)\,dz\,dy \quad (7.28)$$

Now, assuming that $\phi(z,y,T) \to 0$ and $\partial\phi(z,y,T)/\partial T \to 0$ as $y \to \pm\infty$, we can combine (7.28) and (7.27) to give:

$$\frac{\partial c}{\partial T} = \int_{-\infty}^{\infty} \int_{k}^{\infty} (e^z - e^k) \left(-(y+\bar{y}(T)) \left[\phi + \frac{\partial\phi}{\partial z} \right] + \frac{1}{2}\frac{\partial}{\partial z}(\sigma^2(z,T)\phi) \right.$$
$$\left. + \frac{1}{2}\frac{\partial}{\partial z^2}(\sigma^2(z,T)\phi) \right) dz dy$$

Integrating by parts, we arrive at:

$$\frac{\partial c}{\partial T} = \frac{1}{2}e^k\sigma^2(k,T) \int_{-\infty}^{\infty} \phi(k,y,T)dy + e^k \int_{-\infty}^{\infty} \int_{k}^{\infty} (y+\bar{y}(T))\phi(z,y,T)dz dy$$

Taking the first and second derivatives of (7.28) w.r.t k, we arrive at the final expression for the modified Dupire local variance:

$$\sigma^2(k,T) = \frac{\frac{\partial c}{\partial T} - e^k \int_{-\infty}^{\infty} \int_{k}^{\infty} (y+\bar{y}(T))\phi(z,y,T)dz dy}{\frac{1}{2}\left(\frac{\partial^2 c}{\partial k^2} - \frac{\partial c}{\partial k}\right)} \tag{7.29}$$

As per the approach for stochastic local volatility modelling, we solve (7.29) recursively on a 2D ADI grid, solving for the pdf $\phi(z,y,T)$ from time T_i to T_{i+1} and using the result to compute the local volatility at time T_{i+1}, which we then use for the pdf solution from T_{i+1} to T_{i+2}, and so on. The approach is somewhat laborious, with a more efficient approximation detailed in Overhaus et al. [Overhaus et al. (2007)].

7.4.1 *Initial observations*

In the limit of deterministic rates, we must have that the local volatility matches the Dupire local volatility. We can then rewrite (7.29) more succinctly as:

$$\sigma^2(k,T) = \sigma^2_{Dupire}(k,T) - \frac{2e^k \int_{-\infty}^{\infty} \int_{k}^{\infty} (r(T) - f(0,T))\phi(z,r,T)dz dr}{\left(\frac{\partial^2 c}{\partial k^2} - \frac{\partial c}{\partial k}\right)} \tag{7.30}$$

Once again, as per the modified expression for local volatility arrived at with jump to zero modelling, we find that an implied volatility surface which might have resulted in a positive local variance everywhere might now be incompatible with this no arbitrage condition on introducing rate volatility. We can see this more clearly by considering the effect of rate volatility on a flat volatility surface. It can be shown (see exercise), that for spot independent local volatility, the call option implied variance is given by (see exercise):

$$\int_0^T \sigma_F^2(t)dt = \int_0^T \left[\sigma^2(t) + 2\rho\sigma(t)\xi G(\kappa,t,T) + \xi^2 G(\kappa,t,T)^2\right] dt \quad (7.31)$$

where

$$G(\kappa,t,T) = \frac{1}{\kappa}\left[1 - e^{-\kappa(T-t)}\right]$$

In the limit of zero mean reversion, this simply reduces to $G(\kappa,t,T) = T - t$. Where we have non-zero correlation, a boostrapping technique is required to back out the spot volatility. In the simple case of zero correlation, however, we have:

$$\sigma_S = \sqrt{\sigma_F^2 - \xi^2 T^2} \quad (7.32)$$

For a well-defined process we require that σ_S be real, giving $\sigma_F^2 > \xi^2 T^2$. In fact, even for non-zero correlation, the T^2 term will eventually dominate for high enough T, so that there will always come a point where the spot process ceases to be well-defined. This is demonstrated in Figure 7.7 for $\xi = 0.1$ and $\sigma_F = 0.5$, $\kappa = 0$.

Note, however, that mean reversion can rescue us here. In the case of zero correlation again, we have:

$$\sigma_S = \sqrt{\sigma_F^2 - \frac{\xi^2}{\kappa^2}\left(1 - e^{-\kappa T}\right)^2}$$

So provided that $\sigma_F^2 > \xi^2/\kappa^2$ the process will be well-defined for all maturities.

There is, however, an important point to note here. In model risk analysis of the effect of rate volatility on equity exotics, the comparison to simpler models is only fully valid up until the point where calibration to vanilla vols breaks down. On the whole, practitioners tend to invoke some 'rule of thumb' for extrapolation of the vol surface from liquidly traded maturities (typically $< 5Y$ to the sorts of maturities of interest to long-dated exotics (anything up to $15Y$, typically). As this tends not to be done with

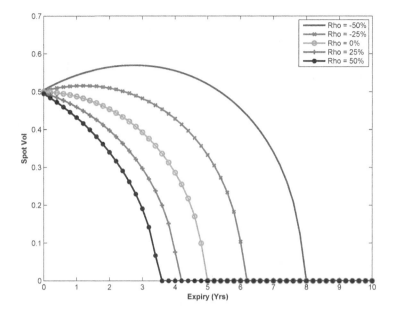

Fig. 7.7   Demonstration of the maturity problem for flat vol with stochastic rates.

a specific rate model in mind, the potential for hybrid model calibration to break down in the long-dated region of interest can be quite high. We will endeavour in this chapter to construct cases where full calibration is possible, though this will limit the range of available short rate volatilities correspondingly.

The above analysis has of course been confined to the simpler case of flat volatility. How much does the picture change when we introduce equity vol skew? Perhaps unsurprisingly, the dominant effect of rate volatility is to provide something close to a parallel shift to the whole vol slice, with the direction depending on the correlation between rates and equity. A representative 5Y surface for a range of ξ at correlations of -50%, 0% and 50% is shown in Figures 7.8, 7.9 and 7.10 respectively. Zero mean reversion has been assumed.

As per the stochastic volatility analysis, the effect of mean reversion is to dampen the effect of the short rate vol. The shift to the implied volatility is correspondingly dampened, as shown in Figures 7.11, 7.12 and 7.13 for a mean reversion level of 10%. This level is somewhat higher than normal long-dated calibrated mean reversion for USD, with typical results of fitting

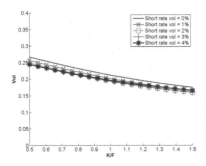

Fig. 7.8 Representative implied volatility slice, 5Y, zero short rate mean reversion, equity-rate correlation -50%.

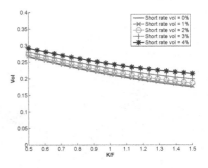

Fig. 7.9 Representative implied volatility slice, 5Y, zero short rate mean reversion, equity-rate correlation 0%.

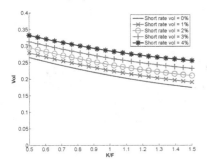

Fig. 7.10   Representative implied volatility slice, 5Y, zero short rate mean reversion, equity-rate correlation 50%.

a single factor Hull–White short rate model to swaption and caplet volatility resulting in mean reversion between around -25% at the short end to 5% in the long end. By contrast, calibrated short rate vol tends to be more stable, averaging around 1%. A similar observation is made by Gurrieri *et al.* [Gurrieri *et al.* (2010)] in their analysis of calibration methods of the Hull–White model. Whilst they in fact impose monotonicity on their fits, they note a short-dated mean reversion of -41% and long-dated mean reversion of 5% for USD as of 8th September 2009. This 'mean fleeing' characteristic of the short end of the USD mean reversion curve, whilst conceptually peculiar, is nothing more than an artefact of calibration, and is not of course in itself an arbitrage opportunity. An excellent discussion of the mechanics of this process is given by Overhaus *et al.* [Overhaus *et al.* (2007)], and will not be re-iterated here. As already mentioned, we will not attempt to include term structure of rate vol and mean reversion in this analysis, but will use calibrated curves as a guide for reasonable ranges these parameters might take.

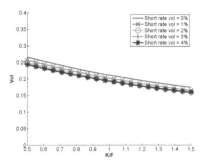

Fig. 7.11 Representative implied volatility slice, 5Y, 10% short rate mean reversion, equity-rate correlation -50%.

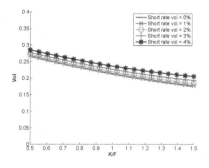

Fig. 7.12 Representative implied volatility slice, 5Y, 10% short rate mean reversion, equity-rate correlation 0%.

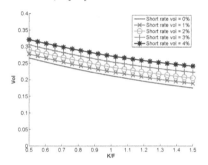

Fig. 7.13 Representative implied volatility slice, 5Y, 10% short rate mean reversion, equity-rate correlation 50%.

Conversely, we would expect the calibrated local volatility to respond in the opposite direction, and indeed it does, as shown in Figures 7.14, 7.15 and 7.16, again at a mean reversion level of 10%.

Whilst it may seem like a straightforward effect, the impact on the different reactions of equity-rate hybrids pre- and post-calibration is crucial, as we shall see in the next section. Before we start looking at these more complicated instruments, however, it's worth revisiting a 'vanilla' trade introduced in Chapter 4, namely the innocuous looking variance swap. Recall that this instrument was supposed to be 'model independent', in principle being replicable through vanilla options. Again, consider the case of flat implied volatility $\widehat{\sigma}(K,T) = \widehat{\sigma}(T)$. The value of a variance swap is given by:

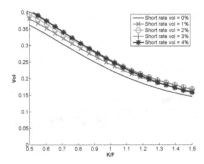

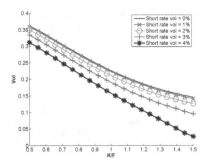

Fig. 7.14   Calibrated local volatility slice, 5Y, 10% short rate mean reversion, equity-rate correlation -50%.

Fig. 7.15   Calibrated local volatility slice, 5Y, 10% short rate mean reversion, equity-rate correlation 0%.

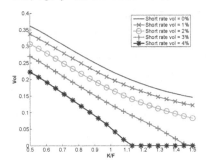

Fig. 7.16   Calibrated local volatility slice, 5Y, 10% short rate mean reversion, equity-rate correlation 50%.

$$V(T) = E_{\mathbb{Q}}\left[\frac{1}{TB_T}\int_0^T \sigma_S^2(t)dt\right] = P(0,T)E_{\mathbb{T}}\left[\frac{1}{T}\int_0^T \sigma_S^2(t)dt\right]$$

Note that the variance swap is written in terms of realised *spot* variance, whilst the implied volatility of a vanilla option corresponds to realised *forward* variance. As it turns out, the model independence of the variance swap depended crucially on these two being the same. With the introduction of stochastic rates, however, this equivalence is manifestly broken. More rigorously, we have for the dividend-free forward $F(t,T)$ in the $\mathbb{T}$-forward measure:

$$\frac{dF(t,T)}{F(t,T)} = \sigma_F(t)dW_t$$

so that, in the spirit of the earlier variance swap derivation we can write:

$$\frac{dF(t,T)}{F(t,T)} - d\log F(t,T) = \frac{\sigma_F^2(t)dt}{2}$$

And proceeding similarly we can write:

$$E_T \left[\frac{1}{T} \int_0^T \sigma_F^2(t)dt \right] = \frac{2}{T} \int_0^\infty \log\left(\frac{F(0,T)}{F(T,T)}\right) \varphi(F(T,T),T)dF(T,T)$$

$$= \frac{2}{T} \int_0^\infty dF(T,T)\varphi(F(T,T),T) \int_{F(T,T)}^{F(0,T)} \frac{dK}{K^2}(K - F(T,T))dK$$

$$= \frac{2}{T} \left[\int_0^{F(0,T)} \widetilde{P}[F(0,T),K,T,\widehat{\sigma}(K,T)] \frac{dK}{K^2} \right]$$

$$+ \frac{2}{T} \left[\int_{F(0,T)}^\infty \widetilde{C}[F(0,T),K,T,\widehat{\sigma}(K,T)] \frac{dK}{K^2} \right]$$

Let us define the 'naive' variance swap price:

$$\frac{V_0(T)}{P(0,T)} =$$

$$\frac{2}{T} \left[\int_0^{F(0,T)} \widetilde{P}[F(0,T),K,T,\widehat{\sigma}(K,T)] \right] \frac{dK}{K^2}$$

$$+ \frac{2}{T} \left[\int_{F(0,T)}^\infty \widetilde{C}[F(0,T),K,T,\widehat{\sigma}(K,T)] \frac{dK}{K^2} \right]$$

But we have, from (7.31):

$$\int_0^T \sigma_F^2(t)dt = \int_0^T \left[\sigma_S^2(t) + 2\rho\sigma_S(t)\xi G(\kappa,t,T) + G(\kappa,t,T)^2\xi^2 \right] dt \quad (7.33)$$

Looking at $\rho = 0$ for tractability, this gives for the var swap price:

$$V(T) = V_0(T) - \int_0^T G(\kappa,t,T)^2\xi^2 dt$$

So, even with perfect calibration of our modified equity process to the implied volatility curve $\widehat{\sigma}(T)$, the price of our 'vanilla' variance swap has turned out to be strongly model dependent. A set of profiles for different levels of correlation, and mean reversion of 10%, is shown against rate vol in Figure 7.17.

7.5 Implicit hybrids

Recall from Chapter 5 the division between products whose exposure to default was *implicit*, by virtue of the sensitivity of the product to default

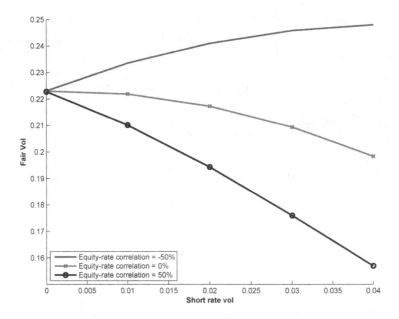

Fig. 7.17   The impact of rate volatility on a 5Y variance swap, different levels of equity-rate correlation.

per se (e.g. deeply out of the money down and out barriers), and *explicit*, through exposure of the product to embedded credit instruments (e.g. convertible bonds). A similar distinction can be drawn for rate modelling. Roughly speaking, we have two principal factors when it comes to introducing stochastic rates to equity exotics:

- The effect of stochastic rates on the calibrated stock process;
- The effect of stochastic rates on embedded interest rate instruments within the payoff.

The first of these factors can be referred to as the *implicit* effect. The two standard products we will consider in analysing these effects in more detail are so-called 'autocallables', where the contract redeems automatically on the stock reaching a pre-determined barrier level, and 'callables', where the holder of the contract has the right to terminate in return for a redemption amount. The latter will of course be more expensive than the former, all other things being equal, though by exactly how much, and in what way, can be quite subtle, as we shall see.

The second factor is clearly an *explicit* dependence. The contract may be as simple as an autocallable which redeems with a delay, e.g. to maturity, introducing an explicit dependence on the correlation between the zero coupon bond to maturity and the stock price at the barrier level. We will consider this variant to the simple immediate redemption autocallable, but will also consider a perhaps more interesting variant, the floating leg of an interest rate swap where each coupon is paid only if a reference equity is above a specified level. These sort of products, exploiting the correlation between rates and equity directly, are becoming increasingly common, notably as 'equity linked notes' where the equity serves to provide leverage on an otherwise low yield fixed income product. We will provide a brief overview of the current product space in the next section.

7.5.1 *Autocallables*

To begin though, let's return to the simple barrier considered back in Chapter 3. Recall the argument for a discrete down and out barrier active at times T_1 and T_2 (the choice will become clear shortly). We have for the probability of knockout:

$$P(S(T_1) < B \cup S(T_2) < B) =$$
$$P(S(T_1) < B) + P(S(T_2) < B) - P(S(T_1) < B \cap S(T_2) < B)$$

Let's begin by considering the effect of stochastic rates on this problem when the local equity volatility is flat. As we saw in Section 7.4.1, in the absence of calibration, the effect of stochastic rate vol is to raise implied volatility levels, provided the correlation is positive. For negative correlation, implied volatility of an option maturity T will actually fall until stochastic rate vol reaches a critical point. The price of the downside digital is simply given by $P(S(T) < B) = 1 - N(\log(F(T)/B)/\hat{\sigma}(T)\sqrt{T} - \hat{\sigma}(T)\sqrt{T}/2)$, which monotonically increases with increasing implied volatility $\hat{\sigma}$ provided $B < F(T)$, with the effect of vol increasing the longer the maturity. We would thus expect, *before* calibration, that the survival probability for a down and out barrier decreases with increasing rate vol for zero and positive correlation, and increases, initially at least, for negative correlation. This is demonstrated in Figure 7.18 for a 5Y, 50% downside barrier, using a 20% vol on the equity. Zero dividends, USD discounting and zero short rate mean reversion are assumed[3].

---

[3]We will assume zero mean reversion for the remainder of the analysis. As we have

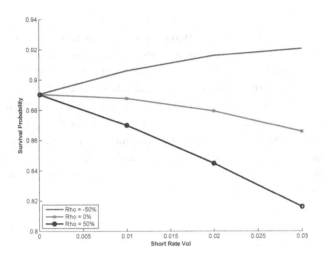

Fig. 7.18   Survival probability, 50% down and out barrier, 5Y, uncalibrated.

As always, however, we are more interested in the calibrated case. As per our analysis of the effects of stochastic volatility on barriers in Chapter 3, the effect is to remove any model dependence for the unconditional digital parts of the survival probability, reducing the whole problem to the probability of staying below the barrier to a later time *given* a barrier breach at an earlier time. From the discussion in Section 7.4.1, we would expect calibrated local volatility to be suppressed for positive correlation, and enhanced for negative correlation. Thinking of the simple two fixing barrier above, the effect of a reduced local vol, *per se*, will be to increase the probability of *staying* below the barrier to T_2 given a breach at time T_1. As the digitals are unaltered, we would then expect the probability of breaching the barrier to decrease with increasing rate vol with positive correlation, or equivalently, the survival probability to increase. The converse should be true, up to the critical short rate vol, for negative correlation. This is shown in Figure 7.19, now calibrated to 20% flat implied vol, with the same option details.

So far so good, but what about conditional stock drift? In previous chapters, this was static, but now we have the further complication that the risk-neutral drift of the stock at some point in the future is conditional

seen, the effect is essentially to dampen the effect of short rate vol, and in itself should be given by calibration to rate instruments. We do not therefore consider it an essential model risk parameter for this chapter.

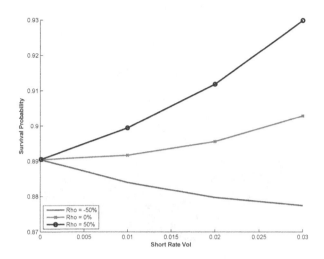

Fig. 7.19 Survival probability, 50% down and out barrier, 5Y, calibrated.

on the prevailing short rate. A picture of the conditional 5Y forward, over a grid of spot heights and short rate deviations x from the instantaneous forward rate, is shown in Figure 7.20.

Clearly, the higher the prevailing short rate, the lower the price of the corresponding zero coupon bond to maturity, and the higher the conditional forward. We might further expect that the joint distribution of short rate and spot would be weighted towards high spot, high rates, and low spot, low rates, for positive correlation, and high spot, low rates and low spot, high rates, for negative correlation. Some contour plots for the joint distribution at the same 1Y point, and a rate vol of 3% are shown in Figures 7.21, 7.22 and 7.23.

One point to note on these distributions, though less clear at the maturity shown, is that the *out-turn* correlation (i.e. the correlation between the *realised* spot and rate values) for zero *local* equity-rate correlation, is not itself zero. In fact, it grows as maturity increases (see exercise). This is intuitively obvious as the distribution of the out-turn spot price depends on the realisation of the cash account $B(T) = \exp\left[\int_0^T r(t)dt\right]$, so that upside rate moves will favour upside spot moves. The distribution for zero equity-rate local correlation at 5Y is shown in Figure 7.24. The positive out-turn correlation is manifest.

Putting this together with the conditional forward picture, we would expect positive equity-rate correlation to favour *lower* conditional forwards,

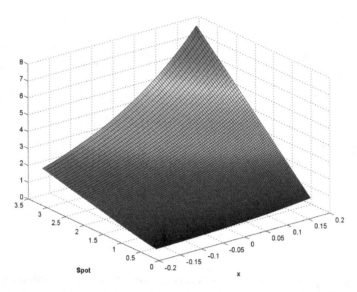

Fig. 7.20   Representation of the conditional forward to 5Y, measured at 1Y from trade inception, $x = r - f(0, t)$.

for downside equity movements. This further increases the probability of the stock staying below the barrier conditional on an earlier breach, and adds to the probability of survival, with the converse true for negative correlation. For *this* analysis then, the conditional drift does not appear to complicate matters.

We now have the machinery for looking at the problem (a) of a simple autocallable where the holder receives a lump sum on the stock breaching the barrier, and a call otherwise and (b) a callable, where the holder can choose (assumed optimally) to terminate the call early in return for a lump sum. The latter is in fact a variant on the former, given that there will exist some boundary, commonly referred to at the *optimal exercise boundary* at which redemption will take place. A graph of the price of a simple 5Y at the money autocallable call, redeeming at 0.2 (compared to a call price of 0.23), for a range of short rate vols and correlations, is shown in Figure 7.25.

7.5.2   Callables: Immediate redemption

In keeping with the survival probability analysis, the value of the early redemption decreases for increasing rate vol and positive correlation, and

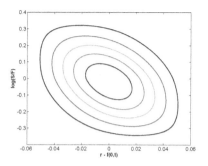

Fig. 7.21 1Y joint short rate-equity distribution, 3% short rate vol, zero mean reversion, equity-rate correlation -50%.

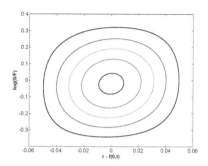

Fig. 7.22 1Y joint short rate-equity distribution, 3% short rate vol, zero mean reversion, equity-rate correlation 0%.

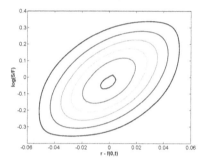

Fig. 7.23 1Y joint short rate-equity distribution, 3% short rate vol, zero mean reversion, equity-rate correlation 50%.

vice versa for negative correlation. What would then happen if holders were allowed to redeem at their discretion? We can begin to understand this by looking at the price of the early redemption autocallable for different barrier levels. This is shown in Figure 7.26 for zero correlation.

There are a couple of points to note here:

- For all correlations, there exists a barrier level for which the price of the autocallable is maximised. One can think about this as follows. For a zero barrier, all prices should clearly converge to the calibrated call level. As we raise the barrier, in effect we've added a downside floor to the deeply out of the money call level, raising the value of the option. As the barrier approaches spot, however, the value of the option is

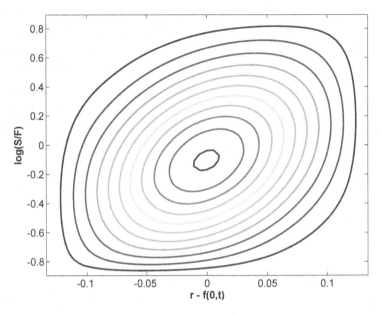

Fig. 7.24   5Y joint short rate-equity distribution, 3% short rate vol, zero mean reversion, equity-rate correlation 0%.

pulled back down to the lower rebate level, giving rising to an optimal barrier level (around 80% in this example).

- Calibration to implied volatility all but removes the model risk of the *optimal* barrier price in the example shown. For barrier levels below this point, the reduced knockout probability reduces the value of the rebate, and the value of the autocallable correspondingly, whilst for levels above this point, the reduced knockout probability reduces the reductive effect of the rebate compared to the regular option price, increasing the value of the autocallable. At the optimal point, these conflicting behaviours effectively cancel out.

Such a picture is of course a considerable simplification, as in reality the optimal exercise boundary is, first, a *surface* in spot and rate space, and second, time dependent. A cross section of the optimal exercise boundary at 2Y for the same option, for zero correlation, is shown in Figure 7.27.

The black region corresponds to early exercise, at which the value of the option is (by definition) equal to the early redemption rebate. Note that as the deviation of the short rate from the instantaneous forward rate becomes negative, the boundary falls off abruptly. This is actually an

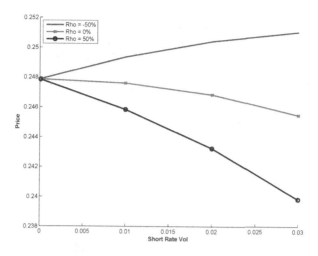

Fig. 7.25 Down and in 0.2 rebate ATM call, 50% barrier, 5Y, calibrated.

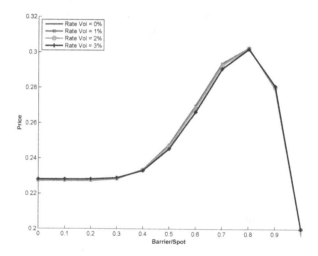

Fig. 7.26 Down and in 0.2 rebate ATM call, multiple barrier levels, 5Y, calibrated.

artefact of models which allow negative short rates. The effect, which is perhaps somewhat contrived, comes from the fact that for strongly negative short rate realisations, it becomes optimal to *receive* the carry on holding the option, rather than exercise early. In the spot domain the picture is somewhat clearer. For higher spot values, the continuation value of the option clearly makes it optimal to hold, and vice versa. As we look ahead towards the option maturity, the continuation value of the option decreases correspondingly, increasing the spot height of the optimal exercise boundary. This is shown for the 3Y slice in Figure 7.28.

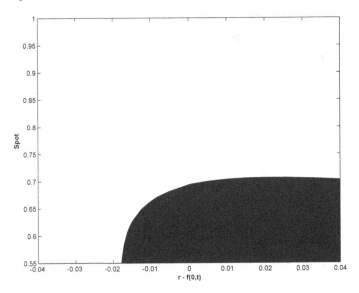

Fig. 7.27   The optimal exercise boundary of a 5Y callable ATM call at 2Y, rebate 0.2, zero equity-rate correlation, 3% short rate vol.

Note that our estimate of the boundary at 80% is not far off. The estimate will, however, be sub-optimal, and indeed such barrier optimisation approaches to early exercise, notably for more complex path dependent, or multi-factor trades requiring Monte Carlo, will always underestimate the early exercise premium.

What of correlation in all this? The 2Y early exercise cross section for 50% and -50% correlation are shown in Figures 7.30 and 7.29 respectively.

The effect of increasing correlation appears to be to raise the level of the exercise boundary in the spot domain. This is consistent with our picture for the autocallable rebate option, where correlation reduced the price of the early rebate. As we increase correlation, the continuation value of the embedded autocallable option would come down, necessitating a high spot level to match the immediate redemption level. The probability of exercise into the sub-option rebate price is thus higher for positive correlation than negative, with a corresponding reduction in the price of the instrument.

For high rate vol, however, the effect of the quadratic term on the local volatility dominates the correlation term, leading to a reduction in the price differences due to correlation on this structure. This is shown in Figure 7.31.

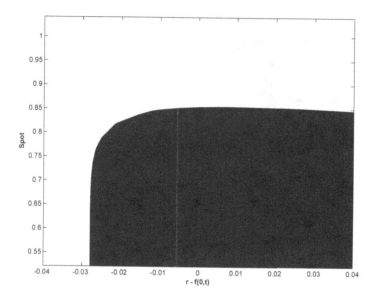

Fig. 7.28   The optimal exercise boundary of a 5Y callable ATM call at 3Y, rebate 0.2, zero equity-rate correlation, 3% short rate vol.

7.5.3 Callables: Delayed redemption

Though there are indeed differences in price due to short rate vol and equity-rate correlation, ultimately they become pretty minor. Essentially we end up with an exercise boundary which is so deeply out of the money that, whilst it does move notably with correlation, the effect on price, following calibration to European options, is small. What would happen, however, if redemption were *delayed* until the maturity of the option? Now we start to come into *explicit* hybrid territory, as the payoff embeds a zero coupon bond. Clearly, the lower the realised short rate, at any given time, the higher will be the value of the redemption, requiring a high spot value for the continuation price to match it. Intuitively then, we would expect a radically different early exercise boundary, sloping upwards towards higher spot for lower rate. This is indeed the case, as shown in Figure 7.32, this time cut at 3Y.

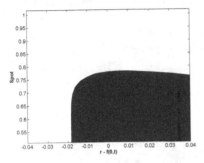

Fig. 7.29   The optimal exercise boundary of a 5Y callable ATM call at 2Y, rebate 0.2, 50% equity-rate correlation, 3% short rate vol.

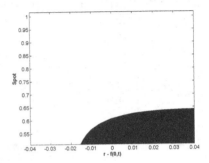

Fig. 7.30   The optimal exercise boundary of a 5Y callable ATM call at 2Y, rebate 0.2, -50% equity-rate correlation, 3% short rate vol.

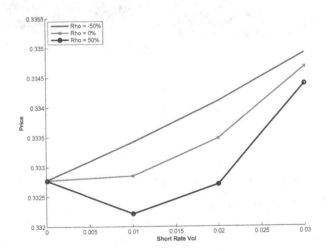

Fig. 7.31   Callable 5Y ATM call, 0.2 rebate, calibrated.

The analysis of the dependance of price on equity-rate correlation and rate vol is now entirely different. For low spot prices near the exercise boundary, the expected early exercise bond value will be higher, *conditional* on the realised spot value, for positive correlation than negative. As rate volatility is increased, this difference is exacerbated, with a corre-

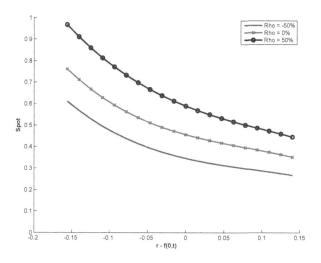

Fig. 7.32   The optimal exercise boundary of a 5Y callable ATM call at 3Y, rebate 0.2 delayed to 5Y.

sponding divergence in price. Indeed, in the case of negative equity-rate correlation, the probability of early exercise, at all, tends to zero for high rate volatility. The price of the product thus tends to the terminal exercise value for negative correlation, but continues to rise for positive. This is shown in Figure 7.33.

Not only do we get opposite behaviour, but the effect of short rate vol and equity-rate correlation is demonstrably stronger. It can be seen, moreover, that the longer the maturity of the option, the greater the effect. The longer we make the maturity of the embedded bond, the greater will be the effect of rate volatility on the value conditional on downward spot moves, widening the price difference between positive and negative correlation, as shown in Figure 7.34. A further complication to the analysis is also given by the calibration itself. For positive and zero correlation, the correction to the local volatility to match option prices will no longer be able to compensate sufficiently the effect of short rate vol without the local variance going negative, as the maturity of the option is increased. Like this, the implied volatility of the regular long-dated call will inevitably rise above the target implied vol level as we increase option maturity, increasing the continuation value of the option itself. The effect is alleviated in the negative correlation case. Figure 7.34, whilst technically an accurate representation of the effect of increased maturity on the stochastic rate effect on callable options, does include the exacerbating effect of calibration breakdown for such products.

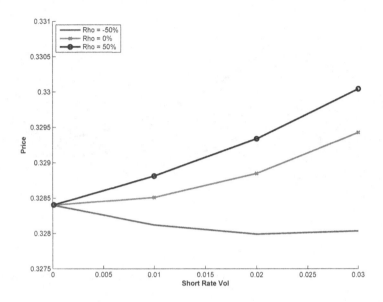

Fig. 7.33   Callable 5Y ATM call, 0.2 rebate delayed to 5Y, calibrated.

It would appear that, through introducing an explicit dependence on rates to our actual payoff, we have significantly altered the model risk sensitivity of the option. We will explore this in more detail in the next section.

7.6   Explicit hybrids

Hybrid products, where the correlation between underlyers from two or more different product areas is exploited explicitly through the payoff construction, have recently grown significantly in popularity. One of the most famous of these was the so-called *Power Reverse Dual Currency Note* (PRDC), popular with Japanese investors in the first half of the last decade, where the investor effectively receives a stream of fx options, which can be cancelled at the discretion of the issuer. Such notes were designed to provide investors with high coupons from the embedded fx optionality (typically USD/JPY), leading to an issuance of around USD 9 billion of these notes in 2003. Their popularity, however, declined markedly in 2008 where increased volatility in the prevailing distressed market put a significant hedging strain on the investment banks issuing these products, through the inherently short cross gamma position between FX volatility, interest rates and FX. For a summary of the decline in this market and the reasons behind it, see Pengelly [Pengelly (2010)].

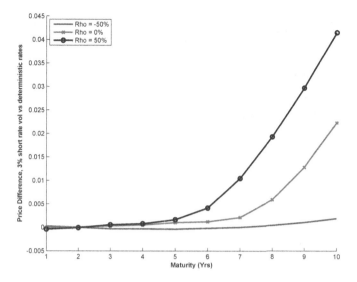

Fig. 7.34 Callable ATM call, 0.2 rebate delayed to maturity, calibrated, increasing maturity, price difference between 3% short rate vol and deterministic valuation.

Typical equity-interest hybrid derivatives include [Overhaus *et al.* (2007); JPMorgan (2010)]:

• 'Best-of' products: e.g. $\max(LIBOR_t, a(S_t/S_0 - 1))$;
• Conditional trigger swaps, where the holder receives a fixed coupon and pays floating, but where the fixed coupon switches conditional on the equity breaching a barrier;
• Hybrid range accrual notes, where the note accrues a fixed coupon *provided* that both Libor trade within a fixed range, and a reference equity (typically an index) trade within a fixed range. An example termsheet is referenced in the bibliography [JPMorgan (2010)].

For the purposes of illustration, we will focus on the hybrid range accrual, where we simply look at the value of a floating rate leg linked to the level of equity spot at each fixing date. Suppose, continuing from the discussion of the previous section, we consider a swap which pays 3M USD Libor for 5Y *provided* the reference equity trades above 50% of its starting level. Recalling the joint distributions illustrated in Section 7.5.1, we would expect that the expected floating rate coupon would be more negative for negative correlation, and positive for positive correlation. Effectively, the downside equity strike removes the contribution to the expected Libor rate from the low equity, high rate region, in the case of negative correlation, and that from the low equity, low rate region for positive correlation. A sample plot of the dependence of this structure on short rate vol and equity-rate correlation is shown in Figure 7.35.

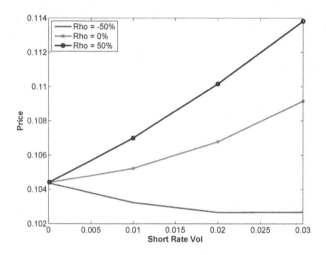

Fig. 7.35   50% downside range accrual on a floating rate USD swap, calibrated.

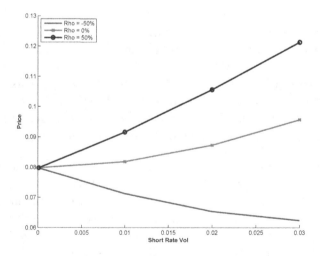

Fig. 7.36   80% downside range accrual on a floating rate USD swap, calibrated.

As we might expect, the difference due to correlation is exacerbated by the moneyness of the downside strike. The closer the downside strike is to the money, the lower the price of the option, but the greater the effect of distribution cut-off, as shown in Figure 7.36.

The difference between -50% correlation and 50% correlation at a rate vol of 3% is as much as a factor of two. As per delayed callables, the effect of equity-rate correlation is enhanced the longer dated the option, and the larger the equity-rate out-turn covariance.

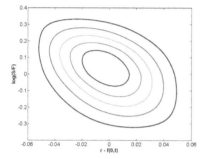

Fig. 7.37 1Y joint short rate-equity distribution, 3% short rate vol, zero mean reversion, equity-rate correlation -50%, negative vol skew.

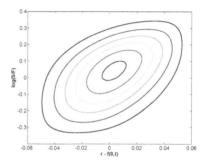

Fig. 7.38 1Y joint short rate-equity distribution, 3% short rate vol, zero mean reversion, equity-rate correlation 50%, negative vol skew.

7.7   A note on vol skew

After the detailed derivation of the incorporation of the Hull–White model into a local volatility framework in Section 7.4, it would seem remiss not to include something on the effect of volatility skew on the preceding analyses. For the cases considered, the effect is qualitatively similar. As we saw in Section 7.4.1, the main effect of interest rate volatility on the local vol is essentially to parallel shift it, with the change to slope and curvature being minor. Whilst the skew will of course intrinsically impact on the barrier breaching probability, the change to that probability will be similar qualitatively to the flat surface case. Likewise, though the joint distributions for positive and negative equity-rate correlation will no longer be centrally symmetric (as shown in Figures 7.37 and 7.38 for a 1Y point), the qualitative behaviour of curtailing the distribution through a barrier, is similar to the flat case. Price vs short rate vol curves for the volatility surface displayed in Section 7.4.1 are shown in Figures 7.39 and 7.40 for the same 5Y delayed callable and 5Y Libor knock-out trades considered above.

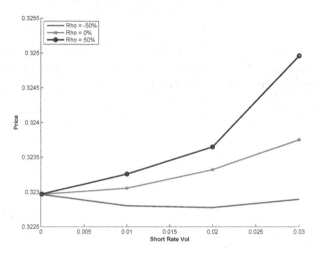

Fig. 7.39   Callable 5Y ATM call, 0.2 rebate delayed to 5Y, calibrated, negative vol skew.

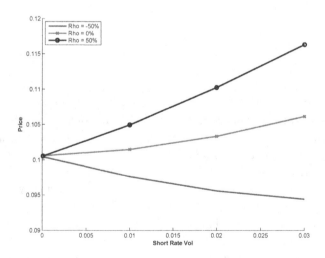

Fig. 7.40   50% downside range accrual on a floating rate USD swap, calibrated, negative vol skew.

7.8 Conclusions

In this chapter we have attempted to explore the effect of stochastic interest rates on a variety of different equity products, ranging from variance swaps to hybrid range accruals. Of all the aspects of model risk in equity derivative seen so far, this has probably been the most complex. Not only do we need to worry about the effects of rate volatility on calibrated equity volatility, but the behaviour of embedded rate instruments, the form of the joint equity-rate distribution and the geometry of early termination boundaries, are *all* strongly influenced by the assumption of stochastic rates, and the nature of their correlation to equity. As we saw in both our historical analysis of interest rates, and the dense market for interest rate derivatives, stochastic rates cannot be overlooked, with their influence of equity derivative valuation a strong function both of the maturity of the option, and the essentially unknown equity-rate correlation.

We have now covered many aspects of the single asset equity problem. In Chapter 3 we looked at the effect of dividend assumptions on barriers and lookbacks. In Chapter 4 we moved onto the impact of stochastic volatility modelling. In Chapter 5 we allowed our diffusion to crash to zero, whilst in Chapter 6 we relaxed this assumption by introducing a jump size distribution. Finally, in this chapter we covered the final term in the Black–Scholes PDE and looked at the importance of stochastic rates. But we're still not done. Over the course of the last decade, a large market for *multiple* asset trading grew up, famously through the collateralised debt obligation market, but also in the equity market itself. Not only were our assumptions on how the individual equities propagated crucial to valuation, but now the way they were *correlated* came to the fore. We will investigate this problem in detail in Chapter 8.

7.9 Exercises

(1) Demonstrate, from a static hedging argument, that the fair rate, at time $t \leq T_1$, for a contract which pays Libor over a period $[T_1, T_2]$ is given by:

$$F(t; T_1, T_2) = \frac{1}{\tau(T_1, T_2)} \left(\frac{P(t, T_1)}{P(t, T_2)} - 1 \right)$$

(2) Denoting the FRA rate $F(t; T_{i-1}, T_i)$ as $F_i(t)$, use question 1 to demonstrate that $F_i(t)$ is a martingale in the $\mathbb{T}_i$ forward measure, defined by:

$$X_t / P(t, T_i) = E_{\mathbf{T}_i} \left[X_{T_i} | \mathcal{F}_t \right]$$

Using the expression for the price of a bond expiring at T_j in terms of one expiring at T_i and the intervening forward rates F_k for $i < k \le j$ (for $i < j$) and $j < k \le i$ (for $j < i$), derive the change of measure result for forward rates given in (7.14).

(3) Using the relation between the discount factor and Libors:

$$P(T_0, T_j) = \prod_{i=1,j} \frac{1}{1 + L_{i-1}\tau(T_{i-1}, T_i)}$$

show that the fair coupon S_T for the fixed leg of a swap paying $S_T\tau(T_{i-1}, T_i)$ at each time T_i, for $1 < i \le n$, against a floating leg paying $L_{i-1}\tau(T_{i-1}, T_i)$, is given by:

$$S_T DV01 = 1 - P(T_0, T_n)$$

where

$$DV01 = \sum_{i=1,n} \tau(T_{i-1}, T_i) P(T_0, T_i)$$

(This is generally referred to as the *swap rate* for the swap of the corresponding maturity and tenor.)

(4) Rewrite the expression for the swap rate from the previous question in terms of a weighted sum over FRA rates spanning the swap period, i.e.

$$S_{\alpha,\beta}(t) = \sum_{i=\alpha+1}^{\beta} w_i(t) F_i(t)$$

where $T_\alpha \le t < T_\beta$, $F_i(t) = F(t; T_{i-1}, T_i)$, and show that the associated weights are given by:

$$w_i(t) = \frac{\tau_i \prod_{j=\alpha+1}^{i} 1/(1 + \tau_j F_j(t))}{\sum_{k=\alpha+1}^{\beta} \tau_k \prod_{j=\alpha+1}^{k} 1/(1 + \tau_j F_j(t))}$$

using the abbreviation $\tau_i = \tau(T_{i-1}, T_i)$. Now, assuming that the variability of the weights is much smaller than the variability of the FRA's derive an expression for the quadratic variation of the swap rate at time T_α evolved from $T = 0$ (this is the Rebonato formula quoted in (7.17)).

(5) Demonstrate, in the case where a rank 2 reduction of the Rebonato FRA correlation matrix is performed, that (7.16) reduces to $\rho_{i,j}(t) = \cos(\theta_i(t) - \theta_j(t))$.

(6) Defining $X(t) = \log(P(t,T)) = -\int_t^T f(t,s)ds$ and applying Itō's lemma, show that:

$$\frac{dP(t,T)}{P(t,T)} = dX_t + \frac{1}{2}(dX_t)^2$$

where, assuming:

$$df(t,T) = \alpha(t,T)dt + \sigma(t,T)dW(t)$$

$$dX_t = r(t)dt - \left[\int_t^T \alpha(t,s)ds\right]dt - \left[\int_t^T \sigma(t,s)ds\right]dW(t)$$

(7) For the short rate given by:

$$r(t) = f(0,t) + \int_0^t \sigma(u,t)\int_u^t \sigma(u,s)dsdu + \int_0^t \sigma(s,t)dW(s)$$

where $E_\mathbb{Q}[dW(s)] = 0$, demonstrate:

$$P(0,t) = E_\mathbb{Q}\left[\exp\left(-\int_0^t r(s)ds\right)\right]$$

(8) Demonstrate that proportional dividends impact only on the forward used in the Black–Scholes call price expression, not the implied vol, regardless of the stochasticity of interest rates.

(9) Show, in the limit of no volatility state dependence, that the implied volatility of a dividend-free call with maturity T, valued with a Hull–White interest rate process, with constant parameters, is given by:

$$\hat\sigma^2(T)T = \int_0^T \left[\sigma^2(t) + 2\rho\sigma(t)\xi G(\kappa,t,T) + \xi^2 G(\kappa,t,T)^2\right]dt$$

where

$$G(\kappa,t,T) = \frac{1}{\kappa}\left[1 - e^{-\kappa(T-t)}\right]$$

(10) Prove that the out-turn covariance between $x_T = \log(S_T/F(0,T))$ and r_T is given by:

$$Cov(x_T, r_T) = \int_0^T \xi e^{-\kappa(T-t)} \left[\xi G(\kappa, t, T) + \rho \sigma_S(t) \right] dt$$

where

$$G(\kappa, t, T) = \int_t^T e^{-\kappa(s-t)} ds$$

This result neatly demonstrates the essential difference between *local* correlation and *implied correlation* (from a Libor-equity outperformance option, for example) in stochastic rate problems.

Chapter 8

Correlation

Since the advent of 'mountain range' options, marketed by Société Générale in 1998, the last decade saw a significant rise in the market for structured multi-asset equity derivatives. The majority of these products, sold predominantly to high net-worth and retail customers by investment banks, benefited from the bull market conditions of the time, typically providing cheap optionality through an embedded short worst-of put or long worst-of call structure. In the highly correlated rising markets of the time, the likelihoods of a knock-out on the worst, or the difference between the worst performer and the average performer, were respectively deemed so small that such options appeared effectively to provide similar payoffs to the more conventional basket equivalents, but for a significantly reduced price. Such products also, however, left the investment banks with large short correlation positions. Indeed, by around September 2007, it was estimated by one senior exotics trader [Thind (2007)], that the aggregate equity derivative correlation exposure across the investment banking industry was between USD 200 million and USD 300 million *short* per correlation *point*. In other words, a spike in average market correlation of 10% would have cost the banking industry somewhere in the region of USD 2–3 billion. Indeed, when correlation (along with implied volatility) did spike up in the worsening conditions of 2008, some dealers reported more than USD 1 billion in losses [Pengelly (2008)].

Roll back to around 2004, and we see that traders, all too aware of the potentially unmanageable one way correlation exposure, attempted to 'buy back correlation', first through dispersion trading through variance swaps (where the investor nets a variance swap on an index against the appropriately weighted sum of variance swaps on the underlyers), and then through outright correlation products such as correlation and covariance swaps (discussed in detail later) [Ramakrishna (2004)]. Though such products were indeed useful in offsetting around 10% of the industry's short correlation position, ironically they came with significant model risk to the one event they were designed to protect against, namely the spiking of correlation in declining markets. In the beginning of 2008, products designed to exploit just such an event, namely best-of puts, paying out a put on the index (typically out of three), which falls the least, began to be marketed as hedges against market crashes [Blees (2008)].

At the time of writing, the correlation position of the industry is significantly reduced compared to the pre-crash levels, with many banks either hedging out or simply disposing of outright directional exposures [Cameron (2010)]. Nonetheless, in this chapter we will reflect on the modelling implications of the correlation dynamics observed through the crash period to some of the products underpinning the crisis. We will see that, far from being limited to periods of distress, the anticorrelated nature of market correlation *itself* with market returns is present even during so-called bullish periods. We will also see that, whilst indeed structured multi-asset products such as best-of and worst-of trades do bear a significant model risk to these dynamics, the model risk on simpler structures, notably the apparently 'pure play' correlation and covariance products is at least as significant. For all the development of structured products in the last decade, the availability of associated flow products against which to calibrate still significantly lags behind. Whilst this situation persists, correlation will continue to be an important source of model risk across the entire spectrum of multi-asset equity derivatives, from humble basket call options, to thirty underlyer autocallable dispersion products.

8.1   Historical analysis

As in previous chapters, we will start by looking historically at the parameter of interest. For a start, how do stocks actually move? For this analysis we will look at the top 100 stocks of the S&P500 which persisted over the last 8 years. To get an idea about the dynamics dominating their co-movement, we will break down the resulting correlation matrix into its principal components. The dominant eigenvector, accounting for 40% of realised variance of the normalised stock returns, is shown in Figure 8.1.

As can be seen from the Gaussian envelope, the distribution of the 100 components of the principal eigenvector is significantly above zero. By

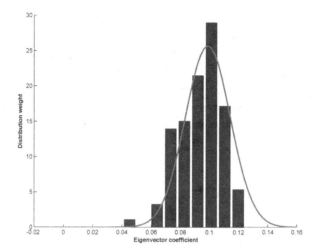

Fig. 8.1 Component distribution for the principal eigenvector of the normalised returns on the top 100 stocks of the S&P500, 2000–2010.

contrast, the component distribution of the second eigenvector, accounting for only 5% of realised variance is shown in Figure 8.2. The mean of the components is evidently not significantly distributed away from zero.

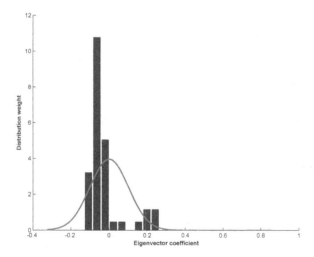

Fig. 8.2 Component distribution for the second eigenvector of the normalised returns on the top 100 stocks of the S&P500, 2000–2010.

Like this, we can start to build up a familiar picture of correlated returns as consisting principally of a parallel shift movement, with a residual noise term on top. Exactly what does this parallel shift correspond to? If we look at a scatter of the returns projected onto this principal eigenmode against the corresponding normalised returns on the index itself (Figure 8.3), we arrive at a simple picture: the principal component of returns on the stocks of the S&P500 is essentially the return on the S&P500 itself.

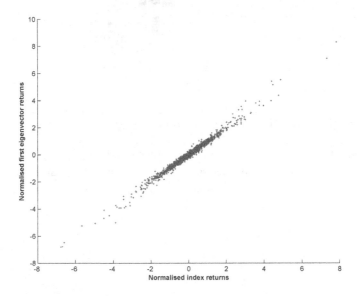

Fig. 8.3   Scatter of the returns on the principal component of returns on the 100 stocks of the S&P500 vs returns on the index, 2000–2010.

We can now begin to build up a simple picture for the dynamics of the stocks of the S&P500, namely:

$$d \log S_t^i = \mu_t^i dt + \sigma_t^i dW_t^i$$
$$d \log S_t^j = \mu_t^j dt + \sigma_t^j dW_t^j$$
$$dW_t^i = \lambda_t^i dV_t + \sqrt{1 - {\lambda_t^i}^2} d\varepsilon_t^i$$
$$dW_t^j = \lambda_t^j dV_t + \sqrt{1 - {\lambda_t^j}^2} d\varepsilon_t^j$$

where dV_t corresponds to the normalised return on the index, uncorrelated with the residual diffusions $d\varepsilon_t^i$. Indeed, the last statement is well supported by the corresponding scatter with the projections onto the second eigenmode, as per Figure 8.4.

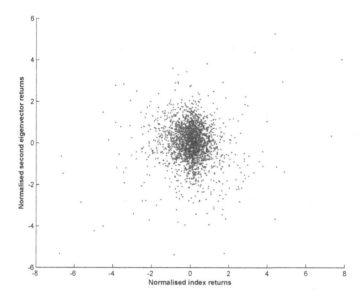

Fig. 8.4 Scatter of the returns on the second component of returns on the 100 stocks of the S&P500 vs returns on the index, 2000–2010.

Such a picture is an example of a so-called *factor model*, which can be written more generally as:

$$x_i = \sum_{j=1,k} \lambda_{ij} V_j + \varepsilon_i$$

where

$$\langle V_i V_j \rangle = \delta_{ij}$$
$$\langle V_i \varepsilon_j \rangle = 0$$
$$\langle \varepsilon_i \varepsilon_j \rangle = \Psi_{i,j}$$

This gives the correlation decomposition:

$$\langle x_i x_j \rangle = \sum_k \lambda_{ik} \lambda_{kj} + \Psi_{i,j}$$

Our picture for stock returns is then a simple one-factor model through which the realised $n \times n$ correlation matrix can be decomposed into an $n \times 1$ vector of factor loadings λ_i:

$$\rho_{ij} = \lambda_i \lambda_j + \Psi_{i,j}$$

This is an extremely powerful result. We have effectively reduced the problem of correlation dynamics from a two-dimensional $n \times n$ problem to a one-dimensional $n \times 1$ problem. Like this, we can adapt the PCA analysis of stock returns directly to stock factor loadings, provided we make a judicious map from the $[-1, 1]$ domain of factor loadings to the $[-\infty, \infty]$ domain of a normal Brownian motion. The obvious choice is $\lambda_i = \tanh(\beta_i)$. We now proceed as follows:

(1) Divide the stock returns into non-overlapping windows such that the number of samples per window is large enough for the standard error of the realised correlation to be small enough to be useful, but small enough to allow enough realised correlation samples to be taken for a valid historical analysis. In line with typical realised volatility analyses, we have taken a 60 business day window (3 months), allowing for 34 correlation samples.

(2) For each correlation sample, compute the realised correlation between the stock returns and the index, as an estimate of the factor loading. Transform this vector of factors to the domain $[-\infty, \infty]$ using $\beta_i = \operatorname{atanh}(\lambda_i)$.

(3) Compute the normal returns $d\beta_i(t_{j+1}) = \beta_i(t_{j+1}) - \beta_i(t_j)$ and calculate the principle components of the resultant correlation matrix.

The results for principal components of the β_i vector are shown in Figure 8.5.

Though not perhaps as clear cut as the component distribution for the principal eigenmode of the stock returns, the corresponding factor loading return eigenmode clearly shows a significant positive average, indicating, perhaps unsurprisingly, that something akin to a parallel shift in the transformed loading space characterises the correlation dynamics (the mode shown accounts for 45% of the realised factor loading variance). Let us map this to a parallel shift plus residual dynamic using the following:

$$d\beta_i = d\langle \beta \rangle + d\xi_i$$

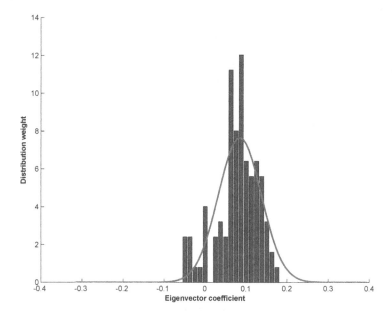

Fig. 8.5 Component distribution for the principal eigenvector of the transformed factor loadings of the top 100 stocks of the S&P500, 2000–2010.

where $\langle\beta\rangle$ is the average of the factor loading returns $d\beta_i$ over the 100 stocks. If we now look at the scatter of normalised $d\langle\beta\rangle$ vs the normalised log returns of the index over the same sampling windows, we get the picture shown in Figure 8.6.

Whilst the sparseness of available data points does make analysis more difficult, it would appear that correlation itself appears to be negatively correlated with the associated index. Note, however, that this does not appear to be confined to periods of market unrest, the dynamic seems to have been present as a matter of course. This is perhaps unsurprising. The more the market falls, the more traders will tend to short stocks to cover themselves against the fall, with correlation between negative stock returns rising accordingly. The analysis is useful in that it does give us some estimate of the factor loading volatility and the factor loading correlation. For the remainder of this chapter, we will take factor loading volatility to refer to the volatility of the returns of the average transformed factor loadings, and factor loading correlation the corresponding correlation to the log returns on the index. Annualising the realised variance of the average factor loading returns, and using standard estimates for the variance of

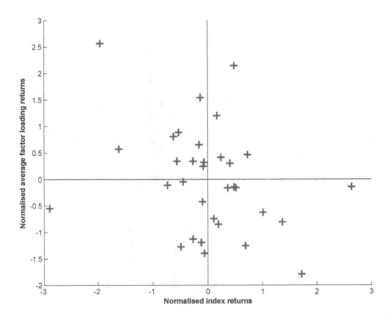

Fig. 8.6   Scatter of the normalised return of average factor loadings vs the normalised return on the S&P500, 2000–2010.

sampled variance[1] gives a factor loading volatility of 25% ± 5%. Using the Fisher transformation for the estimate of correlation error,[2] we obtain an estimate of the factor loading correlation of -30 % ± 20%. Whilst it would clearly be rash to quote a price for an instrument based on these numbers, they do at least provide a basis for model risk analysis.

8.2   Hedging correlation

Before we try to price some products with dynamic correlation, let's address the question of whether there is indeed a valid risk-neutral price for this problem. In keeping with the above analysis, we will assume a model where

---

[1]For n i.i.d random variables y_i sampled from a normal distribution $\mathcal{N}(\mu, \sigma^2)$, the variance of the sampled variance s^2 is given by $\mathrm{Var}[s^2] = \sigma^4 \left(\frac{2}{n-1} + \frac{\kappa}{n} \right)$ where κ is the kurtosis of the distribution.

[2]For a measured correlation coefficient r of two normal variables X and Y sampled from a bivariate normal distribution with correlation ρ, the variable $z = \mathrm{atanh}(r)$ is approximately normally distributed with mean $\mathrm{atanh}(\rho)$ and standard error $1/\sqrt{N-3}$ where N is the sample size.

correlation itself moves according to one stochastic driver only, i.e. $\rho_{ij} = \rho_{ij}(\beta)$ where β is stochastic. The hedging analysis then follows the same pattern as per stochastic volatility. Consider the portfolio Π_t given by $\Pi_t = V_t + \sum_i a_i S_i + bV_t' + cB_t$, with V_t the instrument in question, S_i the underlying stock prices, V_t' the instrument used as a hedge for stochastic correlation and B_t a rolled-up money market account. We then have:

$$dV_t = \frac{\partial V}{\partial t}dt + \sum_i \frac{\partial V}{\partial S_i}dS_i + \frac{1}{2}\sum_{i,j} \frac{\partial^2 V}{\partial S_i \partial S_j}dS_i dS_j$$
$$+ \frac{\partial V}{\partial \beta}d\beta + \frac{1}{2}\frac{\partial^2 V}{\partial \beta^2}d\beta^2 + \sum_i \frac{\partial^2 V}{\partial S_i \partial \beta}dS_i d\beta$$

We then follow the standard hedging arguments:

$$\frac{\partial V}{\partial S_i} + a_i + b\frac{\partial V'}{\partial S_i} = 0$$
$$\frac{\partial V}{\partial \beta} + b\frac{\partial V'}{\partial \beta} = 0$$

to give

$$b = -\frac{\partial V/\partial \beta}{\partial V'/\partial \beta}$$
$$a_i = -\left[\frac{\partial V}{\partial S_i} - \frac{\partial V/\partial \beta}{\partial V'/\partial \beta}\frac{\partial V'}{\partial S_i}\right]$$

For illustration we will assume that β follows a normal Brownian motion, perfectly anticorrelated with a market variable $M_t \sim \mathcal{N}(0, dt)$:

$$d\beta_t = \mu_\beta dt - \sigma_\beta dM_t$$

We will also assume that the stock processes are correlated through M_t:

$$\frac{dS_i(t)}{S_i(t)} = \left[\mu_i(t) - \frac{\sigma_i^2(t)}{2}\right]dt + \sigma_i(t)\left[\lambda_i(\beta_t)dM_t + \sqrt{1 - \lambda_i^2(\beta_t)}d\varepsilon_i\right]$$

giving $E[dS_i(t)d\beta_t] = -S_i\sigma_i(t)\sigma_\beta\lambda_i(\beta_t)dt$.

Using further that $\Pi_t = 0$ to give $cB_t = -[V_t + \sum_i a_i S_i + bV'_t]$, the self-financing condition $d\Pi_t = 0$ yields:

$$
\left[\frac{\partial V}{\partial t} + \sum_{i<j} \frac{\partial^2 V}{\partial S_i \partial S_j}\lambda_i(\beta_t)\lambda_j(\beta_t)\sigma_i(t)\sigma_j(t) + \frac{1}{2}\frac{\partial^2 V}{\partial \beta^2}\sigma_\beta^2 \right.
$$
$$
\left. +\frac{1}{2}\sum_i \frac{\partial^2 V}{\partial S_i^2}S_i^2\sigma_i^2(t) - \sum_i \frac{\partial^2 V}{\partial S_i \partial \beta}S_i\sigma_i(t)\lambda_i(\beta_t)\sigma_\beta - r\left[V - \frac{\partial V}{\partial S_i}\right]\right] \Big/ \frac{\partial V}{\partial \beta}
$$
$$
= \left[\frac{\partial V'}{\partial t} + \sum_{i<j} \frac{\partial^2 V'}{\partial S_i \partial S_j}\lambda_i(\beta_t)\lambda_j(\beta_t)\sigma_i(t)\sigma_j(t) + \frac{1}{2}\frac{\partial^2 V'}{\partial \beta^2}\sigma_\beta^2 \right.
$$
$$
\left. +\frac{1}{2}\sum_i \frac{\partial^2 V'}{\partial S_i^2}S_i^2\sigma_i^2(t) - \sum_i \frac{\partial^2 V'}{\partial S_i \partial \beta}S_i\sigma_i(t)\lambda_i(\beta_t)\sigma_\beta - r\left[V' - \frac{\partial V'}{\partial S_i}\right]\right] \Big/ \frac{\partial V'}{\partial \beta}
$$

recovering the consistent hedging condition reminiscent of Chapter 4. We thus have for the pricing PDE:

$$
\frac{\partial V}{\partial t} + \sum_{i<j} \frac{\partial^2 V}{\partial S_i \partial S_j}\lambda_i(\beta_t)\lambda_j(\beta_t)\sigma_i(t)\sigma_j(t) + \frac{1}{2}\frac{\partial^2 V}{\partial \beta^2}\sigma_\beta^2
$$
$$
+ \frac{1}{2}\sum_i \frac{\partial^2 V}{\partial S_i^2}S_i^2\sigma_i^2(t) - \sum_i \frac{\partial^2 V}{\partial S_i \partial \beta}S_i\sigma_i(t)\lambda_i(\beta_t)\sigma_\beta - r\left[V - \frac{\partial V}{\partial S_i}\right]
$$
$$
= g(\beta_t)\frac{\partial V}{\partial \beta}
$$

for *any* growth factor $g(\beta_t)$. Thus, as per stochastic volatility, we can make an arbitrary choice for the growth of the correlation driver and still maintain risk-neutrality. Just how we choose that growth essentially depends on which options we're trying to calibrate to. As we will see in the rest of the chapter, that choice impacts crucially on the correlation model risk of structured multi-asset products.

8.3 A simple model for dynamic correlation

A natural model which would encapsulate the dynamics arising from the historical analysis of the previous section would be some sort of stochastic volatility analogue for correlation, where correlation itself is derived from a set of dynamic factors which themselves depend on a single normal variable characterising the dominant principal component, itself negatively correlated with market returns. For the purposes of illustration, however, we're going to opt for a simpler model, more akin to *local* volatility, where the factors are a direct function of the market variable V_t itself, namely:

$$\lambda_i(V_t, t) = \operatorname{sgn}(\lambda_i(0,0)) \frac{1 - \tanh(\sigma V_t - \overline{\mu}(t)t - \alpha_i)}{2} \tag{8.1}$$

$$\overline{\mu}(t) = \frac{1}{t} \int_0^t \mu(s)ds$$

$$\alpha_i = \operatorname{atanh}\left[(2\lambda_i(0,0) - 1)\operatorname{sgn}(\lambda_i(0,0))\right]$$

$$dV_t \sim \mathcal{N}(0, dt)$$

We will assume, moreover, that the residual correlation in this single factor model of stock returns, is the identity matrix. A few points to note about this model:

- We assume that correlation is a monotonically decreasing function of the market variable. This is convenient for modelling, but in general would require a richer structure if, for example, index implied volatility were to be matched given underlying stock implied volatilities (see later).
- Factors are bounded between 0 and 1, or 0 and -1: correlation never switches sign. This again is a convenience for model analysis, but is by no means an essential feature of a dynamic correlation model. Historically, equity correlation does tend to be positive. A prolonged negative correlation might be the result of some exceptional corporate activity (e.g. an acquisition), and tends to be rare.
- By constructing our correlation matrix from a set of dynamic factor loadings, the model is *de facto* Cholesky decomposable (the underlying processes will always be real). This is an extremely useful feature of the model, though alternative approaches employing dynamic convex combinations of semi-definite correlation matrices [Langnau (2010)] are equally valid *per se*. That being said, the advantage of a factor based model is that the correlation dynamics can be derived on a *per asset* basis, i.e. for a given asset we can propagate its factor based on a factor loading volatility associated with some market variable. The correlation dynamics of any bespoke multi-asset product can then be derived from these individual factor propagations. Note, however, that in an industrial application an optimal fit of the matrix $\lambda_i(0,0)\lambda_j(0,0)$ would necessitate a non-zero residual correlation matrix to match the initial marked correlation levels.

- The average factor drift $\overline{\mu}(t)$ is calibrated to a single vanilla instrument price at that maturity. Which instrument is used is essentially a trading decision depending on what trades most liquidly. We will assume that instrument to be an at the money geometric basket option for theoretical simplicity, though something like an ATM arithmetic basket, or an outperformance option would be more usual. Note that this model does not contain enough degrees of freedom for the factor drift to be unique for each factor. The calibrated drift for basket ABC would be different for basket ABD, for example. Indeed, the implied correlation for any given pair would not be preserved as we turned on correlation dynamics. In essence, we're treating different basket combinations as single instruments in their own right, each with their own correlation dynamics, and allowing some sort of implied correlation 'anchor point' to be used when analysing model risk. From a conceptual point of view, however, it could be argued that this is a model weakness. A richer treatment which attempted a pairwise implied correlation calibration would greatly add complexity to the model for what are at best illiquidly traded options. For the majority of the analysis in this chapter, we will actually confine our attention to two asset products, for which this problem is patently not an issue.

Note that this model says nothing about the details of the dynamics of the underlyers, it concerns itself only with the method of correlating their normal increments. For this analysis, we will actually use the standard Dupire local volatility model to relate these increments to the actual stock returns, but we could quite happily have employed a stochastic local volatility model or a jump-diffusion model. This separation of the problem of generating correlated normal variates from the problem of transforming those variates to stock returns via the underlying marginal distributions is characteristic of a *copula model*, of which this sort of approach falls under the general title of *factor copula*. Formally, we have the following definition [Schmidt (2006)]:

Definition 8.1. A d−dimensional copula $C : [0, 1]^d \mapsto [0, 1]$ is a function which is a cumulative distribution function (cdf) with uniform marginals, i.e.:

$$C(u_1, \ldots, u_n) = \mathbb{P}(U_1 < u_1, \ldots, U_n < u_n)$$

where $U_i \sim \mathcal{U}(0, 1)$.

On top of this definition, we have *Sklar's theorem*:

Theorem 8.1. *Given the n-dimensional cdf* $H(x_1, \ldots, x_n)$ *with univariate cdfs* $F_{X_1}(x_1), \ldots, F_{X_n}(x_n)$, *then there exists a copula* $C(u_1, \ldots, u_n)$ *such that:*

$$H(x_1, \ldots, x_n) = C(F_{X_1}(x_1), \ldots, F_{X_1}(x_1))$$

for all x_i *in* $[-\infty, \infty]$, $i = 1, \ldots, n$. *If* F_i *is continuous for all* $i = 1, \ldots, n$ *then* C *is unique: otherwise* C *is uniquely determined only on* $RanF_1 \times \ldots \times RanF_n$ *where* $RanF_i$ *denotes the range of the cdf* F_i.

The slightly conceptually easier corollary can be stated in terms of the inverse cdf. Suppose that $F_{X_1}(x_1) = u_1, \ldots, F_{X_n}(x_n) = u_n$, then the copula itself is given by:

$$C(u_1, \ldots, u_n) = H(F_1^{-1}(u_1), \ldots, F_1^{-1}(u_1))$$

which is just joint probability $\mathbb{P}(X_1 < F_1^{-1}(u_1), \ldots, X_n < F_n^{-1}(u_n))$. We can illustrate this through what is probably the most widely used of all copulas, namely the Gaussian copula, given by:

$$C^{Gauss}(u_1, \ldots, u_n) = \Phi_{\Sigma}(\Phi^{-1}(u_1), \ldots, \Phi^{-1}(u_n))$$

where

$$\Phi_{\Sigma}(x_1, \ldots, x_n) = \int_{-\infty}^{x_1} \cdots \int_{-\infty}^{x_n} \frac{1}{(2\pi)^{n/2}|\Sigma|^{1/2}} \exp\left(-\frac{1}{2}\mathbf{y}^T \Sigma^{-1}\mathbf{y}\right) dy_1 \ldots dy_n$$

given a correlation matrix Σ between $\mathcal{N}(0,1)$ variates $y_1, \ldots y_n$. One of the challenges in copula usage is simulation. The Gaussian copula affords an extremely easy prescription. One simply generates a set of *uncorrelated* $\mathcal{N}(0,1)$ normal variates and generates a set of correlated normal variates through Cholesky decomposition (see exercise). The resultant distribution automatically provides the correct joint cdf, simulating the copula. Now, at the risk of re-iterating, what is really powerful about this technique is that at no stage have we said anything about the *actual* marginal distributions of the underlying processes. To map from the joint distribution of normal variates to the actual joint distribution of underlyers, we simply use the transformation:

$$\Psi(S_i) = \Phi(x_i)$$

where $\Psi(S_i)$ is the stock price cdf for the i-th stock defined over the simulation interval. The relationship follows immediately from the conservation of probability $\mathbb{P}(S'_i < S_i < S'_i + \delta S'_i) = \mathbb{P}(x'_i < x_i < x'_i + \delta x'_i)$.

The single factor copula characterised by our model is equally straightforward. Conditional on the realisation of the common factor V, the stock price diffusions W_i are *independent*, allowing us to write for the joint cdf:

$$C(u_1, \ldots, u_n) = \int_{-\infty}^{\infty} \prod_{i=1,n} \Phi\left(\frac{-\lambda_i V + \Phi^{-1}(u_1)}{\sqrt{1 - \lambda_i^2}}\right) \phi(V) dV$$

where $\phi(V) = \frac{1}{\sqrt{2\pi}} e^{-V^2/2}$. The simulation of the copula is simpler still: we just have to take $n+1$ uncorrelated $\mathcal{N}(0,1)$ variates, $\varepsilon_1, \ldots, \varepsilon_n, V$ and use the prescription $x_i = \lambda_i V + \sqrt{1 - \lambda_i^2} \varepsilon_i$. Note a useful biproduct of this approach: the $O(n^2)$ problem of integrating over the n-dimensional multivariate distribution has been reduced to an essentially univariate integral over the product of Gaussian cdfs. For products such as bets on the n-th performer, this can be a huge efficiency saving.

Clearly, this simple factor copula of *constant* factor loadings is still essentially a Gaussian copula: we have merely decomposed the multivariate Gaussian into a product of univariate Gaussians integrated over another Gaussian (see exercise). The simplest way to break the Gaussian form is to make the factor loadings dependent on the common factor, i.e. we could define a modified copula:

$$\tilde{C}(u_1, \ldots, u_n) = \int_{-\infty}^{\infty} \prod_{i=1,n} \Phi\left(\frac{-\lambda_i(V)V + \Phi^{-1}(u_1)}{\sqrt{1 - \lambda_i(V)^2}}\right) \phi(V) dV \qquad (8.2)$$

In effect we have simply modified the simulation to $x_i = \lambda_i(V)V + \sqrt{1 - \lambda_i(V)^2} \varepsilon_i$. The problem with this approach (though not in practice a severe one), is that x_i is no longer a univariate Gaussian. Ferrarese [Ferrarese (2006)] treats a simple two point specification of $\lambda_i(V)$:

$$\lambda_i(V) = \alpha \mathbf{1}(V \leq \theta) + \beta \mathbf{1}(V > \theta)$$

along with a generalisation of x_i: $x_i = \lambda_i(V) + v\varepsilon_i + m$, where $m = -E[\lambda_i(V)V]$ and $v = \sqrt{1 - Var[\lambda_i(V)V]}$ are taken to ensure that x_i has zero mean and unit variance. The simple digital form for the factor loadings then makes the cdf for x_i tractable. Such an approach has the advantage that a non-Gaussian multivariate distribution can be generated in one step, and is popular in the world of collateralised debt obligation pricing. For our purposes however, (a) we're going to need a multiple step Monte Carlo method to deal with path dependent options and (b) making the factor loadings a function of the common factor at the *start* of the step is both a natural development from our historical analysis, as well as a direct analogue to the previsible method of local volatility simulation. Such previsibility also has the convenient property that, conditional on the realisation of the common factor at the start of the Monte Carlo step, the marginal underpinning the stock evolution is automatically distributed $\sim \mathcal{N}(0,1)$, making the conversion to the actual stock marginal trivial.

8.3.1 *Implied distributions*

Before we get onto some initial results for what sort of joint distribution this model gives, it's worth taking a step back and considering what sort of *process* the model implies for correlation. Confining our attention to positive factor loadings for illustration, application of Itō's lemma to $\lambda_i(V)$ gives (see exercise):

$$\frac{d\lambda_i}{2\lambda_i(1-\lambda_i)} = \left[\mu + 2\sigma^2 \left(\frac{1}{2} - \lambda_i\right)\right] dt - \sigma dV_t$$

There are immediately a couple of points to note:

- λ_i is clearly bounded between 0 and 1, as we might expect. Not only does the volatility of the process collapse to zero at these extrema, but so does the drift. In other words, the process ends up getting 'pinned' at either 0 or 1. For the case of two assets, where $\rho = \lambda^2$, perfect and zero correlation act as 'fatal attractors'. Over time, we might expect the distribution of stock returns to converge to a region of zero correlation for positive returns, and perfect correlation for negative returns. This is obviously a considerable restriction, resulting from the overly simplistic nature of the model. An alternative formulation by Driessen *et al.* [Driessen *et al.* (2005)] includes a mean reversion term to correct for this behaviour:

$$d\rho = \kappa(\bar{\rho} - \rho)dt + \sigma_\rho\sqrt{\rho(1-\rho)}dW$$

Whilst for this (Jacobi) process, the volatility clearly also collapses at $\rho = 0$ and $\rho = 1$, the mean reversion term should pull the correlation back to some average level, potentially providing greater flexibility for term structure fitting of implied index correlation, for example. Note, however, that this process suffers from the Feller condition restriction of a CIR process (see Chapter 4). The correlation stays within the interval $(0, 1)$ only if $\kappa\bar{\rho} > \sigma_\rho^2/2$ and $\kappa(1 - \bar{\rho}) > \sigma_\rho^2/2$, whilst ours is bounded by 0 and 1 by construction.

- There is an effective mean reversion effect, within the drift term, with a mean reversion speed of $2\sigma^2$ and a mean reversion level of 0.5, though the effect of this term is crushed as we approach 0 or 1. Again, this is obviously an oversimplification resulting from the simple form for our factor loading function. A function designed for calibration to index volatility would almost certainly require greater sophistication.

In short then, our choice of model is clearly going to be quite restrictive in terms of the range of available term structures for the joint marginal distribution. The function will, however, encapsulate the effect of correlation decreasing for market rallies and increasing for market falls, which will be the main topic for investigation in this chapter. This behaviour is indeed borne out by simulation, as shown in Figure 8.7, shown for a factor loading volatility of 200% (for illustration), 50% initial correlation, at 5Y.

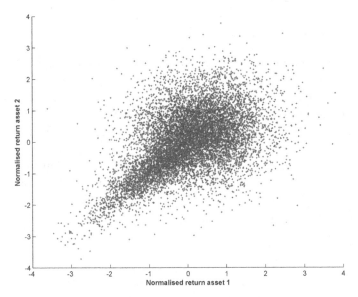

Fig. 8.7   Joint normalised return scatter for a non-Gaussian factor copula, 200% factor loading vol, 50% initial correlation, 5Y maturity.

Our factor loading function has achieved the desired effect. Joint negative returns become concentrated around the $x = y$ line, in line with increased correlation on the downside, whilst joint positive returns become more dispersed, in line with the tendency towards zero correlation on the upside. The effect becomes more pronounced as we extend to higher maturities, though as expected the distribution converges to one of perfect correlation on the downside compared with zero correlation on the upside.

8.3.2 *Implied correlation*

It's instructive to convert these distributions into implied correlation slices, analogously to implied vol surfaces deriving from dynamic volatility models (local vol, stochastic vol etc). To do this in a like-for-like manner, we first need to be sure that the underlying option behind the correlation calculation itself derives from a log-normal process when the dynamics of the model parameters are turned off. This obliges us to consider a *geometric* rather than the more common *arithmetic* basket option. In the latter case the basket spot is commonly defined as:

$$B_{arithmetic}(t) = \sum_i w_i \frac{S_i(t)}{S_i(0)}$$

where $\sum_i w_i = 1$ to ensure the basket starts from unity. In the geometric case, the spot is given by:

$$B_{geometric}(t) = \exp\left[\sum_i w_i \log\left(\frac{S_i(t)}{S_i(0)}\right)\right] = \prod_i \left(\frac{S_i(t)}{S_i(0)}\right)^{w_i}$$

We can see trivially that the distribution of $\log(B_{geometric}(t))$ is itself normal provided the log underlyers are distributed normally, given that the sum of correlated normal variables is itself normal (see exercise). $B_{geometric}(t)$ is thus distributed log-normally. Conversely, as the sum of log-normal variables is not itself log-normal, the arithmetic basket spot will not be distributed log-normally. Even if we had no *local* correlation dynamics then, the *implied* correlation slice would not be flat, breaking the like-for-like comparison with volatility.

Taking the case of flat stock growth and vol for simplicity, from Itō we have:

$$B_{geometric}(t) = \exp\left[\sum_i w_i(\mu_i - \sigma_i^2/2)T\right]\exp\left[\sum_i w_i\sigma_i W_i\right]$$

whence we have:

$$F_B(t) = E\left[B_{geometric}(t)\right] =$$

$$\exp\left[\sum_i w_i(\mu_i - (1 - w_i)\sigma_i^2/2)T\right]\exp\left[\sum_{i<j} w_i w_j \rho_{ij}\sigma_i\sigma_j T\right]$$

$$= \overline{F}_B(t)\exp\left[\sum_i -w_i(1 - w_i)\sigma_i^2 T/2\right]\exp\left[\sum_{i<j} w_i w_j \rho_{ij}\sigma_i\sigma_j T\right]$$

$$\overline{F}_B(t) = \prod_i [F_i(t)/F_i(0)]^{w_i} \tag{8.3}$$

and

$$Var\left[\log(B_{geometric}(t))\right] = \sum_{i,j}\rho_{ij}w_i w_j\sigma_i\sigma_j T = \sigma_B^2 T$$

Giving the undiscounted value of a call on a geometric basket as:

$$C(K,T) = E_{\mathbb{Q}}[(S_B - K,0)^+] = F_B N(d_1) - KN(d_2)$$
$$d_{1,2} = \log(F_B/K)/\sigma_B\sqrt{T} \pm \sigma_B\sqrt{T}/2$$

Note that the geometric basket forward itself depends on correlation. This will be of relevance when considering the replication of covariance swaps later.

Consider now a geometric basket option with *log-normal* underlyers. Defining implied correlation as:

$$\widehat{\rho} = \frac{\sigma_B^2 - \sum_i w_i^2\widehat{\sigma}_i^2}{\sum_{i\neq j} w_i w_j\widehat{\sigma}_i\widehat{\sigma}_j}$$

we would have that local correlation is equal to implied correlation in the case of a geometric basket of two log-normal assets with constant volatility. Whilst the equality would be broken if one or more of the assets had a term structure of implied volatility, there would still be no state dependence. Likewise, even with a term structure of local correlation and a term structure of local volatility but no state dependence in either, the local basket volatility would be state independent, giving a strike independent implied correlation. We thus recover the exact analogue with local volatility: no state dependence in local correlation gives no strike dependence in implied correlation, provided the underlyers are log-normal.

Conversely, non-flat implied correlation, a.k.a *correlation skew*, is given by a state dependent local correlation. In our model, as we introduce extra correlation on the downside, we might expect OTM geometric basket puts to become more valuable, with more of the joint distribution concentrated in the payoff region, and vice versa for OTM calls. Like this, our model of stocks becoming more correlated for downside market moves should give a negative slope to the implied correlation slice, analogously to increased vol on the downside in a local vol model enhancing downside implied volatilities. This is shown in Figure 8.8 for a 2Y geometric basket at increasing levels of factor loading volatility.

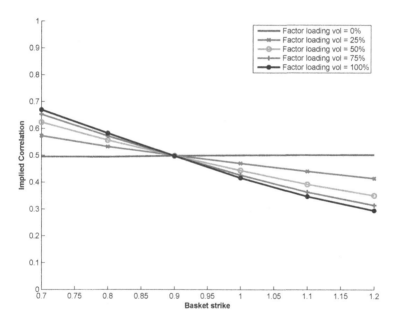

Fig. 8.8   Implied correlation slice at 2Y, geometric basket option of two log-normal assets, increasing factor loading volatility.

As expected, the slice becomes more steeply downward sloping for higher factor loading volatility. Interestingly, the slices (a) intersect at a common point and (b) tend to a limit in the limit of high factor loading vol. The latter is a natural result of the distribution of the factor loading becoming pinned at 0 and 1 for high factor variance. Indeed, we see the same convergence property for increasing maturity, by the same token, as shown in Figure 8.9 for a factor loading volatility of 200%.

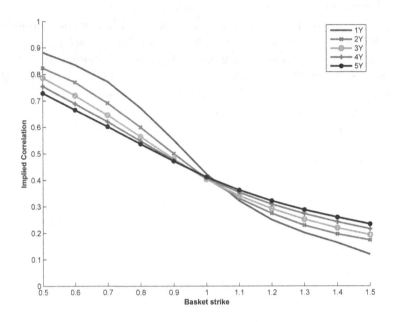

Fig. 8.9   Implied correlation slice term structure, geometric basket option of two lognormal assets, 200% factor loading volatility.

Once again, the limitations of this model in fitting implied basket volatility from the market are evident. Note the suppression of the implied correlation at the ATM strike. In the absence of liquid market data this is not a problem in itself. If, on the other hand, we wish to preserve implied correlation for ATM geometric basket options, a positive correlation drift would be required to compensate. As we shall see in the next section, this calibration is crucial to determining the sensitivity of the instrument to dynamic correlation.

8.4   Rainbow products

As discussed in the introduction to this chapter, much of the short correlation taken in exotics by investment banks in the last decade came from bullish structures employing ranked performance to enhance coupons, or cheapen structures on behalf of clients. Of the more popular structures, the 'mountain range' options invented by Société Générale and simpler 'rainbow' options formed a significant part of the dealer's portfolio. Though the number of variants was large, the two types roughly broke down as follows:

Mountain range options [Quessette (2002)]

- *Altiplano*: An option that entitles one to a large coupon if no stock in a given selection hits a limit in a given period. Otherwise a vanilla basket call. Effectively a knockout on the worst performer.
- *Atlas*: A call on a basket where at maturity some of the best and some of the worst performing stocks are withdrawn. Effectively a rainbow style option with zero weights at the top and bottom of the performance range (see below).
- *Annapurna*: The holder is rewarded if all securities in the basket never fall below a certain price during the relevant time period, i.e. a worst-of knockout.
- *Everest*: Payout based on the worst performing option of a *large* basket of stocks at maturity. Structurally no different to a regular worst-of option, though the Everest tended to be very long term (10–15 years) and on many stocks (10–25), whilst worst-ofs are typically of maturity 2–5 years, on around 3–5 stocks.
- *Himalaya*: One of the most popular of the mountain range trades, and also one of the hardest to analyse [Overhaus (2002)]. A call option on the average of the best performers of a stock selection, but where the best performing stock is withdrawn from the selection after each fixing date. The correlation sensitivity of the product depends critically on the number of periods and assets. For one period, the product is clearly just a best-of call (short correlation) while for the number of periods equal to the number of assets the product simply becomes a basket call (long correlation).

Rainbow options

In many cases the distinction between a mountain range option and a rainbow option is academic, though a rainbow option tends to be European in style, whilst a mountain range option tends to be path dependent. In general, the rainbow spot is defined as:

$$S_{rainbow}(t) = \sum_i w \left[\Pi(S_i(t)/S_i(0)) \right] S_i(t)/S_i(0)$$

where $\Pi(S_i(t)/S_i(0))$ is a function returning the position of the performance of the i-th stock in the basket at maturity, with $w(j)$ a weighting function for the j-th best performance. Of these, the most common rainbow payouts are simply either on the best or the worst. We will concentrate on these products for simplicity. To begin, let's consider a digital call on the worst of two assets. For a non-zero payoff we need *both* assets to perform above the strike price, so that the undiscounted price of such an option should simply be $\mathbb{P}(x_1 > k \cap x_2 > k)$, for performance strike of k against performance $x_i = S_i(T)/S_i(0)$. Manifestly, the higher the correlation between the two assets, the higher the price, so this product should be long correlation. Conversely, given that the best performer digital + the worst performer digital is just the sum of two digitals and thence correlation-neutral, the best performer digital call should be short correlation, which also follows from the relation $\mathbb{P}(A \cup B) = \mathbb{P}(A) + \mathbb{P}(B) - \mathbb{P}(A \cap B)$. Equally, as the call on the worst + the put on the worst is just unity, the corresponding put risks should be the exact mirror images of the calls. This is demonstrated for both best-of and worst-of digitals in Figures 8.10 and 8.11 respectively. In this, and subsequent calculations in this chapter, we have assumed that the assets have identical growth with a flat volatility of 20%.

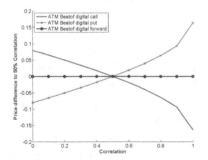

Fig. 8.10 Best-of digital correlation risk, 2Y maturity.

Fig. 8.11 Worst-of digital correlation risk, 2Y maturity.

This picture begins to help us understand how best-of and worst-of calls might react to dynamic correlation. We might expect a best-of call to increase in value as the factor loading volatility is increased from zero, given that the effective correlation in the payoff region declines as a result and the product is short correlation. Indeed this is the case, but by the same token we might expect the best-of put to decrease in value. In fact this is *not* true. We can understand this from put-call parity. The best-of forward on two assets is in fact a forward + an outperformance option, i.e.

$$E_{\mathbb{Q}}[\max(S_1, S_2)] = F_2 + E_{\mathbb{Q}}[\max(S_1 - S_2, 0)] = F_2(1 - N(d_2)) + F_1 N(d_1)$$
$$d_{1,2} = \log(F_1/F_2)/\widehat{\sigma}\sqrt{T} \pm \sigma\sqrt{T}/2$$
$$\widehat{\sigma}^2 = \widehat{\sigma}_1^2 + \widehat{\sigma}_2^2 - 2\rho\widehat{\sigma}_1\widehat{\sigma}_2$$

where the result follows from a change of measure to the S_2 numeraire (see exercise). We thus have that the best-of forward is short correlation, as per the best-of call, except that the best-of forward samples the *entire* joint distribution, including the highly correlated downside, whilst an ATM call (as shown in Figure 8.12) only samples the decorrelated region. This causes the best-of forward to increase in value by less than the best-of call, causing the best-of put to rise in value, albeit less strongly, as we increase factor loading volatility.

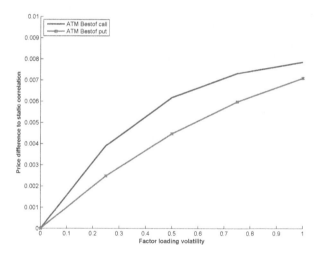

Fig. 8.12   2Y ATM best-of call and put options, vs factor loading volatility, 50% initial correlation.

Already then, we need to be careful with our intuition. When we now *calibrate* to the ATM correlation, so as to leave it stationary under factor loading vol adjustment, the result becomes even less intuitive (Figure 8.13).

The response of both puts and calls is long factor loading volatility, but the magnitude is reversed. Recall that we need to provide a positive correlation drift to keep the ATM correlation fixed. As the put is long correlation risk, and the call short (Figure 8.14), the response of the call is

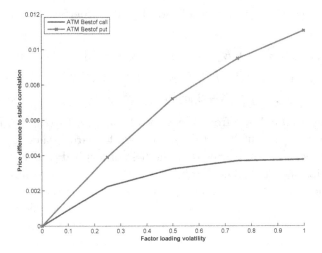

Fig. 8.13   2Y ATM best-of call and put options, vs factor loading volatility, calibrated to 50% ATM correlation.

suppressed, and the put enhanced, reversing the order of magnitude of the response to dynamic correlation.

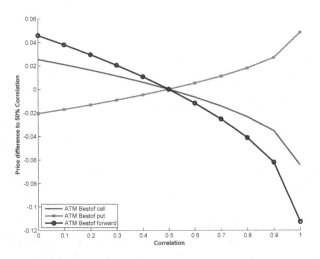

Fig. 8.14   Best-of call correlation risk, 2Y maturity.

Happily at least, the symmetry is preserved when we come to look at worst-ofs, as shown in Figure 8.15.

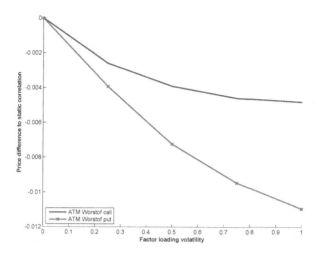

Fig. 8.15   2Y ATM worst-of call and put options, vs factor loading volatility, calibrated to 50% ATM correlation.

To conclude this section, a note about asset number. Recall the expression for the simple factor copula in (8.2). The greater the number of assets, the longer the product of marginal cdfs, and the more sensitive the response of the joint cdf to changes in correlation. We might then expect that an ATM worst-of three call would be more sensitive to factor loading volatility than a worst-of two. Indeed this is so, as shown in Figure 8.16, both for puts and calls. An Everest structure, geared towards the worst-of performer in a large basket of stocks, moreover at long maturity, would be exquisitely sensitive to dynamic correlation. Whilst this is true, correlation model risk is by no means the preserve of the exotic. In the next section we'll look at a product uniquely designed to alleviate the short correlation pressure of the last decade and show that, far from being model risk-free, in many ways its sensitivity is even greater than its exotic counterparts.

8.5   Correlation products

The correlation swap essentially pays out the difference between the average realised correlation on a basket of stocks, and some fair strike, i.e. has a payoff P given by:

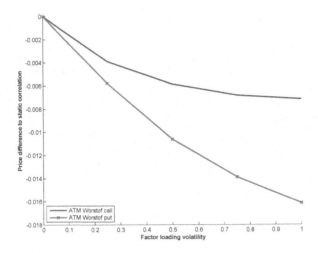

Fig. 8.16   2Y ATM worst-of call and put options, vs factor loading volatility, calibrated to 50% ATM correlation, 3 factors.

$$P_{corrswap} = \frac{2}{N(N-1)} \sum_{i<j} \rho_{ij} - K_{corrswap}$$

$$\rho_{ij} = \frac{\sum_{k=1,M} \log[S_i(t_k)/S_i(t_{k-1})] \log[S_j(t_k)/S_j(t_{k-1})]}{\sqrt{\sum_{k=1,M} \log^2[S_i(t_k)/S_i(t_{k-1})] \sum_{k=1,M} \log^2[S_j(t_k)/S_j(t_{k-1})]}}$$

for M fixings and N assets. These products became popular around 2002 as an efficient means for buying back correlation, compared to the more traditional dispersion methods. In the latter, dealers would buy volatility on an index, or a basket of stocks, through variance swaps or ATM straddles, and short volatility on the individual instruments likewise. The problem with this method is that, whilst indeed you would end up long the correlation between the components of the basket, you would also end up with a short vega position on them, so that the benefits of hedging correlation in a falling market might be outweighed by the corresponding increase in the volatility of the basket components. The correlation swap was not, however, a perfect hedge for the correlation being sold on related products. For example, a dealer short a basket would want to buy back the *covariance* between the individual basket pairs rather than correlation, as this is effectively the risk the basket position is short. As a result, the covariance swap, already common for fx pairs [Carr and Madan (1999)], was introduced to address this hedge short-coming for equities. The payoff is generally given as follows:

$$P_{covswap} = \frac{A}{M} \sum_{k=1,M} \log^2[B(t_k)/B(t_{k-1})] - K_{covarswap}$$

$$- \frac{A}{M} \sum_{k=1,M} [q_1 \log^2[S_1(t_k)/S_1(t_{k-1})] + q_2 \log^2[S_2(t_k)/S_2(t_{k-1})]]$$

where

$$\log[B(t_k)] = w_1 \log[S_1(t_k)] + w_2 \log[S_1(t_k)]$$

and A the annualisation factor.

The choice of the weights against the underlying var swaps is at the trader's discretion. Commonly, the product would be arranged to be vega-neutral with respect to the realised volatility of the two underlyers, giving $q_1 = w_1(w_1 - w_2\sigma_2/\sigma_1)$ and $q_2 = w_2(w_2 - w_1\sigma_1/\sigma_2)$, where σ_i is the square root of the variance swap price for the i-th asset. For the purposes of illustration, however, we'll make the simple choice $q_i = w_i^2$, making the product a pure realised covariance instrument, i.e. (in the limit of large M):

$$P_{covswap} = \frac{1}{T} \int_0^T 2w_1 w_2 \rho(t)\sigma_1(t)\sigma_2(t)dt - K_{covarswap}$$

8.5.1 *Covariance swaps*

We might naively imagine that, given that the covariance swap is essentially a dispersion trade between a two-factor basket variance swap and the weighted sum of the component variance swaps, we should be able to replicate this contract in much the same way as for a single underlyer variance swap (Chapter 4). As it turns out, we *can* replicate a covariance swap, but through a log-*squared*, rather than a log contract on the geometric basket, and only when the underlyers are log-normal. For a start, why does the traditional log contract replication break down? The problem is essentially that the correlation itself enters into the growth of the geometric basket. Applying Itō to $B(t) = \prod_i (S_i(t)/S_i(0))^{w_i}$ we have:

$$\frac{dB(t)}{B(t)} = \left[\sum_i w_i \mu_i(t) + \frac{1}{2} w_i(w_i - 1)\sigma_i(t)^2 + \sum_{i<j} w_i w_j \rho_{i,j}\sigma_i(t)\sigma_j(t)\right] dt$$
$$+ \sum_i w_i \sigma_i(t) dW_i(t) \qquad (8.4)$$

and

$$d\log B(t) = \left[\sum_i w_i \left(\mu_i(t) - \frac{\sigma_i^2(t)}{2}\right)\right] dt + \sum_i w_i \sigma_i(t) dW_i(t) \qquad (8.5)$$

So that combining (8.4) and (8.5), as per a variance swap we have:

$$\frac{dB(t)}{B(t)} - d\log B(t) = \frac{1}{2}\sum_{i,j} w_i w_j \sigma_i(t)\sigma_j(t)dt = \frac{1}{2}\sigma_B^2(t)$$

as expected. So we have:

$$E\left[\int_0^T \sigma_B^2(t)dt\right] = 2E\left[\int_0^T \frac{dB(t)}{B(t)} - \log(B(T)/B(0))\right] \qquad (8.6)$$

But from (8.4):

$$E\left[\int_0^T \frac{dB(t)}{B(t)}\right] = \int_0^T \sum_i w_i \mu_i(t)dt$$
$$+ E\left[\int_0^T \left[\sum_i \frac{1}{2}w_i(w_i - 1)\sigma_i(t)^2\right.\right.$$
$$\left.\left. + \sum_{i<j} w_i w_j \rho_{i,j}\sigma_i(t)\sigma_j(t)\right]dt\right]$$

From (8.3) we have:

$$\log(F_B(T)/B(0)) = \log(\overline{F}_B(T))$$
$$+ \log\left[E\left\{\exp\left[\int_0^T \left[\sum_i \frac{1}{2}w_i(w_i - 1)\sigma_i(t)^2\right.\right.\right.\right.$$
$$\left.\left.\left.\left. + \sum_{i<j} w_i w_j \rho_{i,j}\sigma_i(t)\sigma_j(t)\right]dt\right]\right\}\right] \neq E\left[\int_0^T \frac{dB(t)}{B(t)}\right]$$

as for stochastic X, $E[e^X] \neq e^{E[X]}$. We cannot then complete (8.6) as $2E[\log(F_B(T)/B(T))]$ and the log replication breaks down. The trick then is to come up with a strategy which obviates the state dependent growth problem of the geometric basket spot when we have dynamic correlation active. Suppose we consider the contract $\log^2(B(T)/\overline{F}_B(T))$ (as suggested by earlier work for pricing covariance swaps on foreign exchange pairs [Swishchuk (2004)]):

$$
\log^2[B(T)/\overline{F}_B(T)] = \frac{1}{4}\left[\int_0^T \sum_i w_i \sigma_i(t)^2 dt\right]^2
$$
$$
+ \sum_{i,j} \int_0^T w_i w_j \rho_{ij} \sigma_i(t) \sigma_j(t) dt
$$
$$
- \sum_i \int_0^T w_i \sigma_i^2(t) dt \sum_j \int_0^T w_j \sigma_j(t) dW_j
$$

Hence:

$$
E\left[\log^2(B(T)/\overline{F}_B(T))\right] = \frac{1}{4} E\left[\left[\int_0^T \sum_i w_i \sigma_i(t)^2 dt\right]^2\right]
$$
$$
+ E\left[\sum_{i,j} \int_0^T w_i w_j \rho_{ij} \sigma_i(t) \sigma_j(t) dt\right] \quad (8.7)
$$

So we have, only for deterministic underlyer volatilities:

$$
2E\left[\sum_{i<j} \int_0^T w_i w_j \rho_{ij} \sigma_i(t) \sigma_j(t) dt\right]
$$
$$
= E\left[\log^2(B(T)/\overline{F}_B(T))\right] - T \sum_i w_i^2 V_i(T) - \frac{T^2}{4}\left[\sum_i w_i V_i(T)\right]^2
$$

allowing replication of the covariance swap through a $\log^2(B(T)/\overline{F}_B(T))$ contract and a short position in the weighted sum of variance swaps $V_i(T)$ on the underlyers, and a contract paying the weighted sum of realised variances squared. This is obviously rather contrived, but actually provides a useful check on the accuracy of a dynamic correlation model. If, however, we consider the *difference* in the covariance swap price between dynamic and static correlation, we can cancel off the variance terms giving:

$$Cov_{dyn}(T) - Cov_{stat}(T)$$

$$= \frac{1}{T} \left[E_{dyn} \left[\log^2(B(T)/\overline{F}_B(T)) \right] - E_{stat} \left[\log^2(B(T)/\overline{F}_B(T)) \right] \right] \quad (8.8)$$

where *dyn* and *stat* denote w.r.t the dynamic and static correlation models, and we define:

$$Cov(T) = \frac{2}{T} E \left[\int_0^T \sum_{i<j} \rho_{ij}(t) w_i w_j \sigma_i(t) \sigma_j(t) dt \right]$$

This is an important result. Assuming that we calibrate our correlation model to the ATM implied correlation, with the ATM strike given by $K = \overline{F}_B(T)$, then a model which provides a negatively sloped correlation smile will tend to increase the value of the covariance swap over the static correlation case (see exercise). The result is analogous to the implied volatility skew sensitivity of a variance swap. Note also that as per a variance swap, the weighting rises sharply for deeply out of the money (geometric basket) puts. Not only are these products long factor loading volatility, as shown in Figure 8.17, but frequently dominate the correlation model sensitivity of a portfolio. The effect of correlation skew on the replicating portfolio is shown on the same figure.

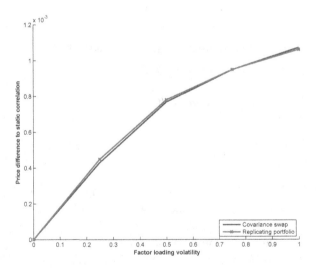

Fig. 8.17   2Y daily sampled covariance swap vs factor loading volatility, calibrated to 50% ATM correlation.

Returning to the issue of calibration, the view on whether or not to calibrate to ATM implied correlation turns out to be crucial for this product. Figure 8.18 shows the corresponding price dependence of the same 2Y covariance swap for zero correlation drift.

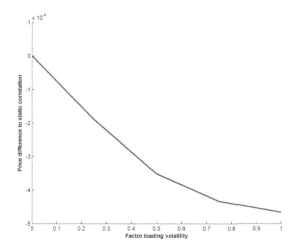

Fig. 8.18   2Y daily sampled covariance swap vs factor loading volatility, zero correlation drift.

The reduction of the implied ATM correlation as we turn on correlation dynamics actually overcompensates the long correlation skew contribution of the implied correlation slope to make the product overall *short* factor loading volatility. Not only is there strong price dependence on the factor loading volatility itself, but the sign of the reaction is a somewhat arbitrary function of whether we consider ATM implied correlation sufficiently liquid to warrant calibration.

Returning to the calibrated case for now, it would appear reasonable to assume that this product is going to be even more sensitive to dynamic correlation when a downward sloping implied volatility surface is introduced to the underlyers, given that ultimately this product depends essentially on the slope of the implied volatility surface for the associated geometric basket. Indeed this is the case, as shown in Figure 8.19. Note that (8.8) no longer holds in this case, due to the state dependence of vol introducing a non-zero effect of correlation dynamics on the first term on the rhs of (8.7) (for negative correlation and volatility skew, as per this example, the effect is to overprice the effect of dynamic correlation).

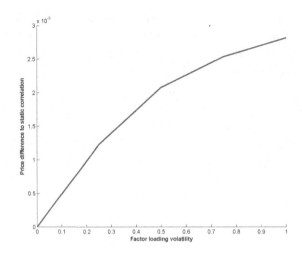

Fig. 8.19   2Y daily sampled covariance swap vs factor loading volatility, calibrated to 50% ATM correlation, negative implied volatility slope on the underlyers.

The volatility surface used is the same as that shown in Figure 2.1 in Chapter 2. Even with this fairly modest amount of vol skew, the price difference to static on the covariance swap is altered by a factor of 3 compared to the flat vol case.

8.5.2   *Correlation swaps*

Unlike the covariance swap, the correlation swap, for all its pure structure is actually harder to hedge. Like volatility swaps, it affords no static replication. Some work, notably by Bossu [Bossu (2005)] has been done to estimate a fair value for the swap in closed form. Bossu uses the realised index variance divided by the average constituent realised variance as a 'proxy' for the average correlation of an index. He observes that the approximation is close in the limit of large basket size and suggests a hedging strategy whereby one goes long c_t/ν_t^I index variance swaps, and short $c_t/\bar{\nu}_t^S$ an equally weighted basket of variance swaps on the underlyer, where c_t is the realised correlation, ν_t^I the realised index variance and $\bar{\nu}_t^S$ the realised average constituent variance, at time t. Whilst such approaches do afford some intuition into how stochastic index volatility and component volatility impact on the price of the correlation swap, they are unfortunately not of great benefit to understanding how dynamic correlation impacts the price of these instruments. This is still an area of ongoing research, but for now we will simply demonstrate the sensitivity of the correlation swap to correlation dynamics, rather than try and explain it precisely. For the case of log-normal underlyers, the sensitivity is, unsurprisingly, equivalent to the covariance swap, as for the two asset basket we simply have a covariance swap inversely weighted by a deterministic volatility term, i.e.:

$$\rho = \frac{\int_0^T \rho\sigma_1(t)\sigma_2(t)dt}{\sqrt{\int_0^T \sigma_1^2(t)dt \int_0^T \sigma_2^2(t')dt'}}$$

The impact of factor loading volatility is shown in Figure 8.20.

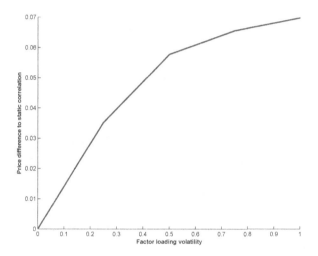

Fig. 8.20   2Y daily sampled correlation swap vs factor loading volatility, calibrated to 50% ATM correlation, flat implied volatility of 20% on the underlyers.

In this example, the increase of realised correlation of around 7% at 100% implied volatility is slightly over the 5% that one would expect for an equally weighted basket on assets with 20% vol for a change in covariance of 0.001, but not greatly. As we might expect, a much larger real effect is seen when one adds in volatility skew. This is shown in Figure 8.21 for the same vol surface as used in Figure 8.19. This time the realised correlation is increased by as much as 20% over the 50% starting correlation.

Paradoxically, it would seem that the simpler the correlation product, the more sensitive it becomes to correlation dynamics. Taking a step back though, this is really just a statement about the underdeveloped nature of correlation hedging, at the time of writing. Imagine that we didn't in

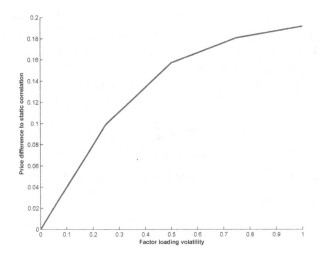

Fig. 8.21   2Y daily sampled correlation swap vs factor loading volatility, calibrated to 50% ATM correlation, negative implied volatility slope on the underlyers.

fact have a liquid market for index options. Different stochastic volatility models would give radically different prices for out of the money options, and by extension volatility and variance products, as only the ATM volatility might be calibrated. If we had a liquid market in bespoke geometric baskets against which to calibrate not only the correlation drift, but the entire dynamics of the correlation process, both correlation and covariance swaps would show very little in the way of correlation model sensitivity, leaving correlation model risk to the more exotic mountain range products, or cliquets on baskets, where the uncertainty in the *forward starting* joint distribution would become the main influence on model risk. To an extent, it might be argued that such a world does exist, at least partially, through the index and single stock option market. Langnau in particular [Langnau (2010)] has developed some ground breaking work to derive a Dupire analogue for a local correlation function defined by the local volatilities of the index underlyers and the local volatility of the index, such that the index implied volatility will be consistently recovered from the underlyer implied volatility surfaces. Analogous to stochastic local volatility, one could then think of correlation model risk as being based on the stochasticity around this local correlation, whilst preserving calibration to implied index volatility. Such an approach would almost certainly greatly reduce the correlation model sensitivity of correlation swaps on the index itself, though correlation and covariance swaps on bespoke sub-baskets of the index would retain model sensitivity until a market for those sub-baskets were created.

8.6 Conclusions

In this chapter we moved beyond the question of the sensitivity of exotic pricing to the model assumptions on the underlyers themselves and attempted to look at the sensitivity to the model correlating them all together. In the wake of the crisis of 2008, this subject has become a key focus of attention, following the painful effects of correlation upturn during periods of market downturn on the predominantly short correlation positions on dealers' exotic books. Motivated by the sorts of instruments underlying that exposure, as well as the instruments designed to hedge it away, we have constructed a toy model of dynamic correlation and applied it to two key classes of multi-asset exotic: rainbow options and outright correlation products. Whilst the sensitivity of the former has been clearly demonstrated, the sensitivity of the latter is no less profound, and if anything more so. Here then is another (and for this book final) aspect of model risk:

> *The simplicity of a product's payoff is no guarantee of its lack of exposure to model risk. The latter may be just as bad as a complex product if the underlying market for calibration is insufficiently developed.*

So, as always, more is less. The deeper and more diverse the range of instruments available for calibration, the less model risky exotic derivatives will be. Sadly, however, we will never be in a position where everything we trade is properly calibrated. In the next, and final chapter of this book, we will take a look at some of the approaches people have come up with for mitigating model risk, and discuss where to go from here.

8.7 Exercises

(1) The joint distribution for n normally distributed correlated variables, with mean μ and covariance Σ, is given by:

$$\phi(\mathbf{x}, \mu, \Sigma) = \frac{1}{(2\pi)^{n/2}|\Sigma|^{1/2}} \exp\left[-\frac{1}{2}(\mathbf{x} - \mu)^T \Sigma^{-1}(\mathbf{x} - \mu)\right]$$

The associated cdf $\Phi(\mathbf{X})$ is given by:

$$\Phi(\mathbf{X}) = \int_{-\infty}^{X_1} \cdots \int_{-\infty}^{X_n} \phi(\mathbf{x}, \mu, \mathbf{\Sigma}) dx_1 \ldots dx_n$$

Show that this integral can be re-expressed as:

$$\Phi(\mathbf{Y}) = \int_{-\infty}^{Y_1} \cdots \int_{-\infty}^{Y_n} \phi(\mathbf{y}, \mathbf{R}) dy_1 \ldots dy_n \qquad (8.9)$$

where $y_i = \frac{x_i - \mu_i}{\sigma_i}$, $Y_i = \frac{X_i - \mu_i}{\sigma_i}$ and

$$\phi(\mathbf{y}, \mathbf{R}) = \frac{1}{(2\pi)^{n/2} |\mathbf{R}|^{1/2}} \exp\left[-\frac{1}{2} \mathbf{y}^T \mathbf{R}^{-1} \mathbf{y} \right]$$

with $\mathbf{R}$ the correlation matrix of $\mathbf{x}$. Consider now the *Cholesky decomposition* $\mathbf{R} = \mathbf{Q}\mathbf{Q}^T$. Defining $\mathbf{z} = \mathbf{Q}^{-1}\mathbf{y}$, demonstrate that (8.9) can be written as:

$$\Phi(\mathbf{Y}) = \prod_i \int_{-\infty}^{(\mathbf{Q}^{-1}\mathbf{Y})_i} \frac{1}{\sqrt{2\pi}} e^{-z_i^2/2} dz_i$$

Based on this result, devise a method for generating a sample from the original correlated normal variates $\mathbf{x}$.

(2) Demonstrate that the matrix $\rho_{ij} = \lambda_i \lambda_j$ is positive semi-definite for all $-1 \leq \lambda_i \leq 1$[3]

(3) Demonstrate that for a two-factor bivariate normal distribution contours of equal probability density are described by an ellipse, and derive an expression for this contour at density height φ.

(4) Demonstrate, *by direct integration*, that the factor copula:

$$C(u_1, \ldots, u_n) = \int_{-\infty}^{\infty} \prod_{i=1,n} \Phi\left(\frac{-\lambda_i V + \Phi^{-1}(u_1)}{\sqrt{1 - \lambda_i^2}} \right) \phi(V) dV$$

---

[3] A square $n \times n$ matrix M is said to be positive definite if $\Re(z^* M z) > 0$ for all non-zero n length complex vectors z, z^* denoting the conjugate transpose, and $\Re$ denoting the real part. For real matrices of the type considered here, this can be simply written $z^T M z > 0$ for all non-zero vectors with real entries. A matrix is said to be positive *semi*-definite, if the strict positivity of $z^T M z$ is relaxed, i.e. we require $z^T M z \geq 0$. Unlike the positive definite case, this allows for the determinant of M to be zero (e.g. perfect correlation).

is itself equivalent to an n-dimensional Gaussian copula with correlation matrix $\rho_{ij} = \lambda_i \lambda_j$. Show further that the corresponding correlation matrix for the factor copula:

$$\Sigma = \begin{pmatrix} 1 & \lambda_1 & \lambda_2 & \ldots & \lambda_n \\ \lambda_1 & 1 & \lambda_1\lambda_2 & \ldots & \lambda_1\lambda_n \\ \vdots & \vdots & \vdots & \vdots & \vdots \\ \lambda_n & \lambda_n\lambda_1 & \lambda_n\lambda_2 & \ldots & 1 \end{pmatrix}$$

is positive semi-definite $\forall \, |\lambda_i| \leq 1$.

(5) For the simple factor loading function given by (8.1), demonstrate that, where the initial factor loading is positive, the process for λ_i is given by:

$$\frac{d\lambda_i}{2\lambda_i(1-\lambda_i)} = \left[\mu + 2\sigma^2\left(\frac{1}{2} - \lambda_i\right)\right] dt - \sigma dV_t$$

(6) Demonstrate that the weighted sum of correlated normal variables $y = \sum_i \alpha_i x_i$ where $x_i \sim \mathcal{N}(\mu_i, \sigma_i^2)$ is itself normal with mean $\mu_y = \sum_i \alpha_i \mu_i$ and variance $\sigma_y^2 = \sum_{i,j} \rho_{i,j} \alpha_i \alpha_j \sigma_i \sigma_j$ (Hint: use Cholesky decomposition together with the characteristic function for a normal variate.)

(7) Using a change of numeraire (see Chapter 7), demonstrate that, in the case where S_1 and S_2 follow geometric Brownian motions with constant volatility, and zero dividends, the undiscounted risk-neutral expectation of the outperformance $P = \max(S_1, S_2)$ is given by:

$$V_{outperf} = F_1 N(d_1) - F_2 N(d_2)$$
$$d_{1,2} = \frac{\log(F_1/F_2)}{\sigma\sqrt{T}} \pm \frac{\sigma\sqrt{T}}{2}$$
$$\sigma^2 = \sigma_1^2 + \sigma_2^2 - 2\rho\sigma_1\sigma_2$$

(8) For the log-squared contract used for covariance swap replication in Section 8.5.1, use replication through calls and puts to demonstrate that a negatively sloped implied correlation smile, linear in $\log(K/\overline{F}_B(T))$ and calibrated to the vol at strike $K = \overline{F}_B(T)$ will always be more expensive than the flat correlation equivalent, to first order.

Chapter 9

Control

Throughout this book, we have seen that attempts at modelling the 'real world' more realistically, no matter how well they might preserve the price of those instruments whose values we *can* see, exacerbate, rather than alleviate our concerns on pricing when it comes to the arena of exotic derivatives. Indeed, we have seen that the estimation of those real-world parameters, such as correlation of correlation and volatility of volatility, is in itself a major challenge. What we may infer from historical data suffers from sample size and ill-posedness (to name but two problems), whilst inference from market data suffers from the very lack of two way price discovery in the exotics market that led to the model risk analysis in the first place. Rarely, if ever, is the historical picture consistent with the market one. Our approach then has not been to suggest 'solutions' to the problem of model risk, it has been simply to try to understand it, and suggest modelling approaches to facilitate that understanding. If one message has come through loud and clear from this work, it is surely this: you've never understood a product's model risk until you've modelled it. We might have thought, for example, that barriers would be exquisitely sensitive to dividend modelling assumptions. Yes, before calibration to European options, but no afterwards. Conversely, we might have taken comfort from the replication strategy on variance swaps that the latter would not be exposed to model risk. Yes, assuming deterministic rates and diffusion, no assuming stochastic rates and jumps. We might have hoped, as a trader managing a large short book of correlation sensitive products, that buying back some of that sensitivity with a simple product like a correlation swap would improve matters. Yes, if correlation is static, categorically not if it's anticorrelated with market moves. So where do we go from here? Given the highly complex and difficult to measure nature of model risk on exotic equity derivatives, what, if anything, can be done to deal with the problem? The truth is, at least as far as this author is concerned, that there is no 'magic bullet' here. We can, however, consider various approaches.

9.1   Elimination

I went to the doctor the other day. I said, 'it hurts when I do that'. He said, 'well don't do that'[1].

The obvious way to eliminate model risk in exotics is just to stop trading exotics. But let's conduct a thought experiment here. Imagine, for the sake of argument, that you're an investment manager charging a fee for managing a client's portfolio. One thing you'd clearly like to guard against is the fall in the value of that portfolio. If you were unsophisticated, you might try to buy put options on each of the stocks in the portfolio, in proportion to their portfolio weight. This would certainly do the job, but would be brutally expensive, particularly considering that in all probability you'd be looking at longer dated options in line with the client's investment horizon. So say you're a bit more savvy and had heard of the benefits of diversification (or maybe even Jensen's inequality, you never know). You'd know that you could buy the protection on the portfolio level much more cheaply than on the individual components. So now you ring up your preferred investment bank and ask for an out of the money *basket* put, with the basket mirroring your portfolio. Supposing, however, that you looked at the growth of the portfolio over the last five years, read the various analysts' views on the stocks in your portfolio and various macroeconomic factors, and took *the view* that the probability of a major fall on any *given* stock was negligible. A yet cheaper option for you, still consistent with your desire to protect your client's interests, would be to buy a knock-in option on the *worst* performer in your basket. Now we're holding an autocallable worst-of structure, with exposure to correlation of correlation, stochastic volatility, jumps and credit events, to name but four. So, through the tailoring of a product to satisfy our desire for cost efficient risk reduction we've taken on, potentially, a substantial exposure to model assumptions. Moreover, as the product has been tailored for us only, there are no real market comparables to benchmark against. But now supposing that we couldn't do any of that, and had to make do with hedging exposure on each of the underlyings through the exchange traded single stock options

---

[1]Tommy Cooper. We should listen to comedians more than we do.

market. The hedging costs we'd have to pass on to our client would be unmanageable. In fact, we probably wouldn't be able to run the business at all, forcing us to run portfolios unhedged. In eliminating model risk, we've ended up increasing market risk. Elimination, whilst employed at times of crisis (e.g. the wholescale unwinding of synthetic credit positions in the wake of the 2008 crash), is not a long term option. A more realistic, and indeed prudent approach, is simply to limit the notional that can be traded on the more model risky of exotics [Allen (2003)]. In times of bullish markets, however, such esoterically set limits may be harder to enforce.

9.2 Reserving

When we've gone through a model risk analysis and come up with an estimate of how much exposure the value of an exotic trading position has to untransparent model parameters, we can simply reserve some of the initial P&L of those trades in an internal account, releasing it to the trading desk at expiry, or on an amortised schedule over the life of the trade. Should no model risk event (such as a market write down of the trade in response to a change of modelling, or re-estimation of model parameters), occur, the desk stands to make a windfall gain. Should such an event occur, the reserve account can act as a cushion for the resulting margin call [Allen (2003)]. This does at least allow the trade to proceed but suffers from a number of significant drawbacks:

- The amount of the reserve will tend to be estimated conservatively, i.e. maximally given the perceived 'worst case' price for the trade given the estimated range of the relevant model parameters. For the more model risky trades, the reserve estimated in this way may make the trade unattractive from the point of view of the seller. This is clearly desirable if the trade *genuinely* incurs that much model risk, but the very nature of model risk makes that estimation hard to perform.
- As we have seen in discussion of cliquet and correlation positions, the trading desk will tend to be a net seller of the product incurring the model reserve. A reserve applied across *all* such products can be highly damaging to the overall P&L of the desk in question. The practical tendency then is for only the largest trades to be reserved in this way, reducing the effectiveness of the process.

- Most firms simply don't have the infrastructure to compute model risk across all exotics. 'Rules of thumb' based on the greeks of the trade (such as the vol gamma reserve on cliquets, or the reserve for correlation skew on multi-asset exotics as a multiple of the correlation risk) are frequently applied in preference. It is unclear in these cases how meaningful the reserve actually is. The fact, for example, that the vol gamma on one trade may exactly offset the vol gamma on another, in no way implies that the model risk with respect to volatility of volatility is zero. The only way to have a proper view on the latter is, of course, to build a model.

As with many accounting approaches, model reserve accounting is a noble theoretical device on paper, but hard to implement effectively in practice. This does not mean, however, that the approach should be abandoned. On the whole, the better the system and structure for estimating model risk, the more effective the approach is. By better we mean:

- That there should exist a model validation group in the firm, responsible for designing models to address the pricing of the exotics portfolios *independently* of the front office quant groups;
- That there should be a consistent, and efficiently updated source of market data, with historical storage of a duration sufficient for robust statistical estimation of the model parameters used in the model risk analysis;
- That there should be a common pricing platform shared by all product groups, reducing the possibility of inaccurate market data used by one business as a result of poor communication from another (e.g. inadequate yield curve construction by the equities business due to the lack of availability of rate instrument marks from the rates business);
- That the pricing platform can easily be switched from one model to another, across entire portfolios, allowing a detailed breakdown of the model risk contribution down to the per-trade level to be made;
- That there should be a substantial computing resource behind the pricing platform allowing for timely model risk calculation across numerous portfolios, ideally covering the entire set of exotic trades.

The investment for such as a system is of course enormous, and frequently the victim of a catch-22 mentality. After all, how do we know we should invest in a system which can compute model risk efficiently unless we know how much the model risk is likely to be? This, as with many problems in finance, is down to management, and at the time of writing, all but a handful of investment banks have actually implemented such a system.

9.3   Model-free approaches

If the problem of model risk is coming from a model, why not have an approach which doesn't rely on one? Is that actually possible? *In principle*, yes, but as with many beautiful ideas, it tends to fall down in practice. The essential idea is that the price of an exotic is driven *entirely* by market observables. This is readily illustrated by reference to Philipp Schönbucher's work on *equity market models* [Schönbucher (1998)][2].

9.3.1   *Calibration to observable dynamics*

For most of this book, our approach has been to postulate extensions to the Dupire framework, apply these enhanced models to a set of exotic trade types, and evaluate the effect of the unobservable extension parameters. At the end of the analysis, we've taken a step back and looked at the implied *dynamics* of market observables such as implied European option volatilities (see Chapters 4 and 6). In the case of stochastic local volatility, it was shown that the relaxation of the deterministic volatility condition of the original Dupire model did not in fact assist in matching actual market implied volatility dynamics, whilst the extension to jump-diffusion did seem more promising in that regard. At least, in both cases, European option prices were matched exactly through local volatility inference, but it would be great if we could match not only prices of vanilla instruments, but their dynamics also. To make a grandiose historical comparison, it was not the existence of the Earth that led to Galileo's reconstruction of the solar system: it was how it *moved*. Whilst a maturation of the exotics market will undoubtedly contribute to model risk reduction, it is tempting to think that a deeper dive into *all* the information encapsulated in the vanilla market might help likewise. Philipp Schönbucher had the foresight to develop this idea as far back as 1998. Though his results were based on the dynamics of a *single* European option strike, the principle is nonetheless quite tantalising. The idea is as follows. Let's suppose that we want to construct a model based entirely on the dynamics of market observables,

---

[2]A similar approach can also be seen in Derman [Derman and Kani (1998)]

and let us assume further that they are the implied volatilities $\hat{\sigma}(t, T, K)$ for options of expiry T and strike K, measured at time t and the spot S_t. We will postulate that all variables evolve diffusively:

$$\frac{dS_t}{S_t} = \mu_t dt + \sigma_t dW_t^S \tag{9.1}$$

$$d\hat{\sigma}(t, T, K) = u(t, T, K)dt + \gamma(t, T, K)dW_t^S + \sum_{i=1}^{N} \nu_n(t, T, K)dW_t^n$$

The aim of the exercise will be to derive the *unobservable* local volatility $\sigma_t = \sigma(S, t, \{\hat{\sigma}(T, K)\})$ based on no arbitrage constraints on the *observable* implied volatility, together with its measured dynamics γ and ν_n, corresponding to the correlation with the spot process, and the volatilities of the principal components of the idiosyncratic evolution, respectively. Schönbucher now considers the simple case when we have only one implied volatility to worry about, and considers, further, constant γ and $\nu = \sqrt{\sum_{i=1}^{n} \nu_n^2}$. We have for the evolution of the call price C_t:

$$dC_t = C_t dt + C_S dS_t + C_{\hat{\sigma}} u_t dt + \frac{1}{2}\sigma^2 S^2 C_{SS} dt + \sigma\gamma S C_{S\hat{\sigma}} dt + \frac{1}{2}\nu^2 C_{\hat{\sigma}\hat{\sigma}} dt$$

where we have used the subscript notation for derivatives. For the undiscounted call to be a martingale under the risk-neutral measure we must have $E_{\mathbb{Q}}[dC_t] = rCdt$. Taking the case of zero dividends on the stock for simplicity, this gives an HJM like condition (Chapter 7) for the drift of the implied volatility:

$$u = \frac{1}{2C_{\hat{\sigma}}} \left(\left(\hat{\sigma}^2 - \sigma^2\right) S^2 C_{SS} - C_{\hat{\sigma}\hat{\sigma}}\nu^2 - 2\gamma\sigma S C_{S\hat{\sigma}} \right)$$

Using the expressions for the corresponding derivatives of a call option $C = SN(d_1) - Ke^{-rT}N(d_2)$ (assuming also flat short rate term structure for illustration), this gives:

$$u\hat{\sigma} = \frac{1}{2\tau}(\hat{\sigma}^2 - \sigma^2) - \frac{1}{2}d_1 d_2 \nu^2 + \frac{d_2\sigma\gamma}{\sqrt{\tau}}$$

where:

$$d_1 = \frac{\log(S/K)}{\hat{\sigma}\sqrt{\tau}} + \frac{\hat{\sigma}\sqrt{\tau}}{2}$$

$$d_2 = d_1 - \hat{\sigma}\sqrt{\tau}$$

$$\tau = T - t$$

Notice that this drift trivially explodes as $\tau \to 0$, at which point the solution for the stochastic differential equation for implied volatility ceases to exist, invalidating the option price. To prevent this 'implied volatility bubble' [Schönbucher (1998)], we impose that the drift be finite as $\tau \to 0$, which can be ensured be fixing that:

$$\hat{\sigma}(T,T)^2 \sigma^2 - 2\gamma f \hat{\sigma}(T,T)\sigma - \hat{\sigma}(T,T)^4 + f^2 \nu^2 = 0$$

where $f = \log(F/K)$ and $F = Se^{r\tau}$. Like this, we end up with a functional relationship between the implied volatility, in the limit of zero time to expiry, and the local volatility:

$$\sigma(f,\hat{\sigma}) = \frac{\gamma f}{\hat{\sigma}} + \sqrt{\hat{\sigma}^2 - \frac{f^2}{\hat{\sigma}^2}(\nu^2 - \gamma^2)} \qquad (9.2)$$

(where we have dropped the arguments of $\hat{\sigma}$ for simplicity). It is intriguing to note that, for constant local volatility and zero equity-implied volatility correlation γ, we have the zero time to expiry limit of implied volatility given by:

$$\hat{\sigma}^2 = \frac{1}{2}\sigma^2 + \sqrt{\frac{\sigma^4}{4} + f^2 \nu^2}$$

in accordance with our work in Chapter 4 where we demonstrated how a volatility smile was a natural consequence of the volatility of implied volatility. Schönbucher then goes on to generalise this result to the case where we have a continuum of implied volatilities, but again, for a single strike, such that, in direct analogy with the short rate models of Chapter 7, we define the short implied volatility:

$$\hat{\sigma}(t) = \lim_{t \to T} \hat{\sigma}_f(t,T)$$

$$\hat{\sigma}_f(t,T) = \frac{\partial}{\partial T}\left[\hat{\sigma}^2(t,T)(T-t)\right]$$

we then have for the local volatility, as per (9.2):

$$\sigma(f,t) = \frac{\gamma f(t)}{\hat{\sigma}(t)} + \sqrt{\hat{\sigma}(t)^2 - \frac{f(t)^2}{\hat{\sigma}(t)^2}(\nu(t)^2 - \gamma(t)^2)}$$

and $f(t) = \lim_{t \to T} f(t,T)$, $\gamma(t) = \lim_{t \to T} \gamma(t,T)$ and $\nu(t) = \lim_{t \to T} \nu(t,T)$, with:

$$f(t,T) = \log[F(t,T)/K]$$

$$\gamma(t,T) = \frac{1}{2(T-t)\widehat{\sigma}(t,T)} \int_t^T \gamma_f(t,s)ds$$

$$\nu(t,T) = \frac{1}{2(T-t)\widehat{\sigma}(t,T)} \int_t^T \nu_f(t,s)ds$$

and the dynamics of the forward implied variance given, analogously again to the HJM instantaneous forward rate, by:

$$d\widehat{\sigma}_f^2(t,T) = u_f(t,T)dt + \nu_f(t,T)dW + \gamma_f(t,T)dW_t^S$$

This would then appear to be a powerful approach to model risk mitigation. If we have a set of implied volatilities today, then, along with knowledge of today's spot, we can in principle derive the unobservable dynamics of the spot process consistently with the measurable dynamics of our observables. Rather than construct a model on an *ad hoc* basis, and invoke model risk as a result, we can price exotics consistently with the dynamics of the options we use for hedging. In the sense that our price is then based entirely on observable quantities, such an approach is sometimes referred to as 'model-free pricing'. Sadly, there are of course complications with this approach:

- The above analysis is applicable to a single option strike, and might be appropriate if, say, we could only hedge vega with ATM calls. The extension to multiple option strikes will clearly complicate the local vol derivation and simulation considerably. A possible approach through surface parameterisation is given by Alexander *et al.* [Alexander and Nogeira (2004)].

- The analysis requires us to have a reasonable knowledge of the dynamics of the short implied volatility. This is of course just as unobservable as local volatility, though, as derived by Schönbucher, this analysis can easily be adapted to finite maturity options, albeit with an arbitrary drift specification for the implied volatility. This choice of drift, however, is essentially as much a model choice as the choice of mean reversion speed in a stochastic volatility process, neither relating simply to observable real-world drifts.

- The analysis assumes diffusion on the market observables, which as we saw in Chapter 6 is unlikely to be valid for spot at least. Indeed, recent data on out of the money options on variance suggests that the assumption is invalid for implied volatilities also. The diffusive assumption on implied vols is really as much a model choice as the diffusive assumption on local vols.

For all the above reservations, the approach is still an interesting one. Whilst we may not in fact be able to rid ourselves of model choice completely, the calibration to both the level and dynamics of market observables may well be a strong constraint on model risk for the future.

9.3.2 *Static replication*

Another conceptually appealing attempt at model-free pricing is *static replication*. We have already seen an example of this in the variance swap replication of Chapter 4, but in this section we will use the somewhat more general framework developed by Derman et al. in 1994 [Derman et al. (1994)]. The idea is to find a representation of a contingent claim's value $P(S, T - t)$ at any instant of time $0 \leq t \leq T$ and stock level S through a static position in options whose maturities span the interval $[t, T]$. On the simplifying assumption that only one strike per maturity is required, we could write this as:

$$P(S, T - t) = \int_t^T \alpha(u)C(S, K(u), u - t)du \qquad (9.3)$$

Derman assumes further that, for some barrier option defined by the barrier function $B(t)$, we can take $K(t) = B(t)$. Special casing the payoff at expiry, he rewrites (9.3) as:

$$P(S, T - t) = \int_t^T \alpha(u)C(S, B(u), u - t)du + \alpha(T)C(S, B(T), T - t)$$

We now consider the payoff of the claim on the actual barrier, denoted $\xi(t)$. Then:

$$\xi(t) = P(B(t), T - t)$$
$$= \int_t^T \alpha(u)C(B(t), B(u), u - t)du + \alpha(T)C(B(t), B(T), T - t) \quad (9.4)$$

Splitting the integral into discrete time sections $t_0 = 0, \ldots, t_N = T$, it can be shown that (9.4) leads to the recurrence relation for the weights $\alpha_i = \alpha(t_i)$:

$$\alpha_i = \frac{\xi_{i-1} - \alpha_{i+1}C(B_i, B_{i+1}, t_{i+1} - t_i) - \ldots - \alpha_N C_N(B_{i-1}, B_N, t_N - t_{i-1})}{C(B_{i-1}, B_i, t_i - t_{i-1})}$$

where C_N denotes the terminal payoff. So, supposing that we had an autocallable structure, paying a fixed rebate conditional on knock-in at a discrete set of times, then in principle we could model this purely with European forward starting options, according to a fixed set of replication weights. Alas, the market for forward starting options is limited, making this approach highly idealistic. Note also that the moment the implied forward volatility on the relevant options changes, the 'static' hedge will have to be rebalanced. This is likely to be quite costly where a large number of barrier fixings are involved. The example does, however, serve to illustrate an important principle, which we have come to time and again throughout this book:

The best way to reduce model risk on exotic derivatives is to have an active market in exotics

---

And that, if nothing else, should be the central message. The exotics market isn't going to disappear, and indeed if the market is to be efficiently hedged, it shouldn't. It *is* the case that, the more sophisticated this market becomes (as it inevitably will by its very nature), the greater will be the significance of those model parameters, which we cannot infer directly from traded instrument.

However, the deeper, and more actively traded the exotics market becomes, the less significant those parameters will be... until the next product comes along!

9.4   Conclusions

It's been a long journey from portfolio based valuation. Our hope is that this book will at least have served to illustrate some of the major model developments in equity derivatives over the last four decades, and have provided a framework for understanding the significance of what we can't measure, as well as what we can, in the valuation of exotic equity derivatives. Note, however, that it is only the framework that has been provided. If you want to understand the model risk embedded in your trading position fully, you're going to have to apply this sort of analysis to every exotic trade that you have. As we have seen, the analysis is complex, and the results frequently surprising. If this remarkable field of finance is to continue to grow robustly in the years ahead, such analysis is indispensable. Of all the things to trust the least when it comes to understanding derivatives, it is surely one's own understanding. Hopefully this book has gone some way to helping us understand a little better.

Appendix A

Solutions to Exercises

A.1 Chapter 1

(1) In the absence of dividends, the forward contract can be replicated by shorting one share, at price S_0, and using the proceeds to buy n zero coupon bonds (bonds which pay unity at maturity and nothing in between). At expiry, the payoff from the bonds should exactly match the cost of unwinding the short position at the agreed forward price F, so that in the absence of borrow costs:

$$n = F \qquad \text{(A.1)}$$

As the net payoff at expiry is zero, the net cost of entering the replicating position must likewise be zero, for the contract to be fair. Denoting the price, at time T_0 of a zero coupon bond which pays unity at T as $P(T_0, T)$, we must then have $nP(T_0, T) = S_0$. Hence, from (A.1), we have for the fair forward price:

$$F = S_0 / P(T_0, T)$$

The price of the zero coupon bond can be deduced by considering a transaction where we short one bond, and invest the proceeds in a money market account $B(t)$ which accrues interest at the risk-free rate $r(t)$. By definition of the account, $dB(t) = B(t)r(t)dt$, so that:

$$B(T) = B(T_0) \exp\left[\int_{T_0}^{T} r(t)dt\right]$$

In the absence of money market based arbitrage, the money market account should be equal to unity at expiry. By virtue of the transaction being costless, we must have $P(T_0, T) = B(T_0)$, hence, as $B(T) = 1$:

$$P(T_0, T) = \exp\left[-\int_{T_0}^{T} r(t)dt\right]$$

In the case where the stock pays a proportional dividend $\tilde{q}(T_i)S(T_i^-)$ at date T_i, we have:

$$S(T_i^+) = S(T_i^-)(1 - \tilde{q}(T_i))$$

where T_i^- denotes the time just before the dividend payment, and T_i^+ the time just after. This condition on the stock price follows trivially from a no arbitrage consideration for the stock holder. Were the stock immediately following the dividend to be above this level, someone who bought the stock just before the ex-date could sell the stock immediately afterwards at a risk-free profit. Likewise, a short seller could lock in a risk-free profit if the converse were true. The risk-neutral strategy is then to invest the dividend at the new stock level, giving for the new stock holding:

$$n(T_i^+) = n(T_i^-)\frac{\tilde{q}(T_i)S(T_i^-)}{S(T_i^-)(1 - \tilde{q}(T_i))} + n(T_i^-) = \frac{n(T_i^-)}{1 - \tilde{q}(T_i)}$$

Let us now define a dividend yield $q(T_i)$ over the interval $(T_i, T_{i+1}]$ given by:

$$q(T_i) = \frac{\tilde{q}(T_{i+1})}{T_{i+1} - T_i}$$

Then:

$$n(T_i^+) = \frac{n(T_{i-1}^+)}{1 - q(T_{i-1})(T_i - T_{i-1})}$$

For a *continuous* dividend yield $dt = T_i - T_{i-1} \to 0$, so that denoting $T_i^+ = t + dt$ and $T_{i-1}^+ = t$:

$$n(t + dt) = \frac{n(t)}{1 - q(t)dt} = n(t)(1 + q(t)dt)$$

in the limit $dt \to 0$. Hence:

$$\frac{dn}{dt} = n(t)q(t)dt$$

Integrating up, we have:

$$n(t) = n(T_0) \exp\left[\int_{T_0}^{t} q(s)ds\right]$$

Now, at the end of a forward contract, we are obliged to buy one share at the agreed forward price. We thus have $n(T) = 1$, giving for the initial share position:

$$n(T_0) = \exp\left[-\int_{T_0}^{T} q(s)ds\right]$$

The value of our initial short stock position is $n(T_0)S_0$, so that, investing *these* proceeds in zero coupon bonds we have $F = n(T_0)S_0/P(T_0, T)$ giving finally:

$$F = S_0 \exp\left[\int_{T_0}^{T} (r(t) - q(t))dt\right]$$

as required. $\qquad\qquad\qquad\qquad\qquad\qquad\qquad\qquad\qquad\qquad\square$

(2) Transforming $x = \log S$, we have:

$$\frac{\partial V}{\partial S} = \frac{1}{S}\frac{\partial V}{\partial x}$$
$$\frac{\partial^2 V}{\partial S^2} = \frac{1}{S^2}\left[\frac{\partial^2 V}{\partial x^2} - \frac{\partial V}{\partial x}\right]$$

Which, substituting into the Black–Scholes equation, gives:

$$\frac{\partial V}{\partial t} + \left[r - \frac{1}{2}\sigma^2 S^2\right]\frac{\partial V}{\partial x} + \frac{1}{2}\sigma^2 \frac{\partial^2 V}{\partial x^2} - rV = 0$$

Transforming further $\tau = \frac{1}{2}\sigma^2(T - t)$, we have:

$$\frac{\partial V}{\partial t} = -\frac{1}{2}\sigma^2 \frac{\partial V}{\partial \tau}$$

giving

$$\frac{\partial V}{\partial \tau} - \left[\frac{2r}{\sigma^2} - 1\right]\frac{\partial V}{\partial x} - \frac{\partial^2 V}{\partial x^2} + \frac{2r}{\sigma^2}V = 0$$

Let us now transform $V(x, \tau)$ as:

$$V(x, \tau) = u(x, \tau)e^{-\alpha x - \beta \tau}$$

Then we have:

$$\frac{\partial V}{\partial x} = e^{-\alpha x - \beta \tau}\left[-\alpha u + \frac{\partial u}{\partial x}\right]$$

$$\frac{\partial^2 V}{\partial x^2} = e^{-\alpha x - \beta \tau}\left[\alpha^2 u - 2\alpha\frac{\partial u}{\partial x} + \frac{\partial^2 u}{\partial x^2}\right]$$

$$\frac{\partial V}{\partial \tau} = e^{-\alpha x - \beta \tau}\left[-\beta u + \frac{\partial u}{\partial \tau}\right]$$

Substituting:

$$\frac{\partial u}{\partial \tau} + \frac{\partial u}{\partial x}\left[\left(1 - \frac{2r}{\sigma^2}\right) + 2\alpha\right] - \frac{\partial^2 u}{\partial x^2}$$

$$+ u\left[-\beta - \alpha\left(1 - \frac{2r}{\sigma^2}\right) - \alpha^2 + \frac{2r}{\sigma^2}\right] = 0$$

Thus, setting:

$$\left(1 - \frac{2r}{\sigma^2}\right) + 2\alpha = 0 \tag{A.2}$$

$$-\beta - \alpha\left(1 - \frac{2r}{\sigma^2}\right) - \alpha^2 + \frac{2r}{\sigma^2} = 0 \tag{A.3}$$

we arrive at the diffusion equation:

$$\frac{\partial u}{\partial \tau} = \frac{\partial^2 u}{\partial x^2}$$

From (A.2) we have $\alpha = a/2$ where:

$$a = \frac{2r}{\sigma^2} - 1$$

From (A.3) we have:

$$\beta = 1 + a + \frac{a^2}{4}$$

as required.   □

(3) Consider the Black–Scholes evolution of the zero cost portfolio $\Pi_t = C_t - \Delta_t S_t + B_t$, assuming that the stock S_t is non-dividend paying:

$$
\begin{aligned}
d\Pi_t &= \frac{\partial C}{\partial t} dt + \frac{\partial C}{\partial S} dS_t + \frac{1}{2} \frac{\partial^2 C}{\partial S^2} dS_t^2 \\
&\quad - \Delta_t dS_t - r(C_t - \Delta_t S_t) dt
\end{aligned}
\tag{A.4}
$$

We have from the Black–Scholes equation, for a call valued with implied volatility $\hat{\sigma}$:

$$
\frac{\partial C}{\partial t} + rS_t \frac{\partial C}{\partial S} + \frac{1}{2} \hat{\sigma}^2 S_t^2 \frac{\partial^2 C}{\partial S^2} - rC(t) = 0
\tag{A.5}
$$

Combining (A.4) and (A.5), we end up with:

$$
d\Pi_t = \frac{1}{2} \frac{\partial^2 C}{\partial S^2} S_t^2 \left[\frac{dS_t^2}{S_t^2} - \hat{\sigma}^2 dt \right]
$$

Thus, in the continuous limit, we have:

$$
E[d\Pi_t] = \frac{1}{2} \Gamma_t S_t^2 \left[\sigma^2 - \hat{\sigma}^2 \right] dt
$$

where

$$
\Gamma_t = \frac{\partial^2 C}{\partial S^2}
$$

Note that this result is independent of measure, as the expression depends only on the *second* moment of stock returns. □

(4) From the expression for the Fourier transform of the option price $\widetilde{V}(\xi, \tau)$, (1.18) and the inverse transform (1.19) we have for the spatial derivatives of $V(x, \tau)$:

$$
\frac{\partial V}{\partial x} = \frac{1}{2\pi} \int_{-\infty}^{\infty} (-i\xi) \widetilde{V}(\xi, \tau) e^{-i\xi x} d\xi
$$

$$
\frac{\partial^2 V}{\partial x^2} = \frac{1}{2\pi} \int_{-\infty}^{\infty} (-\xi^2) \widetilde{V}(\xi, \tau) e^{-i\xi x} d\xi
$$

We have for the time derivative:

$$
\frac{\partial V}{\partial \tau} = \frac{1}{2\pi} \int_{-\infty}^{\infty} \frac{\partial \widetilde{V}(\xi, \tau)}{\partial \tau} e^{-i\xi x} d\xi
$$

Substituting into the Black–Scholes–Merton equation (1.14), with the transformations $x_t = \log S_t$ and $\tau = T - t$, equating the integrand to zero, we have for the *ordinary* differential equation of $\widetilde{V}(\xi, \tau)$:

$$\frac{\partial \widetilde{V}}{\partial \tau} - \left[r(\tau) - q(\tau) - \frac{1}{2}\sigma^2(\tau) \right](-i\xi)\widetilde{V} + \frac{1}{2}\sigma^2(\tau)\xi^2\widetilde{V} + r(\tau)\widetilde{V} = 0$$

which we can integrate to give:

$$\widetilde{V}(\xi, T) = \widetilde{V}(\xi, 0)$$
$$\times \exp\left\{ -\int_0^T \left[i\xi\left(r(s) - q(s) - \frac{1}{2}\sigma^2(s) \right) \right. \right.$$
$$\left. \left. + \frac{1}{2}\sigma^2(s)\xi^2 + r(s) \right] ds \right\}$$

Substituting:

$$\bar{r}(T) = \frac{1}{T}\int_0^T r(s)\,ds$$

$$\bar{q}(T) = \frac{1}{T}\int_0^T q(s)\,ds$$

$$\hat{\sigma}^2(T) = \frac{1}{T}\int_0^T \sigma^2(s)\,ds$$

we have:

$$\widetilde{V}(\xi, T) = \widetilde{V}(\xi, 0)$$
$$\times \exp\left\{ -T\left[i\xi\left(\bar{r}(T) - \bar{q}(T) - \frac{1}{2}\hat{\sigma}^2(T) \right) \right. \right.$$
$$\left. \left. + \frac{1}{2}\hat{\sigma}^2(T)\xi^2 + \bar{r}(T) \right] \right\} \tag{A.6}$$

For the standard Black–Scholes problem, we simply substitute $r = \bar{r}$, $q = \bar{r}$ and $\sigma = \hat{\sigma}$ in (A.6), for which the solution to the call payoff is known to be:

$$C(K,0) = e^{-rT} \left[F(T)N(d_1) - KN(d_2) \right]$$
$$F(T) = S_0 e^{(r-q)T}$$
$$d_1 = \frac{\log(F(T)/K)}{\sigma\sqrt{T}} + \frac{\sigma\sqrt{T}}{2}$$
$$d_2 = d_1 - \sigma\sqrt{T}$$

As the transform of the payoff $\widetilde{V}(\xi,0)$ is transparently independent of process, the solution to the Black–Scholes–Merton equation for the call is clearly of the same form but with the substitutions $r \to \bar{r}(T)$, $q \to \bar{q}(T)$ and $\sigma \to \hat{\sigma}(T)$. $\qquad\qquad\square$

(5) For fixed spot S_T, we have for the call payoff:

$$f(S_T, K) = \begin{cases} S_T - K; \ K < S_T \\ 0; \ K \geq S_T \end{cases}$$

So that:

$$\left. \frac{\partial f}{\partial K} \right|_{S_T} = \begin{cases} -1; \ K < S_T \\ 0; \ K \geq S_T \end{cases}$$

Now, consider the ramp function:

$$g(K) = \begin{cases} 0; \ K > K_+ \\ \frac{K-K_-}{K_+-K_-}; \ K^- \leq K \leq K_+ \\ 0; \ K < K_- \end{cases}$$

Then:

$$g'(K) = \begin{cases} 0; \ K > K_+ \\ \frac{1}{K_+-K_-}; \ K_- \leq K \leq K_+ \\ 0; \ K < K_- \end{cases}$$

So that $\lim_{K_+ - K_+^-} g'(K) = \infty$ and $\int_{\mathbb{R}} dK\, g'(K) = 1$, as per the Dirac delta function $\delta(K - K_+)$. Thus, as $\lim_{K_+ \to K_-^+ = S_T} g(K) = \partial f/\partial K$, we have:

$$\left. \frac{\partial^2 f}{\partial K^2} \right|_{S_T} = \delta(S_T - K)$$

We thus have, for the undiscounted call price $\widetilde{C}(K,T)$:

$$\frac{\partial^2 \widetilde{C}}{\partial K^2}\bigg|_T = \int_0^\infty \delta(S_T - K)\varphi(S_T, T)dS_T = \varphi(K, T)$$

from the property of the Dirac delta function:

$$\int_{\mathbb{R}} f(x')\delta(x - x')dx' = f(x)$$

□

A.2   Chapter 2

(1) Taylor expanding the increment in the undiscounted option price $\widetilde{V}_t$ to second order:

$$d\widetilde{V}_t = \frac{\partial \widetilde{V}}{\partial t}dt + \frac{\partial \widetilde{V}}{\partial x}dx_t + \frac{1}{2}\frac{\partial^2 \widetilde{V}}{\partial x^2}dx_t^2$$

Taking expectations in the risk-neutral measure, for which:

$$dx_t = \left[\mu(t) - \frac{\sigma^2(x, t)}{2}\right]dt + \sigma(x, t)dW_t$$

we have:

$$E_{\mathbb{Q}}[d\widetilde{V}_t] = \frac{\partial \widetilde{V}}{\partial t}dt + \frac{\partial \widetilde{V}}{\partial x}\left[\mu(t) - \frac{\sigma^2(x, t)}{2}\right]dt + \frac{1}{2}\frac{\partial^2 \widetilde{V}}{\partial x^2}\sigma^2(x, t)dt$$

using the property $E_{\mathbb{Q}}[dW_t] := 0$. But from (2.4):

$$\frac{\partial \widetilde{V}}{\partial t} + \left[\mu(t) - \frac{\sigma^2(x, t)}{2}\right]\frac{\partial \widetilde{V}}{\partial x} + \frac{1}{2}\sigma^2(x, t)\frac{\partial^2 \widetilde{V}}{\partial x^2} = 0$$

giving $E_{\mathbb{Q}}[d\widetilde{V}_t] = 0$. We thus have:

$$\widetilde{V}_t = E_{\mathbb{Q}}\left[\widetilde{V}_{t+\delta t}|\mathcal{F}_t\right]$$

We can write this in turn as:

$$\widetilde{V}_t = E_{\mathbb{Q}}\left[E_{\mathbb{Q}}\left[\widetilde{V}_{t+2\delta t}|\mathcal{F}_{t+\delta t}\right]|\mathcal{F}_t\right] = E_{\mathbb{Q}}\left[\widetilde{V}_{t+2\delta t}|\mathcal{F}_t\right]$$

by application of the *tower law*:

$$E\left[E\left[X|\mathcal{F}_j\right]|\mathcal{F}_i\right] = E\left[X|\mathcal{F}_i\right]; \ i \leq j$$

Hence for all times $T \geq t$ we have:

$$\tilde{V}_t = E_{\mathbb{Q}}\left[\tilde{V}_T|\mathcal{F}_t\right] = \int G(x,t;x',t')\tilde{V}(x',t')dx'$$

by definition of the Green's function $G(x,t;x',t')$. □

(2) Consider the situation where, for a given maturity T and strike pair (K_1, K_2) where $K_1 < K_2$, we have $C(K_1,T) < C(K_2,T)$. Suppose we short $1/(K_2 - K_1)$ calls with strike K_2 and use the proceeds to go long the same amount of calls at K_1. As $C(K_1,T) < C(K_2,T)$, this would leave us with a net positive cash balance. At expiry, however, the payoff of this portfolio would be:

$$\Pi(S_T) = \begin{cases} 0; \ S_T < K_1 \\ (S_T - K_1)/(K_2 - K_1); \ K_1 \leq S_T \leq K_2 \\ 1; \ S_T > K_2 \end{cases}$$

For any realisation S_T, $\Pi(S_T) \geq 0$. This strategy will thus leave us net positive cash, for a zero initial investment, constituting a model-free arbitrage. Likewise for puts, if we have $P(K_1,T) > P(K_2,T)$ for $K_1 < K_2$, we would short $1/(K_2-K_1)$ puts at K_1 and use the proceeds to buy the same amount of puts at K_2. Our payoff at expiry would be:

$$\Pi'(S_T) = \begin{cases} 1; \ S_T < K_1 \\ (K_2 - S_T)/(K_2 - K_1); \ K_1 \leq S_T \leq K_2 \\ 0; \ S_T > K_2 \end{cases}$$

which again is non-negative, yielding us a risk-free profit. As this is true for all $K_2 > K_1$, we can take the limit for the call spread no arbitrage condition:

$$\frac{C(K + \delta K, T) - C(K, T)}{\delta K P(0,T)} = -\int_{K+\delta K}^{\infty} \varphi(S_T, T)dS_T$$

$$+ \frac{1}{\delta K P(0,T)} \int_{K}^{K+\delta K}$$
$$(S_T - K)\varphi(S_T, T)dS_T \leq 0$$

In the limit $\delta K \to 0$, this gives:

$$\frac{\partial C}{\partial K} = -P(0,T) \int_K^\infty \varphi(S_T,T)dS_T \le 0$$

Denoting the cumulative distribution function (cdf):

$$\psi(K,T) = \int_0^K \varphi(S_T,T) = 1 - \int_K^\infty \varphi(S_T,T)dS_T$$

the call spread no arbitrage condition gives us the upper bound for the cdf $\psi(K,T) \le 1$. Likewise, the put spread no arbitrage condition gives:

$$\frac{\partial P}{\partial K} = P(0,T) \int_0^K \varphi(S_T,T)dS_T \ge 0$$

which together with the call spread condition gives $0 \le \psi(K,T) \le 1$, as expected for a well behaved probability distribution.

(3) Define the butterfly spread as long one call at strike K_1, short two calls at strike $\widehat{K} = (K_1 + K_2)/2$ and long one call at strike K_2, all calls with the same expiry T. We are given that the call price this maturity is a concave function of strike. For a concave function $f(x)$ we have, by definition:

$$f(x_1)\frac{x_2 - x_3}{x_2 - x_1} + f(x_2)\frac{x_3 - x_1}{x_2 - x_1} < f(x_3); \quad x_1 \le x_3 \le x_2$$

So, we know for $x_1 = K_1$, $x_2 = K_2$ and $x_3 = (K_1 + K_2)/2$:

$$2C(\widehat{K}) > C(K_1) + C(K_2)$$

so that the cost of our butterfly spread is negative. The payoff of this portfolio is:

$$\Pi(S_T) = \begin{cases} 0; \; S_T < K_1 \\ (S_T - K_1); \; K_1 \le S_T \le \widehat{K} \\ (K_2 - S_T); \; \widehat{K} \le S_T \le K_2 \\ 0; \; S_T > K_2 \end{cases}$$

which again is non-negative for all realised S_T. Thus the strategy of shorting two calls at $\widehat{K} = (K_1 + K_2)/2$, and using the proceeds to buy one call at K_1 and one at K_2 would result in a risk-free profit. In the limit of small δK, we can write the no arbitrage condition as:

$$(\delta K)^2 \frac{\partial^2 C}{\partial K^2} \geq 0$$

giving $\varphi(K, T) \geq 0$ from twice differentiation the call integral by strike. In other words, the butterfly spread arbitrage is equivalent to having a well behaved probability distribution $\varphi(S_T, T)$ at maturity T.

(4) The cost of a strategy where we short $1/[K_1 P(T_0, T_1)]$ calls of maturity T_1 and strike K_1, and use the proceeds to go long $1/[K_2 P(T_0, T_2)]$ calls of maturity T_2 and strike K_2 is given by;

$$V = -\frac{1}{K_1} \left[F_1 N(d_1^1) - K_1 N(d_2^1) \right] + \frac{1}{K_2} \left[F_2 N(d_1^2) - K_2 N(d_2^2) \right] \quad \text{(A.7)}$$

where:

$$d_{1,2}^1 = \frac{\log(F_1/K_1)}{\sigma_1 \sqrt{T_1}} \pm \frac{\sigma_1 \sqrt{T_1}}{2}$$

$$d_{1,2}^2 = \frac{\log(F_2/K_2)}{\sigma_2 \sqrt{T_2}} \pm \frac{\sigma_2 \sqrt{T_2}}{2}$$

We have further that the options are at the same moneyness. Hence $F_1/K_1 = F_2/K_2 = \alpha$ simplifying (A.7) to:

$$V(\alpha) = - \left[\alpha N(d_1^1) - N(d_2^1) \right] + \left[\alpha N(d_1^2) - N(d_2^2) \right]$$

At T_1, the first option is either worth zero or $S(T_1) - K_1$. In the former case, the second option clearly has value, so that by unwinding our position we lock in an overall profit. If $S(T_1) > K_1$, our second option is worth:

$$\frac{1}{K_2 P(T_0, T_2)} P(T_1, T_2) \left[S(T_1) \frac{F_2}{F_1} N(d_1'^2) - K_2 N(d_2'^2) \right]$$

$$= \frac{1}{K_1 P(T_0, T_1)} \left[S(T_1) N(d_1'^2) - K_1 N(d_2'^2) \right]$$

where

$$d_{1,2}'^1 = \frac{\log(S_1/K_1)}{\sigma_{1,2} \sqrt{T_2 - T_1}} \pm \frac{\sigma_{1,2} \sqrt{T_2 - T_1}}{2}$$

follows from $K_2 = \frac{F_2}{F_1} K_1$. Note that this derivation assumes deterministic interest rates (giving $P(T_1, T_2) = P(T_0, T_2)/P(T_0, T_1)$) and proportional dividends (giving $F_2(T_1) = S(T_1)F_2/F_1$). Now, consider the function:

$$\widetilde{C}(T) = S(T_1)N(d_1'^2(T)) - K_1 N(d_2'^2(T))$$

We have:

$$\frac{\partial \widetilde{C}}{\partial T} = S(T_1)n(d_1'^2(T))\frac{\sigma_{1,2}}{2\sqrt{T}} > 0 \; \forall \, T > 0$$

i.e. $\widetilde{C}(T)$ is a monotonically increasing function of maturity. Even if our first option ends up in the money, the cost of buying it back in the unwind will be overcompensated by the proceeds of selling the longer maturity option, again yielding a profit. As, per unit strike, the undiscounted value of the shorter maturity option is higher than the corresponding value of the longer maturity option with the same moneyness, we must also have for the initial proceeds $V > 0$. The strategy therefore yields a risk-free profit. □

As this applies for all $T_2 > T_1$, in the limit of small T we have:

$$\frac{\partial}{\partial T}\left[\alpha N(d_1) - N(d_2)\right] > 0$$

So that, given $\alpha n(d_1) = n(d_2)$ we have:

$$\frac{\partial}{\partial T}\left[\sigma(T,\alpha)\sqrt{T}\right] > 0$$

i.e. that the implied variance $s(T,\alpha) = \sigma^2(T,\alpha)T$ must be monotonically increasing along lines of constant moneyness α. □

(5) Applying Itō's lemma to the call payoff function $f(S_T) = (S_T - K, 0)^+$:

$$df_T = \mathbf{1}(S_T - K)dS_T + \frac{1}{2}\delta(S_T - K)dS_T^2$$
$$= \mathbf{1}(S_T - K)S_T\left[\mu(T)dT + \sigma(S_T, T)dW_T\right]$$
$$+ \frac{1}{2}\delta(S_T - K)S_T^2\sigma^2(S_T, T)dT$$

Integrating up, we obtain:

$$f_T = f_0 + \int_0^T \Big[\mathbf{1}(S_t - K)S_t\left[\mu(t)dt + \sigma(S_t, t)dW_t\right]$$
$$+ \frac{1}{2}\delta(S_t - K)S_t^2\sigma^2(S_t, t)dt\Big]$$

Taking expectations in the risk-neutral measure gives:

$$\widetilde{C}(K,T) = f_0 + \int_0^T \left[E_{\mathbb{Q}} \left[\mathbf{1}(S_t - K)S_t\mu(t) \right] \right.$$
$$\left. + \frac{1}{2} E_{\mathbb{Q}} \left[\delta(S_t - K)S_t^2\sigma^2(S_t,t) \right] \right] dt$$

where $\widetilde{C}(T)$ denotes the undiscounted value of a call with maturity T and strike K. Now, we have:

$$E_{\mathbb{Q}} \left[\mathbf{1}(S_t - K)S_t\mu(t)dt \right] = \mu(t) \left[\widetilde{C}(t) - K\frac{\partial \widetilde{C}}{\partial K} \right]$$
$$E_{\mathbb{Q}} \left[\delta(S_t - K)S_t^2\sigma^2(S_t,t) \right] = K^2\sigma^2(K,t)\varphi(K,t)$$

giving:

$$\widetilde{C}(K,T) = f_0 + \int_0^T \left[\mu(t) \left[\widetilde{C}(t) - K\frac{\partial \widetilde{C}}{\partial K} \right] + \frac{1}{2}K^2\sigma^2(K,t)\varphi(K,t) \right] dt$$
$$(A.8)$$

So, differentiating w.r.t T gives us:

$$\frac{\partial \widetilde{C}(K,T)}{\partial T} = \mu(T) \left[\widetilde{C}(T) - K\frac{\partial \widetilde{C}}{\partial K} \right] + \frac{1}{2}K^2\sigma^2(K,T)\varphi(K,T)$$

as obtained earlier. $\square$

(6) In the presence of a stochastic volatility driver α (A.8) is modified to:

$$\widetilde{C}(K,T) = f_0 + \int_0^T dt\mu(t) \left[\widetilde{C}(t) - K\frac{\partial \widetilde{C}}{\partial K} \right]$$
$$+ \int_0^T \frac{1}{2}K^2\sigma^2(K,\alpha,t)\varphi(K,\alpha,t)d\alpha dt$$

Again, differentiating w.r.t T gives us:

$$\frac{\partial \widetilde{C}(K,T)}{\partial T} = \mu(T) \left[\widetilde{C}(T) - K\frac{\partial \widetilde{C}}{\partial K} \right] + \frac{1}{2}K^2 E_{\mathbb{Q}}[\sigma^2|S_T = K]\varphi(K,T)$$

where

$$E_{\mathbb{Q}}[\sigma^2|S_T = K]\varphi(K,T) = \int \sigma^2(K,\alpha,t)\varphi(K,\alpha,t)d\alpha$$

Thus:

$$E_{\mathbb{Q}}[\sigma^2|S_T = K] = \frac{\frac{\partial \widetilde{C}(K,T)}{\partial T} - \mu(T)\left[\widetilde{C}(T) - K\frac{\partial \widetilde{C}}{\partial K}\right]}{\frac{1}{2}K^2\varphi(K,T)} = \sigma^2_{Dupire}(K,T)$$

as derived from Gyöngy's theorem.   □

A.3   Chapter 3

(1) Recall that the subtractive dividend model is specified by the transformation:

$$S_t = (X_t - D(t))Q(t)$$

where

$$D(t) = \sum_{T_0 < T_i \leq t} \tilde{d}_i e^{\bar{r}(T_i,t)(t-T_i)}$$

$$Q(t) = \prod_{T_0 < T_i \leq t} (1 - q_i)$$

$$\tilde{d}_i = \hat{d}_i/Q(T_i)$$

consistent with the dividend process $div_i = \hat{d}_i + q_i S(T_i^-)$. We can write for the undiscounted value of a call option:

$$E_{\mathbb{Q}}\left[(S_T - K, 0)^+\right] = E_{\mathbb{Q}}\left[((X_T - D(T))Q(T) - K, 0)^+\right]$$
$$= Q(T)\widetilde{C}(F_X(T), K_X(T), \sigma_X(K_X,T), T)$$

where

$$\widetilde{C}(F, K, \sigma, T) = FN(d_1) - KN(d_2)$$
$$d_{1,2} = \frac{\log(F/K)}{\sigma\sqrt{T}} \pm \frac{\sigma\sqrt{T}}{2}$$
$$F_X(T) = F_S(T)/Q(T) + D(T)$$
$$K_X(T) = K_S(T)/Q(T) + D(T)$$

Giving:

$$\widetilde{C}\left[F_S(T), K_S, \sigma_S(K_S, T), T\right] = Q(T)\widetilde{C}(F_X(T), K_X, \sigma_X(K_X, T), T) \tag{A.9}$$

or equivalently:

$$\widetilde{C}\left[F_S(T), Q(T)(K_X - D(T)), \sigma_S(Q(T)(K_X - D(T)), T), T\right]$$
$$= Q(T)\widetilde{C}\left[F_X(T), K_X, \sigma_X(K_X, T), T\right]$$

Clearly, for $K_X < D(T)$, no solution to this expression exists, as we are constrained to have $K_S > 0$, by definition of the Black–Scholes formula. $\quad\square$

(2) Assuming one dividend of magnitude D at T_1 and no proportional dividends, flat volatility σ of X_t, and flat rates we can Taylor expand (A.9) to first order to give, for $T > T_1$:

$$\widetilde{C}\left[F_S(T), K_S, \sigma_S(K_S, T), T\right]$$
$$\simeq \widetilde{C}(F_S(T), K_S, \sigma, T) + \frac{\partial \widetilde{C}}{\partial F}De^{r(T-T_1)} + \frac{\partial \widetilde{C}}{\partial K}De^{r(T-T_1)}$$
$$= \widetilde{C}(F_S(T), K_S, \sigma, T) + D\left[N(d_1) - N(d_2)\right]e^{r(T-T_1)}$$

To first order, we can approximate:

$$\widetilde{C}\left[F_S(T), K_S, \sigma_S(K_S, T), T\right]$$
$$\simeq \widetilde{C}\left[F_S(T), K_S, \sigma, T\right] + \left[\sigma_S(K_S, T) - \sigma\right]\frac{\partial \widetilde{C}}{\partial \sigma}$$

giving for the enhancement to implied volatility:

$$\sigma_S(K_S, T) - \sigma \simeq De^{r(T-T_1)}\frac{N(d_1) - N(d_2)}{\partial \widetilde{C}/\partial \sigma}$$

To first order, we can approximate:

$$N(d_1) - N(d_2) \simeq n(d_1)\sigma\sqrt{T}$$

so that, using $\partial \widetilde{C}/\partial \sigma = Fn(d_1)\sqrt{T}$ we have the simple expression:

$$\sigma_S(K_S, T) \simeq \sigma(1 + De^{r(T-T_1)}/F_S(T)) = \frac{\sigma}{1 - \tilde{q}} \tag{A.10}$$

where $\tilde{q} = D/F_S(T^-)$ is the *effective* dividend yield, and we have used, for $T > T_1$, $F_S(T) = F_S(T_1^+)e^{r(T-T_1)}$, with $F_S(T_1^-) = F_S(T_1^+) + D$. Note that this shift is independent of maturity T. $\quad\square$

(3) Using the same approximations of the previous question, and assuming flat rates for simplicity, the shift to the implied volatility of the additive dividend model, for all expiries $T < T_1$ is given by:

$$\sigma_S(K_S, T) \simeq \sigma(1 - De^{-r(T_1-T)}/F_S(T)) = \sigma(1 - \tilde{q})$$

as $F_S(T) = e^{-r(T_1-T)}F_S(T_1^-)$ for $T < T_1$. If we calibrate the surface at T_1, no correction to the implied vol on X_t is required, as $D(t)$ drops by the dividend amount on the dividend ex-date, becoming zero in this case. The implied vol for options expiring prior to T_1 will be reduced by the effective dividend yield, in this case. For the subtractive dividend model, we would have for the calibrated volatility in X_t, $\sigma_X(T_1) = (1 - \tilde{q})\sigma_S(T_1)$, from inversion of (A.10). Assuming linear in variance time interpolation, this would then be the implied volatility of all options expiring prior to T_1, *identically* to the shift in the additive dividend model.   □

(4) (This derivation follows Bos and Vandermark [Bos and Vandermark (2002)].) Consider the spot dividend model for a stock paying one dividend Δ, whose ex-date is τ:

$$\frac{\partial C}{\partial t} + (rS - \Delta\delta(t - \tau))\frac{\partial C}{\partial S} + \frac{1}{2}\sigma^2 S^2\frac{\partial^2 C}{\partial S^2} - rC = 0 \qquad \text{(A.11)}$$

Let us consider solutions to the price of a call expiring at $T > \tau$ of the form:

$$C(S, K) = C_0(S^*, K^*)$$

where C_0 is the Black–Scholes expression for a zero dividend paying stock, and:

$$S^* = S - f(t, T)\Delta\exp(-r(\tau - t)) \qquad \text{(A.12)}$$
$$K^* = K + (1 - f(t, T))\Delta\exp(r(T - \tau)) \qquad \text{(A.13)}$$

Substituting (A.12) and (A.13) into (A.11) gives, for $t < \tau$:

$$\frac{\partial C_0}{\partial t} + \frac{\partial C_0}{\partial S^*}\Delta e^{-r(\tau-t)}\left[-\frac{\partial f}{\partial t} - fr\right] - \frac{\partial C_0}{\partial K^*}e^{r(T-\tau)}\frac{\partial f}{\partial t}$$
$$+ r\left(S^* + f(t)\Delta e^{-r(\tau-t)}\right)\frac{\partial C_0}{\partial S^*} + \frac{1}{2}\sigma^2 S^2\frac{\partial^2 C_0}{\partial S^{*2}} - rC_0 = 0$$

$$\text{(A.14)}$$

But, we also have, by definition of C_0:

$$\frac{\partial C_0}{\partial t} + rS^* \frac{\partial C_0}{\partial S^*} + \frac{1}{2}\sigma^2 S^{*2} \frac{\partial^2 C_0}{\partial S^{*2}} - rC_0 = 0 \qquad \text{(A.15)}$$

Subtracting (A.15) from (A.14) and simplifying, gives:

$$\Delta \frac{\partial f}{\partial t} \left[\frac{\partial C_0}{\partial S^*} + \frac{\partial C_0}{\partial K^*} e^{r(T-t)} \right]$$
$$= \sigma^2 \frac{\partial^2 C_0}{\partial S^{*2}} \left[\Delta S f - \frac{1}{2} \Delta^2 e^{-r(\tau-t)} f^2 \right]$$

Again, using the approximation:

$$\frac{\partial C_0}{\partial S^*} + \frac{\partial C_0}{\partial K^*} e^{r(T-t)} \simeq (T-t)\sigma^2 S \frac{\partial^2 C_0}{\partial S^2}$$

and ignoring the Δ^2 term to lowest-order approximation, we end up with the simple ODE:

$$\frac{\partial f}{\partial t} = \frac{f}{T-t}$$

Given the boundary condition $f(\tau, T) = 1$ (such that the solution is continuous over the ex-date, as required by no arbitrage), we find:

$$f(t,T) = \frac{T-\tau}{T-t}$$

as required. $\qquad \Box$

A.4 Chapter 4

(1) Consider the geometric Brownian motion:

$$\frac{dX_t}{X_t} = \mu dt + \sigma dW$$

From Itō, we have for the evolution of $\log(X_t)$:

$$d\log(X_t) = \left(\mu - \frac{\sigma^2}{2} \right) dt + \sigma dW$$

which we can integrate to give:

$$X_T = X_0 \exp\left[\left(\mu - \frac{\sigma^2}{2}\right)T + \sigma W\right]$$

In general, we can write:

$$E\left[\exp\left(aT + bW\right)\right] = \exp\left[\left(a + \frac{b^2}{2}\right)T\right]$$

provided we are in a measure where $W \sim \mathcal{N}(0, T)$. This can be seen easily by completion of the square of:

$$\frac{1}{\sqrt{2\pi T}} \int_{-\infty}^{\infty} e^{bW} e^{-W^2/2T} dW$$

We can thus write:

$$E[X_T] = X_0 e^{\mu T} = \overline{X}_T$$

and

$$E[\sqrt{X_T}] = X_0 e^{\mu T/2} e^{-\sigma^2 T/8} = \overline{X}_T^{1/2} e^{-\sigma^2 T/8}$$

We have also:

$$E[\log X_T{}^2] - E[\log X_T]^2 = Var[X_T] = \sigma^2 T = \Xi_T^2$$

Hence we arrive at the convexity correction for the expectation of the square root of a log-normal variable:

$$E[\sqrt{X_T}] = \overline{X}_T^{1/2} \exp[-\Xi_T^2/8]$$

as required.   □

(2) Consider the OU process given by (4.12):

$$d\alpha_t = -\kappa\left[\alpha_t - \theta(t)\right]dt + \xi dW_t$$

It's helpful to consider the transformation $y_t = e^{\kappa t}\alpha_t$. Applying Itō, we get:

$$dy_t = e^{\kappa t} \left[\kappa \alpha_t dt + d\alpha_t \right]$$
$$= e^{\kappa t} \left[\kappa \theta(t) dt + \xi dW_t \right]$$

This is just a normal process, which we can integrate directly:

$$y_t = y_0 + \kappa \int_0^t e^{\kappa s} \theta(s) ds + \xi \int_0^t e^{\kappa s} dW_s$$

Transforming back to α_t, we have:

$$\alpha_t = \alpha_0 + \kappa \int_0^t e^{\kappa(s-t)} \theta(s) ds + \xi \int_0^t e^{\kappa(s-t)} dW_s \qquad (A.16)$$

using $\alpha_0 = y_0$, by construction. Now, we are given:

$$\theta(t) = -\frac{\xi^2}{2\kappa} \left(1 + e^{-2\kappa t} \right)$$

We thus have for the first integral:

$$\int_0^t e^{\kappa(s-t)} \theta(s) ds = -\frac{\xi^2}{2\kappa} e^{-\kappa t} \int_0^t e^{\kappa s} + e^{-\kappa s} ds$$

$$= -\frac{\xi^2}{2\kappa^2} e^{-\kappa t} \left[e^{\kappa t} - e^{-\kappa t} \right]$$

$$= -\frac{\xi^2}{2\kappa^2} \left[1 - e^{-2\kappa t} \right]$$

Combining with (A.16), and taking $\alpha_0 = 0$ we get finally:

$$\alpha_t = -\frac{\xi^2}{2\kappa} \left[1 - e^{-2\kappa t} \right] + \xi \int_0^t e^{\kappa(s-t)} dW_s \qquad (A.17)$$

as required. □

The serial covariance ρ_{ij} for an *exponential* OU process, $x_t = e^{\alpha_t}$ is given by:

$$\rho_{ij} = \langle (x_i - \bar{x}_i)(x_j - \bar{x}_j) \rangle$$
$$= E \left[e^{\alpha_i + \alpha_j} \right] - E \left[e^{\alpha_i} \right] E \left[e^{\alpha_j} \right] \qquad (A.18)$$

From (A.17) we have:

$$E\left[e^{\alpha_t}\right] = \exp\left[-\frac{\xi^2}{2\kappa}\left(1 - e^{-2\kappa t}\right)\right]\exp\left[\frac{\xi^2}{2\kappa}\int_0^t e^{2\kappa(s-t)}ds\right]$$

$$= \exp\left[-\frac{\xi^2}{2\kappa}\left(1 - e^{-2\kappa t}\right)\right]\exp\left[+\frac{\xi^2}{4\kappa}\left(1 - e^{-2\kappa t}\right)\right]$$

$$= \exp\left[-\frac{\xi^2}{4\kappa}\left(1 - e^{-2\kappa t}\right)\right]$$

where we have used the *Itō isometry*:

$$E\left[\exp\int_0^t a(s)dW_s\right] = E\left[\frac{1}{2}\exp\int_0^t a^2(s)ds\right]$$

which derives from the fact that $\int_0^t a(s)dW_s$ is itself distributed normally, with variance $\int_0^t a^2(s)ds$, by virtue of the independent increment condition on the Brownian motion $E[dW_s dW_t] = ds\delta_{st}$.

(Note that $E\left[e^{2\alpha_t}\right] = 1$, as stated in our original SLV formulation.) We have then for the second term in (A.18):

$$E\left[e^{\alpha_i}\right]E\left[e^{\alpha_j}\right] = \exp\left[-\frac{\xi^2}{4\kappa}\left(2 - e^{-2\kappa t_i} - e^{-2\kappa t_j}\right)\right] \qquad (A.19)$$

We can rewrite the first term in (A.18) as:

$$E\left[e^{\alpha_i + \alpha_j}\right] = \exp\left[-\frac{\xi^2}{2\kappa}\left(2 - e^{-2\kappa t_i} - e^{-2\kappa t_j}\right)\right]I$$

where

$$I = \exp\left[\xi\int_0^{t_i} e^{\kappa(s-t_i)}dW_s + \xi\int_0^{t_j} e^{\kappa(s'-t_j)}dW_s'\right]$$

Taking $t_i < t_j$, without loss of generality, we can rewrite this as:

$$I = \exp\left[\xi\int_0^{t_i}\left[e^{\kappa(s-t_i)} + e^{\kappa(s-t_j)}\right]dW_s\right]\exp\left[\xi\int_{t_i}^{t_j} e^{\kappa(s-t_j)}dW_s\right]$$

$$= J_1 J_2 \qquad (A.20)$$

again, using the independent increment property of Brownian motions. We now have:

$$J_1 = \exp\left[\frac{\xi^2}{2}\left[e^{-\kappa t_i} + e^{-\kappa t_j}\right]^2 \int_0^{t_i} e^{2\kappa s} ds\right]$$

$$= \exp\left[\frac{\xi^2}{4\kappa}\left[e^{-\kappa t_i} + e^{-\kappa t_j}\right]^2 \left(e^{2\kappa t_i} - 1\right)\right] \qquad (A.21)$$

and

$$J_2 = \exp\left[\frac{\xi^2}{2}\int_{t_i}^{t_j} e^{2\kappa(s-t_j)} ds\right]$$

$$= \exp\left[\frac{\xi^2}{4\kappa}\left[1 - e^{-2\kappa(t_j - t_i)}\right]\right] \qquad (A.22)$$

Combining (A.19) with (A.20), using (A.21) and (A.22) gives us finally for the serial covariance:

$$\langle(x_i - \bar{x}_i)(x_j - \bar{x}_j)\rangle = \exp\left[-2\beta\left(2 - e^{-2\kappa t_i} - e^{-2\kappa t_j}\right)\right]$$

$$\times \exp\left[\beta\left[1 + e^{-\kappa(t_j - t_i)}\right]^2 \left(1 - e^{-2\kappa t_i}\right)\right.$$

$$\left. + \beta(1 - e^{-2\kappa(t_j - t_i)})\right]$$

$$- \exp\left[-\beta\left(2 - e^{-2\kappa t_i} - e^{-2\kappa t_j}\right)\right]$$

with $\beta = \xi^2/4\kappa$. □

(3) Consider the Hull–White volatility process [Hull and White (1987)]:

$$\frac{dS_t}{S_t} = \mu dt + \sigma_t dW_t^S$$

$$\frac{dV_t}{V_t} = \lambda dt + \xi dW_t^V$$

$$V_t = \sigma_t^2$$

We can write for the undiscounted call value, in general:

$$\tilde{C}(K, T) = \int_0^\infty \int_0^\infty (S_T - K, 0)\varphi(S_T, \overline{V}_T) dS_T d\overline{V}_T$$

$$= \int_0^\infty \int_0^\infty (S_T - K, 0)\varphi(S_T | \overline{V}_T) dS_T \varphi(\overline{V}_T) d\overline{V}_T \quad (A.23)$$

For a *given* realisation $\overline{V}_T = \int_0^T V_t dt$, we can write for the terminal stock level:

$$S_T(V_T) = S_0 \exp\left[(\mu - \overline{V}_T/2)T + \int_0^T \sigma_t dW_t^S\right]$$

Let us now split $dW_t^S = \rho dW_t^V + \sqrt{1 - \rho^2} d\varepsilon_t$ where $\langle dW_t^V d\varepsilon_t \rangle = 0$ and $\langle d\varepsilon_t^2 \rangle = dt$. Conditional on some realised $\{dW_t^V\}$ and $\{d\varepsilon_t\}$, we can write the call payoff as:

$$\left[S_0 \exp\left[(\mu - \overline{V}_T/2)T + \int_0^T \sigma_t \rho dW_t^V + \sqrt{1 - \rho^2} I_T\right] - K, 0\right]^+$$

where $I_T = \int_0^T \sigma_t d\varepsilon_t$. Conditional on a realised $\overline{V}_T$, this gives us a call with effective volatility $\sqrt{(1 - \rho^2)\overline{V}_T/T}$ and forward $S_0 \exp\left[\mu T - \rho^2 \overline{V}_T/2 + \int_0^T \sigma_t \rho dW_t^V\right]$. We thus end up with the more general integral expression:

$$\widetilde{C}(K, T) = \int_{-\infty}^\infty \int_0^\infty \widetilde{C}\left[F(\hat{\sigma}_T, J_T, \rho), K, \sqrt{1 - \rho^2}\hat{\sigma}, T\right]$$
$$\times \Phi(\hat{\sigma}_T, J_T) d\hat{\sigma}_T dJ_T$$

where

$$\hat{\sigma}_T = \sqrt{\overline{V}_T/T}$$
$$J_T = \int_0^T \sigma_t dW_t^V$$
$$F(\hat{\sigma}_T, J_T, \rho) = F(T) \exp\left[-\rho^2 \hat{\sigma}^2 T/2 + \rho J_T\right]$$

and $\Phi(\hat{\sigma}_T, J_T)$ is the joint density of $\hat{\sigma}_T$ and J_T. This expression was originally formulated by Willard [Willard (1997)]. For the special case $\rho = 0$ considered in the original Hull–White paper, the dependence of the forward on realised variance and J_T disappears, reducing the expression to a simple expectation of Black–Scholes prices over the distribution of realised variance, as used in Chapter 4.

(4) The integral for the expectation of realised variance is given by the log contract expectation $V(T) = \frac{2}{T} I(T)$ where;

$$I(T) = \int_0^\infty \left[\log\left(\frac{F_T}{S_T}\right) + \left(\frac{S_T - F_T}{F_T}\right)\right] \varphi(S_T) dS_T \qquad (A.24)$$

We can write the first integrand as:

$$\log\left(\frac{F_T}{S_T}\right) = \int_{S_T}^{F_T} \frac{dK}{K}$$

and the second integrand as:

$$\frac{S_T - F_T}{F_T} = -\int_{S_T}^{F_T} S_T \frac{dK}{K^2}$$

allowing us to rewrite (A.24) as:

$$I(T) = \int_0^{\infty} \int_{S_T}^{F_T} \frac{dK}{K^2}(K - S_T)\varphi(S_T)dS_T$$

The integral is represented schematically in Figure A.1, with the direction of inner integration shown with single arrows, and outer integration with a block arrow.

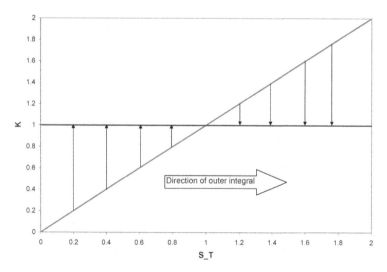

Fig. A.1 Domain of integration for var swap double integral, strike integral inner, spot integral outer, $F_T = 1$ for illustration.

Notice that the direction of integration changes for $S_T > F_T$ (shown as unity for illustration here). Switching the order of integration to spot inner and strike outer gives the schematic shown in Figure A.2.

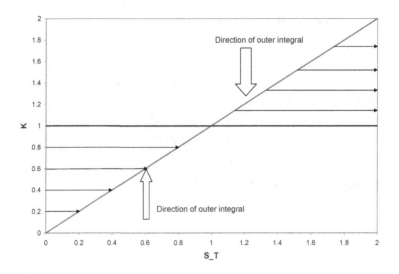

Fig. A.2   Domain of integration for var swap double integral, strike integral outer, spot integral inner.

As the direction of outer integration changes for $K > F_T$, this schematic can be written as:

$$
\begin{aligned}
I(T) &= \int_0^{F_T} \int_0^K \frac{K - S_T}{K^2}(K - S_T)\varphi(S_T)dS_T dK \\
&\quad - \int_{F_T}^{\infty} \int_K^{\infty} \frac{K - S_T}{K^2}(K - S_T)\varphi(S_T)dS_T dK \\
&= \int_0^{F_T} \int_0^{\infty} \frac{K - S_T}{K^2}(K - S_T, 0)^+\varphi(S_T)dS_T dK \\
&\quad + \int_{F_T}^{\infty} \int_0^{\infty} \frac{(S_T - K, 0)^+}{K^2}\varphi(S_T)dS_T dK \\
&= \int_0^{F_T} \frac{P(K,T)}{K^2}dK + \int_{F_T}^{\infty} \frac{C(K,T)}{K^2}dK
\end{aligned}
\tag{A.25}
$$

as per (4.21).   □

Defining $\kappa = K/F_T$, we can rewrite (A.25) as:

$$
I(T) = \int_0^1 \frac{d\kappa}{\kappa^2}\tilde{p}(\kappa, \sigma(\kappa, T), T) + \int_1^{\infty} \frac{d\kappa}{\kappa^2}\tilde{c}(\kappa, \sigma(\kappa, T), T)
$$

where

$$\tilde{p}(\kappa, \sigma(\kappa, T), T) = P(K, T)/F_T$$
$$\tilde{c}(\kappa, \sigma(\kappa, T), T) = C(K, T)/F_T$$

If, under spot movement $S \to S'$, the volatility surface undergoes a 'sticky delta' move, then we have:

$$\sigma(S', KF'_T/F_T, T) = \sigma(S, K, T) \qquad (A.26)$$

Expressing in terms of moneyness κ, we have $\sigma(S, \kappa, T) = \sigma(S, K = \kappa F, T)$. But from (A.26) $\sigma(S, K = \kappa F, T) = \sigma(S', K' = \kappa F'_T, T) = \sigma(S', \kappa, T)$. Under sticky delta movement, implied volatility is therefore constant for fixed moneyness. Like that, $I(T)$ is manifestly invariant under spot movement, giving an identically zero delta. Note that, as the forward delta, $\Delta = N(d_1) = N\left[-\log(\kappa)/\sigma(\kappa)\sqrt{T} + \sigma(\kappa)\sqrt{T}/2\right]$, this movement is equivalent to the volatility for a given forward delta being fixed under spot movement.

(5) Recall from Chapter 3, that, for a constant drift Brownian motion $Y_t = \alpha t + X_t$, (where X_t is driftless and starts at zero) the joint density of the terminal Y_T and the maximum $M_T(Y) = \max_{0 < s \leq T} Y(s)$ was given by:

$$f(Y, M, t) = \exp(-\frac{1}{2}\alpha^2 t + \alpha Y_t)\frac{2(2M - Y)}{\sqrt{2\pi t^3}} \exp\left(-\frac{(2M - Y)^2}{2t}\right)$$

A geometric Brownian motion spot process with constant drift and vol is given by:

$$d\log(S_t) = (\mu - \sigma^2/2)dt + \sigma dW_t$$

This can be transformed to the unit vol Brownian Y_t through the transformations:

$$Y_t = \log(S_t/S_0)/\sigma$$
$$\alpha = (\mu - \sigma^2/2)/\sigma$$

A one-touch barrier can be written as the sum of a digital call and an option which pays unity if the maximum is above the barrier, and the terminal spot is below, i.e.:

$$V = \int_b^\infty \phi(Y) dY + \int_{-\infty}^b dY \int_b^\infty f(Y, M) dM$$
$$= P + Q$$

where $b = \log(B/S_0)/\sigma$ and we drop the underscore T for convenience. We can write:

$$\phi(Y) = \int_Y^\infty f(Y, M) dM$$

as the maximum must be greater than or equal to the terminal Y, by definition. This is just the normal distribution:

$$\phi(Y, T) = \frac{1}{\sqrt{2\pi T}} \exp\left(-\frac{(Y - \alpha T)^2}{2T}\right)$$

giving for the digital:

$$P = 1 - N\left(\frac{b - \alpha T}{\sqrt{T}}\right) = 1 - N(-d_2)$$

where

$$d_2 = \frac{\log(S/B) + \mu T}{\sigma\sqrt{T}} - \frac{\sigma\sqrt{T}}{2}$$

using the shorthand $S = S_0$. The second integral can be solved as:

$$Q = \int_{-\infty}^b dY \frac{1}{\sqrt{2\pi T}} \exp\left(-\frac{1}{2}\alpha^2 t + \alpha Y_t\right) \exp\left[-\frac{(2b - Y)^2}{2t}\right]$$
$$= e^{2b\alpha} N\left(\frac{-b - \alpha T}{\sqrt{T}}\right)$$
$$= \left(\frac{B}{S}\right)^{(2\mu/\sigma^2 - 1)} N(d_1')$$
$$d_1' = \frac{\log(S/B) - \mu T}{\sigma\sqrt{T}} + \frac{\sigma\sqrt{T}}{2}$$

where the second line follows from completion of the square. Thus we have:

$$V = 1 - N(-d_2) + \left(\frac{B}{S}\right)^{(2\mu/\sigma^2 - 1)} N(d_1')$$

as required. $\square$

The vega is given by:

$$
\mathcal{V} = n(-d_2)\frac{\partial d_2}{\partial \sigma} + \frac{\partial}{\partial \sigma}\left[\left(\frac{B}{S}\right)^{(2\mu/\sigma^2-1)}\right]N(d_1')
$$

$$
+ \left(\frac{B}{S}\right)^{(2\mu/\sigma^2-1)}\frac{\partial d_1'}{\partial \sigma}n(d_1')
$$

Using:

$$
\frac{\partial}{\partial x}e^{f(x)} = f'(x)e^{f(x)}
$$

and

$$
\frac{\partial d_2}{\partial \sigma} = -\frac{d_1}{\sigma}
$$

$$
\frac{\partial d_1'}{\partial \sigma} = -\frac{d_2'}{\sigma}
$$

where

$$
d_1 = \frac{\log(S/B) + \mu T}{\sigma\sqrt{T}} + \frac{\sigma\sqrt{T}}{2}
$$

$$
d_2' = \frac{\log(S/B) - \mu T}{\sigma\sqrt{T}} - \frac{\sigma\sqrt{T}}{2}
$$

we arrive at:

$$
\mathcal{V} = -\frac{n(d_2)d_1}{\sigma} - \frac{n(d_1')d_2'}{\sigma}\left(\frac{B}{S}\right)^{(2\mu/\sigma^2-1)}
$$

$$
- \frac{4\mu}{\sigma^3}\log\left(\frac{B}{S}\right)\left(\frac{B}{S}\right)^{(2\mu/\sigma^2-1)}N(d_1')
$$

□

A.5 Chapter 5

(1) Consider a call valued with a forward F and implied vol σ_C, and a put valued with the same forward but an implied vol σ_P, which need not be the same. We have, for the undiscounted option values $\widetilde{C}(K,T)$ and $\widetilde{P}(K,T)$:

$$\widetilde{C}(K,T) - \widetilde{P}(K,T) =$$
$$F(T)\left[N(d_1^C) + N(-d_1^P)\right] - K\left[N(d_2^C) + N(-d_2^P)\right]$$
$$= F(T)\left[1 + N(d_1^C) - N(d_1^P)\right] - K\left[1 + N(d_2^C) - N(d_2^P)\right] \text{(A.27)}$$

If we now have that $F(T)$ satisfies put-call parity for all strikes, then $F(T) = \widetilde{C}(K,T) - \widetilde{P}(K,T) + K$, which can only be true in general if $d_1^C = d_1^P$ and $d_2^C = d_2^P$, as can be seen trivially from (A.27). As the same forward and strike has been used in $d_{1,2}^C$ and $d_{1,2}^P$, we must therefore have $\sigma_C(K,T) = \sigma_P(K,T)$, for all strikes. $\square$

For a state independent jump to zero scenario, the undiscounted call and put prices are given by:

$$\widetilde{C}(K,T) = SP(K,T)\left[F'(T)N(d_1) - KN(d_2)\right] \qquad \text{(A.28)}$$
$$\widetilde{P}(K,T) = SP(K,T)\left[KN(-d_2) - F'(T)N(-d_1)\right] + K(1 - SP(T))$$
$$d_{1,2} = \frac{\log(F'/K)}{\widehat{\sigma}(K,T)\sqrt{T}} \pm \frac{\widehat{\sigma}(K,T)\sqrt{T}}{2}$$
$$F'(T) = F(T)/SP(T)$$

$SP(T)$ the survival probability to maturity T, and $\widehat{\sigma}(K,T)$ the implied volatility corresponding to the underlying diffusion. We thus have:

$$\widetilde{C}(K,T) - \widetilde{P}(K,T) = F(T) - KSP(T) + K(1 - SP(T)) = F(T) - K$$

which again satisfies put-call parity on the *riskless* forward. We should thus have that $\sigma_C(K,T) = \sigma_P(K,T)$ for the implied volatilities backed out from the regular Black–Scholes formulae. The implied volatility given by out of the money puts for $K < F(T)$ and out of the money calls for $K \geq F(T)$ should thus be continuous, regardless of default. $\square$

(2) Let us consider n events occurring over the interval $[0, T]$, each of which occurs independently, with equal probability p. We will define a variable X which augments by unity for each event. From the binomial theorem, we have:

$$\mathbb{P}_n(X = k) = \frac{n!}{(n-k)!k!}p^k(1-p)^{n-k}$$

We have for the expectation of X:

$$E[X] = \sum_{k=0}^{n} k \frac{n!}{(n-k)!k!} p^k (1-p)^{n-k}$$

$$= pn \sum_{k=1}^{n} \frac{(n-1)!}{(n-k)!(k-1)!} p^{k-1} (1-p)^{n-k}$$

$$= pn \sum_{k=0}^{n-1} \frac{(n-1)!}{(n-k-1)!k!} p^k (1-p)^{n-k-1}$$

$$= pn(p + (1-p))^{n-1} = pn$$

Let us denote this expecation λ. We now have:

$$\mathbb{P}_n(X = k) = \frac{n!}{(n-k)!k!} \left(\frac{\lambda}{n}\right)^k \left(1 - \frac{\lambda}{n}\right)^{n-k}$$

$$= \frac{n!}{(n-k)!n^k} \frac{\lambda^k}{k!} \left(1 - \frac{\lambda}{n}\right)^n \left(1 - \frac{\lambda}{n}\right)^{-k}$$

$$= A_k \frac{\lambda^k}{k!} \left(1 - \frac{\lambda}{n}\right)^n \left(1 - \frac{\lambda}{n}\right)^{-k}$$

In the limit of large n, we have:

$$A_k = 1.(1 - 1/n).(1 - 2/n) \ldots (1 - (k+1)/n) \to 1$$

$$\left(1 - \frac{\lambda}{n}\right)^n = 1 - \lambda + \lambda^2 \frac{n(n-1)}{2!n^2} + \ldots$$

$$+ (-1)^r \lambda^r \frac{n(n-1) \ldots (n-r)}{r!n^r} + \ldots$$

$$\to e^{-\lambda}$$

$$\left(1 - \frac{\lambda}{n}\right)^{-k} \to 1$$

giving finally:

$$\lim_{n \to \infty} \mathbb{P}_n(X = k) = e^{-\lambda} \frac{\lambda^k}{k!}$$

□

The moment generating function $m(t) = E\left[e^{tX}\right]$ is then given by:

$$m(t) = \sum_{k=0}^{\infty} e^{-\lambda} \frac{\lambda^k}{k!} e^{tk}$$

$$= e^{-\lambda} \exp\left[\lambda e^t\right]$$

$$= \exp\left[\lambda\left(e^t - 1\right)\right] \tag{A.29}$$

We have that:

$$\frac{d^n m}{dt^n}\bigg|_{t=0} = E[X^n]$$

From (A.29):

$$\frac{dm}{dt} = \lambda m(t) e^t$$

$$\frac{d^2 m}{dt^2} = \lambda m(t) e^t \left(1 + \lambda e^t\right)$$

Giving $E[X] = \lambda$ and $E[X^2] = \lambda + \lambda^2$, given that $m(0) = 1$. Thus both the mean and variance of the Poisson distribution are given by λ. ☐

(3) For a pure jump to zero process with flat hazard rate λ, the undiscounted call price is given by:

$$\tilde{C} = \left(F e^{\lambda T} - K\right) e^{-\lambda T}$$

for $F e^{\lambda T} > K$ and zero otherwise (from (A.28)). For an ATM call $F = K$, this gives $F\left(1 - e^{-\lambda T}\right)$. Using the approximation for an ATM call $C \simeq F\sigma\sqrt{T}/\sqrt{2\pi}$, this gives for the ATM implied volatility:

$$F\frac{\sigma\sqrt{T}}{\sqrt{2\pi}} \simeq F\left(1 - e^{-\lambda T}\right)$$

$$\Rightarrow \sigma \simeq \lambda\sqrt{2\pi T}; \ \lambda T \ll 1$$

☐

Were we to have a situation where the ATM implied vol were significantly below this value, we could short an option which pays the forward at expiry only in the event of default, and go long a regular ATM put. In the case of no default, the put would pay out. In the case of default, the put would be cancelled by the default option. In either event, the payout is zero or positive, from a net positive initial cash position. Such situations are therefore indicative of arbitrage possibilities.

(4) For very low strike $K \ll F$, the Black–Scholes put can be approximated by:

$$P(K, T) \simeq K N(-d_2)$$

(from simple first-order Taylor expansion). We have, however, for a defaulting put, in the limit of low K that:

$$P(K,T) \simeq K(1 - e^{-\lambda T})$$

We thus have that $d_2 = -c = -N^{-1}\left(1 - e^{-\lambda T}\right)$. Writing $\sigma(K,T)\sqrt{T} = x$ this gives:

$$\frac{\log(F/K)}{x} - \frac{x}{2} = -c$$

which we can solve as a quadratic equation to give:

$$x = c\left(1 + \sqrt{1 + 2\log(F/K)/c^2}\right) = \sqrt{2\log(F/K)}$$

in the limit $K \to 0$. In other words, implied volatility for non-zero probability of jump to zero must always go to infinity as strike goes to zero. Any volatility extrapolation which ascribes a finite vol at zero strike must therefore be underpricing out of the money puts.   □

(5) In terms of the Green's function conditional on survival, the option price for state x_0 and time t_0 can be written as:

$$V(x_0, t_0) = Df(t_0, T) \int V(x_T, T)G(x_0, t_0; x_T, T)dx_T$$

$$+ \int_{t_0}^{T} Df(t_0, t)V^*(t) \int G(x_0, t_0; x_t, t)\lambda(x_t, t)dx_t dt$$

where $Df(t_0, t)$ is the discount factor from t_0 to t. Differentiating w.r.t T, we have:

$$0 = Df(t_0, T) \int \left[-r(T)V(x_T, T)G(x_0, t_0; x_T, T) \right.$$

$$+ \frac{\partial}{\partial T}V(x_T, T)G(x_0, t_0; x_T, T)$$

$$\left. + \frac{\partial}{\partial T}G(x_0, t_0; x_T, T)V(x_T, T) \right]dx_T$$

$$+ Df(t_0, T)V^*(T) \int G(x_0, t_0; x_T, T)\lambda(x_T, T)dx_T$$

Using the backward equation for $V(x_t, t)$, this gives:

$$0 = Df(t_0, T) \int -r(T)V(x_T, T)G(x_0, t_0; x_T, T)dx_T$$

$$+Df(t_0, T) \int G(x_0, t_0; x_T, T)dx_T \times$$

$$\left[-\frac{1}{2}\frac{\partial^2 V}{\partial x_T^2}\sigma^2(x_T, T) - \left(\mu(T) + \lambda(x_T, T) - \frac{\sigma^2(x_T, T)}{2}\right)\frac{\partial V}{\partial x_T} \right.$$

$$\left. +(r(T) + \lambda(x_T, T))V_T - \lambda(x_T, T)V_T^* \right]$$

$$+Df(t_0, T) \int \frac{\partial}{\partial T}G(x_0, t_0; x_T, T)V(x_T, T)dx_T$$

$$+Df(t_0, T)V^*(T) \int G(x_0, t_0; x_T, T)\lambda(x_T, T)dx_T$$

Cancelling terms, we get:

$$0 = \int G(x_0, t_0; x_T, T)dx_T$$

$$\times \left[-\frac{1}{2}\frac{\partial^2 V}{\partial x_T^2}\sigma^2(x_T, T) - (\mu(T) + \lambda(x_T, T) - \sigma^2(x_T, T)/2)\frac{\partial V}{\partial x_T} \right.$$

$$\left. +\lambda(x_T, T)V_T \right]$$

$$+ \int \frac{\partial}{\partial T}G(x_0, t_0; x_T, T)V(x_T, T)dx_T$$

So that, again, integrating by parts, and using the condition that the Green's function and its spatial derivative vanish at $x_T = \pm\infty$, we get:

$$\frac{\partial G(x_0, t_0; x_T, T)}{\partial T}$$

$$= -\frac{\partial}{\partial x_T}[(\mu(T) + \lambda(x_T, T) - \sigma^2(x_T, T)/2)G(x_0, t_0; x_T, T)]$$

$$+\frac{1}{2}\frac{\partial^2}{\partial x_T^2}[\sigma^2(x_T, T)G(x_0, t_0; x_T, T)] - \lambda(x_T, T)G(x_0, t_0; x_T, T)$$

which, under change of variable $S_T = e^{x_T}$ recovers the Fokker–Planck equation (5.17). □

(6) The payoff of a European convert, conversion ratio n, face value N_0 is given by $\max(nS, N_0) = n\max(S - N_0/n, 0) + N_0$. The value, for flat hazard rate, short rate, vol and no divs is given by:

$$V = ne^{-(r+\lambda)T}\left(F'N(d_1) - KN(d_2)\right) + N_0 e^{-(r+\lambda)T}$$
$$= ne^{-(r+\lambda)T}\widetilde{C}(K,T) + N_0 e^{-(r+\lambda)T}$$

where $F' = Fe^{\lambda T}$ and $K = N_0/n$. We know, from put-call parity, that $\widetilde{C} = F' - K + \widetilde{P} > F' - K$. Thus:

$$V > ne^{-(r+\lambda)T}(F' - K) + N_0 e^{-(r+\lambda)T} = ne^{-(r+\lambda)T}F' = nS$$

It is thus never optimal to exercise the convert early, regardless of non-zero credit spread. □

A.6 Chapter 6

(1) We have that X is distributed $\sim \mathcal{N}(\mu, \sigma^2)$. We can consequently write for the moment generating function:

$$m(t) = E\left[e^{tX}\right]$$
$$= \int_{-\infty}^{\infty} e^{tX}\frac{e^{-\frac{(X-\mu)^2}{2\sigma^2}}}{\sqrt{2\pi}\sigma}dX$$
$$= \frac{1}{\sqrt{2\pi}\sigma}e^{\mu t+\sigma^2 t^2/2}\int_{-\infty}^{\infty} e^{-\frac{(X-(\mu+\sigma^2 t))^2}{2\sigma^2}}dX$$
$$= e^{\mu t+\sigma^2 t^2/2}$$

We consequently have $\log(m(t)) = \mu t + \sigma^2 t^2/2$ from which we can see trivially:

$$\kappa_1 = \mu$$
$$\kappa_2 = \sigma^2$$
$$\kappa_n = 0; \ \forall\, n > 2$$

□

(2) We have for the Merton jump process:

$$\frac{dS_t}{S_t} = \mu dt + \sigma dW_t + (e^J - 1)dN_t$$

Let us consider the delta hedged strategy:

$$\Pi_t = V_t - \Delta S_t + B_t$$

where $\Delta = \partial V/\partial S$. We have for the evolution of the strategy:

$$d\Pi_t = \left[\frac{\partial V}{\partial t} dt + \frac{\partial^2 V}{\partial S^2} \sigma^2 S^2 dt \right] (1 - dN_t)$$
$$+ \left[(V(Se^J, t) - V(S,t)) - \Delta S(e^J - 1) \right] dN_t + r(\Delta S_t - V_t) dt$$

where we have assumed no dividends, flat model parameters, and that the portfolio is rebalanced continuously. Using $E_\mathbb{Q}[dN_t] = \lambda dt$, and that N_t and J are independent, we can write (to $O(dt)$):

$$E_\mathbb{Q}[d\Pi_t] = \frac{\partial V}{\partial t} dt + \frac{\partial^2 V}{\partial S^2} \sigma^2 S^2 dt$$
$$+ \left[(E_J[V(Se^J,t)] - V(S,t)) - \Delta S(E_J[e^J] - 1) \right] \lambda dt$$
$$+ r(\Delta S_t - V_t) dt$$

Equating this expectation to zero recovers the Merton equation:

$$\frac{\partial V}{\partial t} + \frac{\partial V}{\partial S} S \left(r - \lambda (E_J[e^J] - 1) \right) + \frac{\partial^2 V}{\partial S^2} \sigma^2 S^2$$
$$= V(r + \lambda) - \lambda E_J[V(Se^J, t)]$$

$\square$

(3) First, let us re-express the call in terms of a stock and covered call:

$$(S_T - K, 0)^+ = S_T - \min(S_T, K)$$

We then have for the undiscounted call price:

$$\widetilde{C}(K,T) = F_T - E_\mathbb{Q}[\min(S_T, K)]$$

Writing $x = \log(S_T/F(T))$ and $k = \log(K/F(T))$, we can re-write the covered call as $\min(S_T, K) = F(T)e^k \min(e^{x-k}, 1)$. We then have for the risk-neutral expectation:

$$E_\mathbb{Q}[\min(S_T, K)] = F(T)e^k \int_{-\infty}^{\infty} \min(e^{x-k}, 1) G(x, \tau) dx$$

using the assumption that the Green's function $G(x_0, t_0; x_T, T)$ is space and time homogeneous, as per (6.11). Writing this in terms of the Fourier transforms of G and $h(x) = \min(e^x, 1)$ gives:

$$E_\mathbb{Q}\left[\min(S_T, K)\right] = F(T)e^k \int_{-\infty+i\gamma}^{\infty+i\gamma} e^{-i\xi k}\hat{h}(-\xi)\widehat{G}(\xi,\tau)d\xi$$

The Fourier transform of $h(x,\tau)$ is given by:

$$\hat{h}(\xi) = \int_{-\infty}^{0} e^x e^{i\xi x}dx + \int_{0}^{\infty} e^{i\xi x}dx$$

$$= \frac{1}{i(\xi - i)} - \frac{1}{i\xi}$$

$$= \frac{1}{\xi(\xi - i)}$$

provided $0 < \Im\xi < 1$, the lower bound required for the second integrand to vanish as $x \to \infty$, the upper bound for the first integrand to vanish as $x \to -\infty$. As the transform of the Green's function is well-defined for all ξ, we have that the strip of regularity for $\hat{h}(-\xi)\widehat{G}(\xi,\tau)$ is $-1 < \gamma < 0$ (as the strip for $\hat{h}(\xi)$ is $0 < \gamma < 1$). We can thus make the judicious choice:

$$E_\mathbb{Q}\left[\min(S_T, K)\right] = F(T)e^k \int_{-\infty-i/2}^{\infty-i/2} e^{-i\xi k}\frac{\widehat{G}(\xi,\tau)}{\xi(\xi + i)}d\xi$$

Changing variable to $\xi' = \xi + i/2$ gives:

$$E_\mathbb{Q}\left[\min(S_T, K)\right] = F(T)e^{k/2} \int_{-\infty}^{\infty} e^{-i\xi' k}\frac{\widehat{G}(\xi' - i/2, \tau)}{\xi'^2 + 1/4}d\xi'$$

From the definition of $\widehat{G}(\xi)$, we have that $\Re(e^{-i\xi k}\widehat{G}(\xi,\tau)) = \Re(e^{+i\xi k}\widehat{G}(-\xi,\tau))$ and $\Im(e^{-i\xi k}\widehat{G}(\xi,\tau)) = -\Im(e^{+i\xi k}\widehat{G}(-\xi,\tau))$, giving:

$$E_\mathbb{Q}\left[\min(S_T, K)\right] = F(T)e^{k/2} \int_{-\infty}^{\infty} \Re\left[e^{-i\xi' k}\widehat{G}(\xi' - i/2, \tau)\right]\frac{1}{\xi'^2 + 1/4}d\xi'$$

Giving for the undiscounted call price $\widetilde{C}(K, T) = F(T)c(k, T)$ where:

$$c(k,\tau) = 1 - e^{k/2}\frac{1}{\pi}\int_{0}^{\infty} \frac{d\xi}{\xi^2 + \frac{1}{4}}\Re\left[e^{-ik\xi}\widehat{G}(\xi - i/2, \tau)\right]$$

$\square$

(4) We have for the Itō integral of the function $f(X_t)$ a jump-diffusion $X_t = X_t^c + J_t$:

$$
\begin{aligned}
f(X_t) &= f(X_0) + \int_0^t f'(X_s)dX_s^c + \frac{1}{2}\int_0^t f''(X_s)\sigma_s^2 ds \\
&\quad + \sum_{0<s\leq t}[f(X_s) - f(X_{s-})]
\end{aligned}
$$

Considering the time interval $[t, t+dt]$ incorporating a single jump, with indicator $dN_t = \{0, 1\}$ we can write:

$$
f(X_{t+dt}) = f(X_t) + f'(X_t)dX_t^c + \frac{1}{2}f''(X_t)\sigma_t^2 dt + [f(X_t) - f(X_{t-})]dN_t
$$
(A.30)

Let us now consider the process $S_t = e^{X_t}$. From (A.30):

$$
\begin{aligned}
dS_t &= S_t dX_t^c + \frac{1}{2}S_t\sigma_t^2 dt + S_t(e^{J_t} - 1)dN_t \\
&= S_t\left(\mu_t + \frac{1}{2}\sigma_t^2\right) + S_t\sigma_t dW_t + S_t(e^{J_t} - 1)dN_t
\end{aligned}
$$

But we have for the Merton stock process:

$$
\frac{dS_t}{S_t} = \mu_S dt + \sigma_S dW_t + (e^J - 1)dN_t
$$

giving $\sigma_t = \sigma_S$ and $\mu_t = \mu - \sigma_S^2/2$, so that we have for the evolution of $X_t = \log(S_t)$:

$$
d\log(S_t) = (\mu_S - \sigma_S^2/2)dt + \sigma_S dW_t + JdN_t
$$

$\square$

(5) We have for the evolution of the Green's function under Merton jump-diffusion:

$$
\begin{aligned}
&-\frac{\partial G(x,t;z,T)}{\partial T} - \frac{\partial}{\partial z}(\mu(T)G(x,t;z,T)) + \frac{1}{2}\frac{\partial^2}{\partial z^2}(\sigma^2(T)G(x,t;z,T)) \\
&- \lambda G(x,t;z,T) + \lambda E_{J'}[G(x,t;z-J',T)] = 0
\end{aligned}
$$
(A.31)

And for the undiscounted call price:

$$\widetilde{C}(x,t;K,T) = \int_{-\infty}^{\infty} (e^z - K, 0)\, G(x,t;z,T)dz \tag{A.32}$$

Using:

$$\mu(t) = g(t) - \frac{\sigma^2(t)}{2} - \lambda(E_{J'}[e^{J'}] - 1)$$

we can apply (A.31) to (A.32) and separate out the λ independent terms as per the original Dupire formulation to give:

$$-\frac{\partial \widetilde{C}}{\partial T} + g(T)\left[\widetilde{C} - K\frac{\partial \widetilde{C}}{\partial K}\right]$$

$$+ \frac{1}{2}\sigma^2(K,T)K^2\frac{\partial^2 \widetilde{C}}{\partial K^2} + \lambda\left(E_{J'}[e^{J'}] - 1\right)K\frac{\partial \widetilde{C}}{\partial K}$$

$$- \lambda E_{J'}[e^{J'}]\widetilde{C} + \lambda\int \widetilde{C}(Fe^J, K, T)\phi(J)dJ = 0 \tag{A.33}$$

Defining:
$k = K/F(t,T)$ and $\widehat{c}(t,T,\alpha,k) = \widetilde{C}(t,T,\alpha F(t,T), kF(t,T))/F(t,T)$,
we have:

$$\frac{\partial \widetilde{C}}{\partial T} = F(T)\left[\frac{\partial \widehat{c}}{\partial T} + g(T)\widehat{c} - g(T)k\frac{\partial \widehat{c}}{\partial k}\right]$$

$$\frac{\partial \widetilde{C}}{\partial K} = \frac{\partial \widehat{c}}{\partial k}$$

$$\frac{\partial \widetilde{C}}{\partial K^2} = \frac{1}{F(t,T)}\frac{\partial^2 \widehat{c}}{\partial k^2}$$

simplifying (A.33) to:

$$-\frac{\partial \widehat{c}}{\partial T} + \frac{1}{2}\sigma^2(k,T)k^2\frac{\partial^2 \widehat{c}}{\partial k^2} + \lambda(E_{J'}[e^{J'}] - 1)k\frac{\partial \widehat{c}}{\partial k}$$

$$- \lambda E_{J'}[e^{J'}]\widehat{c} + \lambda\int \widehat{c}(t,T,e^J,k)\phi(J)dJ = 0$$

where we have used the shorthand notation $\widehat{c} = \widehat{c}(t,T,1,k)$. Defining further $E_{J'}[e^{J'}] = e^{\mu_J}$ and $\lambda' = \lambda e^{\mu_J}$, we get

$$-\frac{\partial \widehat{c}}{\partial T} + \frac{1}{2}\sigma^2(k,T)k^2\frac{\partial^2 \widehat{c}}{\partial k^2}$$

$$+ (\lambda' - \lambda)k\frac{\partial \widehat{c}}{\partial k} - \lambda'\widehat{c} + \lambda\int \widehat{c}(t,T,e^J,k)\phi(J)dJ = 0$$

We can expand the last integral as:

$$\int \widehat{c}(t, T, e^J, k) \phi(J) dJ = I = \frac{1}{\sqrt{2\pi\delta}} \int e^J \widehat{c}(t, T, 1, ke^{-J}) e^{-\frac{(J - \mu'_J)^2}{2\delta^2}} dJ$$

$$\mu'_J = \mu_J - \frac{\delta^2}{2}$$

Completing the square, we can write:

$$I = \frac{1}{\sqrt{2\pi\delta}} e^{\mu'_J + \delta^2/2} \int \widehat{c}(t, T, 1, ke^{-J}) e^{-\frac{(J - (\mu'_J + \delta^2))^2}{2\delta^2}} dJ$$

and using the transformation $J = \delta z + \mu'_J$ gives:

$$I = e^{\mu_J} \int \widehat{c}(t, T, 1, ke^{-\delta z - \mu_J + \delta^2/2}) n(z - \delta) dz$$

giving finally:

$$-\frac{\partial \widetilde{c}}{\partial T} + (\lambda' - \lambda) k \frac{\partial \widetilde{c}}{\partial k} + \frac{1}{2} \sigma^2(T, k) k^2 \frac{\partial^2 \widetilde{c}}{\partial k^2}$$

$$+ \lambda' \left(\int_{-\infty}^{\infty} \widetilde{c}(t, T, ke^{-\mu_J + \delta^2/2 - \delta z}) \phi(z - \delta) dz - \widetilde{c} \right) = 0$$

where $\widetilde{c}(t, T, k) = \widehat{c}(t, T, 1, k)$. □

(6) We have the expression for Dupire variance given in Chapter 2:

$$\sigma^2(z, T) = \frac{\frac{\partial}{\partial T}\big|_z (\widehat{\sigma}^2 T)}{1 + \widehat{\sigma} T \frac{\partial^2 \widehat{\sigma}}{\partial z^2} + T d_1 d_2 \left(\frac{\partial \widehat{\sigma}}{\partial z}\right)^2 - \frac{2z}{\widehat{\sigma}} \frac{\partial \widehat{\sigma}}{\partial z}} \qquad \text{(A.34)}$$

where $z = \log(K/F(T))$. The absence of arbitrage is equivalent to the positivity of this quantity everywhere. Consider the sticky delta transformation:

$$\widehat{\sigma}'(K, T) = \widehat{\sigma}(KS/S', T)$$

We have:

$$\widehat{\sigma}'(z, T) = \widehat{\sigma}'(F'e^z, T) = \widehat{\sigma}(F'e^z S/S', T) = \widehat{\sigma}(Fe^z, T) = \widehat{\sigma}(z, T)$$

as for a proportional dividend model $F'/F = S'/S$. As the implied vol surface is thus fixed against z, so is the local variance, from (A.34). An implied vol surface which is non-arbitrageable for a given spot will thus stay non-arbitrageable under a sticky delta move, provided dividends are proportional. □

(7)

$$\int_{-\infty}^{\infty} J^3 \omega(J) dJ = \frac{1}{\sqrt{2\pi}\delta} \int_{-\infty}^{\infty} J^3 e^{-\frac{(J-\mu'_J)^2}{2\delta^2}} dJ$$

$$= \frac{1}{\sqrt{2\pi}\delta} \int_{-\infty}^{\infty} (J - \mu'_J + \mu'_J) J^2 e^{-\frac{(J-\mu'_J)^2}{2\delta^2}} dJ$$

$$= \frac{1}{\sqrt{2\pi}\delta} \left[2\delta^2 \int_{-\infty}^{\infty} J e^{-\frac{(J-\mu'_J)^2}{2\delta^2}} dJ \right.$$

$$\left. + \int_{-\infty}^{\infty} \mu'_J J^2 e^{-\frac{(J-\mu'_J)^2}{2\delta^2}} dJ \right]$$

$$= 2\delta^2 \mu'_J + \mu'_J (\delta^2 + \mu'^2_J)$$

$$= \mu'_J (\mu'^2_J + 3\delta^2)$$

$\square$

(8) We have for the CPPI strategy:

$$\frac{F_i}{F_{i-1}} = \left[1 + L_{i-1} \left(\frac{S_i}{S_{i-1}} - 1 \right) + (1 - L_{i-1}) \left(\frac{P_i}{P_{i-1}} - 1 \right) \right] \quad \text{(A.35)}$$

$$L_i = m \frac{F_i - P_i}{F_i} \quad \text{(A.36)}$$

Combining (A.35) and (A.36) gives:

$$F_i = F_{i-1} + m(F_{i-1} - P_{i-1}) \left(\frac{S_i}{S_{i-1}} - 1 \right)$$

$$+ (F_{i-1}(1 - m) + m P_{i-1}) \left(\frac{P_i}{P_{i-1}} - 1 \right)$$

Consider now the move on the risky asset $S_i/S_{i-1} - 1 = -1/m$. We have:

$$F_i = P_{i-1} + (F_{i-1}(1 - m) + m P_{i-1}) \left(\frac{P_i}{P_{i-1}} - 1 \right)$$

Consider now situations where the fund is still above the bond floor at t_{i-1}. Writing $F_{i-1}/P_{i-1} = \alpha > 1$ we have:

$$F_i - P_i = (P_{i-1} - P_i)(1 - \alpha - m(1 - \alpha))$$

Assuming $P_i > P_{i-1}$ (i.e. non-negative interest rates), $F_i < P_i$ if $1 - \alpha - m(1 - \alpha) > 0$. Denoting $\alpha = 1 + \beta$; $\beta > 0$, this gives $\beta m > \beta$, i.e. $m > 1$. Thus, for leveraged funds $(m > 1)$, a relative downward stock move of greater than $1/m$ will cause the fund to fall beneath the bond floor.   □

Note, if $m = 1$ then the fund will exactly hit the floor, and can go no further. ATM puts on the fund will thus have identically zero price.

A.7 Chapter 7

(1) The payoff of the forward rate agreement (FRA), struck at T_1 and paying at T_2 on a unit notional, can be written:

$$\tau(T_1, T_2)\,(F - L(T_1, T_2))$$

where F is the FRA strike, and $L(T_1, T_2)$ the annualised floating rate applicable between T_1 and T_2. The value of this contract at time T_1 is:

$$V(T_1) = P(T_1, T_2)\tau(T_1, T_2)\,(F - L(T_1, T_2))$$

where $P(T_1, T_2)$ is the discount factor from T_1 to T_2. But, by definition, we have:

$$P(T_1, T_2) = \frac{1}{1 + L(T_1, T_2)\tau(T_1, T_2)}$$

giving

$$V(T_1) = P(T_1, T_2)\,(F\tau(T_1, T_2) + 1) - 1$$

In other words, the FRA can be replicated by going long $F\tau(T_1, T_2) + 1$ units of zero coupon bonds, expiring at T_2, and going short one unit of cash. The value of the FRA at time t must therefore be:

$$V(t) = P(t, T_2)\,(F\tau(T_1, T_2) + 1) - P(t, T_1)$$

For this to be fair, we must have $V(t) = 0$, giving:

$$F = \frac{1}{\tau(T_1, T_2)}\left(\frac{P(t, T_1)}{P(t, T_2)} - 1\right) \tag{A.37}$$

□

(2) We define the $\mathbb{T}_i$ measure via the tradable $X(t)$ and the numeraire $P(t,T_i)$:

$$\frac{X(t)}{P(t,T_i)} = E_{\mathbb{T}_i}\left[X(T_i)|\mathcal{F}_t\right] \qquad (A.38)$$

Rearranging (A.37):

$$F(t;T_1,T_2) = \frac{1}{\tau(T_1,T_2)P(t,T_2)}\left[P(t,T_1) - P(t,T_2)\right]$$

As both the ZCB paying at T_1 and the one at T_2 are tradables, the difference $V(t;T_1,T_2) = P(t,T_1) - P(t,T_2)$ must also be tradable. We have then, from (A.38):

$$\frac{V(t)}{P(t,T_2)} = E_{\mathbb{T}_2}\left[V(T_2)|\mathcal{F}_t\right]$$

in other words:

$$F(t;T_1,T_2) = E_{\mathbb{T}_2}\left[F(T_2;T_1,T_2)|\mathcal{F}_t\right]$$

demonstrating that $F(t;T_1,T_2)$ is a $\mathbb{T}_2$ martingale, and indeed, in general $F(t;T_i,T_j)$ is a $\mathbb{T}_j$ martingale. $\qquad\square$

Let us now consider the quantity $Y(t) = F_k(t)P(t,T_k)/P(t,T_i)$. For $i < k$ we have, by definition of the FRA rate:

$$P(t,T_k) = P(t,T_i)\prod_{j=i+1}^{k}\frac{1}{1+\tau_j F_j(t)}$$

As $P(t,T_k)$ is tradable we must have that $P(t,T_k)/P(t,T_i)$ is driftless in the $\mathbb{T}_i$ forward measure. We have also that $F_k(t)P(t,T_k)$ is tradable (see above), so:

$$E_{\mathbb{T}_i}\left[dF_k(t)\frac{P(t,T_k)}{P(t,T_i)} + dF_k(t)d\left(\frac{P(t,T_k)}{P(t,T_i)}\right)\right] = 0 \qquad (A.39)$$

To $O(dt)$, we have:

$$E_{\mathbb{T}_i}\left[dF_k(t)d\left(\frac{P(t,T_k)}{P(t,T_i)}\right)\right]$$

$$= E_{\mathbb{T}_i}\left[-dF_k(t)\sum_{j=i+1}^{k}\frac{\tau_j dF_j(t)}{1+\tau_j F_j(t)}\frac{P(t,T_k)}{P(t,T_i)}\right]$$

$$= -\sum_{j=i+1}^{k}\rho_{j,k}F_j(t)\sigma_j\sigma_k\frac{\tau_j}{1+\tau_j F_j(t)}Y(t) \qquad (A.40)$$

where we have assumed:

$$\frac{dF_k(t)}{F_k(t)} = \sigma_i(t)dZ_k(t)$$

with $E_{\mathbb{T}_k}[dZ_k(t)] = 0$

For $Y(t)$ to be a martingale under $\mathbb{T}_i$, we need to have (from (A.39) and (A.40)):

$$E_{\mathbb{T}_i}[dZ_k(t)] = \sum_{j=i+1}^{k}\rho_{j,k}F_j(t)\sigma_j\sigma_k\frac{\tau_j}{1+\tau_j F_j(t)}$$

which we can achieve through the drift adjustment:

$$dZ_k(t) = \sum_{j=i+1}^{k}\rho_{j,k}F_j(t)\sigma_j\frac{\tau_j}{1+\tau_j F_j(t)}dt + d\widetilde{Z}_k(t)$$

with $E_{\mathbb{T}_i}[d\widetilde{Z}_k(t)] = 0$. For $i > k$ we have:

$$P(t,T_k) = P(t,T_i)\prod_{j=k+1}^{i}1+\tau_j F_j(t)$$

which going through the same mechanics as for $i < k$ gives:

$$dZ_k(t) = -\sum_{j=k+1}^{i}\rho_{j,k}F_j(t)\sigma_j\frac{\tau_j}{1+\tau_j F_j(t)}dt + d\widetilde{Z}_k(t)$$

For $i = k$, no drift adjustment is required, by definition, so we recover:

$$dF_k(t) = \sigma_k(t)F_k(t) \sum_{j=i+1}^{k} \frac{\rho_{k,j}\tau_j\sigma_j(t)F_j(t)}{1+\tau_j F_j(t)}dt$$
$$+ \sigma_k(t)F_k(t)dZ_k(t), \; i < k, t \le T_i$$
$$dF_k(t) = \sigma_k(t)F_k(t)dZ_k(t), \; i = k, t \le T_{k-1}$$
$$dF_k(t) = -\sigma_k(t)F_k(t) \sum_{j=k+1}^{i} \frac{\rho_{k,j}\tau_j\sigma_j(t)F_j(t)}{1+\tau_j F_j(t)}dt$$
$$+ \sigma_k(t)F_k(t)dZ_k(t), \; i > k, t \le T_{k-1}$$

where the t inequalities follow from the condition that both the numeraire and the forward rate should be active at t. $\qquad\square$

(3) The value of the floating leg of an interest rate swap at T_0, can be written:

$$V_{floating} = \sum_{i=1,n} L(T_{i-1},T_i)\tau(T_{i-1},T_i)P(T_0,T_i)$$

Writing $x_i = L(T_{i-1},T_i)\tau(T_{i-1},T_i)$, we can rewrite this as:

$$V_{floating} = \sum_{i=1,n} x_i \prod_{j=1,i} \frac{1}{1+x_j}$$

Let us denote this quantity V_n. We have:

$$V_n + P(T_0,T_n) = \sum_{i=1,n} x_i \prod_{j=1,i} \frac{1}{1+x_j} + \prod_{j=1,n} \frac{1}{1+x_j}$$
$$= \sum_{i=1,n-1} x_i \prod_{j=1,i} \frac{1}{1+x_j} + \prod_{j=1,n-1} \frac{1}{1+x_j}$$
$$= V_{n-1} + P(T_0,T_{n-1})$$

We thus have $V_n + P(T_0,T_n) = V_1 + P(T_0,T_1) = (1+x_1)/(1+x_1) = 1$, giving:

$$V_n = 1 - P(T_0,T_n)$$

The value of the fixed leg is simply:

$$V_{floating} = S_T \sum_{i=1,n} \tau(T_{i-1},T_i)P(T_0,T_i) = S_T DV01$$

so that the fair value for the swap rate S_T is given by:

$$S_T DV01 = 1 - P(T_0, T_n)$$

□

(4) Taking a set of FRA expiries as $\{T_i\}$ with $i > 1$ and defining the bounding indices of a swap α and β by $T_\alpha \leq t < T_\beta$, we can write for the value of the fixed and floating legs at time t:

$$V_{floating}(t) = \sum_{i=\alpha+1}^{\beta} F_i(t)\tau_i \prod_{j=\alpha+1}^{i} \frac{1}{1 + \tau_j F_j(t)}$$

$$V_{fixed}(t) = \sum_{i=\alpha+1}^{\beta} S_{\alpha,\beta}(t)\tau_i \prod_{j=\alpha+1}^{i} \frac{1}{1 + \tau_j F_j(t)}$$

We thus have for the swap rate:

$$S_{\alpha,\beta}(t) = \sum_{i=\alpha+1}^{\beta} w_i(t) F_i(t)$$

where

$$w_i(t) = \frac{\tau_i \prod_{j=\alpha+1}^{i} 1/(1 + \tau_j F_j(t))}{\sum_{k=\alpha+1}^{\beta} \tau_k \prod_{j=\alpha+1}^{k} 1/(1 + \tau_j F_j(t))}$$

□

We will assume, in general:

$$dF_i(t) = F_i(t) \left(\mu_i(t)dt + \sigma_i(t)dW_i(t) \right)$$

Now, let us assume that the weights $w_i(t)$ are slowly varying, so that $w_i(t) \simeq w_i(0)$, giving:

$$dS_{\alpha,\beta}(t) = \sum_{i=\alpha+1}^{\beta} w_i(0) F_i(t) \left(\mu_i(t)dt + \sigma_i(t)dW_i(t) \right)$$

giving for the variance of $dS_{\alpha,\beta}(t)$:

$$Var\left[dS_{\alpha,\beta}(t)\right] = S_{\alpha,\beta}^2(t) \sum_{i,j=\alpha+1}^{\beta} \frac{w_i(0)w_j(0)F_i(t)F_j(t)\sigma_i(t)\sigma_j(t)\rho_{i,j}dt}{S_{\alpha,\beta}^2(t)}$$

We will approximate further $F_i(t)F_j(t)/S^2_{\alpha,\beta}(t) \simeq F_i(0)F_j(0)/S^2_{\alpha,\beta}(0)$, to give:

$$Var\left[d\log S_{\alpha,\beta}(t)\right] = \sum_{i,j=\alpha+1}^{\beta} \frac{w_i(0)w_j(0)F_i(0)F_j(0)\sigma_i(t)\sigma_j(t)\rho_{i,j}dt}{S^2_{\alpha,\beta}(0)}$$

Integrating up, we arrive at the approximation for the swaption implied volatility:

$$\sigma^2_{\alpha,\beta} = \frac{1}{T_\alpha}\sum_{i,j=\alpha+1}^{\beta} \frac{w_i(0)w_j(0)F_i(0)F_j(0)\rho_{i,j}}{S^2_{\alpha,\beta}(0)} \int_0^{T_\alpha} \sigma_i(t)\sigma_j(t)dt$$

□

(5) For the rank two formulation of Rebonato correlation, we have:

$$\frac{dF_i(t)}{F_i(t)} = \sigma_i(t)(b_t^{i1}dZ_t^1 + b_t^{i2}dZ_t^2)$$

We thus have for the covariance $\langle d\log[F_i(t)]\,d\log[F_j(t)]\rangle$:

$$\begin{aligned}
&\langle d\log[F_i(t)]d\log[F_j(t)]\rangle \\
&= \sigma_i(t)\sigma_j(t)dt\left(b_t^{i1}b_t^{j1} + b_t^{i2}b_t^{j2}\right) \\
&= \sigma_i(t)\sigma_j(t)dt\left[\cos[\theta_i(t)]\cos[\theta_j(t)] + \sin[\theta_i(t)]\sin[\theta_j(t)]\right] \\
&= \sigma_i(t)\sigma_j(t)dt\cos[\theta_i(t) - \theta_j(t)]
\end{aligned}$$

giving for the correlation $\rho_{i,j}(t) = \cos[\theta_i(t) - \theta_j(t)]$. □

(6) Define $X(t) = \log[P(t,T)] = -\int_t^T f(t,s)ds$. We have $P(t,T) = e^{X(t)}$, so that from Itō's lemma:

$$dP(t,T) = e^{X(t)}dX_t + \frac{1}{2}e^{X(t)}dX_t^2$$

giving

$$\frac{dP(t,T)}{P(t,T)} = dX_t + \frac{1}{2}dX_t^2$$

Let us consider the integral:

$$I(t) = \int_{\alpha(t)}^{\beta(t)} g(t,s)ds$$

We then have:

$$I(t+dt) = \int_{\alpha(t+dt)}^{\beta(t+dt)} g(t+dt,s)ds$$

$$= \int_{\alpha(t+dt)}^{\beta(t)} g(t+dt,s)ds + \left[\int_{\alpha(t+dt)}^{\beta(t+dt)} g(t+dt,s)ds \right.$$

$$\left. - \int_{\alpha(t+dt)}^{\beta(t)} g(t+dt,s)ds \right]$$

$$= \int_{\alpha(t)}^{\beta(t)} g(t+dt,s)ds - \left[\int_{\alpha(t)}^{\beta(t)} g(t+dt,s)ds \right.$$

$$\left. - \int_{\alpha(t+dt)}^{\beta(t)} g(t+dt,s)ds \right]$$

$$+ \left[\int_{\alpha(t+dt)}^{\beta(t+dt)} g(t+dt,s)ds - \int_{\alpha(t+dt)}^{\beta(t)} g(t+dt,s)ds \right]$$

$$= \int_{\alpha(t)}^{\beta(t)} g(t+dt,s)ds + [\beta_t g(t+dt,\beta(t)) - \alpha_t g(t+dt,\alpha(t))]dt$$

where $\alpha_t = d\alpha/dt$, $\beta_t = d\beta/dt$.

In the limit $dt \to 0$:

$$I(t+dt) - I(t)$$

$$= \int_{\alpha(t)}^{\beta(t)} [g(t+dt,s) - g(t,s)]ds$$

$$+ [\beta_t g(t,\beta(t)) - \alpha_t g(t,\alpha(t))]dt$$

(This is the general form of the Leibniz integral rule.) We thus have:

$$X(t+dt) - X(t) = -\int_{t}^{T} [f(t+dt,s) - f(t,s)]ds + f(t,t)dt$$

$$= r(t)dt - \left[\int_{t}^{T} \alpha(t,s)ds \right] dt - \left[\int_{t}^{T} \sigma(t,s)ds \right] dW(t)$$

$$\square$$

(7) We have for the integrated short rate:

$$r(t) = f(0,t) + \int_{0}^{t} \sigma(u,t) \int_{u}^{t} \sigma(u,s)dsdu + \int_{0}^{t} \sigma(s,t)dW(s)$$

We then have:

$$E_{\mathbb{Q}}\left[\exp\left(-\int_0^t r(s)ds\right)\right] =$$
$$\exp\left(-\int_0^t f(0,s)ds\right)\exp\left(-\int_0^t ds\int_0^s \sigma(u,s)\int_u^s \sigma(u,s')ds'du\right)$$
$$\times E_{\mathbb{Q}}\left[\exp\left(-\int_0^t ds\int_0^s \sigma(s',s)dW(s')\right)\right]$$
$$= P(0,t)I_1(t)I_2(t)$$

where

$$I_1(t) = \exp\left(-\int_0^t ds\int_0^s du\,\sigma(u,s)\int_u^s \sigma(u,s')ds'\right)$$
$$I_2(t) = E_{\mathbb{Q}}\left[\exp\left(-\int_0^t ds\int_0^s \sigma(s',s)dW(s')\right)\right]$$

Focusing on the second integral, we have:

$$I_2(t) = \exp\left(\frac{1}{2}E_{\mathbb{Q}}\left[\left(-\int_0^t ds\int_0^s \sigma(s',s)dW(s')\right)^2\right]\right)$$
$$= \exp\left(\frac{J(t)}{2}\right)$$

where

$$J(t) = E_{\mathbb{Q}}\left[\int_0^t ds\int_0^s \sigma(s',s)dW(s')\int_0^t dy\int_0^y \sigma(x,y)dW(x)\right]$$
$$= J_1(t) + J_2(t)$$

where

$$J_1(t) = E_{\mathbb{Q}}\left[\int_0^t ds\int_0^s \sigma(s',s)dW(s')\int_0^s dy\int_0^y \sigma(x,y)dW(x)\right]$$
$$J_2(t) = E_{\mathbb{Q}}\left[\int_0^y ds\int_0^s \sigma(s',s)dW(s')\int_0^t dy\int_0^y \sigma(x,y)dW(x)\right]$$

which we get by splitting the outer integrals over (y,s) between the domains $y < s$ and $y \geq s$ respectively.

By interchange of variables $y \leftrightarrow s$ and $s' \leftrightarrow x$, we can see that $J_1(t) = J_2(t)$, so that $I_2(t) = \exp[J_1(t)]$. Using the fact that $y < s$ and $E_{\mathbb{Q}}[dW(s')dW(x)] = ds'\delta_{s'x}$ we can write:

$$J_1(t) = \int_0^t ds \int_0^s dy \int_0^y \sigma(s',s)\sigma(s',y)ds'$$

$$= \int_0^t ds \int_0^s ds' \int_{s'}^s \sigma(s',s)\sigma(s',y)dy$$

$$= \int_0^t ds \int_0^s du\sigma(u,s) \int_u^s \sigma(u,s')ds'$$

where the second line follows from change of order of integration. We therefore have $I_1(t)I_2(t) = 1$, recovering the result:

$$E_{\mathbb{Q}}\left[\exp\left(-\int_0^t r(s)ds\right)\right] = P(0,t)$$

$\square$

(8) For a proportional dividend paying stock, we have that the stock falls by an amount $q_i S(t_i^-)$ at each dividend ex-date. In the risk-neutral measure, the integrated stock price is then given by:

$$S_t = S_0 \exp\left[\int_0^t \left(r(s) - \frac{\sigma_S(s)^2}{2}\right)ds + \sigma_S(s)dW_s\right]Q(t)$$

where $Q(t) = \prod_{0 < t_i \leq t}(1 - q_i)$. Rewriting this as $S_t = X_t Q(t)$, we can see that X_t/B_t is manifestly a martingale under $\mathbb{Q}$. We should then have for the integrated value:

$$\frac{X_t}{P(t,T)} = \frac{X_0}{P(0,T)} \exp\left[\int_0^t \sigma_F(s,T)dW_s - \frac{1}{2}\int_0^t \sigma_F^2(s,T)ds\right]$$

where $E_{\mathbb{T}}[dW_t] = 0$ as $X_t/P(t,T)$ must be a martingale in $\mathbb{T}$ if X_t/B_t is a martingale in $\mathbb{Q}$. We have for the volatility of the conditional forward on X_t:

$$\sigma_F^2(t,T) = \sigma_S^2(t) - 2\rho(t)\sigma_S(s)\sigma_P(t,T) + \sigma_P^2(t,T)$$

We thus have for the call price:

$$C_0 = P(0,T)E_{\mathbb{T}}\left[(X_TQ(T) - K, 0)^+\right]$$
$$= P(0,T)Q(T)E_{\mathbb{T}}\left[(X_T - K/Q(T), 0)^+\right]$$
$$= P(0,T)Q(T)\left[F_X(T)N(d_1) - \frac{K}{Q(T)}N(d_2)\right]$$

where

$$d_{1,2} = \frac{\log(F_X(T)Q(T)/K)}{\widehat{\sigma}_F(T)\sqrt{T}} \pm \frac{\widehat{\sigma}_F(T)\sqrt{T}}{2}$$

with

$$\widehat{\sigma}_F^2(T)T = \int_0^T \sigma_F^2(t,T)dt$$

Using $F_XQ(T) = F_S(T)$, we recover the familiar Black–Scholes expression $C_0 = P(0,T)\left[F_S(T)N(d_1) - KN(d_2)\right]$. In other words, for state independent local volatility, the presence of proportional dividends has no effect on the volatility used in the Black–Scholes call formula. The adjustment is only to the forward.

(9) Taking the dividend-free stock process to be a tradable, we have that:

$$E_{\mathbb{T}}\left[d\left(\frac{S_t}{P(t,T)}\right)\right] = 0$$

From Itō, we have:

$$d\left(\frac{S_t}{P(t,T)}\right)$$
$$= \frac{dS_t}{P(t,T)} - \frac{S_t}{P^2(t,T)}dP(t,T) + \frac{S_t}{P^3(t,T)}dP^2(t,T) - \frac{dS_t dP(t,T)}{P^2(t,T)}$$

As both S_t and $P(t,T)$ are tradable, we have, in the risk-neutral measure $\mathbb{Q}$:

$$\frac{dS_t}{S_t} = r(t)dt + \sigma_S(t)dW_t^S$$
$$\frac{dP(t,T)}{P(t,T)} = r(t)dt + \sigma_P(t,T)dW_t^P$$

giving:

$$\frac{dF(t,T)}{F(t,T)} = \sigma_S(t)dW_t^S - \sigma_P(t,T)dW_t^P + \sigma_P^2(t,T)dt - \rho_{SP}\sigma_S(t)\sigma_P(t,T)dt$$

where $F(t,T) = S_t/P(t,T)$.

As the money market account B_t is also a tradable, we have $E_\mathbb{T}[d(B_t/P(t,T))] = 0$. From Itō, as $dB_t = r(t)dt$:

$$d\left(\frac{B_t}{P(t,T)}\right) = \frac{dB_t}{P(t,T)} - \frac{B_t}{P^2(t,T)}dP(t,T) + \frac{B_t}{P^3(t,T)}dP^2(t,T)$$

$$= \frac{B_t}{P(t,T)}\left[\sigma_P^2(t,T)dt - \sigma_P(t,T)dW_t^P\right]$$

As this is driftless under $\mathbb{T}$ we must have:

$$dW_t^P = d\widetilde{W}_t^P + \sigma_P(t,T)dt$$

where $d\widetilde{W}_t^P$ is driftless under $\mathbb{T}$. This then gives:

$$\frac{dF(t,T)}{F(t,T)} = \sigma_S(t)dW_t^S - \sigma_P(t,T)d\widetilde{W}_t^P - \rho_{SP}\sigma_S(t)\sigma_P(t,T)dt$$

As this is also driftless under $\mathbb{T}$, we must have:

$$dW_t^S = d\widetilde{W}_t^S + \rho_{SP}\sigma_P(t,T)dt$$

where $d\widetilde{W}_t^P$ is driftless under $\mathbb{T}$. We arrive finally at:

$$\frac{dF(t,T)}{F(t,T)} = \sigma_S(t)d\widetilde{W}_t^S - \sigma_P(t,T)d\widetilde{W}_t^P$$

So that:

$$F(T,T) = S_T = F(0,T)\exp\left[\int_0^T \sigma_F(t,T)d\widetilde{W}_t^F - \frac{\sigma_F^2(t,T)}{2}dt\right]$$

This gets us to the familiar Black–Scholes formula

$$C_0 = P(0,T)\left[F(0,T)N(d_1) - KN(d_2)\right]$$

where $d_{1,2} = \log(F(0,T)/K)/\hat{\sigma}_F(T)\sqrt{T} \pm \hat{\sigma}_F(T)\sqrt{T}/2$ and:

$$\hat{\sigma}_F^2(T)T = \int_0^T \left[\sigma_S^2(t) - 2\rho_{SP}(t)\sigma_S(t)\sigma_P(t,T) + \sigma_P^2(t,T)\right]dt \quad \text{(A.41)}$$

Recall the expression for the integrated short rate $r_t = x_t + \bar{x}_t$ where $d\bar{x}_t = \kappa(\bar{r} - \bar{x})dt$ and $dx_t = -\kappa x_t dt + \xi dW_t$. We have for x_s:

$$x_s = x_t e^{-\kappa(t-s)} + \int_t^s e^{-\kappa(s-u)} \xi dW_u$$

giving for $P(t,T)$:

$$P(t,T) = E_{\mathbb{Q}}\left[\exp\left(-\int_t^T r_s ds\right)\middle|\mathcal{F}_t\right]$$

$$= \exp\left(-\int_t^T \bar{x}_s ds - x_t G(\kappa,t,T)\right)$$

$$\times E_{\mathbb{Q}}\left[\exp\left(-\int_t^T \xi G(\kappa,s,T)dW_s\right)\middle|\mathcal{F}_t\right]$$

$$= A(t,T)\exp\left(-x_t G(\kappa,t,T)\right)$$

$$G(\kappa,t,T) = \int_t^T e^{-\kappa(s-t)}ds = \frac{1}{\kappa}\left[1 - e^{-\kappa(T-t)}\right]$$

From Itō, this gives:

$$dP(t,T) = \frac{\partial P(t,T)}{\partial t}dt - G(\kappa,t,T)P(t,T)dx_t + \frac{1}{2}\frac{\partial^2 P(t,T)}{\partial x_t^2}dx_t^2$$

giving for the bond volatility:

$$\sigma_P(t,T) = \xi G(\kappa,t,T) \tag{A.42}$$

and the bond-equity correlation $\rho_{SP}(t) = -\rho_{Sr}(t)$. Substituting this correlation, and (A.42) into (A.41) yields finally:

$$\hat{\sigma}^2(T)T = \int_0^T \left[\sigma_S^2(t) + 2\rho_{Sr}\sigma_S(t)\xi G(\kappa,t,T) + \xi^2 G(\kappa,t,T)^2\right]dt$$

$\square$

(10) From the previous question, we have:

$$\log[S_T/F(0,T)] = \int_0^T \sigma_S(t)d\widetilde{W}_t^S + \xi G(\kappa,t,T)d\widetilde{W}_t^r - \frac{\sigma_F^2(t,T)}{2}dt$$

and

$$r_T = \bar{r}(T) + \int_0^T e^{-\kappa(T-s)} \xi d\widetilde{W}_s^r$$

where $\bar{r}(T) = E_T[r_T]$. This gives us for the covariance of $X_T = \log[S_T/F(0,T)]$ and r_T:

$$\mathbb{Cov}(x_T, r_T) = \int_0^T \rho\xi\sigma_S(t)e^{-\kappa(T-t)}dt + \int_0^T \xi^2 e^{-\kappa(T-t)}G(\kappa, t, T)dt$$

$$= \int_0^T \exp[-\kappa(T-t)]\xi\left[\xi G(\kappa, t, T) + \rho\sigma_S(t)\right]dt$$

$$\square$$

A.8   Chapter 8

(1) We have the joint distribution for n normally distributed variables $x_i \sim \mathcal{N}(\mu_i, \sigma_i^2)$ with covariance matrix $\Sigma_{ij} = R_{ij}\sigma_i\sigma_j$ given by:

$$\phi(\mathbf{x}, \mu, \mathbf{\Sigma}) = \frac{1}{(2\pi)^{n/2}|\mathbf{\Sigma}|^{1/2}} \exp\left[-\frac{1}{2}(\mathbf{x} - \mu)^T \mathbf{\Sigma}^{-1}(\mathbf{x} - \mu)\right] \quad \text{(A.43)}$$

and the associated cdf $\Phi(\mathbf{X})$ given by:

$$\Phi(\mathbf{X}) = \int_{-\infty}^{X_1} \cdots \int_{-\infty}^{X_n} \phi(\mathbf{x}, \mu, \mathbf{\Sigma})dx_1 \ldots dx_n \quad \text{(A.44)}$$

To begin, we can write the inverse of Σ_{ij} as:

$$\Sigma_{ij}^{-1} = C_{ij}/|\mathbf{\Sigma}|$$

where C_{ij} is the matrix of co-factors given by:

$$C_{ij} = (-1)^{i+j}M_{ij}$$

with M_{ij} the determinant of the submatrix of Σ_{ij} obtained by removing the i-th row and j-th column from Σ_{ij}. By inspection of Σ_{ij}, we can see that C_{ij} is given by:

$$C_{ij} = \frac{\prod_i \sigma_i^2}{\sigma_i\sigma_j}C_{ij}^R$$

where C_{ij}^R is the co-factor of the correlation matrix R_{ij}. The result follows from the fact that the determinant of a matrix a_{ij} is given by:

$$|\mathbf{A}| = \sum_{i_1,\ldots,i_n=1}^{n} \epsilon_{i_1,\ldots,i_n} a_{1,i_1} \ldots a_{1,i_n}$$

with $\epsilon_{i_1,\ldots,i_n}$ the Levi–Civita symbol equal to 1 for even permutations of $i_1,\ldots,i_n$, -1, for odd permutations, and zero for any two indices the same. As permutation of indices leaves the magnitude of C_{ij} unchanged, we can factor it out against C_{ij}^R. Manifestly, the magnitude for C_{11} is then simply $\prod_{i\neq 1} \sigma_i^2 = (\prod_i \sigma_i^2)/\sigma_1^2$. The result for C_{ij} is general can then be obtained by index permutation.

Writing $y_i = (x_i - \mu_i)/\sigma_i$ we then have:

$$(\mathbf{x} - \mu)^T \mathbf{\Sigma}^{-1} (\mathbf{x} - \mu) = \sum_{i,j} y_i \sigma_i \Sigma_{ij}^{-1} y_j \sigma_j$$

$$= \frac{\prod_i \sigma_i^2 \sum_{i,j} y_i C_{ij}^R y_j}{|\mathbf{\Sigma}|}$$

$$= \frac{|\mathbf{R}| \prod_i \sigma_i^2}{|\mathbf{\Sigma}|} \sum_{i,j} y_i R_{ij}^{-1} y_j$$

But from the multiplicative properties of determinants, that multiplication of a row or column by α multiplies the entire determinant by α, we can see that:

$$|\mathbf{\Sigma}| = \prod_i \sigma_i^2 |\mathbf{R}| \tag{A.45}$$

giving:

$$(\mathbf{x} - \mu)^T \mathbf{\Sigma}^{-1} (\mathbf{x} - \mu) = \mathbf{y}^T \mathbf{R}^{-1} \mathbf{y}$$

We also have $\prod_i dx_i = \prod_i \sigma_i dy_i$ allowing us to rewrite (A.44) as:

$$\Phi(\mathbf{X}) = \Phi(\mathbf{Y}) = \int_{-\infty}^{Y_1} \ldots \int_{-\infty}^{Y_n} \phi(\mathbf{y}, \mathbf{R}) dy_1 \ldots dy_n$$

with
$Y_i = \frac{X_i - \mu_i}{\sigma_i}$ and

$$\phi(\mathbf{y}, \mathbf{R}) = \frac{1}{(2\pi)^{n/2}|\mathbf{R}|^{1/2}} \exp\left[-\frac{1}{2}\mathbf{y}^T\mathbf{R}^{-1}\mathbf{y}\right]$$

□

Now let us consider the Cholesky decomposition $\mathbf{R} = \mathbf{Q}\mathbf{Q}^T$ and define $\mathbf{z} = \mathbf{Q}^{-1}\mathbf{y}$. We have:

$$\mathbf{y}^T\mathbf{R}^{-1}\mathbf{y} = \mathbf{z}^T\mathbf{Q}^T(\mathbf{Q}^T)^{-1}\mathbf{Q}^{-1}\mathbf{Q}\mathbf{z}$$
$$= \sum_i z_i^2 \qquad (A.46)$$

We have moreover, from the property that the volume of an n-dimensional parallelepiped spanned by vectors $\mathbf{a}^1, \ldots, \mathbf{a}^n$ is given by $|\mathbf{A}|$ where $A_{ij} = \mathbf{a}_j^i$, that $dy_1 \ldots dy_n = |\mathbf{Q}|dz_1 \ldots dz_n = |\mathbf{R}|^{1/2}dz_1 \ldots dz_n$. Together with (A.46) and the definition of z we can write finally:

$$\Phi(\mathbf{Y}) = \prod_i \int_{-\infty}^{(\mathbf{Q}^{-1}\mathbf{Y})_i} \frac{1}{\sqrt{2\pi}} e^{-z_i^2/2} dz_i$$

□

The procedure for sampling from a correlated set of normals $\sim \mathcal{N}(\mu_i, \sigma_i^2)$ is then evident. We generate a set of uncorrelated unit normals $z_i \sim \mathcal{N}(0, 1)$, and apply Cholesky decomposition to generate the corresponding set of correlated unit normals y_i. As z_i are uncorrelated, the probability that $\mathbf{z} < \mathbf{Z}$ is just $\prod_i \mathbb{P}(z_i < Z_i)$. Thus the probability that the Cholesky generated $y_i < Y_i$ is:

$$\prod_i \mathbb{P}(z_i < (\mathbf{Q}^{-1}\mathbf{Y})_i) = \Phi(\mathbf{Y}) = \Phi(\mathbf{X})$$

where we map back to the $\mathcal{N}(\mu_i, \sigma_i^2)$ normals x_i via $x_i = \sigma_i y_i + \mu_i$. The procedure will thus generate a scatter of x_i with the correct cdf, and hence sample the multivariate distribution correctly.   □

(2) Recall that for a real valued square matrix $\mathbf{M}$ to be positive semi-definite, then for any non-zero real valued vectors $\mathbf{z}$, we must have $\mathbf{z}^T\mathbf{M}\mathbf{z} \geq 0$. Using eigenvalue decomposition $\mathbf{M} = \mathbf{Q}^T\mathbf{\Lambda}\mathbf{Q}$, where $\mathbf{Q}\mathbf{Q}^T = \mathbf{I}$ and $\mathbf{\Lambda} = \text{diag}(\alpha_i)$ we can see this implies $\sum y_i^2\alpha_i^2 \geq 0$ where $\mathbf{y} = \mathbf{Q}\mathbf{z}$. As this must be true for any z, we must have $\alpha_i \geq 0$ for each α_i. For a non-zero eigenvector $\mathbf{x}$, the eigenvalue relationship

$\mathbf{Mx} = \alpha\mathbf{x}$ implies $|\mathbf{M} - \alpha\mathbf{I}| = 0$. We need to solve for the eigenvalues of $\rho_{i,j} = \lambda_i\lambda_j$ for $i \neq j$ and 1 otherwise. It's helpful to write this as $A_{ij} + \lambda_i\lambda_j$ where $A_{ij} = \text{diag}(1 - \lambda_i^2)$. We can the make use of the *matrix determinant lemma*:

$$|\mathbf{A} + \mathbf{u}\mathbf{v}^T| = |\mathbf{A}|(1 + \mathbf{v}^T\mathbf{A}^{-1}\mathbf{u})$$

where both $\mathbf{u}$ and $\mathbf{v}$ are of length n, and $\mathbf{A}$ is an $n \times n$ real valued matrix.

Proof. Consider the product:

$$\begin{pmatrix} \mathbf{I} & 0 \\ \mathbf{v}^T & 1 \end{pmatrix} \begin{pmatrix} \mathbf{I} + \mathbf{u}\mathbf{v}^T & \mathbf{u} \\ 0 & 1 \end{pmatrix} \begin{pmatrix} \mathbf{I} & 0 \\ -\mathbf{v}^T & 1 \end{pmatrix}$$
$$= \begin{pmatrix} \mathbf{I} & \mathbf{u} \\ 0 & 1 + \mathbf{v}^T\mathbf{u} \end{pmatrix}$$

So that as the first and third matrix are unit determinant we have:

$$|\mathbf{I} + \mathbf{u}\mathbf{v}^T| = 1 + \mathbf{v}^T\mathbf{u}$$

Then, as $|\mathbf{A} + \mathbf{u}\mathbf{v}^T| = |\mathbf{A}||\mathbf{I} + \mathbf{A}^{-1}\mathbf{u}\mathbf{v}^T|$, from (A.47) we have $|\mathbf{A} + \mathbf{u}\mathbf{v}^T| = |\mathbf{A}|(1 + \mathbf{v}^T\mathbf{A}^{-1}\mathbf{u})$. $\qquad\square$

Denoting $\lambda_i = \lambda_i$, we thus have, for $\mathbf{C} = \mathbf{A} - \alpha\mathbf{I} + \lambda\lambda^T = \rho - \alpha\mathbf{I}$:

$$|\mathbf{C}| = |\mathbf{A} - \alpha\mathbf{I}|(1 + \lambda^T(\mathbf{A} - \alpha\mathbf{I})^{-1}\lambda^T)$$
$$= \prod_i (1 - \lambda_i^2 - \alpha)\left(1 + \sum_i \frac{\lambda_i^2}{1 - \lambda_i^2 - \alpha}\right) \qquad (A.47)$$

Note further that the eigenvalues of a symmetric real valued matrix (or in general a Hermitian matrix $\mathbf{A} = \mathbf{A}^\dagger$) are real, we have that the condition for ρ_{ij} to be positive semidefinite is simply that there exists no real valued solution α to $|\mathbf{C}| = 0$ where $\alpha < 0$. As $-1 \leq \lambda_i \leq 1$, this is evident from (A.47). We thus know that all eigenvalues of ρ_{ij} must be real and greater than or equal to zero, completing the proof that ρ_{ij} is positive semi-definite. $\qquad\square$

(3) From (A.43), we can write for the bivariate normal distribution:

$$\phi(z_1, z_2) = \frac{1}{2\pi\sigma_1\sigma_2\sqrt{1-\rho^2}} \exp\left[-\frac{1}{2}\left(\frac{z_1^2\sigma_2^2 + z_2^2\sigma_1^2 - 2\rho\sigma_1\sigma_2 z_1 z_2}{\sigma_1^2\sigma_2^2(1-\rho^2)}\right)\right]$$

where $z_i = x_i - \mu_i$. For a given value φ of $\phi(z_1, z_2)$, we have:

$$\frac{z_1^2}{\sigma_1^2} + \frac{z_2^2}{\sigma_2^2} - \frac{2\rho z_1 z_2}{\sigma_1 \sigma_2} = k$$

where

$$k = 2(\rho^2 - 1) \log \left[2\pi \sigma_1 \sigma_2 \sqrt{1 - \rho^2} \varphi \right]$$

Transforming to $y_i = z_i/\sigma_i$, we have:

$$y_1^2 + y_2^2 - 2\rho y_1 y_2 = k \tag{A.48}$$

i.e. $\mathbf{y}^T \mathbf{R} \mathbf{y} = k$ where

$$\mathbf{R} = \begin{pmatrix} 1 & -\rho \\ -\rho & 1 \end{pmatrix}$$

The eigenvalues λ_i, of $\mathbf{R}$ are given by $(1 - \lambda^2) = \rho^2$, giving $\lambda = 1 \pm \rho$. The corresponding eigenvalue decomposition is then:

$$\mathbf{R} = \begin{pmatrix} 1/\sqrt{2} & 1/\sqrt{2} \\ -1/\sqrt{2} & 1/\sqrt{2} \end{pmatrix} \begin{pmatrix} 1 + \rho & 0 \\ 0 & 1 - \rho \end{pmatrix} \begin{pmatrix} 1/\sqrt{2} & -1/\sqrt{2} \\ 1/\sqrt{2} & 1/\sqrt{2} \end{pmatrix}$$

so that writing $\alpha_1 = (y_1 - y_2)/\sqrt{2}$ and $\alpha_2 = (y_1 + y_2)/\sqrt{2}$ we can rewrite (A.48) as:

$$\frac{\alpha_1^2}{c_1^2} + \frac{\alpha_2^2}{c_2^2} = 1$$

with $c_1 = \sqrt{k/(1 + \rho)}$ and $c_2 = \sqrt{k/(1 - \rho)}$. This is simply an ellipse in (y_1, y_2) along axes $y_1 = y_2$ and $y_1 = -y_2$, with the eccentricity given by $e = \sqrt{1 - c_2^2/c_1^2} = \sqrt{2\rho/(\rho - 1)}$. Note that, for $\rho \to 1$, we obtain the solution $y_1 = y_2$, and likewise for $\rho \to -1$, $y_1 = -y_2$, regardless of φ, as we might expect from the perfectly correlated and anticorrelated limits, where x_1 and x_2 become deterministically related.

(4) We have for the $n + 1$-dimensional factor copula:

$$C(u_1, \ldots, u_n) = \int_{-\infty}^{\infty} \prod_{i=1,n} \Phi \left(\frac{-\lambda_i V + \Phi^{-1}(u_1)}{\sqrt{1 - \lambda_i^2}} \right) \phi(V) dV$$

Let's begin by expanding the cdf's:

$$C(u_1, \ldots, u_n) = \frac{1}{(2\pi)^{n/2} \prod_i \sqrt{1 - \lambda_i^2}}$$

$$\times \int_{-\infty}^{\infty} \prod_{i=1,n} \int_{-\infty}^{Y_i} \phi\left(\frac{y_i - \lambda_i V}{\sqrt{1 - \lambda_i^2}}\right) dy_i \phi(V) dV$$

where $Y_i = \Phi^{-1}(u_1)$. Expanding the inner integrals over y_i and switching inner and outer integrals, we have:

$$C(u_1, \ldots, u_n) = \frac{1}{(2\pi)^{n/2} \prod_i \sqrt{1 - \lambda_i^2}} \prod_{i=1,n} \int_{-\infty}^{Y_i} \exp\left[-\frac{y_i^2}{2(1 - \lambda_i^2)}\right] dy_i$$

$$\times \int_{-\infty}^{\infty} \exp\left[-\frac{1}{2}\left[V^2\left(1 + \sum_i \frac{\lambda_i^2}{1 - \lambda_i^2}\right)\right.\right.$$

$$\left.\left. -2V \sum_i \frac{y_i \lambda_i}{1 - \lambda_i^2}\right]\right] dV \tag{A.49}$$

We can rewrite the V integrand as:

$$\exp\left[-\frac{1}{2}\left(1 + \sum_i \frac{\lambda_i^2}{1 - \lambda_i^2}\right)\left(V - \sum_i \frac{y_i \lambda_i/(1 - \lambda_i^2)}{1 + \sum_j \lambda_j^2/(1 - \lambda_j^2)}\right)^2\right]$$

$$\times \exp\left[\frac{1}{2}\left(1 + \sum_i \frac{\lambda_i^2}{1 - \lambda_i^2}\right)\left(\sum_i \frac{y_i \lambda_i/(1 - \lambda_i^2)}{1 + \sum_j \lambda_j^2/(1 - \lambda_j^2)}\right)^2\right] \tag{A.50}$$

Making use of the matrix determinant lemma again, we have for the determinant of ρ_{ij}:

$$|\rho| = \prod_i (1 - \lambda_i^2)\left(1 + \sum_i \frac{\lambda_i^2}{1 - \lambda_i^2}\right)$$

which together with (A.50) allows us to write (A.49):

398   *The Value of Uncertainty: Dealing with Risk in the Equity Derivatives Market*

$$\frac{1}{(2\pi)^{n/2}|\rho|^{1/2}} \int_{-\infty}^{Y_1} \cdots \int_{-\infty}^{Y_n} dy_1 \ldots dy_n \prod_i \exp\left[-\frac{y_i^2}{2(1-\lambda_i^2)}\right]$$

$$\times \exp\left[\frac{\prod_i(1-\lambda_i^2)}{2|\rho|}\left(\sum_i \frac{y_i\lambda_i}{1-\lambda_i^2}\right)^2\right]$$

$$= \frac{1}{(2\pi)^{n/2}|\rho|^{1/2}} \int_{-\infty}^{Y_1} \cdots \int_{-\infty}^{Y_n} dy_1 \ldots dy_n \exp\left[\sum_{i,j} y_i y_j c_{ij}\right]$$

Concentrating on the y_i^2 terms:

$$c_{ii} = \frac{1}{2\prod_i(1-\lambda_i^2)|\rho|}\left[\lambda_i^2 \prod_{i\neq j}(1-\lambda_j^2)^2\right.$$

$$\left. - |\rho|\prod_{i\neq j}(1-\lambda_j^2)\right]$$

$$= \frac{1}{2|\rho|}\prod_{i\neq j}(1-\lambda_j^2)\left(-1-\sum_{i\neq j}\frac{\lambda_j^2}{1-\lambda_j^2}\right)$$

$$= -\frac{1}{2|\rho|}\widetilde{C}_{ii}$$

where $\widetilde{C}_{ij}$ is the matrix of co-factors of ρ_{ij}. Likewise, for the cross terms:

$$c_{ij} = \frac{1}{2|\rho|\prod_m(1-\lambda_m^2)}\lambda_i\lambda_j \prod_{k\neq i}(1-\lambda_k^2)\prod_{l\neq j}(1-\lambda_l^2)$$

$$= \frac{1}{2|\rho|(1-\lambda_i^2)}\lambda_i\lambda_j \prod_{l\neq j}(1-\lambda_l^2)$$

$$= \frac{1}{2|\rho|}\lambda_i\lambda_j \prod_{l\neq i\neq j}(1-\lambda_l^2)$$

$$= -\frac{\widetilde{C}_{ij}}{2|\rho|}$$

where the last equality can be seen by inspection of the determinant comprising the (i,j)-th co-factor element. Putting this all together we end up with:

$$\sum_{i,j} y_i y_j c_{ij} = -\frac{1}{2} \mathbf{y}^T \rho^{-1} \mathbf{y}$$

giving:

$$C(u_1, \ldots, u_n) = \frac{1}{(2\pi)^{n/2} |\rho|^{1/2}} \int_{-\infty}^{Y_1} \ldots$$
$$\int_{-\infty}^{Y_n} dy_1 \ldots dy_n \exp\left[-\frac{1}{2} \mathbf{y}^T \rho^{-1} \mathbf{y}\right]$$

as per the n-dimensional Gaussian copula with correlation matrix ρ_{ij}.
□

Rewriting the $n+1$-dimensional factor copula correlation as:

$$\Sigma = \begin{pmatrix} 1 & \lambda_0 \lambda_1 & \lambda_0 \lambda_2 & \ldots & \lambda_0 \lambda_n \\ \lambda_1 \lambda_0 & 1 & \lambda_1 \lambda_2 & \ldots & \lambda_1 \lambda_n \\ \vdots & \vdots & \vdots & \vdots & \vdots \\ \lambda_n \lambda_0 & \lambda_n \lambda_1 & \lambda_n \lambda_2 & \ldots & 1 \end{pmatrix}$$

with $\lambda_0 = 1$, and using (A.47), the eigenvalue problem reduces to $|\mathbf{C}| = 0$ where:

$$|\mathbf{C}| = \prod_{i=1}^n (1 - \lambda_i^2 - \alpha) \left[1 - \alpha - \alpha \sum_{i=1}^n \frac{\lambda_i^2}{1 - \lambda_i^2 - \alpha} \right]$$

Again, we see that for $\alpha < 0$ and $\lambda_i^2 < 1$, $|\mathbf{C}| > 0$, so that any eigenvalue solution must be real and non-negative, i.e Σ is positive semi-definite. □

(5) We have for the factor loading function of equation ((8.1)):

$$\lambda_i(V_t, t) = \text{sgn}(\lambda_i(0,0)) \frac{1 - \tanh(\sigma V_t - \bar{\mu}(t)t - \alpha_i)}{2}$$

Applying Itō, we have:

$$d\lambda_i = \frac{\partial \lambda_i}{\partial t} dt + \frac{\partial \lambda_i}{\partial V} dV + \frac{1}{2} \frac{\partial^2 \lambda_i}{\partial V^2} dV^2$$

Denoting $x = 1 - \tanh(\sigma V_t - \bar{\mu}(t)t - \alpha_i)$ and $s = \text{sgn}(\lambda_i(0,0))$ we have:

$$\frac{\partial \lambda_i}{\partial t} = \frac{1}{2} s\mu(t)\text{sech}^2(x)$$
$$\frac{\partial \lambda_i}{\partial V} = -\frac{1}{2} s\sigma \text{sech}^2(x)$$
$$\frac{\partial^2 \lambda_i}{\partial V^2} = s\sigma^2 \text{sech}^2(x) \tanh(x)$$

So, using $\tanh(x) = 1 - 2\lambda_i s$, and $\operatorname{sech}^2(x) = 1 - \tanh^2(x)$, we have:

$$d\lambda_i = \frac{1}{2}\operatorname{sech}^2(x)s\left[(\mu(t)dt - \sigma dV_t) + \sigma^2 \tanh(x)dt\right]$$

$$= 2\lambda(s - \lambda)\left[\left(\mu(t) + \left(\frac{1}{2} - s\lambda\right)2\sigma^2\right)dt - \sigma dV_t\right]$$

We thus have:

$$\frac{d\lambda_i}{2\lambda_i(1 - \lambda_i)} = \left[\mu + 2\sigma^2\left(\frac{1}{2} - \lambda_i\right)\right]dt - \sigma dV_t; \ \lambda_i(0,0) \geq 0$$

$$\frac{d\lambda_i}{2\lambda_i(1 + \lambda_i)} = \left[-\mu - 2\sigma^2\left(\frac{1}{2} + \lambda_i\right)\right]dt + \sigma dV_t; \ \lambda_i(0,0) < 0$$

as required for the case where $\lambda_i(0,0) \geq 0$. $\qquad\square$

(Note that the corresponding collapse of drift and vol occurs for $\lambda_- = 0, -1$, with a mean reversion level of -1/2.)

(6) Consider the weighted sum of normally distributed variables $y = \sum_i \alpha_i x_i$ where $x_i \sim \mathcal{N}(\mu_i, \sigma_i^2)$. The characteristic function for y is given by:

$$f(t) = \int e^{-ity}\phi(x_1, \ldots, x_n)dx_1 \ldots dx_n$$

where $\phi(x_1, \ldots, x_n)$ is the n-dimensional joint Gaussian distribution given in (A.43). Again, writing $z_i = (x_i - \mu_i)/\sigma_i$, we have:

$$f(t) = \int e^{-it\sum_i \alpha_i(\sigma_i z_i + \mu_i)}\phi'(z_1, \ldots, z_n)dz_1 \ldots dz_n$$

$$= e^{-it\mu_y} \int e^{-it\sum_i \alpha_i \sigma_i z_i}\phi'(z_1, \ldots, z_n)dz_1 \ldots dz_n$$

$$\mu_y = \sum_i \alpha_i\mu_i$$

where

$$\phi'(z_1, \ldots, z_n) = \frac{1}{(2\pi)^{n/2}|\mathbf{R}|^{1/2}}\exp\left[-\frac{1}{2}\mathbf{z}^T\mathbf{R}^{-1}\mathbf{z}\right]$$

We now employ Cholesky decomposition $z_i = \sum_k a_{ik}z_k'$ once more to give:

$$f(t) = e^{-it\mu_y} \int e^{-it \sum_i \sum_k \alpha_i \sigma_i a_{ik} z'_k} \phi'(z'_1, \ldots, z'_n) dz'_1 \ldots dz'_n$$

Where $\phi'(z'_1, \ldots, z'_n) = \prod_i n(z'_i)$, with $n(x)$ the standard normal. Rearranging the sum in the exponent, we can rewrite $f(t)$ as:

$$f(t) = e^{-it\mu_y} \prod_i \int e^{-it z'_i \tilde{\sigma}_i} n(z'_i) dz'_i$$

where $\tilde{\sigma}_i = \sum_j a_{ji} \sigma_j \alpha_j$. We have for the characteristic function of an $\mathcal{N}(\mu, \sigma^2)$ distributed variable:

$$g(t, \mu, \sigma) = e^{-it\mu} \frac{1}{\sqrt{2\pi}} \int e^{-it\sigma} e^{-z^2/2} dz$$
$$= e^{-it\mu - t^2\sigma^2/2}$$

We have, likewise for $f(t)$:

$$f(t) = e^{-it\mu_y - t^2 \sigma_y^2/2}$$

where

$$\mu_y = \sum_i \alpha_i \mu_i$$
$$\sigma_y^2 = \sum_i \tilde{\sigma}_i^2 = \sum_i \sum_{j,k} \sigma_j \alpha_j a_{ji} a_{ki} \sigma_k \alpha_k = \sum_{j,k} \alpha_j \alpha_k \sigma_j \sigma_j \rho_{j,k}$$
$$= \sum_{i,j} \rho_{i,j} \alpha_i \alpha_j \sigma_i \sigma_j$$

$y = \sum_i \alpha_i x_i$ is thus normally distributed with mean $\alpha_i \mu_i$ and variance $\sum_{i,j} \rho_{i,j} \alpha_i \alpha_j \sigma_i \sigma_j$, as required. $\qquad\square$

(7) Consider the outperformance payoff

$$P(S_1, S_2) = \max(S_1, S_2)$$

We have for the value V_0 at time $t = 0$:

$$V_0 = P(0, T) E_\mathbb{T} [\max(S_1(T), S_2(T))]$$

where $E_\mathbb{T}$ denotes expectation in the $\mathbb{T}$-forward measure. Let us now define the change of measure $d\mathbb{T}/d\mathbb{S}_2$ and the associated process:

$$\zeta_t = E_{\mathbb{S}_2}\left[\frac{d\mathbb{T}}{d\mathbb{S}_2}\middle|\mathcal{F}_t\right] = \frac{P(t,T)}{S_2(t)}$$

Then we have, by change of measure:

$$E_{\mathbb{T}}\left[\max(S_1(T), S_2(T))\right] = E_{\mathbb{S}_2}\left[\max(S_1(T), S_2(T))\zeta_T\right]\zeta_0^{-1}$$
$$= \frac{E_{\mathbb{S}_2}\left[\max\left(\frac{S_1(T)}{S_2(T)}, 1\right)\right]}{P(0,T)/S_2(0)}$$

giving:

$$V_0 = S_2(0)E_{\mathbb{S}_2}\left[\max\left(\frac{S_1(T)}{S_2(T)}, 1\right)\right] \qquad (A.51)$$

But we know, *in the absence of* dividends, that both S_1 and S_2 are tradable, hence:

$$S_1(0) = P(0,T)E_{\mathbb{T}}\left[S_1(T)\right] = S_2(0)E_{\mathbb{S}_2}\left[\frac{S_1(T)}{S_2(T)}\right]$$

giving $E_{\mathbb{S}_2}\left[S_1(T)/S_2(T)\right] = S_1(0)/S_2(0)$, i.e. S_1/S_2 is a martingale in the $\mathbb{S}_2$ measure. If we then also have that S_1 and S_2 follow geometric Brownian motions with constant volatility σ_1 and σ_2 respectively, that, in the $\mathbb{S}_2$ measure:

$$d[\log(S_1/S_2)] = -\frac{\sigma^2}{2}dt + \sigma dW_t$$

where $E_{\mathbb{S}_2}[dW_t] = 0$ and $\sigma^2 = \sigma_1^2 + \sigma_2^2 - 2\rho\sigma_1\sigma_2$. Integrating, we have $S_1(T)/S_2(T) = S_1(0)/S_2(0)\exp\left[-\sigma^2 T/2 + \sigma W\right]$, which together with (A.51) gives:

$$V_0 = S_2(0)\left[\frac{S_1(0)}{S_2(0)}N(d_1) - N(d_2)\right]$$
$$= S_1(0)N(d_1) - S_2(0)N(d_2)$$
$$= P(0,T)\left[F_1 N(d_1) - F_2 N(d_2)\right]$$

where

$$d_{1,2} = \frac{\log(F_1/F_2)}{\sigma\sqrt{T}} \pm \frac{\sigma\sqrt{T}}{2}$$
$$\sigma^2 = \sigma_1^2 + \sigma_2^2 - 2\rho\sigma_1\sigma_2$$
$$F_1 = E_{\mathbb{T}}\left[S_1(T)\right]$$
$$F_2 = E_{\mathbb{T}}\left[S_2(T)\right]$$

$\square$

(8) We have, from integration by parts, that:

$$\int_0^{S^*} f''(K)\,(K - S_T, 0)^+\, dK$$
$$= [f'(S^*)(S^* - S_T) - (f(S^*) - f(S_T))]\,\mathbf{1}(S^* - S_T) \quad \text{(A.52)}$$

and

$$\int_{S^*}^{\infty} f''(K)\,(S_T - K, 0)^+\, dK$$
$$= [f'(S^*)(S^* - S_T) - (f(S^*) - f(S_T))]\,\mathbf{1}(S_T - S^*) \quad \text{(A.53)}$$

so that, combining (A.52) and (A.53) we have:

$$\int_0^{S^*} f''(K)\,(K - S_T, 0)^+\, dK$$
$$+ \int_{S^*}^{\infty} f''(K)\,(S_T - K, 0)^+\, dK = f'(S^*)(S^* - S_T) - (f(S^*) - f(S_T))$$

giving

$$f(S_T) = f(S^*) + f'(S^*)(S_T - S^*)$$
$$+ \int_0^{S^*} f''(K)\,(K - S_T, 0)^+\, dK + \int_{S^*}^{\infty} f''(K)\,(S_T - K, 0)^+\, dK$$

(A derivation of this formula can also be found in Lipton [Lipton (2001)].) Taking $S^* = F_T$ we can write:

$$E_{\mathbb{T}}[f(S_T)] = f(F_T) + \int_0^{F_T} f''(K)\widetilde{P}(K,T)dK + \int_{F_T}^{\infty} f''(K)\widetilde{C}(K,T)dK$$

using $E_{\mathbb{T}}[S_T] = F_T$, and $\widetilde{C}(K,T)$ and $\widetilde{P}(K,T)$ the undiscounted call and put prices, as always. We can now write for the replication strategy of the contract $f(S_T) = \log^2(S_T/F_T)$:

$$V(T) = E_{\mathbb{T}}[f(S_T)]$$
$$= 2\int_0^{F_T} \frac{1}{K^2}\left[1 - \log\left(\frac{K}{F_T}\right)\right]\widetilde{P}(K,T)dK$$
$$+ 2\int_{F_T}^{\infty} \frac{1}{K^2}\left[1 - \log\left(\frac{K}{F_T}\right)\right]\widetilde{C}(K,T)dK$$

$$\text{(A.54)}$$

Transforming to $z = \log(K/F_T)$, we can rewrite (A.54) as:

$$V(T) = 2 \left[\int_{-\infty}^{0} (1-z)\tilde{p}(z,T)e^{-z}dz + \int_{0}^{\infty} (1-z)\tilde{c}(z,T)e^{-z}dz \right]$$

where $\tilde{p} = \tilde{P}/F_T$ and $\tilde{c} = \tilde{C}/F_T$. Now let us consider a vol slice in z, given by $\hat{\sigma}(z) = \hat{\sigma}_0 - \alpha z$. Then to first order, using $\partial\tilde{p}(z,T)/\partial\hat{\sigma} = \partial\tilde{c}(z,T)/\partial\hat{\sigma} = \sqrt{T}n(d_1)$, we have:

$$V(T) = V_0(T) + 2\alpha\sqrt{T} \left[\int_{-\infty}^{\infty} z(z-1)n(d_1(\hat{\sigma}_0))e^{-z}dz \right] \qquad (A.55)$$

where $V_0(T)$ is the value of the contract priced with flat vol $\hat{\sigma}_0$. Using $d_1(\hat{\sigma}_0) = -z/\hat{\sigma}_0\sqrt{T} + \hat{\sigma}_0\sqrt{T}/2$, we can solve (A.55) to give:

$$V(T) = V_0(T) + \alpha\hat{\sigma}_0^3 T^2 \left[3 + \frac{\hat{\sigma}_0^2 T}{2} \right]$$

So, for $\alpha > 0$ on the implied geometric basket volatility slice, to first order the covariance swap with correlation skew will always be more expensive than that priced with static correlation. $\square$

Bibliography

Akgiray, V. and Booth, G. (1986). Stock price with discontinuous time paths: an empirical examination, *Financial Review* **21**, pp. 163–184.

Albanese, C. and Chen, O. (2005). Pricing equity default swaps, *Risk* **18**, pp. 83–87.

Alexander, C. and Nogeira, L. (2004). Stochastic local volatility, in *Second IASTED International Conference*, pp. 136–141.

Allen, S. (2003). *Financial Risk Management: a practitioner's guide to managing market and credit risk* (Wiley Finance, ISBN 978-0471219774).

Altman, E., Resti, A. and Sironi, A. (2002). The link between default and recovery rates: effects on the procyclicality of regulatory capital ratios, Tech. rep., Bank for International Settlements, http://www.bis.org/publ/work113.htm.

Andersen, L. (2007). Efficient simulation of the Heston stochastic volatility model, Tech. rep., Bank of America Securities, http://papers.ssrn.com/sol3/papers.cfm?abstract_id=946405.

Andersen, L. and Andreasen, J. (2000). Jump-diffusion processes: volatility smile fitting and numerical methods for option pricing, *Review of Derivatives Research* **4**, pp. 231–262.

Andersen, L. and Brotherton-Ratcliffe, R. (2001). Extended Libor market models with stochastic volatility, Tech. rep., Gen Re Securities, http://papers.ssrn.com/sol3/papers.cfm?abstrat_id=294853.

Andersen, L. and Buffum, D. (2002). Calibration and implementation of convertible bond models, Tech. rep., Bank of America Securities.

Andersen, L. and Piterbarg, V. (2010). *Interest Rate Modeling* (Atlantic Financial Press, ISBN 978-0984422104).

Arvanitis, A. and Gregory, J. (2003). *Credit: The Complete Guide to Pricing, Hedging and Risk Management* (Risk Books, ISBN 978-1899332731).

Ayache, E., Forsyth, P. and Vetzal, K. (2003). The valuation of convertible bonds with credit risk, Tech. rep., University of Waterloo.

Bakshi, G., Cao, C. and Chen, Z. (1997). Empirical performance of alternative option pricing models, *Journal of Finance* **52**, pp. 2003–2049.

Ball, C. and Torous, W. (1985). On jumps in common stock prices and their impact on call option pricing, *Journal of Finance* **40**, pp. 155–173.

Bates, D. (1991). The crash of 87: was it expected? the evidence from options markets, *Journal of Finance* **46**, pp. 1009–1044.

Bates, D. (1996a). Jumps and stochastic volatility: exchange rate processes implicit in deutschmark options, *Review of Financial Studies* **9**, pp. 69–108.

Bates, D. S. (1996b). *Testing option pricing models, Statistical Methods in Finance*, Vol. 14 (North Holland, Amsterdam), pp. 567–611.

Baumol, W., Malkiel, B. and Quandt, R. (1966). The valuation of convertible securities, *Quarterly Journal of Economics* **80**, pp. 48–59.

Baxter, M. and Rennie, A. (1997). *Financial calculus* (Cambridge University Press, ISBN 0-521-55289-3).

Beckers, S. (1981). A note on estimating the parameters of the diffusion-jump model of stock returns, *Journal of Financial and Quantitative Analysis* **16**, pp. 127–140.

Bergomi, L. (2004). Smile dynamics, *Risk* **September**, pp. 117–123.

Bergomi, L. (2005). Smile dynamics ii, *Risk* **October**, pp. 67–73.

Bergomi, L. (2009). Smile dynamics iv, *Risk* **December**, pp. 94–100.

Black, F. (1995). Interest rates as options, *Journal of Finance* **50**, pp. 1371–1376.

Black, F. and Cox, J. (1976). Valuing corporate securities: some effects of bond indenture provisions, *Journal of Finance* **31**, pp. 351–367.

Black, F. and Karasinski, P. (1991). Bond and option pricing when short rates are lognormal, *Financial Analysts Journal* **47**, pp. 52–59.

Black, F. and Scholes, M. (1973). The pricing of options and corporate liabilities, *Journal of Political Economy* **81**, pp. 637–654.

Blees, W. (2008). The creative hedge, `http://www.risk.net/risk-magazine/feature/1498441/the-creative-hedge`.

Bollerslev, T. (1986). Generalized autoregressive conditional heteroskedasticity, *Journal of Econometrics* **31**, pp. 307–327.

Bos, M. and Vandermark, S. (2002). Finessing fixed dividends, *Risk* **September**, pp. 157–158.

Bos, R., Gairat, A. and Shepeleva, A. (2003). Dealing with discrete dividends, *Risk* **January**, pp. 109–112.

Bossu, S. (2005). Arbitrage pricing of equity correlation swaps, Tech. rep., Equity Derivatives Group, JP Morgan.

Brace, A., Gatarek, D. and Musiela, M. (1997). The market model of interest rate dynamics, *Mathematical Finance* **7**, pp. 127–155.

Brennan, M. and Schwartz, E. (1977). Convertible bonds: valuation and optimal strategies for call and conversion, *Journal of Finance* **32**, pp. 1699–1715.

Brigo, D. and Mercurio, F. (2006). *Interest rate models - theory and practice, with smile, inflation and credit* (Springer Verlag, ISBN 978-3540221494).

Buehler, H. (2007). Volatility and dividends, Tech. rep., Institut fur Mathematik, TU Berlin.

Buehler, H., Dhouibi, A. and Sluys, D. (2010). Stochastic proportional dividends, Tech. rep., JP Morgan.

Cameron, M. (2010). Surviving skew, http://www.risk.net/risk-magazine/feature/1720194/surviving-skew.

Carr, P. and Chou, A. (1997). Hedging complex barrier options, Tech. rep., New York University and Enuvis Inc.

Carr, P., Geman, H., Madan, D. and Yor, M. (2002). The fine structure of asset returns: an empirical investigation, *Journal of Business* **75**, pp. 305–332.

Carr, P. and Lee, R. (2010). Hedging variance options on continuous semimartingales, *Finance and Stochastics* **14**, pp. 179–207.

Carr, P. and Madan, D. (1999). Introducing the covariance swap, *Risk* **February**, pp. 47–51.

Carr, P. and Wu, L. (2003). The finite moment log stable process and option pricing, *Journal of Finance* **58**, 2, pp. 753–778.

Carverhill, A. (1994). When is the short rate Markovian? *Mathematical Finance* **4**, pp. 305–312.

Castagna, A. and Mercurio, F. (2007). The vanna-volga method for implied volatilities, *Risk* **January**, pp. 106–111.

Chen, N. and Kou, S. (2009). Credit spreads, optimal capital structure, and implied volatility with endogenous default and jump risk, *Mathematical Finance* **19**, pp. 343–378.

Christie, D. (2002). Accrued interest and yield calculations and determination of holiday calendars, Tech. rep., SWX Swiss Exchange.

Cont, R. and Fonseca, J. (2002). Dynamics of implied volatility surfaces, *Quantitative Finance* **2**, pp. 45–60.

Cont, R., Fonseca, J. and Durrleman, V. (2002). Stochastic models of implied volatility surfaces, *Economic Notes* **31**, pp. 361–377.

Cox, J., Ingersoll, J. and Ross, S. (1985). A theory of the term structure of interest rates, *Econometrica* **53**, pp. 385–407.

Cox, J. C. (1996). The constant elasticity of variance option pricing model, *Journal of Portfolio Management* **22**, pp. 15–17.

Crosby, J. (2011). Variance derivatives and estimating realised variance from high-frequency data, Tech. rep., UBS Investment Bank Ltd and Glasgow University.

Davis, M. and Lischka, F. (1999). Convertible bonds with market risk and credit risk, Tech. rep., Tokyo-Mitsubishi International.

Davydov, D. and Linetsky, V. (2001). Pricing and hedging path dependent options under the cev process, *Management Science* **47**, pp. 949–965.

Dempster, A., Laird, N. and Rubin, D. (1977). Maximum likelihood from incomplete data via the em algorithm, *Journal of the Royal Statistical Society* **39**, pp. 1–38.

Derman, E. (1994). Valuing convertible bonds as derivatives, Tech. rep., Goldman Sachs.

Derman, E. (1999a). More than you ever wanted to know about volatility swaps, *The Journal of Derivatives* **6-4**, pp. 9–32.

Derman, E. (1999b). When you cannot hedge continuously: the corrections of Black–Scholes, *Risk* **1**, pp. 82–85.

Derman, E., Ergener, D. and Kani, I. (1994). Static options replication, Tech. rep., Goldman Sachs Quantitative Strategies Research Notes.

Derman, E. and Kani, I. (1994). The volatility smile and its implied tree, *Risk* **7**, 2, pp. 32–39, 139–145.

Derman, E. and Kani, I. (1996). The ins and outs of barrier options: part 1, *Derivatives Quarterly* **Winter**, pp. 55–67.

Derman, E. and Kani, I. (1998). Stochastic implied trees: arbitrage pricing with stochastic term and strike structure of volatility, *International Journal of Theoretical and Applied Finance* **1**, 1, pp. 61–110.

Driessen, J., Maenhout, P. and Vilkov, G. (2005). Option-implied correlations and the price of correlation risk, Tech. rep., Finance Group, University of Amsterdam and Finance Department, INSEAD.

Duffie, D. and Singleton, K. (1999). Modeling term structures of defaultable bonds, *The Review of Financial Studies* **12**, pp. 687–720.

Duncan, J., Randal, J. and Thomson, P. (2009). Fitting jump diffusion processes using the em algorithm, Tech. rep., Lane Cove, Australia and Victoria University of Wellington, New Zealand and Statistics Research Associates Ltd, New Zealand.

Dupire, B. (1994). Pricing with a smile, *Risk* **7**, 1, pp. 18–20.

Dupire, B. (2005). Lecture 11: Volatility expansion, http://www.math.nyu.edu/~benartzi/Slides11.ppt.

Engle, R. (1982). Autoregressive conditional heteroscedasticity with estimates of variance of United Kingdom inflation, *Econometrica* **50**, pp. 987–1008.

Engle, R. and Lee, G. J. (1999). A permanent and transitory component model of stock return volatility, in *Cointegration, Causality, and Forecasting: A Festschrift in Honor of Clive W. J. Granger* (Oxford University Press), pp. 475–497.

Engle, R. and Ng, V. (1993). Measuring and testing the impact of news on volatility, *Journal of Finance* **48**, pp. 1749–1778.

Eom, Y. H., Helwege, J. and Huang, J.-Z. (2004). Structural models of corporate bond pricing: an empirical analysis, *The Review of Financial Studies* **17**, pp. 499–544.

Eraker, B., Johannes, M. and Polson, N. (2000). The impact of jumps in volatility and returns, Tech. rep., University of Chicago and Columbia University.

Fama, E. (1965). The behaviour of stock market prices, *Journal of Business* **38**, pp. 34–105.

FASB (2008). Fas 157-3: Determining the fair value of a financial asset when the market for that asset is not active, Tech. rep., The Financial Accounting Standards Board.

Ferrarese, C. (2006). *A comparative analysis of correlation skew modeling techniques for CDO index tranches*, Master's thesis, King's College, London, United Kingdom.

Finkelstein, V. (2002). Assessing default probabilities from equity markets, Tech. rep., Goldman Sachs, http://www.creditgrades.com/resources/pdf/Finkelstein.pdf.

Frishling, V. (2002). A discrete question, *Risk* **January**, pp. 115–116.

Gatheral, J. (1999). The volatility skew: arbitrage constraints and asymptotic behaviour, Tech. rep., Merrill Lynch.

Gatheral, J. (2006). *The volatility surface: a practitioner's guide* (Wiley Finance, ISBN 978-0471792512).

Global Fixed Income Research (2010). Default, transition and recovery: 2009 annual global default study and rating transitions, Tech. rep., Standard & Poor's, http://www.standardandpoors.com/ratings/articles/en/us/?assetID=1245207201119.

Gurrieri, S., Nakabayashi, M. and Wong, T. (2010). Calibration methods of the Hull–White model, Tech. rep., Risk Management Department, Mizuho Securities.

Gyöngy, I. (1986). Mimicking the one-dimensional marginal distributions of processes having an ito differential, *Probability Theory and Related Fields* **71**, pp. 501–516.

Hagan, P., Kumar, D., Lesniewski, A. and Woodward, D. (2002). Managing smile risk, *Wilmott* **September**, pp. 84–108.

Hagan, P., Lesniewski, A. and Woodward, D. (1999). Equivalent black volatilities, *Applied Mathematical Finance* **6**, pp. 147–157.

Harrison, J. and Pliska, S. (1981). Martingales and stochastic integrals in the theory of continuous trading, *Stochastic Processes and their Applications* **11**, pp. 215–260.

He, C., Kennedy, J., Coleman, T., Forsyth, P., Li, Y. and Vetzal, K. (2005). Calibration and hedging under jump diffusion, Tech. rep., J.P. Morgan Securities Inc. and University of Waterloo, Canada and Cornell University, USA.

Heath, D., Jarrow, R. and Morton, A. (1987). Bond pricing and the term structure of interest rates: a new methodology, Tech. rep., Cornell University.

Henry-Labordere, P. (2009). Calibration of local stochastic volatility models to market smiles, *Risk* **September**, pp. 112–117.

Heston, S. and Nandi, S. (1997). A closed-form GARCH option pricing model, Tech. rep., Federal Reserve Bank of Atlanta.

Hull, J. (2008). *Options, futures and other derivatives* (Prentice–Hall, ISBN 978-0136015864).

Hull, J. and White, A. (1987). The pricing of assets with stochastic volatilities, *Journal of Finance* **42**, pp. 281–300.

Hull, J. and White, A. (1990). Pricing interest rate securities, *The Review of Financial Studies* **3**, pp. 574–592.

Hull, J. and White, A. (1995). The impact of default risk on the prices of options and other derivative securities, *Journal of Banking and Finance* **19**, pp. 299–322.

IMF (2009). International Monetary Fund, World Economic Outlook Database, http://www.imf.org/external/pubs/ft/weo/2009/02/weodata/index.aspx.

Ingersoll, J. (1977). A contingent-claims valuation of convertible securities, *Journal of Financial Economics* **4**, pp. 289–322.

ISDA (1998). EMU and market conventions: recent developments, .

ISDA (2009). ISDA market survey results 1987-present, http://www.isda.org/
    statistics/pdf/ISDA-Market-Survey-historical-data.pdf.

ISDA (2010). ISDA news, http://www.isda.org/newsletters/Issue6-2010/
    Issue6-2010mainframe.html.

Jackworth, J. C. and Rubinstein, M. (2001). Recovering stochastic processes from
    option prices, Tech. rep., London Business School.

Jackworth, J. C. and Rubinstein, M. (2003). Recovering probabilities and risk
    aversion from option prices and realized returns, Tech. rep., Universitat
    Konstanz, University of California at Berkeley.

James, J. and Webber, N. (2000). *Interest rate modeling* (Wiley Finance, ISBN
    0-471-97523-0).

Jamshidian, F. (1997). Libor and swap market models and measures, *Finance
    and stochastics* **1**, pp. 293–330.

Jarrow, R., Lando, D. and Turnbull, S. (1997). A Markov model for the term
    structure of credit risk spreads, *The Review of Financial Studies* **10**, pp.
    481–523.

Jarrow, R. and Turnbull, S. (1995). Pricing derivatives on financial securities
    subject to credit risk, *Journal of Finance* **50**, pp. 53–85.

Javaheri, A. (2005). *Inside Volatility Arbitrage* (Wiley Finance, ISBN 0-471-
    73387-3).

Jeffery, C. (2004). Reverse cliquets: end of the road? *Risk* **February**, pp. 20–22.

Jex, M., Henderson, R. and Wang, D. (1999). Pricing exotics under the smile,
    Risk **November**, pp. 72–75.

JPMorgan (2010). Callable Range Accrual Notes linked to six-month USD Li-
    bor   and
    the S&P500 Index due October 14, 2025, http://investor.shareholder.
    com/JPMorganChase/secfiling.cfm?filingID=891092-10-4171.

Kato, T. and Yoshiba, T. (2000). Model risk and its control, Tech. rep., The Bank
    of Tokyo-Mitsubishi and the Institute for Monetary and Economic Studies,
    Bank of Japan.

Kim, I. J., Ramaswamy, K. and Sundaresen, S. (1993). Does default risk in
    coupons affect the valuation of corporate bonds? A contingent claims
    model, *Financial Management* **22**, pp. 117–31.

Krekel, M. (2003). The pricing of Asian options on average spot with aver-
    age strike, Tech. rep., Fraunhofer ITWM, Department of Finance, Kaiser-
    lautern, Germany.

Kyprianou, A., Schoutens, W. and Wilmott, P. (2005). *Exotic option pricing and
    advanced Levy models* (John Wiley and Sons, ISBN 978-0470016848).

Langnau, A. (2010). A dynamic model for correlation, *Risk* **April**, pp. 74–78.

Lardy, J.-P. (2002). A simple model to assess default probabilities from eq-
    uity markets, Tech. rep., JP Morgan, http://www.creditgrades.com/
    resources/pdf/E2C_JPM_CDconference.pdf.

Lee, R. (2004). Implied volatility: statics, dynamics, and probabilistic interpre-
    tation, in *Recent Advances in Applied Probability* (Springer).

Leland, H. and Toft, K. B. (1996). Optimal capital structure, endogenous bankruptcy, and the term structure of credit spreads, *Journal of Finance* **51**, pp. 987–1019.

Leland, H. E. (1985). Option pricing and replication with transaction costs, *Journal of Finance* **5**, pp. 1283–1301.

Lesniewksi, A. (2008). The forward curve, Tech. rep., New York University, http://math.nyu.edu/~alberts/spring07/Lecture1.pdf.

Lewis, A. (2001). A simple option formula for general jump-diffusion and other exponential levy processes, Tech. rep., Envision Financial Systems and Optioncity.net.

Lintner, J. (1965). The valuation of risk assets and the selection of risky investments in stock portfolios and capital budgets, *Review of Economics and Statistics* **47**, pp. 13–37.

Lipton, A. (2000). Pricing and risk-managing exotics on assets with stochastic volatility, Tech. rep., Forex Product Development Group, Deutsche Bank.

Lipton, A. (2001). *Mathematical methods for foreign exchange* (World Scientific Press, ISBN 978-981-02-4823-9).

Lipton, A. (2002a). Assets with jumps, *Risk* **September**, pp. 149–153.

Lipton, A. (2002b). The vol smile problem, *Risk* **February**, pp. 61–65.

Lipton, A. and McGhee, W. (2002). Universal barriers, *Risk* **May**, pp. 81–85.

Lipton, A. and Rennie, A. (2011). *The Oxford handbook of credit derivatives* (Oxford University Press, ISBN 978-0-19-954678-7).

Lipton, A. and Sepp, A. (2009). Credit value adjustment for credit default swaps via the structural default model, *The Journal of Credit Risk* **5**, pp. 123–146.

Litterman, R. and Iben, T. (1991). Corporate bond valuation and the term structure of credit spreads, *The Journal of Management* **spring**, pp. 52–64.

Longstaff, F. and Schwartz, E. (1992). A two-factor interest rate model and contingent claims valuation, *The Journal of Fixed Income* **3**, pp. 16–23.

Longstaff, F. and Schwartz, E. (1995). A simple approach to valuing risky fixed and floating rate debt, *Journal of Finance* **3**, pp. 789–819.

Lyon, P. (2005). Mixed messages, *Risk* **June**, pp. 14–15.

Madan, D., Ren, Y. and Qian Qian, M. (2007). Calibrating and pricing with embedded local volatility models, *Risk* **September**, pp. 138–143.

Madan, D. and Unal, H. (1996). Pricing the risks of default, Tech. rep., The University of Maryland.

Mayle, J. (1993). *Standard securities calculation methods: fixed income securities formulas for price, yield and accrued interest* (SIFMA, ISBN 1-882936-01-9).

Merton, R. (1973). The theory of rational option pricing, *Journal of Finance* **4**, pp. 141–183.

Merton, R. (1974). On the pricing of corporate debt: the risk structure of interest rates, *Journal of Finance* **2**, pp. 449–471.

Merton, R. (1976). Option pricing when underlying stock returns are discontinuous, *Journal of Financial Economics* **3**, pp. 125–144.

Mikhailov, S. and Noegel, U. (2003). Heston's stochastic volatility model implementation, calibration and some extensions, *Wilmott magazine* **July**, pp. 74–79.

Miltersen, K., Sandermann, K. and Sondermann, D. (1997). Closed-form solutions for term structure derivatives with log-normal interest rates, *Journal of Finance* **52**, pp. 409–430.

Modigliani, F. and Pogue, G. (1974a). An introduction to risk and return, *Financial Analysts Journal* **March**, pp. 68–80.

Modigliani, F. and Pogue, G. (1974b). An introduction to risk and return, *Financial Analysts Journal* **May**, pp. 69–85.

Moody's, G. C. R. (2000). Moody's approach to evaluating distressed exchanges, Tech. rep., Moody's Investors Service, `http://www.moodyskmv.com/research/files/wp/distressed_exch.pdf`.

Mossin, J. (1966). Equilibrium in a capital asset market, *Econometrica* **34**, pp. 768–783.

Muromachi, Y. (1999). The growing recognition of credit risk in corporate and financial bond markets, Tech. rep., NLI Research Institute.

Musiela, M. and Rutkowski, M. (1997). *Martingale methods in financial modeling* (Springer, , ISBN 978-3540209669).

Naik, V. and Lee, M. (1990). General equilibrium pricing of options on the market portfolio with discontinuous returns, *Review of Financial Studies* **3**, pp. 493–521.

Nyborg, K. (1996). The use and pricing of convertible bonds, *Applied Mathematical Finance* **3**, pp. 167–190.

OCC (2011). Supervisory guidance on model risk management, Tech. rep., Office of the Comptroller of the Currency.

O'Kane, D. and Turnbull, S. (2003). Valuation of credit default swaps, Tech. rep., Lehman Brothers, `http://www.brokerbase.eu/credit-derivatives/cds.pdf`.

Overhaus, M. (2002). Himalaya options, *Risk* **March**, pp. 101–104.

Overhaus, M., Bermudez, A., Buehler, H., Ferraris, A., Jordinson, C. and Lamnouar, A. (2007). *Equity hybrid derivatives* (Wiley Finance, ISBN 978-0471770589).

Pengelly, M. (2008). Sunk by correlation, `http://www.risk.net/risk-magazine/feature/1497285/sunk-correlation`.

Pengelly, M. (2010). Banks pull out of PRDC market, `http://www.risk.net/risk-magazine/news/1589083/banks-pull-prdc-market`.

Pickard, D., Kempthorne, P. and Zakaria, A. (1986). Inference for jump diffusion processes, in *ASA Business and Economics Section*, pp. 107–111.

Piterbarg, V. (2003). A stochastic volatility forward libor model with a term structure of volatility smiles, Tech. rep., Bank of America.

Piterbarg, V. (2007). Markovian projection for volatility calibration, *Risk* **April**, pp. 84–89.

Poensgen, O. (1965). The valuation of convertible bonds, *Industrial Management Review* **7**, pp. 77–92.

Poulsen, R. (2006). Barrier options and their static hedges: simple derivations and extensions, *Quantitative Finance* , pp. 327–335.

Press, J. (1967). A compound events model for security prices, *Journal of Business* **40**, pp. 317–335.

Privault, N. (2009). Stochastic analysis in discrete and continuous settings: with normal martingales, http://www.ntu.edu.sg/home/nprivault/MA5182/notes.pdf.

Quessette, R. (2002). New products, new risks, *Risk* **March**, pp. 97–100.

Ramakrishna, S. (2004). New products, new buyers, http://www.risk.net/risk-magazine/feature/1498392/new-products-buyers.

Rebonato, R. (1999a). On the simultaneous calibration of multifactor lognormal interest rate models to black volatilities and to the correlation matrix, *The Journal of Computational Finance* **2**, pp. 5–27.

Rebonato, R. (1999b). *Volatility and correlation, 2nd Edition* (Wiley, ISBN 0-470-09139-8).

Rebonato, R. (2002a). *Modern pricing of interest rate derivatives* (Princeton University Press, ISBN 0-691-08973-6).

Rebonato, R. (2002b). Theory and practice of model risk management, Tech. rep., Royal Bank of Scotland.

Ross, S. (1976). The arbitrage theory of capital asset pricing, *Journal of Economic Theory* **13**, pp. 343–362.

Schmidt, T. (2006). Coping with copulas, Tech. rep., Department of Mathematics, University of Leipzig.

Schoenmakers, J. and Coffey, C. (2000). Stable implied calibration of a multifactor Libor model via a semi-parametric correlation structure, Tech. rep., Weierstrass Institute, Preprint n. 611.

Schönbucher, P. (1998). *A market model for stochastic implied volatility*, Ph.D. thesis, Bonn University.

Schönbucher, P. (2003). *Credit derivatives pricing models* (Wiley Finance, ISBN 978-0470842911).

Sepp, A. (2006). Extended creditgrades model with stochastic volatility and jumps, Tech. rep., Northwestern University, http://papers.ssrn.com/sol3/papers.cfm?abstract_id=1412327.

Sepp, A. (2010). An approximate distribution of delta-hedging errors in a jump-diffusion model with discrete trading and transaction costs, Tech. rep., Bank of America Merrill Lynch.

Sharpe, W. F. (1964). Capital asset prices: a theory of market equilibrium under conditions of risk, *Journal of Finance* **19**, pp. 425–442.

Shparber, M. and Resheff, S. (2004). Valuation of cliquet options, Tech. rep., The Leon Recanati Graduate School of Business Administration.

Shreve, S. (2004). *Stochastic Calculus for Finance II: continuous time models* (Springer, ISBN 978-0387401010).

Swishchuk, A. (2004). Modeling of variance and volatility swaps for financial market with stochastic volatility, http://math.ucalgary.ca/~aswish/StochVolatSwap.pdf.

Takahashi, A., Kobayashi, T. and Nakagawa, N. (2001). Pricing convertible bonds with default risk, *Journal of Fixed Income* **11**, pp. 20–29.

Thind, S. (2007). Concerns rise over correlation trades, `http://www.risk.net/asia-risk/news/1508815/concerns-rise-correlation-trades`.

Treynor, J. (1961). Toward a theory of the market value of risky assets, Unpublished manuscript.

Tsiveriotis, K. and Fernandes, C. (1998). Valuing convertible bonds with credit risk, *Journal of Finance* **8**, pp. 95–102.

Vasicek, O. (1977). An equilibrium characterisation of the term structure, *Journal of Financial Economics* **5**, pp. 177–188.

Weil, R., Segall, J. and Green, D. (1968). Premiums on convertible bonds, *Journal of Finance* **23**, pp. 445–463.

West, G. (2009). Exotic equity options, Tech. rep., Financial Modeling Agency.

Whetten, M. (2006). Cds recovery basis: issues with index auctions & credit event valuations, Tech. rep., Nomura Fixed Income Research, `http://www.securitization.net/pdf/Nomura/CDSRecovery_12Apr06.pdf`.

Willard, G. (1997). Calculating prices and sensitivities for path-dependent derivative securities in multi-factor models, *Journal of Derivatives* **5**, pp. 45–61.

Wilmott, P. (1998). *Derivatives: The Theory and Practice of Financial Engineering* (John Wiley & Sons, ISBN 978-0471983668).

Wu, L. and Zhang, F. (2002). Libor market model: from deterministic to stochastic volatility, Tech. rep., Claremont Graduate University and Hong Kong University of Science and Technology.

Wystup, U. (2002). Ensuring efficient hedging of barrier options, Tech. rep., Commerzbank Treasury and Financial Products, `http://www.mathfinance.de/seminars/risk/barriers2002/efficientHedgingBarriers.pdf`.

Wystup, U. (2008). Vanna-volga pricing, Tech. rep., MathFinance AG, `http://www.mathfinance.com`.

Index

About the Author

George Kaye is an independent financial consultant with over a decade of experience as a quantitative analyst ('quant') in the investment banking industry. Starting at Credit Suisse First Boston's Product Development Group in 1999, George quickly specialised in the field of equity derivatives, building models and infrastructure for the trading desks. In 2006, he left to join the Derivative Analysis Group of Goldman Sachs, where his responsibilities focused on building a methodology for model risk analysis of the firm's equity derivatives positions. In 2010 he returned to the front office, working in the equity derivatives section of the Quantitative Analysis Group of UBS Investment Bank, leaving at the end of 2011 to build his own derivatives software company, Derivitec Ltd.